HARDPRESS.NET
HOME OF HARD-TO-FIND BOOKS

The Philological Essays of the Late Rev. Richard Garnett, of the British Museum
by Richard Garnett

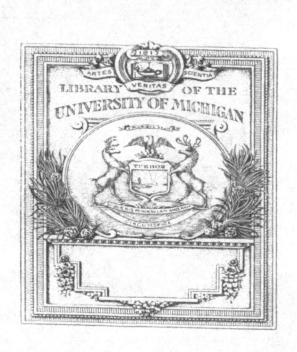

THE

PHILOLOGICAL ESSAYS

OF THE LATE

REV. RICHARD GARNETT

OF THE BRITISH MUSEUM.

———

EDITED BY HIS SON.

———

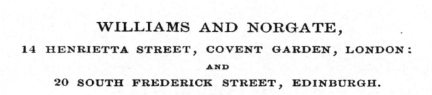

WILLIAMS AND NORGATE,

14 HENRIETTA STREET, COVENT GARDEN, LONDON:

AND

20 SOUTH FREDERICK STREET, EDINBURGH.

1859.

PRINTED BY B. G. TEUBNER, LEIPZIG.

CONTENTS.

IV

MEMOIR

OF THE, LATE

REV. RICHARD GARNETT.

The subject of this biography was born, July 25., 1789, at Otley in Wharfedale — a locality distinguished alike for natural beauty and the independent, intelligent character of the inhabitants, and in or near which his family, supposed to have originally come from Westmoreland, have been resident for several centuries. His father, Mr. William Garnett, was a manufacturer of paper, and is still remembered as a man of unusual ability and force of character; his mother's maiden name was Rhodes. At an early age, he was sent to the grammar-school of his native place, an establishment whose condition at that period was so different from what it is at present, that the reputation he in due time acquired of being better qualified to teach his master than the latter to teach him must by no means be taken as denoting a very advanced stage of scholarship. As was to be expected, his original destination was to a life of business, it being intended to place him with a house engaged in foreign commerce. This proved ultimately most advantageous, as it led to his being sent to Leeds and placed with an Italian gentleman named Facio, for the sake of receiving instruction in the principal Continental languages. Here the foundation of his subsequent linguistic attainments was laid by a thorough acquisition of French and Italian; he also attained considerable proficiency in German. His literary affections, however, were at this period of his life decidedly engrossed by the Italian poets, and much is yet extant to evince the warm admiration he entertained for many of these, and for Petrarch in particular. By the time he quitted Mr. Facio (about 1803) the intentions entertained respecting his destination in life had undergone a change, and he remained several years at home, assisting his father in his manufactory. But it soon appeared that this was not at all his vocation. He was, indeed, far from deficient either in the industry or the prudence requisite for success in trade, and no one could be less inclined to the disdain which some men of more erudition than sense have affected to entertain for commercial pursuits. But his residence with Mr. Facio had powerfully stimulated his native enthusiasm for literature, and when he found the indulgence of this incompatible with the position of a manufacturer, he hesitated not to exchange the latter for the former, even though the comforts of home, the society of those most dear to him, the prospect of affluence and the satisfaction of a settled position in life had to be resigned at the same time. Nor was this all. Not only had he to go forth for a season upon the world, but the attainment of his wishes demanded an amount of labour which few, perhaps, would have possessed resolution to encounter. His ultimate goal was the Church — a profession for which his inborn piety and habitual seriousness seemed to have marked him out from the cradle, but from which his high sense of duty and responsibility, as well as the feeling of combined modesty and self-respect which never, throughout his life, permitted him to undertake anything which he did not feel certain of being able to perform with credit, could not but withhold him till he should feel his qualifications for the position far more in accordance with his own lofty standard than was ever the case during his residence at Otley. He must have felt, also, that the want of serviceable connections, as well as of the showy accomplishments of the popular divine, debarred him from every chance of distinction, save such as might be the meed of unusual merit and acquirements. Before all things, it was necessary to obtain a thorough acquaintance with Latin, of which he knew little, and with Greek, of which he knew nothing. This — as well as a competent knowledge of technical divinity and no despicable amount of Hebrew — was the work of something less than four years, much occupied with other tasks. In 1809 he quitted his father's roof to teach at the school of the Rev. Evelyn Falkner, Southwell — in 1813 he was ordained by the Archbishop of York, after an examination in which he displayed an amount of knowledge, especially Scriptural, declared by that prelate's chaplain to have surpassed every thing that, in his official capacity, had previously come under his notice. Traces of the severity of his application at Southwell survive in the mass of marginal notes that cover his books, as well as in his recorded feat of mastering the whole Iliad in a month. "I finished it," he remarked to one of his brothers, "but it nearly finished me."

His first pastoral charge was at Hutton Rudby, in Cleveland, whither he went as curate to the Rev. Mr. Grice. It would have been difficult to find a more congenial spot than this quiet, secluded hamlet, with its grey old church picturesquely situated on a knoll rising in front of an amphitheatre of wood, the blunt contour of the Cleveland hills in the distance, and the foaming Leven at its foot. Add to this that some of his warmest friendships were contracted here, and it will not seem surprising that he should have regretted to exchange the tranquil scene for manufacturing, bustling Blackburn, whither he repaired in 1815 as curate of the Parish Church and second master of the Grammar School. Here too, however, he was not long without contracting intimacies that rendered his residence extremely happy. The most important of these, no doubt, was that which speedily united him with his Vicar, the Rev. Dr. Whitaker, a man of original character, a kind heart, and abundant learning, whose histories of Craven and Whalley entitle him to a place in the first class of British antiquaries. Dr. Whitaker doubtless rejoiced to find a congenial spirit in his curate, and his advice and encouragement must have been of essential service to the young student, who received an additional and melancholy proof of the regard in which he was held in the Doctor's dying request that he would preach his funeral sermon (1821). The late excellent Rev. S. J. Allen, subsequently Vicar of Easingwold, and author of "Lectures in defence of the Church of England," may also be named among his most intimate and valued Blackburn friends. The sphere of his attachments, however, was by no means confined to this locality. He had never ceased to maintain a most affectionate intercourse with his family, and his native place afforded him at least one other friend for whom he invariably entertained the highest regard, and whose name a disastrous fate has identified with the history of British discovery in Africa. This was Mr. Joseph Ritchie — the grandson of the Dr. Ritchie frequently mentioned in Wesley's journals, and the unfortunate companion of Captain Lyon's unsuccessful attempt to penetrate into Central Africa by way of Fezzan. As a medical student, Mr. Ritchie at one time resided in the metropolis, and mixed much in literary circles,* and it may easily be imagined how invaluable his correspondence (which has been preserved, and is remarkable for liveliness of expression and independence of thought) must have been to the secluded student at Southwell, the most retired of towns, where, while the grey Minster still endures in undecaying beauty, the stately archiepiscopal

---

* An allusion to him will be found in Milnes's Life of Keats — also in Haydon's Memoirs, vol. I., p. 388.

a *

palace lies in ivied ruin, and which is perhaps the only place
in the kingdom where a railway has been closed from actual
want of passengers.

1824 and 1825 were important years in Mr. Garnett's life.
In the first he was united to his first wife, Margaret, daughter
of the Rev. Godfrey Heathcote, of Southwell. In the second
he made his first appearance as a writer by publishing a
series of articles on the Hamiltonian system of tuition in the
Kaleidoscope, a literary journal issued at Liverpool. The
present writer has a dim recollection of having seen the
numbers containing these essays, but the copy has long
been lost, and he knows not where to find another. As
will appear in the sequel, they were by no means laudatory
of Mr. Hamilton, who would seem to have met with a full
measure of the caustic severity which sciolists of all descriptions were tolerably certain of encountering at the hands
of his critic. About this time also commenced Mr. Garnett's
correspondence with Southey, whose acquaintance he had
made a few years previously. That this acquaintance soon
ripened into cordial esteem, is evinced, among other testimonies, by the following passage in a letter from the Lau-
reate to Mr. Rickman, dated April 10., 1826, and printed in
Mr. Warter's collection of Southey's correspondence, Vol. III.,
pp. 540—541 · —

'The packet which comes herewith contains a note of introduction to Turner* for Mr. Garnett, who is a curate at Blackburn, and a very remarkable person. He did not begin to learn
Greek till he was twenty, and he is now, I believe, acquainted,
with all the European languages of Latin or Teutonic origin, and with sundry Oriental ones. I do not know any man
who has read so much which you would not expect him to have
read. He is very likely to distinguish himself in his vocation
by exposing the abominable falsifications of such men as Milner
and Lingard, whom he has industry enough to ferret out throughout all their underhand ways. The Bishop of Chester** knows
him, and I hope will give him some small preferment, on which
he may have leisure for turning his rare acquirements to good
use. He was the schoolfellow and intimate friend of that poor
Ritchie who lost his life in one of the African expeditions.'

The nature of Southey's correspondence with Mr. Garnett
will be explained by the allusions to Milner and Lingard.
Lancashire, as the reader may be aware, is the most Roman

---

* Sharon Turner, the historian, whose friendship also Mr. Garnett
had the good fortune to acquire.
** Dr. Blomfield, afterwards Bishop of London.

Catholic county in Great Britain. Its rude and uncivilized condition at the Reformation prevented the new doctrines from making progress until much of the zeal with which they were originally urged had evaporated, and hence the number of the Catholic gentry is so great that, since the Emancipation Act has rendered them eligible, nearly half the county sheriffs' have belonged to the ancient faith. There are also a great number of Irish immigrants, attracted by the pressing demand for labour and the geographical position of the county. It is not, then, surprising that the clergy of the rival communions should frequently come into collision; that, — especially at a period when "the Catholic question" was *the* question of the day — each should resort to the aid of the press for the discomfiture of its opponents, nor, assuredly, that Mr. Garnett's learning and abilities should have been employed on behalf of the Church to which his attachment, however temperate and rational, was always firm and cordial. It may, however, be affirmed with certainty that his motives for engaging in the controversy were not quite the same as those of most of his coadjutors. He never felt any uneasiness at the apparent progress of the Church of Rome; there is nothing in his writings to show that he doubted either the justice or the expediency of Emancipation; nor could he ever discover the Pope in the Apocalypse, or any incompatibility between the precepts of Catholicism and a good life attended by the Divine favour. No man, in a word, was ever less of a bigot, or less obnoxious to the charge of narrow-mindedness. His was the *literary* branch of the controversy; his prodigious reading had ranged over the whole field of ecclesiastical history and hagiology; and, himself a man of the purest integrity, he felt indignant at the disingenuousness with which too many Roman Catholic controversialists* have striven to misrepresent facts disadvantageous to their cause, as well as the mendacity so unscrupulously employed to procure the canonisation of some whose saintly virtues might have been thought to suffice without the aid of supposititious miracles. Perhaps the most masterly of Mr. Garnett's many powerful contributions to the "Protestant Guardian," is the series of papers devoted to the exposure of the mass of falsehood accumulated around the venerable name of Francis Xavier — and it is not without a sigh that the Editor refrains from offering any example of the vast erudition, masculine energy

---

* This is not meant as an indiscriminate censure. Mr. Garnett frequently eulogises the candour of Tillemont, and holds him up as an example and rebuke to less scrupulous writers.

of diction and scathing sarcasm buried in the forgotten columns of an obscure provincial journal.

Southey's letters principally relate to his own and Mr. Garnett's share in the Roman Catholic Controversy — under the
date, however, of March 31., 1825, he thus alludes to the
latter's remarks on the Hamiltonian system: —

'I thank you for your Hamiltonian controversy — a subject
concerning which I knew very little before; but it is always
worth while to know upon what gross error, or misapprehended
truth, any popular delusion or system of quackery is founded. If
there be anything useful in his method, I apprehend it can be
nothing more than would be attained by following old Lilly's in-
structions for beginning as soon as possible to exercise the pupil
in literal translation. You have made a lively and amusing pamphlet.'

Southey was the means of introducing Mr. Garnett to the
Rev. J. Blanco White, who soon became one of his most
valued friends and correspondents. Some passages of this
excellent man's letters are sufficiently interesting in themselves and characteristic of the writer, to warrant their insertion even in this brief memoir: —

7 Paradise Row, Chelsea.
June 16th. 1826.

My dear Sir,
'I take the pen in hopes of forwarding this letter under a Government frank together with a copy of my answer to Mr. Butler,
which I beg you to accept. You will see that I have taken the
liberty of inserting in a note the passage from Villani which you
had the goodness to send me. There is nothing so painful to me
as the necessity of carrying on a controversy of this kind. My
health suffers considerably from it. My mind was agitated while
writing, and now that the Letter is published, I fear that in my ve-
hemence I may have exceeded the limits of Christian moderation.
I certainly did not allow my feelings to direct my pen without en-
deavouring to weigh what the nature of the subject and all its
circumstances required.....
...When do you intend to favour us with your intended work?
From the sketch I had the pleasure of reading, I feel assured that
it will be of the greatest service to the good cause.'

Oriel College, Oxford.
March 19th. 1827.

My dear Sir,
'Your very kind letter has been for some time in my hands,
though I have not been so fortunate in regard to the pamphlet.
My intimate friend, the Rev. Mr. Butler, whom I believe you saw

at my Chelsea lodgings, has promised me to send it by the first opportunity; and I hope to have the pleasure of reading it ere long.....

...... I believe I told you in London that having determined to fix myself somewhere out of that great Babylon, I had chosen Oxford as my residence. This determination I put in execution in October last, and after very near six months' residence, I have every reason to be satisfied with it. My degree enables me to join the Society at Oriel College, which I consider as my home; though I do not live within its walls, and being allowed to dine in the Hall, I can live with more economy here than in London. My health is little more or less the same as formerly, subject to daily sufferings, and constant weakness......

...... You have seen, I suppose Dr. Philpotts' Letter to Canning. It is written with uncommon ability, and has, I believe, great effect. I hope you will soon publish your intended work — be cautious, however, how you deal with the book-sellers. I have been exceedingly ill-treated by Mr.———— '

Oxford, Aug. 20th, 1827.

My dear Sir,

'I feel very much obliged to you for the two Nos. of the Protestant Guardian, which I conceive to be a very useful publication. Your letters on the Breviary are remarkable for that kind of accurate knowledge which you have a peculiar ability to collect and digest. If the Roman Catholics, in the mass, were open to conviction, I do not know anything more likely to produce it than the rooted love of falsehood and deception which their church displays in the Breviary. Your letters will be useful not only in a controversial point of view, but also as specimens of historical criticism.....

..... I am sorry to find that Colburn is advertising a work by me. I had intended to write something as a supplement to Doblado; but as I grow older Spanish subjects become more and more painful to me; and having attempted them in different views, I find myself under the necessity of relinquishing the work.

Have you seen my Letter to the converted Roman Catholics? It is a mere trifle; but I believe that in the controversy with Romanists it is of the greatest importance to show the great question at issue — the supreme authority on matters of Faith — as detached as possible from all collateral points. Such is the object of my little tract. I do not think that it has attracted the notice of the public, which makes me suspect that I have missed the true way of treating that important point.'

It will be seen that Mr. Garnett at this time meditated, and had probably nearly completed, a substantial work on the Roman

Catholic controversy. But the hand of domestic calamity was now to intervene. In July, 1826, he had quitted his curacy for the incumbency of Tockholes, near Blackburn, on which occasion an exceedingly handsome testimonial, the subscription for which was by no means confined either to his own congregation or to persons professing the same religious sentiments, was presented to him, accompanied by a highly flattering address. Nor were other marks of the esteem of his fellow-townsmen wanting: —

'Sure we are, said the *Blackburn Mail*, that if a conscientious discharge of duty, dictated by the loftiest principles, and accompanied by soundness of judgment, kindness of heart, and superior yet unobtrusive attainments as a scholar and divine, can secure esteem either in public or social life, the subject of this gratifying tribute will be surrounded where he is going, and wherever his lot may be cast, by as sincere well-wishers as he leaves behind.'

The subject of *this* gratifying tribute, had not, however, been long at Tockholes before the scene began to overcloud, and in October, 1828, the deepest gloom was thrown over his mind by the untimely death of his wife,* followed within three months by that of his only child, an infant daughter. These calamities changed the whole current of his existence. Controversy was thrown aside, never to be resumed, and he eagerly sought an opportunity of quitting a spot once beloved beyond all others, but where everything now reminded him of his melancholy bereavement. This desire was gratified through the friendly intervention of the venerable Dr. Woodhouse, Dean of Lichfield, a relative of his departed wife. In May, 1829, Tockholes was exchanged for a Priest-Vicarship in Lichfield Cathedral, and he entered upon an entirely new sphere of social intercourse and literary activity. The following letter from Blanco White needs no comment: —

---

* Margaret Garnett could claim the honours of a literary ancestry, her grandfather, Dr. Ralph Heathcote, having been an eminent divine in the 18th. century (see Nicholls, 'Literary Anecdotes,' vol. III, pp. 531—544.) and the blood of Simon Ockley, the famous Orientalist, and Mompesson, the heroic vicar of Eyam, also flowing in her veins. Her own character was thus sketched by one who knew her well: — "A lady who will be long and deeply regretted by every class of society amongst us, whose several orders she was formed to attach to herself, and to each other, by her gentle, cheerful, and charitable disposition, her unfeigned and exalted piety, her exemplary discharge of duty domestic or social, and the humble and unostentatious but active and persevering exercise of every Christian virtue." This gentleness, however, co-existed with much sagacity and intellectual vigour, and a remarkable talent for repartee.

Oxford, Nov. 10th., 1828.

My dear Sir,

'Had it been in my power to administer to you any consolation by letter when I heard of your great affliction, you may believe that no press of business would have prevented my writing. The sympathy which I felt would, however, have induced me to send you a word of condolence, if I had known where to address you. I feel therefore very much obliged to you for letting me know that you are now in your former residence; and am glad to find that you are determined to occupy your mind on literary subjects.....

..... Would you like, for instance, to write an account of some of the Spanish Chronicles? The embassy to Tamerlane by Ruy Gonzalez de Clavijo is full of curious matter. Gibbon was not able to consult it. The Chronicle of Don Alvaro de Luna is also very interesting, especially if compared with that of Don Juan II, written by the Condestable's enemies. The reign indeed of Juan II. is one of the most remarkable in Spanish history. If you wish to have my copy of the Chronicles, I will send them to you by coach or waggon. I have them here, and if you write so that I may receive your letter before the 20th you shall have them immediately.'

It does not appear that this friendly offer was attended by any immediate result. It may, however, have been owing to Mr. White that Mr. Garnett, soon after his removal to Lichfield, became a contributor to the Encyclopædia Metropolitana, then in course of publication under the direction of the Rev. Edward Smedley — author, among other works, of an admirable "History of the Reformed Religion in France." To the Encyclopædia Mr. Garnett contributed several chapters on the ecclesiastical history of the fourth century, as well as a review of the theological literature of the same epoch. At a later period, when, after the death of Mr. Smedley, the superintendence of the undertaking had passed into the hands of the late Rev. H. J. Rose, his connection with it was resumed, and he supplied several miscellaneous articles, the most important being those on "Superstition," "University," and "Writing." A letter from Mr. Rose, referring to the second of these essays, seems worthy of preservation from the interest of the subject and the clear enunciation of the writer's views — views, it should be added, substantially in harmony with those of his contributor: —

'..... As to the professional and tutorial systems I think your remarks are just, although they will bear modification — i. e., as it seems to me, it is not possible properly to teach mathematics or many other branches of science by oral lectures, but many of the accessory branches of knowledge are well communicated in

that way.   By accessory I mean those branches of knowledge
which are not the staple commodity of the education given, and
are not required from young men.   Thus, I think, as mathematics
and classics are required from young men, they cannot be effi-
ciently taught by vivâ voce lectures.   Those who are careless
would get no profit from such lectures — nor perhaps can they be
fully taught even to those who wish for improvement and information.   But take botany for example.   The public lectures give
very excellent outlines of the science, the professor examines and
gives the cream (to use a vulgar phrase,) of all the new discoveries and brings them before his class — and he gives examples
either by drawing or by dissected flowers to illustrate the principles of the science, and, although a person would not become a
first rate botanist by attending a course, he obtains a considerable
stock of knowledge and is set upon his journey towards acquiring
a full knowledge of the subject.   In this way public oral lectures
are admirable — so in chemistry, geology, &c. &c.   In short I
think in all cases where *to communicate the knowledge of a science* is
the desideratum, public oral lectures are of admirable use, though
not sufficient in themselves.   But where *the effect on the mind of
the student* is the principal matter, there public lectures will generally be of little utility, and therefore the *great* business of an
University must necessarily be carried on chiefly by some such
expedient as a tutorial system.   But public lectures by the pro-
fessors of the University are always to be united with this system
as keeping up a high tone, and giving a stimulus to college lec-
turers.'

This, however, belongs to a later period of Mr. Garnett's
life.   From the time of his arrival in Lichfield, his studies
were almost entirely directed into a philological channel.
The study of languages had, indeed, always been his favourite occupation — we have already seen Southey's testimony
to the extent of his linguistic acquirements in 1826, and the
mass of notes covering the pages of his Spanish dictionary
attests the zeal with which he had applied himself to the idiom
of Cervantes in particular.   Hitherto, however, philological
lore had been amassed as a means, not as an end, and tongues
acquired not for their own sake, but for that of the literary
monuments they possessed.   This was now to cease, and the
future Quarterly reviewer entered upon his new career at
the most auspicious period imaginable, when Rask and Grimm
and W. Humboldt and many an illustrious fellow-labourer were
beginning to shed a light upon the science sufficient to dis-
play, without exhausting, the treasures awaiting the first
fortunate explorers of its virgin realms.

No further occurrence of importance marked Mr. Garnett's

existence till 1834, when a second marriage (with Rayne, daughter of John Wreaks Esq., of Sheffield, and mother of his three surviving children,) insured the felicity of his remaining years. The following year witnessed the appearance of his first contribution to the Quarterly Review, which is also the first piece published in the annexed collection. The sensation it occasioned in learned circles was very great, and he was not long without gratifying proof of the attention it excited on the Continent. It also procured him the friendship and epistolary communications of several scholars devoted to similar pursuits, among whom are especially to be named Sir F. Madden, of the British Museum, and Hensleigh Wedgwood Esq., the latter of whom was induced by his admiration for the article to address a long and valuable letter to the as yet unknown author, of which, as well as of several subsequent communications of much interest, the Editor (by permission) has availed himself in his scanty annotations. Two additional articles succeeded in 1836, in the autumn of which year the Dean and Chapter of Lichfield presented him to the vicarage of Chebsey, a village in the neighbourhood of Stafford. His residence in this agreeable locality was, however, of short duration, he being, in February 1838, appointed Assistant Keeper of the Department of Printed Books in the British Museum, an office then vacant through the resignation of the Rev. H. F. Cary, the distinguished translator of Dante. He had now at length attained a position in entire harmony with his desires, and the remaining twelve years of his existence glided by in calm uneventful happiness, occupied in the discharge of his official duties, the persevering prosecution of philological researches, and the education of his children, to which no man could have been more devoted. He maintained a regular correspondence with the late Professor Molbech, of Copenhagen, a man of character and pursuits kindred to his own, and exchanged letters at intervals with other men of learning, The following letter from John Mitchell Kemble is at once too interesting and too characteristic to be omitted: —

My dear Mr. Garnett,

'I am at length prisoner at large, that is, my tether extends to the whole area of my bedroom, which is something for a man who has been nearly ten days in bed: and so, having ascertained that I am in a fair way of recovery, I set to again with redoubled vigour. The longer Bewcastle inscription, of which Holmes* sent

---

* The late John Holmes Esq., Assistant Keeper of MSS. in the British Museum.

me a copy, from the Gentleman's Magazine of 1742, is a *crux*; but
I have the key to it thus far — the inscription is in Latin, and
refers to one Baldgar, who was somebody's father and somebody's
brother.   Interesting information, this! But we will hope it will
not stop here.

If you have any bowels of compassion, and any specimens of
Northumbrian Anglo-Saxon, you will lend me the latter for a few
days. I am working at my grammar, literally from memory, having given Thommerel all I had of the Durham book, and my tran-
scripts in hand being nearly confined to Vesp. A. 1, which is not
pure Northumbrian: thus I am in what the Yankees in their vernacular call "a precious nip and frizzle of a fix." Nor can I,
in my present condition, haunt the Museum for the purpose of col-
lating and collecting. This rere-winter troubles me: I was beginning to think of striking my tents and migrating when lo! frost
and snow forbid me.   One comfort is that it will kill the
grubs in the earth: they have been a sort of locust plague in my
little Egypt for the last three years. *Per contra* is alarm for the
laurels, and the horse chestnut buds, which were beginning to swell
and look gummy. So the Gods give us all things mingled; neither
white nor black, but speckled! I have been reading Ettmüller carefully: I dare say he is quite right in many of his remarks upon my
preface, but I do not think him fair to me, considering that in the
main he adopts my views, and without them would probably have
had none of his own. However in this I suppose I undergo the
common fate of predecessors. The main question — was Beowulf
an Angle, i. e. a Mercian poem? remains I think as I left it. That
Wermund is Garmund I continue to assert: that the Offa of the
poem is the Offa *primus* of the Mercian line I reassert: that he *is*
the Offa of Saxo I am certain, and Ettmüller cautiously avoids
the consequences from the lines "syððan geómor wóc, haelethum
tó helpe, Henninges maeg, nefa Swerting," and the allusion in
the travellers' song to the duel on the Eider. Nor does the existence of a tribe of Geáts in Sweden prove much, till we rid ourselves of Geát the eponymus, and God of the Saxons in England.
The identification of Hygelác necessarily modifies a very few of
my views; but in my preface I treated him as one of the personages who *might* be historical, and certainly was not mythic. That
Hygd is a lady I still think open to doubt, though Thorpe has
always held the affirmative. It is not without importance that the
right of succession in the eldest son is recognised throughout the
poem: as far as I can judge this was the Mercian i. e. Angle law,
and was certainly not the Saxon, the latter taking from the royal
family him who suited them best. Ettmüller's translation I have
not yet read attentively: I should think the Germans would find it
as easy to learn the A.-S. as the language into which it is *fordutched!*

This letter is undated, but from the mention of Ettmüller's edition of Beowulf was probably written in the spring of 1841. In the following year one of Mr. Garnett's warmest wishes was realised by the formation of the Philological Society, due in great measure to the exertions of his sincere friend and indefatigable fellow-labourer E. Guest, Esq., and of which he long continued one of the most active members. The whole of his papers are reprinted in this volume. In 1848 he furnished his last contribution to the Quarterly, and in the July of the following year, discussed his friend Mr. Cureton's "Corpus Ignatianum" in the Edinburgh Review. The article is not reprinted here, as being scarcely in harmony with the general character of the collection; yet, as the precise value of the Syriac text published by Mr. Cureton seems still a subject of controversy, it may not be inexpedient to place Mr. Garnett's opinion on record: —

To the above lucid and convincing statement we shall merely add that similar conclusions drawn from similar evidence would have been acquiesced in at once in the case of a profane author. Let us suppose that certain passages occurring in a play of Euripides, known only from one or two manuscripts of the fourteenth century, had been pronounced spurious by Bentley and Porson on the ground of their faulty versification, barbarous phraseology, and allusions to events of the period of Augustus and Tiberius; and that, when these were cleared away, all the rest was worthy of the reputed author, and suitable to the age in which he lived. This criticism, if well supported by facts, would certainly be entitled to consideration. But suppose further that, years after the death of these critics, manuscripts six or seven centuries older should be produced from an Egyptian catacomb, in which the precise passages excepted against were omitted, to the manifest improvement of what remained, the literary world would immediately admit that Bentley and Porson had been in the right, and would unite in applauding their learning and sagacity. But in the theological world such convictions are established much more slowly, for in that world, unfortunately, there is always a larger class of men who will resolutely shut their ears against the demonstrations of common sense, rather than renounce one of their favourite idols. [After some remarks on the retention of the celebrated verse of the "Three Heavenly Witnesses" as a case in point, the writer continues:] We are told by Guibert, Abbot of Nogent in the tenth century, that it was not safe to question the current popular legends of miracles; as the old women not only reviled bitterly those who did so, but attacked them with their spindles! The Corpus Ignatianum will excite something of a similar feeling — though the feeling will probably not be manifested in precisely the same manner. There may not be material

inkstands thrown at the editor's head, but there will be brandish-
ing of pens, and a considerable amount of growling in cliques and
coteries. However, *magna est veritas*, and those who assail it will
in the end damage nobody but themselves.

ED. REV. No. CLXXXI.

This, with the exception of the concluding papers on the
Nature and Analysis of the Verb, was Mr. Garnett's last
literary labour. In 1848 he had begun to suffer habitually
from catarrh, and by the winter of 1849 it was but too
evident that his health was declining. Still the progress of
decay was very gradual, and his sons, at least, had little
suspicion of its extent till the means of comparison between
the actual and former state of their parent's health were
afforded by a visit to Otley in June 1850, when it appeared
that he who in the previous September had been accustomed
to walk upwards of four miles daily to visit his aged mother-
in-law, was then unable to go much beyond the garden.
On his return to London, however, he attempted to resume
his official duties, and it was only at the pressing instance
of the present Principal Librarian (at that time Keeper of
the Printed Books, and ever the warm-hearted friend of him
and his,) that he consented to apply to the Trustees for
leave of absence. This was immediately granted, but the
decline of his health could not be arrested, and terminated
in a peaceful death on September 27. 1850. He was interred
in Highgate Cemetery.

There are many and obvious reasons why the present
writer should refrain from attempting any estimate of the
extent and importance of his father's philological and ethnological labours. Not the least weighty is that the work has
to a considerable extent been already performed by a pen
as competent as his own is the reverse. The Editor's pleasure
in adducing the following important testimony can only be
equalled by that which he feels in recording that Dr. Latham was himself the first to draw his attention to its existence, and suggest its insertion in the present publication: —

The chief writings that, either by suggestions, special indications, or the exposition of known facts, have advanced Keltic ethnology, now come under notice; and first and foremost amongst
them the writings of the philologue so often quoted — Mr. Garnett. These have touched upon the grammatical structure, the
ethnological relations of the stock in general, and the details of its
constituent elements.....

1. The oblique character of the pronouns of the persons of verbs is his palmary contribution to philology — to philology, however, rather than to ethnology.

2. His other notices are: —

a. In favour of the language of ancient Britain being that of ancient Gaul, and of both being British rather than Gaelic.

b. In favour of the Picts having been Britons rather than either Gaels or Germans.

c. In illustration of the affinities of Keltic tongues with the German, Slavonic, and other undoubted members of the Indo-European stock, and with the Albanian, Armenian, and other branches beyond it..... '

..... And here I may be allowed to express the hope, not only that Mr. Garnett's papers on the Keltic tongues, but that all his writings on philological subjects may be published. *They are by far the best works in comparative grammar and ethnology of the century.*
    Latham's Edition of Prichard on the Eastern origin of the Celtic nations. Pp. 371—372.

Extreme weight is universally accorded to the philological judgments of Dr. Donaldson. He thus expresses himself in his New Cratylus (page 47, 2nd edition): —

'Mr. Garnett, whose comprehensive and truly philosophical analysis of the constituent elements of language was first made known in a notice of Dr. Prichard's Celtic work, has since then developed his views in various contributions to the records of the *London Philological Society*, and we do not know where to look for sounder or more instructive examples of linguistic research.'

The reader of the papers thus highly eulogised must, however, bear in mind that they by no means appear in the form which the author would have wished to impart to them. As examples of scientific research, they are perhaps the most valuable of his writings, but in a literary point of view, he must be judged, if he is to be judged candidly, by his contributions to the "Quarterly Review." In these he was enabled to follow the natural bent of his mind by mingling the *dulce* with the *utile* — anecdote, allusion, humour were all in place — and it may be asserted with some confidence that the science on which he wrote never before or since gained so much in agreeableness with so little loss of profundity. There is a sort of dry warm raciness about these pleasant papers, "like clear sherry, with kernels of old authors thrown into it," as Hazlitt says of the prose of the writer's friend Southey. This tone would not have suited papers read before a learned Society, and hence, Mr. Garnett's productions of this nature are rather to be regarded as abstracts of treatises he could have written than substantial literary productions. It is much to be regretted that he was never enabled to work them up into essays after the mayner of his articles in the Quarterly, when his extraordinary powers of illustration and amplification* would assuredly have transformed the brief memoranda into a fascinating book. A yet more serious cause for regret is his inability to carry out a design he long entertained of producing an independent work on English provincial dialects — a task of national importance which still remains unperformed, notwithstanding the abundance of materials. No reader of the essay on the subject reprinted in this volume will question his remarkable qualifications for such an undertaking.

The pleasant duty remains of thanking those to whose friendly assistance the Editor has been indebted during the prosecution of his task. His acknowledgments are due, in the first place to the Philological Society for permitting the reprint of Mr. Garnett's papers from their published Transactions, and to Mr. J. Murray for a similar favour as regards the articles which appeared in the Quarterly Review. He has also to express his especial obligations to Dr. Latham, to Dr. Donaldson, to T. Watts, Esq., of the British Museum, to Hensleigh Wedgwood, Esq., the Treasurer, and F. J. Furnivall, Esq., the Secretary of the Philological Society.   R. G.

    April 20., 1858.

---

* Notwithstanding the amount of his philological attainments, Mr. Garnett was anything but a *mere* linguist. It would have been difficult to find anything with which he was not more or less conversant, from Sanscrit and Mathematics to chess and the manufacture of artificial flies (he was an enthusiastic angler.) The extent of his acquaintance with elegant literature is best shown by the copiousness of illustration from this source, observable in his more finished writings. His library may be said without exaggeration to have contained examples of every printed language, and every species of composition.

ENGLISH LEXICOGRAPHY.

[*Quarterly Review*, *September*, 1835.]

1. *A Dictionary of the English Language.* By S. Johnson, LL. D. With numerous Corrections and Additions, by the Rev. H. J. Todd, A. M. 4 vols. 4to. London. 1818.
2. *A Dictionary of the English Language.* By Noah Webster, LL. D. 2 vols. 4to. New York. 1828. Reprinted, London, 1832.
3. *A New Dictionary of the English Language.* By Charles Richardson. Parts I. and II. London. 1835.

Though we were never enrolled in Pinkerton's corps of *mighty Goths*, being neither believers in his theories, nor admirers of the spirit and temper in which he maintained them, we do not mean to deny that we feel a strong partiality for almost every branch of the great Gothic and Teutonic family, by whatever appellation it may be designated. We may, perhaps, be a little out of humour at present with the Belgians * — but we have a great regard for the Dutch, a still greater for the Germans, and an absolute enthusiasm for all the sons of Odin, whether Danes, Swedes, Norwegians, or Icelanders. Our Gallic neighbours, or rather the doctors of one of their literary sects, may still affect to doubt 'si un Allemand peut avoir de l'esprit' — but if even these fine gentlemen reflect on the part acted by the Germans and their kindred on the theatre of the world since Arminius struck Rome the blow from which she never recovered, they can hardly deny them power and valour, and a knowledge of the arts by which dominion is acquired and preserved. Our interest on behalf of this remarkable race extends not only to their history and civil polity, but also to their language, in all its branches We well remember our delight at the discovery that Justin and Justinian originally bore the respectable names of Upright and Stock. We look upon Ulphilas's Mœso-Gothic Gospels as one of the most precious relics of antiquity, and would have every word of genuine Teutonic descent carefully preserved, whether spoken by the prince or the peasant.

---

* An allusion to the conservative politics of the Review. ED.

Of course, we include English in our list of favourites, and believe, as in duty bound, that, take it for all in all, there is no tongue superior to it in the whole European circle. We are disposed, also, to take it as we find it, and are very far from wishing to banish any terms of southern descent that can produce proper warrants of naturalization. We are fully sensible of the advantage of possessing such words as *flower*, *florid*, *flourishing*, along with their counterparts *bloom*, *blooming*, *blow*, *blossom* ; and feel — as every one must — that the union of the two classes furnishes a strength and richness of diction, and a choice of terms to express primary and secondary ideas, compared with which the vocabulary of the French and the Italians is poverty itself. But, after all, terms of Saxon and Northern origin constitute the sinews of our speech, and must be the most attentively studied by those who would form clear ideas of its genius and structure. Indeed, one principal reason why we prize a knowledge of the German and Scandinavian dialects, and would recommend it to others, is that they throw a light on the analogies of our own language, and the principles of its grammar, which cannot be obtained from any other source. We know that it is easy to sneer at such pursuits, and to ask — who but a dull pedant can see any use in confronting obscure and antiquated English terms with equally obscure German ones, all which might, without any great injury, be consigned to utter oblivion? It would have been equally easy to ask fifty or sixty years ago — and would at that time have sounded quite as plausibly — what can be the use of collecting and comparing unsightly fragments of bone that have been mouldering in the earth for centuries? But now, after the brilliant discoveries of Cuvier and Buckland, no man could propose such a question without exposing himself to the laughter and contempt of every man of science. Sciolists are very apt to despise what they do not understand; but they who are properly qualified to appreciate the matter know that philology is neither a useless nor a trivial pursuit, — that, when treated in an enlightened and philosophical spirit, it is worthy of all the exertions of the subtlest as well as most comprehensive intellect. The knowledge of words is, in its full and true acceptation, the knowledge of things, and a scientific acquaintance with a language cannot fail to throw some light on the origin, history, and condition of those who speak or spoke it. Who knew anything about the gipsies, till an examination of their language proved beyond all doubt that they came from the banks of the Indus? Who knows anything certain about the Pelasgi?

And who does not perceive that two connected sentences of their language would tell us more clearly what they really were than all that has hitherto been written about them? The Irish antiquaries give magnificent accounts of the learning and civilization of their ancestors two or three thousand years ago; but when we find that their language, in some respects a copious as well as beautiful one, is utterly destitute of scientific terms, and cannot convey the import of them without a clumsy periphrasis, we are enabled to appreciate such statements at their real value.

We are aware that Dugald Stewart, while combating the metaphysical conclusions of Horne Tooke, thought proper to speak somewhat slightingly of etymological investigations. With all due respect for such authority, we think that he took an insufficient as well as an unfair view of the matter. When he represents the cultivation of this branch of knowledge as unfavourable to elegance of composition, refined taste, or enlargement of the mental faculties, he seems to have forgotten the grammatical and etymological speculations of Plato, Cæsar, and Cicero — and that the collection and comparison of the provincialisms of Germany was a favourite employment of the illustrious Leibnitz. We fully assent to Mr. Stewart's strictures on the absurdity of Tooke's favourite position, that words ought *always* to be used in their primitive signification. A wise man employs the language of the country according to its current acceptation, as he uses the national coin according to its current value, taking care in both cases to choose the genuine and reject the counterfeit. But when Mr. Stewart tries to make it appear that it is better in many cases to remain ignorant of the original meaning of words than to know it, we think him singularly unfortunate both in his position and in the illustration which he brings forward to support it. The learned Professor says: —

'The argument against the *critical* utility of these etymological researches might be carried much farther, by illustrating their tendency with respect to our poetical vocabulary. The power of *this* (which depends wholly on association) is often increased by the mystery which hangs over the origin of its consecrated terms; as the nobility of a family gains an accession of lustre, when its history is lost in the obscurity of the fabulous ages.

'A single instance will at once explain and confirm the foregoing remark. Few words, perhaps, in our language have been used more happily by some of our older poets than *harbinger;* more particularly by Milton, whose "Paradise Lost" has rendered even the organical sound pleasing to the fancy —

1 *

> "And now of love they treat, till th' evening star,
> Love's *harbinger*, appear'd."

How powerful are the associations which such a combination of ideas must establish in the memory of every reader capable of feeling their beauty; and what a charm is communicated to the word, thus blended in its effect with such pictures as those of the evening star, and of the loves of our first parents!

'When I look into Johnson for the etymology of *harbinger*, I find it is derived from the Dutch *herberger*, which denotes one who goes to provide lodgings or a harbour for those that follow. Whoever may thank the author for this conjecture, it certainly will not be the lover of Milton's poetry. The injury, however, which is here done to the word in question, is slight in comparison of what it would have been, if its origin had been traced to some root in our own language equally ignoble, and resembling it as nearly in point of orthography.' — *Philosophical Essays*, p. 195.

This is elegantly and plausibly expressed, and will doubtless appear very convincing to a certain class of readers. In our opinion the criticism is radically unsound, and more worthy of Lord Chesterfield than of Dugald Stewart. In fact, the implicit adoption of the principle involved in it would make us quarrel with half our national vocabulary, which must, in the nature of things, have been applied to low and familiar objects, when it was the language of a rude and barbarous people. Let us apply the canon to another expression, much more homely in its origin and associations than *harbinger*. We need not inform our readers who wrote the following passages —

> 'Though the *yesty* waves
> Confound and swallow navigation up.'

> 'These are thy toys, and, as the snowy flake,
> They melt into thy *yeast* of waves, which mar
> Alike the Armada's pride, or spoils of Trafalgar.'

With all due reverence for Partridge's maxim — *de gustibus* — we cannot help maintaining that no man can perceive the full power of the above nervous expressions, unless he knows precisely what *yeast* means; and, moreover, that the critic who would quarrel with them on account of the connexion of the word with malt, hops, and beer-barrels, and propose the substitution of *froth*, *foam*, or any similar milk and water expression, had better shut up Shakspeare and Byron, and devote himself to the study of French tragedies. It seems as absurd to quarrel with a forcible and appropriate poetical epithet on account of the homeliness of its origin, as it would be to despise a beautiful butterfly, because it was once a caterpillar; and, to pursue the analogy, it is as interesting and instructive to trace the progress of language from rudeness to refinement, as to watch the successive transformations of the various tribes of insects.

Once more: Mr. Stewart describes philologists as a useful sort of inferior drudges, who may often furnish their betters with important data for illustrating the progress of laws, of arts, and of manners, or for tracing the migrations of mankind in ages of which we have no historical records. It does not seem to have occurred to him that it is very possible for the profound philologist, and the enlightened antiquary or historian, to be united in the same person; and that he who derives this species of knowledge from the fountainhead, must possess a great superiority over him who has it at second or third hand, as all can testify who know and are able to appreciate the profound researches of such men as the late illustrious Humboldt.* Had Mr. Stewart himself possessed a little more of this sort of knowledge, he would never have brought forward that most extraordinary theory of the origin of Sanscrit, which he supposes to be a mere factitious language, manufactured by the Bramins on the model of the Greek. This, we are willing to admit, is the most flagrant absurdity that has emanated from the Scotch school since the days of Monboddo.

Our anxiety to vindicate a favorite pursuit has rather led us astray from our purpose, which is, to make some remarks on the present state of English Lexicography. We shall not laboriously attempt to demonstrate the value of a good dictionary, or to show that there is as much reason for compiling a good one of the English language as of any other. Even supposing that we did not require such a work for ourselves, it must at all events be wanted by those foreigners who take an interest in our literature. In most parts of Europe, a knowledge of English is now a necessary part of a liberal education, and the scholars of Germany and Denmark are not satisfied with a meagre school vocabulary, but go to the best and most original sources of information, wherever they can procure them. It is, therefore, of great importance to them that the words of our language should be carefully collected and correctly explained, as they cannot always have recourse, like ourselves, to living sources of information. We heartily wish, for their sakes, as well as for our own credit, that they had some better guidance

---

* Wilhelm Humboldt—not the author of "Kosmos." ED.

than they can command at present. We fear that our best
means and appliances are far from trustworthy, and we feel
rather inclined to agree with a worthy Hibernian of our
acquaintance, who declared that the only good English dictionary we posess is Dr. Jamieson's *Scottish* one. None of
our lexicographers has equalled, or even approached, the
venerable Doctor's industry in collecting words, or his skill
and care in explaining them; and though etymology is his
weakest point, he has, even in this department, a decided
superiority over his southern competitors. Etymology and
philology do not seem to thrive on British ground. We were
indebted to a foreigner (Junius) for the first systematic and
comprehensive work on the analogies of our tongue, and it
is humiliating to think how little real improvement has been
effected in the two centuries that have since elapsed. We
have manifested the same supineness in other matters connected with our national literature. We have allowed *a Bavarian* to print the first edition of the Old Saxon evangelical harmony — the most precious monument of the kind, next
to the Mœso - Gothic Gospels — *from English manuscripts*. In
like manner, we are indebted to *a Dane* for the first printed
text of Beowulf, the most remarkable production in the whole
range of Anglo-Saxon literature; and we have to thank another Dane for our knowledge of the principles of Anglo-
Saxon versification, and for the only grammar of that language which deserves the name. We have had, it is true,
and still have, men who pride themselves on their exploits
in English philology, but the best among them are much on
a par with persons who fancy they are penetrating into the
profoundest mysteries of geology, while they are only ga-
thering up the pebbles that lie on the earth's surface.* We
admit that Horne Tooke dug more deeply than his competitors, and by no means without success; but, for want of
practical knowledge, he often laboured in the wrong vein,
and as often failed to turn the right one to the utmost advantage.

One principal cause for the little progress hitherto made
in this branch of science is, that it has too often been studied
as physiology was before the time of Galileo and Bacon.
It was found easier to guess than to explore; consequently,
almost every etymologist — instead of forming his system

---

* We are far from intending to include all our *Anglo-Saxon* scholars of
the present day in this censure. We admired, and sincerely regret, Mr.
Conybeare. Some others of them — especially Mr. Kemble and Mr. Thorpe
— have also done good service in this department, and we sincerely hope
hat they will live to do a great deal more.

from a copious and careful induction of facts — sets out with a determination to reduce everything to a certain preconceived chimerical theory. One starts with the doctrine, that Celtic was certainly spoken in Paradise; another assumes the identity of Irish with Phœnician; a third undertakes to prove that Welsh is the oldest daughter of the Hebrew. Murray clearly sees all languages lurking in nine uncouth monosyllables — like forests of oaks in a few acorns; Voss is content with extracting Greek from a couple. On this, a German philologist, of a better stamp, sarcastically observes, that we may just as well undertake to derive every word in our language from the vowel A; and that, if such theories are to be tolerated at all, the *simplest* must necessarily be the best. All extravagances of this sort deserve to be classed with Darwin's process for manufacturing animal bodies from irritable fibres; and make us long for the re-appearance of Aristophanes on earth, to put the dreaming authors — λεπτοτάτων λήρων ἱερεῖς — in the Clouds.

Another great source of failure has been, that nearly all our English etymologists took up their trade without sufficient capital; and showed themselves grievously deficient in the various kinds of knowledge requisite to pursue it with success. It is not sufficient to collect a mass of apparently similar words, according to their initial letters in dictionaries; an etymologist ought to know the affinity and different degrees of affinity between languages — to study the genius and grammatical structure of each — and, above all, to possess a certain intuitive quickness of perception, combined with sound judgment, capable of distinguishing the real from the imaginary. Without this faculty of discrimination, mere ponderous learning is often worse than useless — the more a man knows, the more blunders he is likely to commit. We have a 'signal example of this in our countryman Hickes. Few works exhibit more zeal and industry than his 'Thesaurus;' and those who can separate the wheat from the chaff may glean from it a great deal of valuable information. Nevertheless, we should be sorry to send a *fellow-creature* thither for elementary instruction. Though he had so little discrimination as to confound old Saxon and Francic — the very north and south poles of the Germanic dialects — he, in an unlucky hour, took upon himself to determine *ex cathedrâ* the different periods of the Anglo-Saxon language, and to classify its written monuments according to their different degrees of purity or impurity. His method of proceeding was summary enough: he first constructed a grammatical and critical system of his own, on the most erroneous and imperfect data; and then proceeded to stigmatise everything that did not seem to accord with it, as Dano-Saxon, and corrupt. As he was unable to distinguish between archaisms and poetical forms, and actual corruptions, he has included under the above head innumerable compositions which do not exhibit a single Danish peculiarity, grammatical or verbal; some of them, in fact, being written before the Danish invaders were seen or heard of. Most unfortunately, he has been looked up to as a paramount authority for more than a century; consequently, his labours have been, in many respects, more injurious than beneficial. We do not hesitate to say, that a man may learn more of the genius of the Anglo-Saxon language, and of the true principles of its grammar, from Rask, in a single week, than he will be likely to do in a year from the ponderous, ill-digested, and bewildering compilation of Hickes.

Of course, not much was to be expected from the successors of Hickes, who had his faults without a tithe of his learning or industry. Some of them seem to have been qualified for the office they undertook, in the same way as the macers in the Scottish courts, 'of whom,' as the author of Redgauntlet records, 'it is expressly required that they shall be persons of *no knowledge.*' Not only do they manifest a gross ignorance of the grammatical structure of the languages they have to deal with, but a total want of perception of their most obvious analogies. The changes in corresponding words of kindred languages are not arbitrary and capricious, but regulated by fixed and deeply-seated principles; especially in the radical words of the more ancient dialects. When we meet with a simple verbal form in Anglo-Saxon, we know beforehand in what shape it may be expected to occur in Icelandic, as well as what further modification it is likely to undergo in Danish and Swedish. Of this sort of knowledge — the very foundation of all rational etymology — our word-catchers do not seem to have had the smallest tincture, and consequently they are perpetually allowing themselves to be seduced by imaginary resemblances into the most ludicrous mistakes. One of their deficiencies is extraordinary enough in these days of universal diffusion of knowledge. We have taken some pains in making ourselves acquainted with our recent lexicographers and glossarists, and find great reason to doubt whether any two of the whole tribe have so much as a school-boy acquaintance with modern German. It is well known that this language is of the utmost importance to the philologist, not only on account of the extent of its vocabulary and the number and value of its ancient literary monuments, but further, because the best works on almost every branch of the subject are only accessible to a person acquainted with it. Perhaps the writings of Grimm, Bopp, and their coadjutors — men who seem likely to effect the same sort of revolution in European philology that Cuvier wrought in the sciences of comparative anatomy and geology — have scarcely had time to make their way among our scholars: but how comes it that so little use has been made of works which have been forty or fifty years before the public? We indeed occasionally meet with references to Schilter, Haltaus, Wachter, and Richey, whose *Latin* furnishes some clue to their meaning; but we have looked in vain for an etymology from the valuable Bremisch-Sächsisches Wörterbuch — the Holsteinisches Idiotikon — the elaborate work of Stalder on the dialects of Switzerland; and what is still more extraordinary, we have not found the smallest notice taken of the celebrated dictionary of Adelung — which, as a comprehensive etymological depository, perhaps claims precedence over every European work of the same class. We can only account for this by concluding that the *key* to those treasures was wanting. The explanations and definitions are *German* — σφόδρα Τεύτονες — consequently, any attempt of the uninitiated to give us the benefit of them would have had the success of George Primrose's well-meant attempt to teach the Dutch English.

It is, however, time to take some notice of the different works we are professing to review. The limits of an article necessarily preclude all detailed analysis of their contents; we shall, therefore, give our opinion of their respective merits as briefly as we can. Concerning Mr. Todd's labours, we do not think it necessary to say much. He has shown much industry in collecting words from our old writers; and has made sundry corrections, which are not without their value. In short, it is easy to perceive that he has read many books, and remembers a great deal of what he has read; and that he is sufficiently accurate in matters connected with his own particular department. But his acquaintance with the language is more scholastic than vernacular; and he too frequently reminds us of Lightfoot, who, after drawing up a most learned and elaborate topographical description of Jerusalem, was completely lost on the road to his own field. He has most especially failed in adapting his work to the present state of *science*. Innumerable terms of art are wholly omitted, and the explanations of many that are given are either defective or absolutely erroneous; in short, he seems to think that the terminology of science remains nearly what it was in the days of George II. The department of British botany, in which precision was both necessary and easily attainable, is executed throughout in the most slovenly and incomplete manner. Instead of the nomenclature of Linnæus, Mr. Todd has either given the exploded and forgotten definitions of Miller's dictionary, or none at all; consequently, a foreigner would, in a vast majority of instances, be unable to discover what is meant. Let the following familiar words — respecting which one would think there could be no mistake — serve as a sample: —

1. 'COCKLE (*coccel*, Sax.; *lolium*, *zizania*, Lat.), a weed that grows in corn. The same with corn-rose, a species of poppy.'

Here is a confusion of three distinct plants, — *Lolium temulentum*, or darnel — *Agrostemma githago*, the corn-cockle — and *Papaver rhœas*, the wild poppy.

2. 'WAYBREAD (*plantago*), a plant.'

What plant? — Is it *Plantago* MAJOR — *media* — *lanceolata* — *coronopus* — or *maritima*? A reference to the Saxon *wegbræd*, or the German *wegebreit*, would have shown that the proper orthography is way*brede*; and also have served to identify the *species*.

3. 'CRANBERRY, the whortleberry or bilberry.'

No more than a *raspberry* is a *blackberry* — as every man, woman, or child, that has tasted a cranberry-tart, can testify. We hope it is unnecessary to tell our readers in what the difference consists; but we ask seriously, whether foreigners, who find these gross blunders in our most accredited dictionaries, will not have cause to say, that Englishmen neither know their own language, nor the most common natural productions of their own country?

As specimens of English natural history, the above are doubtless bad enough; they are, however, by no means the worst samples of the march of information among us. Our readers are probably aware that an Almanac is annually published under the superintendence of the Society for the Diffusion of Useful Knowledge — with sufficiently lofty pretensions, and bearing in front the names of an ex-Lord Chancellor, and we know not how many cabinet ministers. The one published in 1832 is garnished with a calendar of British zoology, furnished, we suppose, by a professor of the London University* — certainly by some one to whom the

---

* The time has long gone by — if it ever existed — when the teaching of University College could be censured with justice. It may be feared, however, that, as a *popular* branch of knowledge, natural history (except as regards sea-slugs) is little more advanced now than in 1835. ED.

sound of Bow-bell is more familiar than the zoology of this or any other country. Among the natural phenomena in January, we are gravely informed that the *hearth-cricket*, the *bed-flea*, and the *cheese-mite* may be seen in their respective haunts, *particularly on fine days*! Undoubtedly! and so may bugs and other little creatures familiar to man! In February, 'the grayling ascends rivers from the sea.' We believe grayling are about as plentiful in the sea as herrings are in Virginia Water. In June 'the sheep — *Ovis aries* — is shorn and washed!' — (*qu.* washed and shorn?) a piece of *natural* history worthy of the wight who pronounced St. Paul's a great *natural curiosity*. In November, 'hares remain much in their *dens*' — (fearful places, no doubt); and the in-June-shorn-and-washed *ovis aries* 'pairs' (we thought the ram was *vir gregis*), 'and utters its *peculiar call*' — being, we suppose, *silent* at all other seasons. In December, the different species of swallows — like Horrebow's owls — 'are *not* found:' we needed no ghost to tell us that. Surely such stuff as this — and there is plenty of the same sort — is not much better than Francis Moore's astrology! A botanical and floral register, in a subsequent Almanac, is pretty much of the same calibre. If the countrymen of Linnæus get hold of these publications — which they will naturally regard as containing the concentrated wisdom of the *Society* — what an elevated idea they will have of the state of knowledge among us! — But we must come back to our dictionaries.

We had seen Dr. Webster's work so highly praised, particularly by his countrymen, that we were led to form high expectations of its merit. These expectations have, in a great measure, been disappointed. We give the author credit for great industry — some of which is not unsuccessfully directed. He has added many words, and corrected many errors, especially in terms relating to natural history and other branches of modern science. But the general execution of his work is poor enough. It contains, indeed, the words in common use, with their ordinary acceptations, but conveys no luminous or correct views of the origin and structure of the language. Indeed, as an attempt to give the derivation and primary meaning of words it must be considered as a decided failure; and is throughout conducted on perverse and erroneous principles. The mere perusal of his Preface is sufficient to show that he is but slenderly qualified for the undertaking. There is everywhere a great parade of erudition, and a great lack of real knowledge; in short, we do not recollect ever to have witnessed in the same compass a greater number of crudities and errors, or more pains taken to so little purpose.

In his sketch of languages, he describes Basque as a pure
dialect of the old Celtic: it is neither allied to the Celtic nor
to any other European family of tongues.* He states further,
that he 'has no particular knowledge of the Norwegian, Icelandic, and the dialects or languages spoken in Switzerland,
further than that they belong to the Teutonic or Gothic family.' Could a man who professes to have spent half his
life in comparing languages be ignorant that Iceland is the
venerable *parent* of the whole Scandinavian tribe; and, consequently, of first rate importance in tracing the origin of
words? He discovers that the prefixed *a* in *awake, ashamed,*
&c. is formed from the Anglo-Saxon *ge* — with which it has
not the smallest connexion; and, moreover, that the same
particle (*ge*) is retained in the Danish and in *some* German
and Dutch words. It is notoriously of the most extensive use
in Dutch and German — and the very few Danish words in
which it occurs are one and all borrowed from the Lower
Saxon. With equal felicity he asserts that the prefix *be* is of
extensive use in Danish and Swedish. Just as much as *hyper*
and *peri* are in Latin; *be* like *ge* is in those two languages
a *borrowed* particle, and from the same quarter. He thinks
the negative prefix *o* in Swedish is *probably* a contracted word,
being unable to perceive its identity with the German and
English *un.* As might be supposed from these specimens —
Dr. Webster's application of the northern tongues to English
etymologies is often erroneous and perverse enough — it is,
however, upon the whole, better than we should have anti-
cipated from one so slenderly acquainted with their structure
and peculiarities. He has taken great pains in collecting and
comparing synonymes from different languages, and is often
sufficiently happy in the explanation of individual terms.
But the ambitious attempt to develope the radical import of
words was an undertaking far beyond his strength and acquirements. In nineteen instances out of twenty his explanations are founded on a mere *petitio principii,* and frequently
they are too ludicrous to deserve a serious refutation. Our
readers may judge of them by the following sample: —

'Heat usually implies excitement; but as the effect of heat as
well as of cold is sometimes to *contract* — I think *both* are sometimes
from the *same radix.*'

We fear the doctor had forgotten the fable of the satyr and
the traveller, when he penned the above choice sentence.

The main feature of the doctor's work — and the point on

---

* It is now usually considered as a member of the Turanian class of languages. ED.

which he evidently most prides himself — is a laborious parallel between Hebrew — with its kindred dialects — and those European languages from which English is derived. We hesitate not to say that it is a waste of time and labour to attempt to establish an analogy between two classes so totally unlike in their component elements, as well as their entire mechanism and grammatical structure. There are, it is true, a certain number of verbal resemblances, which, when carefully examined, generally prove more apparent than real. It is seldom that an affinity can be proved, and when a remote one does exist, the discovery of it rarely throws any light on the origin or philosophy of languages like ours. We will produce a single example of the fallacy of trusting to resemblances of this sort. In Matth. i. 2. *et seq.*, the Syriac translator renders ἐγέννησε by אולד (*auled* or *avled*); in the modern Danish version we find *avlede*, apparently so closely resembling the Syriac term, in sound, spelling, and signification, that many a smatterer in etymology would jump to the conclusion of a community of origin. But an examination of the grammatical inflexions proves that there is not the smallest affinity between the two. The roots have just *one letter* in common, and the apparent similarity is, in fact, a proof of real difference, being accidentally brought about in each word by a totally opposite process of inflexion. Yet, unskilful as it would be to identify the above words with each other, it would hardly be so bad as deriving *preach* [Lat. prædico] from the Hebrew *barak* — to bless — or *establish* [Lat. sto !!!] from *yatzab* — which Dr. Webster does without the smallest symptoms of remorse, or apparent suspicion of the absurdity and impossibility of the thing. These specimens may make us thankful that the doctor's 'Synopsis of the Principal Uncompounded Words in *Twenty* Languages' is ' not published — and perhaps never will be.' It would certainly be a formidable addition to the mass of etymological trash already before the world.

The above strictures on the application of Oriental languages to etymology must, of course, be understood to refer to those of the Semitic family. With respect to Persian, the case is very different, and though Dr. Webster's etymologies from this source are not always to the purpose, they are more frequently so than those from Hebrew and Arabic. In fact, the Persian language is an undoubted descendant of Sanscrit, or some ancient tongue closely allied to it: wofully disfigured and corrupted, it is true, but still retaining sufficient traces of its origin. It is, therefore, capable of furnishing valuable materials for the illustration of the great

Indo-European tribe, if used skilfully and soberly, but the
mischief is, that half-learned philologists are always attempting to make some kind of coin pass for more than its real
worth.   Various attempts, for example, have been made to
deduce German — *en ligne droite* — from the old Persian.
Von Hammer, if we recollect rightly, maintains most perti-
naciously, that not only the language, but the German men
and the German horses are from this quarter, being the undoubted descendants of the warriors and steeds of Darius
the son of Hystaspes.   The verbal coincidences between the
two languages are indeed so numerous, that a sufficiently
plausible theory may be constructed by any one who takes
care to exhibit everything that suits his purpose, and to keep
all the rest out of sight, according to the established practice of system-mongers.   But when carefully and impartially
examined, they only go to prove a remote collateral affinity.
The majority may be accounted for by a common descent
from Sanscrit or its parent, and the points of dissimilarity
are much more numerous than those of agreement. Still the
latter are well worthy of notice, not only as illustrative of
the history and affinities of language, but also of the manners, customs, and religious opinions of antiquity; and occasionally we are amused by meeting with things of this
sort, where we should hardly expect, *à priori*, to find them.
We will produce a couple of instances which have not, to
our recollection, been noticed before.

We have observed that the Semitic languages do not throw
much light on those of Europe.   This remark, however, does
not necessarily apply to the exotic terms that have found
their way into some Semitic dialects. In a remarkable Syro-
Chaldaic lectionarium in the Vatican library, supposed by
Adler to be in the Jerusalem dialect, ὑποδήματα, Luke xv. 22,
is rendered שׁוּרִין, that is, in a more European dress, *shuuin*,
or *shooin* — precisely the word which a West Riding Yorkshireman uses for *shoes*.   Hence, it appears, that those Hie-
rosolymitan Christians, if such they were, not only, to use
the Beaufoy phrase had their feet *accommodated* with shoes,
but, moreover, had a very tolerable sort of English name for
them.   The termination *in* is the Chaldee or Syriac plural:
the word itself cannot be referred to any known Semitic root.
It is not very easy to explain how this Germanic word got
into an Aramean dialect, but we believe the history of its
progress thither would be both curious and instructive, if it
were possible to trace it.

Much has been written to little purpose, respecting the
origin of *Yule*.   We are not without a suspicion that the fol-

lowing curious passage may in some way be connected with it. The substance of the story is in the Shah Nameh, but we prefer Castell's account, we know not whence derived, as more clear and consistent. In his Persian lexicon are the following articles: —

'SHEB YELDA. Anni nox longissima. SEDEH ET SEDHEH. Sextus decimus dies mensis Behmen [*i. e.* medii mensis hyemis] magis solennis et festus. Item, Nox quædam festa qua ignes solenni ritu exstruunt; al. *sheb sayeh*, et *sheb yelda* [see above]; Turc. *sayeh-bindsy* dictum. Tempore Regis Husbenk [Hoshung] magnus extitit draco, ut aiunt; quem ipse rex lapide petens forte fortuna alium lapidem jactu tetigit; quorum lapidum collisione ignis excitatus, qui herbas et arbores circumcirca consumpsit, earumque incendio draco ille periit. Læti incolæ sumpserunt de hoc igne, et veluti triumphales ignes ubique extruxerunt. Qui mos ab eo tempore ad hoc usque solemnis mansit.'

The story is not a bad one, though not quite so marvellous as Baron Munchausen's destruction of the bear by the collision of two flints. We lay no great stress on the verbal resemblance between *yelda* and *yule,* which may be wholly casual, but. we consider the similarity of the two festivals, and especially the exact correspondence of the season of celebration, as very remarkable. If we mistake not, Firdusi deduces the whole system of fire-worship from this source — we think the other the more plausible version of the matter — we do not say more *true.* The feast was evidently, in its origin, in honour of the sun's passing the winter solstice. The story of the dragon we conceive to be an ancient mythus that has appeared in more than one shape, and as we vehemently suspect, also to be traced to an astronomical origin. The most obvious parallel is the destruction of the Lernæan Hydra by Hercules. In both cases we have a monster subdued by a professed hero-errant, and by the assistance of fire; it happens too, oddly enough, that Iolaus, or Iolas, who furnished Hercules with the burning brands from the adjoining forest, bears a name very capable of *petrifaction.* A clever mythologist might construct a *theory* out of much scantier materials. If the author of Nimrod, for instance, takes the matter in hand, we have no doubt of his explaining every part of it as ingeniously as he resolved St. Cuthbert into an avatar of *Cush the bright.* He would have little difficulty in identifying Hercules with Hoshung — the hydra with the dragon — Iolaus with the stone — or the stone with Iolaus — *ad libitum*; or, in proving that the Persian *Sheb yelda* — the Theban *Iolæa* — and the Scandinavian *Yule,* were originally one and the same festival; and finally, that the re-

suscitation, or rejuvenescence of Iolaus, charioteer of Herçu-
les (*i. e.* of the *sun*), has a reference to the renewal of the
solar year.   We do not presume to decide such recondite
questions, but merely wish to suggest, that a careful examination of the Indian and Persian traditions might perhaps
throw some light on the mythology of Scandinavia, where we
find the same blending of Sabianism, pantheism, and worship of deified heroes as in that of Greece, Egypt, and Hindostan, and resemblances in detail too numerous to be always accidental.

To those who care more about the business of real life
than the genealogy of gods and demigods, it may be more
interesting to learn that Persia was not only, like Scotland,
literally a land of *cakes* * — with frontiers called *marzha* or
marches, under the care of a *marzuban* or *custos confinium* (Anglicè, warden of the marches) — but that the inhabitants
were moreover well acquainted with the truly English games
of tipcat** and leap-frog.   They who maintain that our an-

_____

* Kak, panis biscoctus. — Castell. Lex. Pers. col. 434. The word is also
found in Syriac, Arabic, and Chaldee, evidently borrowed from the Persian.
— Vide Michaelis' edition of Castell's Syriac Lexicon, p. 404. In the Germanic languages *cake* is significant, being formed from *cook,* like πέμμα from
πεπτω ; as is manifest in Lower Saxon, *koken,* to cook, *kauke,* a cake, and
still more plainly in the Scottish form, *cookie.* It would be curious to trace
the exact degrees of relationship between the Persian and Teutonic terms
and the Latin *coquo.* Compare Sanscrit *pac,* to cook, Phrygian *bekos,* bread,
and our own *bake.*

** We transcribe the following articles for the benefit of those who have
not access to that extraordinary monument of ill-requited learning, — Castell's Lexicon Heptaglotton.

'Chelu chub (q. d. paxillus et baculus), Lusus genus puerorum; ligni
teretis extremum alio ligno percutiunt, atque ita in aërem subsiliens pro-
pellunt.' — Lex. Pers. col. 211.   This game was formerly well known in
Yorkshire under the appellation of *trippets.*   In the southern countries it is
called tipcat; in Northumberland trippet and coit.

'Mezhid, Mezid et Mezideh.   Lusus nomen quo aliqui quotcunque proni,
ad genua manibus compositis consistunt, quorum extremus semper cæteros
omnes supra dorsum transilit, et primo loco se eodem modo rursus consti-
tuit.' — col. 508.   We leave it to persons better versed in the antiquities of
popular sports than ourselves to decide whether the above were among the
games invented by the Lydians in the time of the great famine, which enabled them to pass every alternate day during eighteen years without eating. — Vide Herodot. lib. 1, col. 94.

The following passage proves that the *plough-drill* is neither an English
invention nor a very recent one : —

'Kesht karideh; ager aratus, seminatusque simul — ut in Curdistan —
dum aratur, per exiguum foramen desuper granum decidit quovis momento
ante vomerem, et parum à latere, quod subversâ deinde terrâ obtegitur.'—
Lex. Persicum, col. 458.

It seems the barbarous Kurds are at least no novices in agriculture.

cestors were once tributaries of 'the Grand Cyrus,' are welcome to suppose that those words and things accompanied
the Sakai Sunu, or Sacæ, on their passage from the banks
of the Jaxartes to the shores of the Baltic; and that our adjective *bad*, a word only found in Persian and English, is
from the same quarter.

On the whole, Dr. Webster's quartos were hardly worthy
of being reprinted in England. Of the next work on our
list, Mr. Richardson's, we are inclined, on many accounts,
to judge favourably. We do not consider it perfect, either
in point of plan or execution, but we hope it is likely to
become the *foundation* of a better dictionary than we have
hitherto possessed — and that, in the mean time, the honourable zeal of the author may be properly encouraged by the
public. His selection of words is, in the main, judicious,
and he has shown laudable industry in the collection of authorities for their different acceptations. We still adhere to
the opinion which we formerly expressed, that it would be
a more scientific, and in all respects a preferable arrangement, to give the significations of words in the *natural* order
of succession, for we hold Grandgoustier's golden rule — '*de
commencer par le commencement*' — to be as applicable to
etymology as any other subject. A *chronological table of
authors* would enable every reader to classify the quotations
according to their respective ages; and it is of much more
consequence to ascertain what a word originally meant, than
to know by what English *author* now extant it happened to
be first used. We think, moreover, that there is too often
a scantiness in Mr. Richardson's definitions, calculated to
leave imperfectly informed persons, and especially foreigners,
at a loss; and that the more remote senses of words, which
are precisely those that most need explanation, are often
wholly overlooked. For example, under *Aberration*, no notice
is taken of the astronomical and optical employment of the

The missionary Garzoni, who resided in Kurdistan from 1764 to 1782, describes the valleys and champaign country as being at that time in a high
state of cultivation. As his 'Grammatica e Vocabolario della Lingua
Kurda' is in few hands, the following extract from the preface may not be
unacceptable to our readers : —

'Li paesi Kurdi sono tutte montagne altissime appartenenti al monte
Tauro, con le loro bellissime valli, fertili di frutta e riso. I loro monti so-
pratutto abbondano di ottima galla, della quale li mercanti esteri ne fanno
un gran commercio, trafficandola nella Asia minore, in Soria, in Aleppo, indi
in Europa; per li buoni pascoli abbondano pure d'ottime pecore, e capre,
in cui consiste la maggior entrata. Le pianure poi à piè de' monti, tanto
dalla parte di Persia, quanto dalla parte di Mesopotamia, sono fertilissime
di grano, lino, bombace e sesamo.' — p. 5.

term; and under *Alchymy,* the primary meaning is left to be collected from an absurd and erroneous etymology of Vossius, and the secondary one, viz., 'a factitious or mixed metal,' from a passage in Milton, unintelligible to common readers. We could easily show that Mr. Richardson has omitted many words employed by the writers of the middle ages — but we do not find fault with this; — we rather object to his having admitted too many. In our opinion, archaic and provincial terms belong rather to a glossary than to a standard dictionary of a cultivated language. A repository of such words, to be of any real value, ought to be complete; and it is easy to perceive what dreadful confusion it would cause, to blend a huge mass of antique and dialectical forms with the English of the present day. We conceive the following would be a proper division of the different periods of our tongue: — 1. An Anglo-Saxon lexicon, concluding with the eleventh century. 2. A glossary of archaic, and, what is much the same thing, provincial English, to the end of the fifteenth century. 3. Classical and modern English, from A. D. 1500, to the present time. Words belonging to the second period must of course be referred to for the *illustration* of those in the third—but ought not to be classed with them.

We shall not enter into any detailed examination of the etymological portion of Mr. Richardson's work, the defects of which are not so much chargeable on himself, as on the guide whose dicta he implicitly follows. He appears to take it for granted that the author of the Diversions of Purley proves every thing that he asserts, and that all rational and philosophical English etymology must be founded on his system. As we think there are no sufficient grounds for this persuasion, and that the general prevalence of it would be more likely to impede the improvement of sound philology than to promote it, we shall avail ourselves of the present opportunity of making some strictures on this celebrated work, which has been praised and censured without sufficient discrimination.

It cannot be denied that Tooke has done some service to the cause of English philology. He has successfully exposed the dreaming theories of Harris and Monboddo. He has made valuable remarks on various grammatical subjects, and is frequently sagacious and happy in the explanation of particular words. Even his errors and paradoxes are not without their use. They are supported with an ingenuity that compels us to admire when we feel obliged to withhold our assent, and not unfrequently contain approximations to truth which more wary and cautious inquirers may turn to good account. In short, we know few books more instructive than

the Diversions of Purley, to those who are able and willing
to think for themselves; but those who are content to take
up their opinions on trust, that is to say, the great majority
of readers, are as likely to be misled by its author as directed aright. No one appears to have formed a more accurate
estimate of the merits and defects of the work, than the late
accomplished editor* of Warton's History of English Poetry
— whose remarks are so distinguished by moderation and
candour, as well as by their general truth and discrimination,
that we make no apology for laying them before our readers.

'To those who will be at the trouble of examining Mr. Tooke's
theory, and his own peculiar illustration of it, it will soon be evident, that, though no objections can be offered to his general results, yet his details, more especially those contained in his first
volume, may be contested nearly as often as they are admitted.
The cause of this will be found in what Mr. Tooke has himself related, of the manner in which those results were obtained, combined with another circumstance, which he did not think it of importance to communicate, but which, as he certainly did not feel
its consequences, he could have no improper motive for concealing.
The simple truth is, that Mr. Tooke, with whom, like every man
of an active mind, idleness — in his case, perhaps, the idleness
of a busy political life — ranked as an enjoyment, only investigated his system at its two extremes, the root and the summit, the
Anglo-Saxon, and English from the thirteenth century downwards,
— and having satisfied himself on a review of its condition in
these two stages, that his previous convictions were on the whole
correct, he abandoned all further examination of the subject. The
former, I should feel disposed to believe, he chiefly studied in
Lye's vocabulary — of the latter, he certainly had ample experience. But in passing over the intervening space, and we might
say for want of a due knowledge of those numerous laws which
govern the Anglo-Saxon grammar — and no language can be familiar to us without a similar knowledge — a variety of the fainter
lines and minor features, all contributing to give both form and
expression to our language, entirely escaped him; and hence the
facilities with which his system has been made the subject of attack, though in fact, it is not the system which has been vulnerable,
but Mr. Tooke's occasionally loose application of it.' — *Warton's
History of English Poetry*, vol. ii. pp. 493-4. ed. 1824.

To this we assent, with some little limitation. We are of
opinion that Tooke signally failed in establishing some leading points of his system, and that his knowledge of ancient
English literature was more multifarious than accurate. He

* Richard Price, Esq. ED.

2*

frequently mistakes the meaning of his English quotations, as well as of his Scottish ones, and often draws sweeping and utterly unwarrantable conclusions from the blunder of a printer, or a mere misconception of his own. What Mr. Price observes of his Anglo-Saxon scholarship is equally applicable to his acquaintance with the German and Scandinavian dialects. There is sufficient evidence that he did not possess an accurate grammatical knowledge of any one of those languages, and of their general analogies and distinguishing peculiarities he knew nothing at all. It is, therefore, not wonderful that he fell into many gross mistakes; there is more cause to be surprised that he was so often in the right.

Our limits do not permit us to enter into any detailed analysis of Tooke's work, — we shall merely produce some instances of what we conceive to be practical errors, and leave our opinion of his principles to be collected from our strictures on their particular application. Mr. Price observes that the details in the first part of his work, namely, his much vaunted analysis of particles, may be contested nearly as often as they are admitted. We venture to go further, and to pronounce that it is, both in principle and execution, the most erroneous and defective part of the system, and that it contains very little indeed that can be safely relied upon.

One copious source of error, affecting more or less every branch of Tooke's system, is the assumption that Anglo-Saxon and its sister dialects may be practically regarded as original languages, and, consequently, that the bulk of the abbreviated forms of speech, which we call particles, may be traced to verbs or nouns, actually existing in one or more of that tribe. All this is more easily asserted than proved: in fact, we have almost invincible evidence that the assumption is a downright *petitio principii* and totally erroneous. Collateral dialects, so closely related as those in question, as certainly prove the existence of a parent language, as the co-existence of brothers and sisters implies a father before them; and as we have reason to suppose that Hecuba had a mother, though we do not know who she was, it is at least possible, that this more ancient Teutonic, or whatever we choose to call it, might not itself be an original tongue, but a scion from a still older form of speech. If, therefore, Anglo-Saxon is a *nata natarum*, a language several descents removed from a primæval one now lost, but in all likelihood closely related to Sanscrit, is it to be supposed that all its component elements are self-existent and self-derived? Must all the primitive circulating medium be cast into the crucible and recoined? May not some of the pieces have come down to us, somewhat clipped and defaced, as might be expected, but still substantially the same coin? A little further consideration will show that, next to the numerals and pronouns, no words are more likely to have been thus transmitted than particles, especially *prepositions*, which are absolutely necessary both to the precision and facility of languages constructed like ours. They bear a close analogy to the symbols in algebra, and language would be as unintelligible without words denoting the *separation* and *connexion* of particulars, as the demonstrations of the analyst without signs denoting positive, negative, and proportional quantities. Prepositions, therefore, must have existed from a very early period, and if our ancestors found a quantity of suitable ones ready made to their hands, we see no earthly reason why they should reject them *in toto*. Let us examine how far this *à priori* reasoning is borne out by facts in a particular instance. If we search for the origin of the preposition *over*, we find the equivalent words *ofer*, *yfir*, and *upar*, in the oldest monuments of the Anglo-Saxon, Icelandic and German. Three or four centuries earlier occurs the Gothic *ufar*, then the Latin *super*, and Greek ὑπέρ, and in Sanscrit, the most ancient and unmixed language of the whole class, *upari*,* all precisely in the same signification. We entertain not the smallest doubt of the original identity of all the above words, and would as soon believe that the Athenians sprung out of the ground like mushrooms, as that *ofer* is formed from an indigenous Anglo-Saxon root, totally unconnected with the Sanscrit. That we may not appear to rest our cause on a solitary instance, we shall examine a number of Tooke's etymologies of particles, beginning with the prepositions, the most ancient and simple words of the class.

'THROUGH. No other than the Gothic substantive *dauro*, or the Teutonic substantive *thuruh*, and, like them, means *door*, *gate*, *passage*.'

To say nothing of confounding Teutonic *turi* (door) with the Old Saxon *thuruh* (through), it is sufficient to observe, that in the very Gothic dialect here appealed to, — *through* and *door* are different words, and from different roots, as is clearly shown by Ulphilas's *thairh* aggvu *daur* (Matth. vii.

---

* Compare Persian *eber*.

13.), — *through* the strait *door*. It is, indeed, easy to assert that *th* is here substituted for *d,* and equivalent to it, but before we assent to this, we desire to have an unequivocal instance of such a change in the initial consonants of contemporary words in any Teutonic language. Medial and final consonants are variously modified, but initials are tenaciously preserved unaltered, by Goths, Saxons, and Scandinavians, and we have no more right to assume the identity of *thairh* and *daur,* than we have to confound *thorn* and *turn,* in English. We venture to substitute the following etymology, more as probable, than absolutely certain. Sanscrit, *tri,* transgredi, (of which Latin *trans* seems a participial form); old Swedish, *tœra, permeare, transire*; Gothic, *thairks,* foramen, and *thairh,* whence Anglo - Saxon, *thurh*; English, *through*. Compare Welsh, *trwy* — Gaelic and Irish, *troimh, tre, trid,* through — and probably Gothic *thaurn,* Anglo-Saxon, *thorn,* spina, *q. d.* the *piercer*. We may just observe that the Sanscrit, *tri,* appears to be the root of the comparative affix *tara* (Greek, τερος, Persian, *ter*), *q. d. exceeding,* or exactly equivalent to our *passing* strange, *passing* fair.

'OF. A fragment of Gothic, *afara, posteritas.* ANGLO-SAXON, *afora, proles.*'

No more than the Latin *post* is from English *posterity ,* as will appear from the following synonyms. Sanscrit, *apa*; Greek, ἀπὸ; Latin, *ab*; Old German, *aba, apa*; Gothic, Icelandic, *af*; ANGLO-SAXON, *of*. The Gothic noun *afar* is two descents removed, being from the particle *afar, post,* which is evidently *derived* from *af*.

'To, is the Gothic substantive *taui* or *tauhts, i. e.,* act, effect, result, consummation. Which Gothic substantive is indeed no other than the past participle *tauid,* or *tauids,* of the verb *taujan,* agere. In the Teutonic this verb is written *tuan* or *tuon,* whence the modern German *thun,* and its preposition varying like the verb, *tu.* In Anglo-Saxon the verb is *teogan,* and preposition *to.*'

This assemblage of errors and crudities is enough to make one exclaim with Toinette, *Ignorantus, ignoranta, ignorantum !* The Gothic particle, here entirely overlooked, is *du* — *taujan* is not the Teutonic *tuon,* but *zawjan,* quite a distinct verb. The German preposition is not *tu,* but *zu* — the Anglo-Saxon *teogan* does not mean *to do,* but *to draw* or *tow* (German, *ziehen*); and finally, the particle *to* cannot be derived from *do* in any Germanic dialect, old or new, without a gross violation of the elementary principles of language. Let our readers just compare the following parallel forms —

	Verb.	Preposition.
Gothic,		du.
Old German,	tuan, tuon,	za, zi, zuo.
Old Saxon and Anglo-Saxon,	don,	te, to.
Modern German,	thun,	zu.
Dutch,	doen,	te, toe.
English,	do,	to.

Surely this dissimilarity, running as it does through so many languages, is a pretty strong proof of a radically distinct origin! Respecting the true etymon of *to*, the best philologists have nothing but conjectures to offer, and we purposely refrain from adding to the number.

'By is the imperative byð of the ANGLO-SAXON *beon*, to be.'

This is not only an assertion without proof, but as extravagant a proposition as ever was advanced. *By* simply denotes juxtaposition; *be* can convey no other idea than that of essential identity; — and how those two notions are to be reconciled with each other, we are unable to perceive. It is comparatively small criticism to remark that, after all, byð is not the *imperative* of *beon*, but the *indicative present, est*. The most probable etymon of *by* appears to be the Sanscrit *abhi*. Another form, *api*, seems the prototype of the Greek ἐπὶ, and the old Latin *ape*: Gloss. Philoxeni *ape*, παρὰ.

'BEYOND, the imperative *be* with the past participle *geond*, of the verb *gan, gangan,* or *gongan*, to go, and means, *be passed*.'

A Saxon past participle in *ond* would be as strange a phenomenon as a Latin past participle in *ans* or *ens*. We believe that *geond* belongs to the class of pronominal particles, a numerous family that Tooke does not seem to have dreamt of. Gothic *jainar*, ἐκεῖνος, *jaind, jaindre*, ἐκεῖ, ἐκεῖσε, Bavarian *ent, enont*, from the demonstrative pronoun *ener*, German *jener*. It is remarkable that this pronoun does not appear in Anglo-Saxon, though we have it in the English *yon*, whence *yond, yonder, beyond*. The Anglo-Saxon *geond* (beyond), and *geond* (through), are apparently the same word, having reference, in the former instance, to a certain remote point, and in the latter, to the intervening space. In like manner, *over* may either include the sense of *trans* or *per*, according to the context.

It would be tedious to enter into a minute examination of every individual preposition. Tooke's etymologies of *down* and *about* are very properly corrected by his editor, and we could easily show that his resolutions of *from, for, without, under*, are grossly erroneous; that those of *in* and *out* are

unsupported by evidence and without intrinsic probability;
and that the root of *against* is not a past participle, but a
noun substantive. *Between* and *betwixt* are in the main correctly explained; and in his etymology of *with*, which we
allow to be highly ingenious and plausible, he is right as
to the primary signification, but greatly mistaken in making
it, *more suo*, a verb in the imperative mood.

We must dispatch the remaining particles as briefly as
we can, consistently with a due examination of Tooke's principles, which are most fully developed in his theory of conjunctions. For the little virtuous peace-making particle IF,
which he places in front of his array, he appears to have
felt a peculiar affection, if we may judge from the pains
that he takes to establish its genealogy. In fact, we believe
that this word was the foundation of his whole system.
Having discovered, as he thought, that *if* is the imperative
of *give*, he naturally enough concluded that other particles
might be accounted for by the same process. Accordingly,
he expends a profusion of labour and perverse ingenuity in
detecting imperatives where none ever existed, or possibly
could. In the present instance, a comparison of the cognate
languages proves that *if* is neither an imperative of *give* nor
of any other verb; consequently, any system founded on
that basis is a mere castle in the air. It is unnecessary to
repeat Dr. Jamieson's statement of the matter, which is, in
our opinion, perfectly decisive against Tooke's etymology.*
We shall merely observe, that the great variety of ancient
forms makes it extremely difficult to determine the precise
etymon. Some are not unlike the Sanscrit *iva* — sicut —
others have plainly the form of *nouns* — e. gr. the old German *ibu*, *ipu*, may be resolved into the ablative or instrumental case of *iba*, *ipa*, dubium. Compare the Icelandic *efa*,
to doubt, *efi*, a doubt, *ef*, if.

'BUT.' There is no single word which Tooke has laboured
with more diligence and acuteness than this, none concerning which he delivers his conclusions more confidently, and,
we venture to say, none in which he has more signally and
demonstrably failed in establishing them. His theory of two
buts — one the imperative of *botan*, and the other the imperative of Anglo-Saxon *beon*, combined with *utan* — q. d. *be out*,
is a chimera from beginning to end. We assert most con-

---

* Vide Jamieson's Scottish Dictionary, vol. i. art. Gif. The Doctor
justly observes that neither the Gothic *jabai*, the Alemannic *ibu*, *ob*, *oba*,
nor the Icelandic *if* or *ef*, can be formed from the verbs denoting *to give* in
those languages. The Frisic and Old Saxon synonyms are equally unfavourable to Tooke's hypothesis.

fidently, that *but* is, under every shade of signification, simply *bi utan* (exactly the Greek παρεκτὸς), under which form it plainly appears in Old Saxon. This compound term is peculiar to the Saxon and Belgic dialects; in Scandinavian and Old German we find the simple forms *utan, uzzan*; and a decisive argument against all necessity for two English *buts* is that *utan* and *uzzan*, originally denoting *extra*, are unequivocally employed in the various senses of *vero, sed, nisi, præter*, and *sine*. In fact, the office of *but*, under all its modifications, is merely to *discriminate* — sometimes with more, and sometimes with less, precision. In the beginning of a sentence it usually denotes transition, in the middle it is commonly adversative; and in each case, any word authorized by the custom of the language, conveying the idea of *distinction*, may be used to express it. Thus the Greek ἀλλὰ denotes diversity; the modern German *sondern*, separation: the Icelandic *helldür* (potius), Dutch *maar*, French *mais*, Spanish *mas*, and several others imply *preference*. It is worthy of notice, that the Latin *sed** anciently signified *without* (sine), as our *but* still does in some provincial dialects.

Did our limits permit, we could easily show that the conjunction *as* is not, as Tooke affirms, equivalent to *that*, but to *thus* or *so*; that *and* cannot be derived from *anan*, to give, because no such verb exists; that *though* is in all probability a pronominal particle; and *since* no corruption of *seen* or *seeing*, but simply *after that*. We further maintain that *else, unless*, and *least* have not the smallest connection with *lesan*, to dismiss. The first is a genitive absolute form of *elle*, alius, reliquus; the second, merely *on less* — i. e. *at* or *for less* (French *à moins*, Danish *med mindre*, literally *with less*); and the original form of the third, Anglo-Saxon *thy læs*, exactly corresponds with Latin *eò minus*. We think we could, moreover, show that Tooke's resolution of English pronouns into Anglo-Saxon verbal forms, is as preposterous in principle as it is thoroughly erroneous in its details. Most of our European pronouns are found already existing in the most ancient Sanscrit monuments, and frequently under nearly identical forms. Let our readers compare our Anglo-Saxon article *se, seo, that*, Gothic *sa, so, thata*, with the Sanscrit *sa, sā, tad*, or *tat*, and analyse their respective *inflections*. They will then be able to judge how far *se* is likely

---

* ' Eam pecuniam eis *sed fraude* suâ solvito.'—Fragm. Leg. xii. Tabular. apud Scaliger. ad Festum. *Se* in the same signification is of more common occurrence—' *se* dolo malo;' ' se fraude esto.' Both forms seem to be merely ablatives of *sui*, q. d. *by itself, apart*; consequently including the same idea of separation as Germ. *sondern*.

to come from *seon*, or *the* from *thean*, or any Saxon verbs
whatever.   Our readers may not be displeased to know the
sentiments of two of the first philologists in Europe , Bopp
and Grimm, on some of the above points. The former, after
observing that the bulk of words composing the Sanscrit
language are formed from monosyllabic verbal roots, adds,
that 'we cannot refer to this source either the *numerals* , the
pronouns, or the majority of the *prepositions* and other particles, most of which last class may be traced with more or
less certainty to *pronominal* roots.'   On the prepositions and
prepositional particles Grimm remarks ——

   'We are far from being able to trace their origin and peculiar
formation in all cases. The oldest , like the pronouns with which
a number of them are undeniably connected, belong to the more
obscure parts of language — those of more recent formation may
be more easily deduced from substantives or adjectives.'

On the whole, then, we are of opinion that Tooke has signally failed in some of his leading conclusions respecting
our English particles.   He overlooked the share which pronouns have in their formation; he sought the origin of the
prepositions where it is no more to be found than the source
of the Nile is in Egypt; and he forced upon many particles
a verbal signification which they are not capable of bearing.
According to Plutarch, the Delphian *EI* supported the tri-
pod of truth; we fear that Tooke's *if imperative* led him into
a labyrinth of error.   Indeed, we doubt whether any genuine simple preposition or conjunction ever was, in point
of fact, a verb imperative, or could be in the nature of
things.   Imperatives are often employed as interjections or
interjectional adverbs — never, we conceive, as conjunctions,
properly so called — still less as prepositions or pronouns.
We have not leisure to examine Tooke's explanations of
English adverbs, much less to point out all the errors of detail
in the second part of his work. In the principles there laid
down we agree with him to a certain extent.   It seems curious, yet it is an undoubted fact, that we can discover no
nouns, denoting material objects, of a strict primary signification; all whose origin can be traced conveying a secondary or relative idea.   A fox, for example, is a particular
animal, distinguishable by well recognized characters from
every other; but the name by which we designate it is not
a primitive word, originally and essentially appropriate to
the species, or even to the genus.   On the contrary, Grimm
has shown, that in English and German, *fox* simply denotes
hairy; in Sanscrit, the feminine noun *lomasā — q. d., villosa,*

from *lomas* (hair) — means a fox; while the masculine *lomasă* (*villosus*), denotes quite a different animal, a *ram*. In other languages, *e. g.* in the Icelandic *refr*, and Persian *roubah*, the idea of hairiness quite disappears, and Reynard is designated by another single quality, *thievishness*. The reason of this is obvious. Though a fox is an individual, he is composed of an aggregate of particulars, which no simple word is capable of expressing. We therefore denote this complex idea by a term expressive of some single quality; and though the term may. in itself be equally characteristic of a rat or a squirrel, it answers every purpose of oral communication, as long as people agree to employ it in the same sense. Tooke had consequently no difficulty in showing, that many names of material objects are mere verbal nouns. He has also shown that many adjectives were originally participles; though he too frequently refers those of remote origin to English or Saxon roots. There is, however, one part of his work calculated, as we think, to convey false notions, both of language and philosophy. We find in all languages a number of what are commonly called *abstract* nouns — that is, nouns not significative of sensible or material objects, but of mental conceptions. Tooke's peculiar grammatical and metaphysical notions rendered him anxious to get rid of them; accordingly, he made an indirect attempt to prove that no such words really exist. It is indeed true that the ideas expressed by them have only a relative, not an independent or positive existence. Without space there can be no extension — without matter there can be neither length, breadth, nor thickness; but matter being granted, the above properties of it necessarily follow. Our *senses*, it is true, cannot discern them, except as attributes of a material object; but the whole science of pure geometry proves that the *mind* is capable of conceiving them *abstractedly* — that is, without the smallest reference to matter. The words denoting such ideas form, therefore, a distinct as well as a highly important and interesting class; and the facility and nicety of discrimination with which the Indo-European tongues — especially Sanscrit, Greek, and German — are capable of expressing them, add greatly to their richness and beauty, and give them a marked superiority over all the Semitic family.

Tooke only attempted a small portion of our English abstract nouns, in anything like a direct method; but this portion was too hard for him. He resolves those ending in *th* into third persons of verbs, though no word can at the same time be a noun substantive and a verb in any person; and he all along confounds agent and patient, subject and predicate, in the most arbitrary and illogical manner. We shall not now stop to examine whether month is *mooneth*, fifth *fiveth*, or knave (German, *knabe*, a *youth*!!) which he has dragged in among the *abstracts* — *ne hafath*, *qui nihil habet*; but we will just bestow a few words on his famous etymology of *truth*. We are not going to animadvert on the moral and metaphysical part of the question, which has been sufficiently done already, but merely to view it in a philological light.

The whole of Tooke's case rests on two assumptions: first, that to *trow* simply denotes to *think* or *believe*; secondly, that *truth* originally meant, and still does mean, what *is trowed*, and nothing more: and on the strength of these conclusions, neither of which he has proved, he flatters himself that the old-fashioned notion of *truth* is totally exploded. We venture to think that the following statement is rather more germane to the matter. Sanscrit *dhru*, to be established — *fixum esse*; whence, *dhruwa*, certain — i. e. *established*; German, *trauen*, to rely, trust; *treu*, faithful, true — πιστός; Anglo-Saxon, *treow*, fidus,—*treowth*, fides—πίστις—both subjectively and objectively; English, *true*, *truth*. To these we may add, Gothic, *triggvus*, — Icelandic, *tryggr*, — fidus, securus, tutus: all from the same root, and all conveying the same idea of stability or security. *Truth*, therefore, neither means what is *thought* nor what is *said*, but that which is *permanent*, *stable*, and is and ought to be *relied upon*, because, upon sufficient data, it is capable of being demonstrated or shown to exist. If we admit this explanation, Tooke's assertions, that there is nothing but truth in the world; — in other words, that there is no difference between truth and falsehood; that without mankind there could be no truth, *i. e.* without mankind there could be no other mode of existence; and that two contradictory propositions may be true because *believed* by the utterers,— which amounts to saying, that a thing may be and not be at the same time — become *vox et præterea nihil*. In all inquiries after *truth* the question is, not what people, who may or may not be competent to form an opinion, *think* or *believe*, but what *grounds* they have for believing it. A man may feel persuaded that two and two make five, or that the angles of a triangle are equal to three right angles; but he can neither *prove* these propositions to others, nor have them demonstrated to himself, because they come under the Houhynymn category of *things that are not*. Mr. Stewart observes, that Tooke avoids all reference to mathematical science; we trow that he had good reasons for this omission.

We think we have shown that Tooke's doctrines are not

to be admitted without restriction; and that his application of them is far from being universally correct. It may perhaps be said, that it is easier for a man to find fault with the doings of other etymologists than to produce anything more to the purpose himself. But though it would be *pessimi exempli*, and fatal to the whole craft of reviewing, to admit that no man is entitled to criticise a poem unless he is able to write one, we shall, on the present occasion, imitate the example of 'Milburn, the fairest of critics,' and give those, who may think themselves aggrieved by us, their revenge. They may, if they please, consider the following detached articles as a specimen of a new Etymologicon Anglicanum, and deal with them as they think fit. At all events, the observations may serve as an extension of our critique on the books we have been professing to review, and as a vehicle for communicating some etymologies which, whether right or wrong, do not appear to be generally known.

ABRAID, BRAID.—Our etymologists have given the various significations of these words more or less correctly, and referred some of them to the Icelandic and Anglo-Saxon *bregda*. No one has, as far as we know, attempted to assign the primary sense, or to classify the numerous and seemingly unconnected acceptations.* This, we think, may be done as follows. The Icelandic verb *bregda*, and its corresponding noun *bragd*, denote — 1. sudden, quick motion — whence *braid*, a start; 2. removal — 'the kerchiefe off her hede she *braide*;' 3. transition, change to a different state of things — *v. t. q.*, 'out of her sleep she *braide*;' 4. change of countenance, gesture — whence the provincial term to *braid* of one's parents — *i. e.*, resemble them — *vultu vel gestu referre*; 5. change produced by artificial means, to *braid*, *nectere* — hence metaph., as Dr. Webster well observes; 6. deceit, to deceive — *nectere dolos*. The simple verb also denotes to reproach — whence our *upbraid* — the precise force of which is not quite obvious; it seems to include the idea of a sudden stroke or attack. Boucher's fancy of a connection between *abraid* and *broad* is quite out of the question. We give this, out of a multitude of instances, to show the light thrown on

---

* 'The original application of *braid* is to a loud noise, to almost any description of which it is constantly applied in our older writers. Hence it is transferred to the accompanying motion which is the cause of that noise. In Douglas' Virgil it is said of the winds breaking out of Aeolus' cavern that they forth *brayed* in ane rout.'
Letter from H. Wedgwood, Esq., to the author.

our language by the Icelandic, which has hitherto been most strangely neglected by our lexicographers.

AGOG. — We shall say nothing of the innumerable conjectures respecting this word, except that Mr. Richardson's derivation from the Gothic *gaggan*, to go, is against all analogy. He ought to have known that this verb is in reality *gangan*, and cannot possibly be the parent of either *gag* or *gog*. We believe that the Roxburghshire phrase, *on gogs*, adduced by Mr. Brockett, points to the true origin; viz., Icelandic, *à gægium* — on the watch or look-out — from the neuter passive verb *gægiaz*, to peep or prey.

AISTRE, ESTRE. — This word has long been a *crux etymologorum*; even Adelung confesses that he has nothing satisfactory to offer respecting it. Though found in one form or other all over the north of Europe, it is evidently not a native, but an exotic term of art. We believe the following to be the true history of it. Italian, *lastra* (*tabula lapidea*), a stone or marble slab used for flooring — *lastricare*,, to lay a stone floor; *lastrico*, a pavement or stone floor — λιϑόστρωτος. By a confusion between the initial consonant and the article, common in Italian (comp. *azzurro*, from *lazur*, *ninferno* for *inferno*), *lastrico* became *astrico* — a word preserved by Florio and Torriano, though omitted by Alberti and the 'Vocabolario della Crusca.' In this form the Italian architects employed in our ecclesiastical edifices imported it into the transalpine regions, where, under the further mutations of *aesterich*, *estrich*, *astre*, *estre*, *aistre*, it appears at various times under the following gradation of meanings: — 1. stone floor, pavement, paved causeway; 2. plaster-floor, also ceiling; 3. hearth, fire-place; 4. apartment; 5. dwelling-house. It is curious to see how nearly people often approach the truth without being able to find it. Schmeller traces the word to *astrico*, but no further; and Adelung actually refers to Ducange for *lastra*, without suspecting that it furnishes a clue to the whole matter. We leave those who have leisure and opportunity to inquire whether the original form is *lastra* or *astra*. Frisch gives *aster*, lapis quadratus; but we can find no other authority for the word.

ALDER. — 'French, *aulne*, *aune*; Italian, *alno*; Spanish, *alamo*; Latin, *alnus*: so called *quod alatur amne.*'—Richardson.

Neither a complete etymology, nor entirely correct. The Spanish synonym is *aliso*, not *alamo*, which means a *poplar*; and the following are surely more nearly related to an English word than terms of Latin extraction: Anglo-Saxon, *ælr* (also *alor*, *alr* — apparently dialectical forms); old High German, *elira*, and, by transposition, *erila*; modern German, *erle*; Lower Saxon, *eller* (still used in Yorkshire and Scotland); Icelandic, *œln*, *elni* (resembling the Latin); Swedish, *al* (the simple root); Danish, *elle*. This is a sample of the care of our lexicographers in collecting Teutonic etymologies. Though the above synonyms illustrate several curious points relating to the formation of language, not one is given by Todd or Richardson; and Dr. Webster only has the Anglo-Saxon *alr* — not so genuine a form as *œlr*. We adduce this word chiefly for the sake of showing how unsafe it is to catch at mere resemblances in sound or spelling. Schmeller, in his valuable Bavarian Dictionary, observes, that the termination *ter* or *der* is a relic of an ancient word denoting *tree* — *holun–der*, elder-tree; *wachol–der*, juniper-tree. It might seem an obvious deduction from analogy, that *alder* is also *al–tree*; but this, though plausible enough, would be an erroneous conclusion. The *d* in *alder* is of very recent date, being introduced, *euphoniæ gratiâ*, to prevent the unpleasant collision between *l* and *r*. The Germans seem to have transposed their *elira* for the same reason. The derivation of *alnus* from *alo* does not seem very probable; it is more likely to be connected with a class of words denoting *moisture* — uligo, ulva, &c.

   *ASHLER STONES. — 'Stones as they come from the quarry.' — Todd, Webster. Meant, we suppose, to prove Pope's dictum, that a dictionary-maker does not know the meaning of *two words* put together. If any inquisitive foreigner should happen to learn that our most superb public edifices — St. Paul's and York cathedrals, for example — are *ashler–work*; that is, constructed (as here defined) of *stones as they come from the quarry*; what an elevated opinion he must form of English architecture! No one, as far as we know, has attempted an etymology of the word; which seems to be confined to the British islands: we believe it to be Celtic. The Gaelic is *clach shreathal* (pronounced *shreāl*); *i. e.*, stone laid in *rows* — from *sreah*, a row. We have another Celtic term still more extensively diffused — viz., *gavelock*, a large crow used by masons and quarrymen. A lynx-eyed antiquary might here find materials for some speculation respecting the native country of the workmen employed in the construction of our old castles and cathedrals. But indeed, speaking seriously — though we suspect Sir Francis Palgrave exaggerates the amount of the Celtic element in our actual language — we can have no doubt that that element is a very considerable one; and that the author, if there ever shall be

---

* More commonly spelt *ashlar*. ED.

one, of a complete English Lexicon, will be, *inter alia*, a Celtic scholar. *

AVERAGE. — We believe our English termination has here helped to confound three perfectly distinct words. The old law-term denoting the service which a tenant was bound to render to his lord with teams and carriages, is from Latin. barb. *averium*, originally, goods, property; in a secondary sense, *jumentum*; Scoticè, *aiver* (compare *chattel* and *cattle*). The marine term — French, *avarie*, is the German *haferey*; Lower Saxon, *haverije* — meaning, in the first instance, *harbour dues*; more commonly, a contribution towards loss or damage incurred at sea; ** and in a still more extensive acceptation, a mean proportion between unequal quantities. Lastly, *average* or *averish*, after-grass, stubble — a sense, we believe, confined to the Anglian and Northumbrian counties — is the Icelandic *afrett* or *afrettr*; Danish, *afred*, *aevret* — primarily, an inclosure, also pasturage — after-grass. We are ashamed to say, that a whole bevy of provincial glossarists have acquiesced in the portentous mongrel etymology of *hiver, eatage*! Tell it not at Copenhagen! Had they resolved the parallel term *eddish* into *eatage*, it would have been more to the purpose. This is a word of remote antiquity. In Ulphilas, we find *atisks*, *seges*; in Anglo-Saxon, *edisc*, *vivarium*; in the Leges Bajuvariorum, *ezzisczun* — apparently, park or paddock-fence; in various glosses of the eighth and ninth centuries *ezzisc*, *ezzisca*, *seges*; and in the modern Bavarian, *ätzen*, to depasture — *ätz*, *eddish*, aftermath — and *essisch*, a common field; all from the verbs *etan*, *ezzan*, *essan*, to eat. In *average* the primary import is inclosure — the derivative, food or pasturage — in *eddish*, originally food, there is a curious fluctuation between the two meanings. It is not unworthy of notice, that in Greek χόρτος means both *gramen* and *hortus*: if food or pasturage is the original sense, the Persian *khorden*, to eat, furnishes a plausible etymology.

AWARD. — Of the various etymologies proposed for this word, we shall merely observe, that Tooke's — 'a determination *à qui c'est à garder*'—is the clumsiest and worst. *Award* has evidently a subjective, not an objective meaning; and an etymon that confounds the two ideas, seems neither lo-

---

* The hint thus given was eventually followed up by the author himself. See the papers on the languages of the British islands in this volume. ED.
** 'Tout dommage survenu à des marchandises.' *Bescherel. Dict. Nat.* It also denotes damage sustained by vessels — see the report on the condition of Prince Napoleon's yacht in the appendix to Lord Dufferin's "Letters from Hihg Latitudes."

gical nor very probable. We have nothing certain to offer in lieu of it; but, like Rumour, we have 'a couple of *supposes.*'* *Qvardi*, in Icelandic, is a half-ell, statute measure, whence the verb *aqvarda*, to allot; *i. e.*, to give a man his measure. If we suppose this to have come in with the Northmen, and to have become a forensic term, it follows, that when our barristers and commissioners make their *awards*, they are dealing out justice by the *half-ell*. They who think this *trop boutiquier*, may take refuge in the Lower Saxon *warden*, to fix the *worth*, to estimate. In the Rouchi or Valenciennes dialect, which has borrowed a good deal from the Belgic, *auvarde* is an *expert*, or legal appraiser —
'Utrum horum mavis accipe!'

BIRCH. — This tree of knowledge bears a name analogous to the one so well known at Eton and Westminster, not only in all the German and Slavonic tongues, but also in the Sanscrit — *b'hurjja*. On this foundation Klaproth builds an argument for the northern origin of the dominant race in Hindostan. It seems birch was the only tree the invaders recognized, and could name, on the south side of the Himalaya; all others being new to them. The inference may be right or wrong — it is, at all events, ingenious.

BLIND. — We admit the ingenuity of Tooke's derivation from *blinnan*, to stop, but, like Miss Edgeworth's hero, Mr. Macleod, we think it may be *dooted* — for the following reasons: — 1. *blinnan* does not mean to stop up, *obturare*, but simply to cease, discontinue; 2. it is not a simple verb, but in reality *be-linnan*, as is proved by the old high German gloss *pi-linnan*, *cessare*, and the Icelandic *linnan*, the preposition *be* or *bi* not being known in this language; nevertheless the adjective is exactly the same, *blindr*, though it is not easy to see how it could be formed from the simple *linnan*. We say nothing respecting the real etymology, because we believe that nothing is known of it beyond the Mœso-Gothic *blinds*. Schmitthenner's reference of it to *blenden*, *occœcare*, seems to be a hysteron-proteron. *Blenden* is a causative verb, denoting to *make blind*, like *raise* from *rise*, *set* from *sit*, consequently of more recent origin than the adjective. Grimm's derivation from *blandan*,** to confuse, is more probable, but not quite convincing.

---

* I do not think you need go any farther than *garder* to look for *award*. You look for a fair conclusion amongst the troubles submitted to your award. Look is constantly used in this sense in Robert of Gloucester. e. gr. "To stonde at lokinge (by the award) of the bishop Watre."'
Letter from H. Wedgwood, Esq., to the author.
** (I think *blend* is the same as *blandan*, rather to 'mingle' than to 'con-

3

COTTER. — Our readers are doubtless aware that the appellations, *Cotarii, Coscez, Bordarii,* in Domesday, have caused our antiquaries a great deal of perplexity. We do not undertake to settle the entire question, but we may perhaps furnish something like a clue to one of the terms. In Lower Saxony, the former abode of our ancestors, the following classes existed late in the eighteenth century: — 1. *bauer*, the Anglo-Saxon *ceorl*, one who holds and cultivates a farm of not less than a carucate or ploughgate of land, commonly about thirty acres; 2. *halbmeyer*, in Brunswick *halbspänner*, a smaller farmer occupying only half the amount; 3. *käterkother, kotsass, kossat*, one who holds a cottage and a quantity of land not exceeding the fourth part of an ordinary farm, having no plough or team, and, consequently, no land under tillage; 4. *brinksitter*, who has nothing but a cot, and a small garden or croft, sometimes called *handfröhner*, from being chiefly occupied in servile manual labour for his feudal superior. The above words are used with some occasional latitude of application, but we believe that we have given the original meanings. There is no etymological connexion between *bordarius* and *brinksitter*, the former being derived from *bord*, a cottage, the latter from *brink*, a small croft; nor do they appear to have denoted the same class of persons; but we have not the smallest doubt of the *original* identity of *coscez* with *kossat*, or *kotsass*. It is evident that the Anglo-Saxons brought the term with them from Germany, and, consequently, that something like the same gradations of society existed among them in their Pagan state as at the time of our national survey. We believe that a careful study of the old Lower Saxon, Frisic, Danish, and Icelandic laws would amply repay the legal and constitutional antiquary as well as the philologist.*

CURL. — Among various etymologies for this word, only one of which is to the purpose, Mr. Todd gives pleasantly enough, Danish *krille*, which means to *itch!* The Icelandic *krulla* does, indeed, signify to curl, but this is as etymologically distinct from *krille* as κρνὸς is from κριός. The primary meaning of the word seems to have ceen hitherto overlooked. We conceive that our *curl*, the Scottish *curling* (a

---

fuse' primarily. N. (For this and subsequent notes distinguished by the initial N the editor is indebted to E. Norris Esq. Secretary to the Royal Asiatic Society).

* We may take this opportunity of directing the attention of the reader curious in such matters to a valuable little tract on *Ancient Juries*, lately published by Mr. Repp, an Icelander of extensive learning, employed in the Advocate's Library at Edinburgh.

game on the ice), with the verb to *hurl*, including the Cornish *hurling* (a sort of cricket), are merely different forms and modifications of *roll*. In Schmeller's Dictionary we find *krollen*, to curl the hair; *horlen*, *hurlen*, to roll, to play at skittles. *Scroll* is also of the same family,' exactly answering to Latin *volumen*. Compare *troll*, *stroll*, &c.

DEARTH. — Tooke, in his antipathy to *abstracts*, explains dearth into *dereth*, Anglo-Saxon *derian*, nocere. This we hold to be just as felicitous as the Bishop of Winchester's guess that a *lugg* meant a *cathedral*. * It is a noun formed from the adjective *dear*, like *caritas* from *carus*, and etymologically speaking, neither denotes *suffering* nor *scarcity*, but simply *costliness, high price* — Old German, *tiur*, precious, *tiuran*, to hold dear, glorify. The German equivalent for *derian* is *derjan* or *daron*, lædere — as distinct from *tiur* and *dear* as light is from darkness.

EXCEPT. — It has been the fashion since the appearance of the Diversions of Purley to call *except, save*, and similar expressions, *verbs* in the imperative mood. Dr. Webster, though he professes to have made no use of Tooke's writings, frequently advances the same *doctrines* in nearly the same *words*, and is very severe on grammarians who regard such words as conjunctions. In the examples, 'Israel burned none of them *save* Hazor only' — 'I would that all were as I am, *except* these bonds' — he considers it as certain that *save* and *except* are transitive verbs with an object following them. We hesitate not to say that they cannot be verbs, imperative or indicative, because they have no *subject*, and that a verb could not be employed in any language that distinguishes the different persons without a gross violation of idiom. This will clearly appear if, in the vulgar Latin version of the latter sentence, 'Opto omnes fieri tales, qualis et ego sum, exceptis vinculis his,' we substitute 'excipe vincula hæc,' or any other person of *excipio*. The fact is, that in the above instances *save* is an adjective with the force of a participle (Latin, *salvus*), and *except* an abbreviated participle; in short, these and many similar forms were originally *ablatives absolute*, a construction as familiar in Anglo-Saxon, Old German, and Icelandic, as in Latin, but necessarily less apparent in modern languages, in which the distinctions of case are obliterated. The following examples, all taken from existing versions of the New Testament, show the progress of the ablative participle to an indeclinable word. Icelandic '*undanteknum thessum böndum*,' exactly equi-

---

* Vide Fortunes of Nigel, vol. iii. c. 9, p. 250.

3 *

valent to *exceptis vinculis his* — Italian, *eccettuate queste catene,* preserving the number and gender, but losing the case; Spanish, *salvo estas prisiones*; Portuguese, *excepto estas prizoēns*; German, *ausgenommen diese Bände*, where all distinction of number, case, and gender is lost. Such phrases as *demus ita esse*, French *supposons qu'il vienne*, sometimes rendered in English by verbs and sometimes by conjunctions, are *different constructions*, totally unconnected with the point in debate.

HAGGLE. — Mr. Todd refers this word to the French *harceler*; and Dr. Webster tries to connect it through the medium of *higgle* with the Danish *hykle*, to play the hypocrite. *Hykle* is borrowed from the German *heucheln*, and neither agrees with our English word in form nor meaning. A derivation furnished by Schmeller is somewhat curious. *Häkeln*,* literally to *hook*, also applied to a sort of boys'-play, in which each inserts his hooked forefinger into that of his opponent, and tries to drag him from his standing — whence metaphorically to *strive*, *wrangle*. According to this etymon, *haggling* is 'playing at *finger-hookey*.'

LOUD. — Mr. Tooke confidently refers this word to the Anglo-Saxon *hlowan*, to low, and exults greatly at the discovery that some of our old writers wrote it *lowd*. They who are acquainted with the capricious orthography of the middle ages will be able to appreciate this sort of evidence at its real worth. Until it is shown by what process *hlud* can be extracted from *hlowan*, which we do not think a very easy task, we shall prefer believing that *loud* does not mean what is *lowed* or *bellowed*, but what is *heard*. We do not, indeed, find any simple verb, *hluan*, or *hluen*, to hear; but there are the following traces of one — Gothic *hliuma*, the ear, evidently a verbal noun — Old German, *hliumunt*, hearsay, report; *hlosen*, to listen; — and many others. On this supposition, the Anglo-Saxon *hlud*, Old German, *hlut*, Modern German *laut*, *loud*, also, *sound*, will denote *quod aure percipitur*. It is, at least, certain that a similar verb has nearly gone the round of the European languages: — Greek κλύω, Latin *cluo, clueo, inclytus*, Lithuanian *klausyti*, Irish *cluinim*, Welsh *clywed*, besides several Sclavonic words. The root of all is to be found in the Sanscrit *sru*, to hear, in which the *s* is *palatal*, consequently organically allied to the initial consonant of κλύω and its fellows.

MUCH, MORE. — According to Tooke, '*more, most*, are from the

---

* Compare *hackle* ED.

Anglo-Saxon *mowe*, a *mow*, or *heap*, *q. d. mower*, *mowest*. *Much* is abbreviated from *mokel*, *mykel*, *mochel*, *muchel*, a diminutive of *mo*.'

More strange, we fear, than true! We know the Greeks had their δουλότερος, and similar words, but nobis non licet esse tam disertis. We affirm, without fear of contradiction, that there is not an instance of a substantive in the comparative or superlative degree, in a single Germanic dialect of which we have any knowledge. The remainder of the statement is equally incredible. It would be difficult to show how the Gothic *mikils*, a word known to be more than fourteen hundred years old, was manufactured from either *mo* or *mow*; and such phrases as *se mycel Atlas*, that is, according to our oracle, Atlas the *little mow*, sound as odd to us, as *meritorius*, *respectable*, *worthy* of the *gallows*, did to Golownin's Japanese pupils. The real positive of *more* must be sought in a very different quarter. Sanscrit, *maha*, great, a present participle of *mah*, to grow, increase; Persian *mih*; Greek μέγας, μέγαλος; Gothic, *mikils*; Old German, *mihhil*; Icelandic, *mikill*; Anglo-Saxon, *micel*; Latin, *magnus*. For the comparative, we have Greek, μείζων; Gothic, *maiza*; Latin, *major*; Icelandic, *meiri*; Old German, *mero*; Anglo-Saxon, *mara* — *cum multis aliis*. If these comparatives are not from a more simple and primitive form than the positives now extant, the medial consonant may be dropped *euphoniæ gratiâ*. It re-appears in μέγιστος, and *maximus*, *i. e.*, *mag-simus*, but not in Gothic, *maisis*, nor any of its Germanic brethren. This example may direct us where to look for the verbal roots of many of our simple adjectives.

'ODD. *Owed*, wanted to make up another pair.' 'ORT, ORTS, from Anglo-Saxon, *orettan*, deturpare, *i. e.*, made vile or worthless.' — *Tooke*.

Just as much as Cinderella's *cock-tailed mice* were identical with the *coctiles muri* of Semiramis. *Odd* does not signify deficiency but surplus; *ort* has not the least connexion with *orettan*; and both are, in fact, different forms of the same word. In Icelandic, *oddr*, is a point, cuspis; Danish, *odd*, the same; Swedish, *udd*, a point, also *odd* in the English sense. In German, the primary meaning of *ort* is also *point*. To establish a connexion between the two, we must have recourse to the Bavarian dialect. In this, *ort* not only denotes *point*, but also *beginning*, the *end* of a *thread* or *skein* — and what is most to our purpose, *ort oder eben*, is exactly our *odd or even*. In *odd*, the idea is that of unity, a single point, hence one over; *orts* are waste or superfluous *ends*,

*leavings.** The latter is the German form, the former the
Scandinavian, in which the *r* is *assimilated* to the following
consonant, by a very common process in Icelandic — *e. gr.,
broddr*, a sting, Anglo-Saxon, *brord*; *rödd*, voice, Anglo-
Saxon, *reord*.

SPICK and SPAN. — These words have been sadly tortured
by our etymologists — we shall, therefore, do our best to
deliver them from further persecution. Tooke is here more
than usually abusive of his predecessors; however, Nemesis,
always on the watch, has permitted him to give a lumber-
ing, half Dutch, half German, etymology, of *'shining new
from the warehouse'* — as if such simple colloquial terms were
formed in this clumsy round-about way. Spick-new is simply
nail—new, and span-new, *chip—new*. Many similar expressions
are current in the north of Europe; *fire—new*, *spark—new*,
splinter—new, also used in Cumberland; High-German, *nagel-
neu*, eqivalent to the Lower Saxon *spiker—neu*, and various
others.** The leading idea is that of something quickly
produced or used only once. The Icelandic *spann* signifies
not only *chip*, but *spoon*, whence we may infer, that as the
Latin *cochlear* denotes the employment of a *shell* to convey
pottage to the mouth, our unsophisticated ancestors once used
a *chip* for the same important purpose. We hope none of
our 'exclusives' will quarrel with the word or the thing on
this account; for our part, we think that those little disclo-
sures of ancient manners are not the least interesting part
of etymology.

STEPFATHER. — Tooke refers this with great confidence to
the Danish *stedfader*, *q. d., pater vicarius*; proving that he
knew little either of the history or analogy of language.
Stedfader is a corrupt word of yesterday: the genuine term
stivfader is legitimately connected with all the older dialects;
and we would sooner believe, on the authority of Mascarille,
that the Armenians change *nis* into *rin*, than that our ancestors ever converted *sted* into *step*. We have no doubt
that Junius is right in referring the word to *steop, orphanus*.
The simplest, and consequently the original forms, Icelandic,
stiupr, Old German, *stiuf*, do not denote step-father or mo-

---

* "When numbers are considered as odd or even they seem to be considered as placed in two rows — and if the ends of the rows are even with
each other, we call the number even; if one row projects beyond the other
it is an odd number; and the Icelanders have yddia to *project* from udd.
I don't think you alluded to the expression odds and ends, which is a
common one."

Letter from H. Wedgwood, Esq., to the author.

** Compare *bran-new from the fire*, (brenning) N.

ther, but step-child, orphan; and all doubt respecting the parent-verb is removed by the Carlsruhe glossary of the eighth century, in Graff's Diutiska, which gives us *pim arstiuphil suniu* = ultra urbabor (orbabor) filio. — We take this opportunity of observing, that those who wish to investigate the original forms and significations of the Teutonic tongues, must seek them in the vocabularies of the eighth and ninth centuries, where they are sometimes more plainly developed than in the Gothic of Ulphilas. The mere English or Latin scholar, however, had better let them alone, as it requires considerable knowledge of languages, and a certain skill in conjectural criticism, to use them to any good purpose. For example, *potho*, *apostolus*, conveys no idea to those who do not know that *Bothe*, in modern German, is a messenger; and *lancnasech, aquilus*,* has by some been interpreted *eagle*, and by others, *dark-coloured, dusky*; whereas, it means neither, but *having a long (aquiline) nose*. In a very ancient glosssary preserved at St. Gall, we find *singularis*, *epur* — to understand which, we must remember the German *eber*, a boar, and the Italian *cinghiale*, or French *sanglier*, wild boar. This, which was written in the seventh century, illustrates the early formation of the rustic Roman; and the following specimens equally show the antiquity of some familiar terms in our own language : — *Clausura*; *piunte* (pound); *scopa*; *pesamo* (besom); *pala*; *scufla* (shovel); *sublimitare*; *drisgusli* (threshold) : — *stool, thronus*, seems to have lost a little of its pristine dignity.

WRITE. — The Germans undoubtedly derived their verb *schreiben*, and probably the art of writing with pen and ink, from the Romans. But the existence of an older verb, *rizan*, originally, like the Anglo-Saxon *writan*, Icelandic *rita*, denoting *sculpere, incidere*, as well as the general diffusion of Runic characters among the various tribes, seem to imply that they were not wholly without letters before the Roman period. Otfried accurately discriminates between the two words. In the account of the woman taken in adultery, he says, 'Christ *reiz* mit demo fingero,' — *digito exaravit*; but Pilate's, What I have written, is 'thaz ih *scrib*,' — *quod scripsi*. *Graben* appears from the glossaries to have been similarly employed to denote *literas incidere*, also *to write*. The preterite of *graben, gruob, grub*, furnishes an etymology

---

* Farmatia (pharmacia), *poisun*, seems to show that the compiler of this glossary was not an *apothecary*. The author of Douglas would have been delighted with "nectareus, *van clarette*," unless he had discovered that *claret* does not here mean Lafitte or Château Margaux, but *sweetened wine, clary*.

for Grub Street, which we would recommend the inmates of that classical region by all means to adopt.

Sed manum de tabula — We have endeavoured to show that the field of English philology is far from being exhausted, and we should be glad to see it treated with something of the same rigorous and scientific application of principles and copious induction of particulars, that have been exercised upon some of the sister tongues. Much has been done and is still doing by the Germans and Danes, which ought to excite our emulation, and which we may turn to our own advantage.

ENGLISH DIALECTS.

[*Quarterly Review*, February 1836.]

1. *Provincial Glossary.* By Francis Grose, Esq. London. 1811.
2. *Supplement to the Provincial Glossary of Francis Grose, Esq.* By Samuel Pegge, Esq. London. 1814.
3. *An Attempt at a Glossary of some Words used in Cheshire.* By Roger Wilbraham, Esq. London. 1826.
4. *Observations on some of the Dialects in the West of England.* By James Jennings. London. 1825.
5. *The Hallamshire Glossary.* By the Rev Joseph Hunter. London. 1829.
6. *The Dialect of Craven. With a copious Glossary.* By a Native of Craven. 2 vols. 8vo. London. 1828.
7. *The Vocabulary of East Anglia.* By the late Rev. Robert Forby. 2 vols. 8vo. London. 1830.
8. *A Glossary of North Country Words.* By John Trotter Brockett, F. S. A. Newcastle-upon-Tyne. 1829.
9. *An Etymological Dictionary of the Scottish Language.* By John Jamieson, D.D. 2 vols. 4to. Edinburgh. 1808.
10. *Supplement to ditto.* 2 vols. 4to. 1825.
11. *Glossary of Archaic and Provincial Words.* By the late Rev. Jonathan Boucher. 4to. Parts I. and II. London. 1832, 1833.

It is justly observed by Johnson — whose theoretical ideas of philology were, like those of many teachers and preachers, much better than his practical performances — that the language of our northern counties, though obsolete, (i. e., discontinued in written compositions,) is not barbarous. On another occasion the Doctor told Boswell, that his meditated dictionary of *Scottish* words would be a very useful contribution towards the history of the English language. For our part, we never refer to that extraordinary work, Cotgrave's French Dictionary — the value of which is perhaps now better known in France than in England — without a feeling of regret that its author did not employ the same industry and research in collecting the obsolete and dialectical words of his native tongue. Not a few works, both in

verse and prose, current in his time, and containing, doubtless, valuable materials for the illustration of the literature
of the Elizabethan period, are irretrievably lost; and since
then many genuine Saxon words have gradually disappeared
from the language of common life, especially in the southern and midland counties, which, if carefully preserved,
would have freed the present race of antiquaries and critics
from a great deal of uncertainty and error. However, it
avails nothing to lament the archaisms which have sunk in
the ocean of oblivion, together with Wade and his boat
Guingelot.   We cannot, perhaps, repair the injury we have
sustained in this way, but we may check its increase by
making a diligent collection of those which still survive.
The books named at the head of the present article show
various attempts of this sort have been made, and in various quarters.   They possess, as might be expected, different degrees of literary merit; but all furnish materials of
some value to the philologist and the critic, and will doubtless be thankfully received by those who are aware of the
importance of the subject.

We consider it superfluous to discuss the causes of dialect
in the abstract, or to attempt to establish a clear and positive distinction between the vaguely employed terms *dialect*
and *language*.   The apparently simple question, — is Gaelic
a tongue *per se*, or a mere dialectical variety of Irish? is
not without its intricacies — nay, not without its perils —
to a peaceably disposed man.   Within the English pale the
matter is sufficiently clear; all agree in calling our standard
form of speech the English language, and all provincial deviations from it — at least all that assume a distinct specific
character — dialects.   How and when those different forms
originated has never yet been fully explained: there is, however, no doubt that some of them existed at a very early
period.   Bede observes, that Ceawlin was the West Saxon
form of Cælin; and a nice observer may detect diversities
of grammatical and orthographical forms in our Anglo-Saxon
MSS., according to the province of the transcriber.*   The
remarks of Higden on the subject, though neither very profound, nor, as we think, quite correct, are by no means
devoid of interest: —

'Although the English, as being descended from three German tribes, at first had among them three different dialects;
namely, southern, midland, and northern: yet, being mixed in the

---

* The late Mr. Price promised a work on the Anglo-Saxon dialects: we
do not know whether his collections on the subject are still in existence.

first instance with Danes, and afterwards with Normans, they have in many respects corrupted their own tongue, and now affect a sort of outlandish gabble — (*peregrinos captant boatus et garritus*). In the above threefold Saxon tongue, which has barely survived among a few country people,* the men of the east agree more in speech with those of the west — as being situated under the same quarter of the heavens — than the northern men with the southern. Hence it is that the Mercians or Midland English — partaking, as it were, the nature of the extremes —· understand the adjoining dialects, the northern and the southern — better than those last understand each other. The whole speech of the Northumbrians, especially in Yorkshire, is so harsh and rude, that we southern men can hardly understand it.'**

We see here that Higden (writing about A. D. 1350) was only aware of the existence of three different forms, which he regards as analogous to the dialects spoken by the Jutes, Old Saxons, and Angles, by whom the island was colonized. It is, however, certain that there were in his time, and probably long before, five distinctly marked forms, which may be classed as follows: — 1. Southern or Standard English, which in the fourteenth century was perhaps best spoken in Kent and Surrey by the body of the inhabitants.*** 2. Western English, of which traces may be found from Hampshire to Devonshire, and northward as far as the Avon. 3. Mercian, vestiges of which appear in Shropshire, Staffordshire, and South and West Derbyshire, becoming distinctly marked in Cheshire, and still more so in South Lancashire. 4. Anglian, of which there are three subdivisions — the East Anglian of Norfolk and Suffolk; the Middle Anglian of Lincolnshire, Nottinghamshire, and East Derbyshire; and the North Anglian of the West Riding of Yorkshire — spoken most purely in the central part of the mountainous district of Craven. 5. Northumbrian; of which we shall treat more fully in the sequel. This sketch is only to be considered as an approximation to a geographical arrange-

---

* This, literally interpreted, would denote that the Anglo-Saxon language was not yet quite extinct.
** Polychronicon R. Higdeni, ap. Gale, pp. 210, 211.
*** "The only MS. I recollect, which presents us with an autograph specimen of a dialect at a certain period, is that of the Kentish speech written by Dan. Inchbold of Northgate, Canterbury, in 1320, and preserved among the Arundel MSS. This exhibits all the pecularities of the East Somersetshire dialect; when therefore you state that the standard English was best spoken in the 14th century by the body of inhabitants in Kent and Surrey, you must confine your remark to the upper classes of the laity and clergy."

Letter from Sir F. Madden to the author.

ment; for in this, as in all other countries, dialects are apt to get out of bounds, or to mix with their neighbours. For example — the pronunciation in the parishes of Halifax and Huddersfield is decidedly Mercian; while that of North Lancashire, Westmoreland, and Cumberland exhibits many Anglian peculiarities, which may have been occasioned in some degree by the colonies* from the south planted in that district by William Rufus.

We refrain from entering at present into the obscure and difficult subject of the origin and early history of the West-Saxon, Mercian, and Anglian dialects; especially as valuable materials for its illustration will shortly be laid before the public. When we are in possession of Layamon and the semi-Saxon gospels, illustrated, as we doubt not they will be, by the care and skill of Sir Frederick Madden and Mr. Kemble, we trust they will clear up many points connected with the early history of our language that are now involved in a good deal of uncertainty. We have not space to point out the distinctive peculiarities of our provincial dialects, consisting chiefly in minutiæ of grammar and pronunciation, which it is sometimes difficult to render intelligible. Those of the West of England are exhibited by Mr. Jennings, and those of East Anglia by Mr. Forby, in the introductions to their respective Glossaries. Some information respecting the Halifax dialect will be found in Watson's history of that town; or in the Appendix to Mr. Hunter's 'Hallamshire Glossary.' It may not be unacceptable to some of our readers to know that Robert of Gloucester's language is decidedly West Saxon,** that the peculiarities of 'Pier's Plouhman's Vision' belong to the Mercian dialect; and that Manning's version of Langtoft's 'Chronicle' is written in the English of his age, with a pretty copious sprinkling of Middle Anglian. We know of no production of the middle ages in the Yorkshire Anglian or the Lancashire Mercian. Of the latter there is not even a decent vocabulary, though it is highly important to the philologist,

---

* Saxon Chronicle, A. D. 1092. A comparison of Anderson's ballads with Burns's songs will show how like Cumbrian is to Scottish, but how different. We believe that Weber is right in referring the romance of Sir Amadas to this district. The mixture of the Anglian forms, *gwo*, *gwon*, *hwons*, *boyd-word*, (in pure Northumbrian, *gae*, *gane*, *banes*, *bod worde*,) with the northern term *tynt*, *kent*, *bathe*, *mare*, and many others of the same class, could hardly have occurred in any other part of England.

** It is worth observing that the language of Layamon — just one step removed from Anglo-Saxon — bears an unequivocal analogy to the present West of England dialect; a pretty strong proof that the distinguishing peculiarities of the latter are not modern corruptions.

on account of its peculiar grammatical structure and its many genuine Saxon terms. However, a tolerably correct idea of it may be formed from Collier's justly celebrated 'Dialogue between Tummus and Meary;' which is not only a faithful exhibition of the dialect, but perhaps the truest picture of the modes of thought and habits of the class of people described in it, in their native breadth and coarseness, that has hitherto appeared. The mixture of population consequent upon the spread of the cotton manufacture has greatly deteriorated the purity of the Lancashire speech; but our worthy friend the Laird of Monkbarns might still have found the genuine Saxon guttural in the mouths of old people. A single word still remains generally current, as a memorial of its former prevalence — namely Leigh, a town near Wigan; pronounced nearly like the German *leich*, both by gentle and simple.

The most important of our provincial dialects is undoubtedly the Northumbrian — both on account of the extent of the district where it prevails, and its numerous and interesting written monuments. It is the speech of the peasantry throughout Northumberland, Durham, the North and East Ridings of Yorkshire, nearly the whole of the extensive Wapontake of Claro in the West Riding, and the district called the Ainsty or liberties of the city of York. What is spoken in Cumberland, Westmoreland, and Lancashire, to the north of the Ribble, is substantially the same dialect, but with many verbal varieties, and a less pure pronunciation. It is, as might be expected, more like English to the south of the Tees, and more like Scotch as we approach the Tweed, but its essential peculiarities are everywhere preserved. It is unquestionably — pace Ranulphi Higdeni dixerimus — the most pleasing of our provincial forms of speech, especially as spoken in the North and East Ridings of Yorkshire. The Durham pronunciation, though soft, is monotonous and drawling; and that of Northumberland is disfigured by the burr and an exaggerated Scotch accent.

The resemblance between this dialect and the lowland Scotch will strike every one who compares Mr. Brockett's glossary with Dr. Jamieson's dictionary, or Minot's poems with Barbour's Bruce. In fact, it is still a matter of debate among our literary antiquaries, whether some of our metrical romances—'Sir Tristrem,' for example*—were written

---

* The writer's views respecting the dialect of Sir Tristrem were subsequently fully stated in a long note to the edition of Warton's English Poetry published by Mr. R. Taylor in 1840. Ed.

to the north or the south of the Tweed. In our opinion,
both may be practically considered as forming one and the
same dialect. The vocabularies, it is true, are not perfectly
identical, many words being used in Scotland which are
unknown in England, and *vice versâ*; but the verbal forms,
the grammatical constructions, and all other distinguishing
characteristics are the same in both countries. And now
questions arise on which much Christian ink has been shed,
and no small acrimony displayed: Where was this dialect
first manufactured, and out of what materials? — Was it imported into Scotland from England, or into England from
Scotland, or did it grow up in both countries simultaneously?

We thought, on concluding many years back an examination of the points of history and geography involved in
the above questions, that they had all been set at rest long
ago by Usher and Lloyd; and notwithstanding the arguments
adduced by Dr. Jamieson — the present champion of the
Pinkertonian hypothesis — we think so still. On one side
we have the positive testimony of contemporary authors —
on the other, the dreams of Pinkerton, and the assertions
of Dempster and Hector Boethius: men who thought it the
duty of an historian — like that of an ambassador — to tell
lies for the good of his country. We could easily show that
the cardinal argument for the Scandinavian origin of the
Picts — the very corner-stone of Dr. Jamieson's theory — is
a three-fold begging of the question; but we consider it superfluous to discuss a point, which, after all, we do not
feel concerned to prove or disprove.* Whatever might be
the race or language of the Picts, it is difficult to deduce
the origin of the Scoto-Northumbrian dialect from them — for
this weighty reason, that two of the three millions who speak
it inhabit districts where that people never had a permanent
settlement during any known period of their history. We
first find them mentioned at the end of the third century,
in conjunction with the Irish. Their precise abode is not
specified, but we know that they did not occupy either Lothian or Galloway during the latter part of the fourth century. In the time of Valentinian, the ancient frontier of

---

* We the more willingly waive this subject at present, because we know
that a work in which it is largely discussed will shortly issue from the
press. We allude to Mr. William Skene's Essay on the Highlanders of
Scotland, which obtained the Highland Society of London's gold medal
for 1835 — but which the author is understood to be bringing before the
public at large in a much extended form. (ª)

(ª) For some remarks on this book see the essay on the languages of the British islands. Ed.

Antoninus was restored by the establishment of the new province of Valentia, having the Clyde and the Forth for its northern boundary. After the usurpation of Maximus, the barbarians beyond the frontier made repeated irruptions, which were successively repelled, till the final departure of the Roman forces, in the time of Honorius, left the northern part of the province at their mercy for several years. We have tolerably express testimony as to the proper territory of the Picts at this period. Gildas, speaking of their destructive invasion when the Roman forces were withdrawn, describes them as *a transmarine nation from the north* — words which Dr. Jamieson seizes upon in confirmation of his theory of their Scandinavian origin. Bede, however, who had evidently this passage of Gildas before him, will inform us in what sense his expressions are to be understood, — 'We call these people (the Scots and Picts) *transmarine* — not because they were situated out of Britain, but because they were separated from the territory of the *Britons* by the intervention of two *arms of the sea*, of considerable length and breadth; one of which penetrates the land of Britain on the side of the eastern sea, the other of the western.' Thus, according to the idea of Bede, who knew a great deal more about the Picts than we do — 'transmarine from the north' — means neither more nor less than from the other side of the Friths of Forth and Clyde. As Dr. Jamieson lays great stress on Bede's account of the Scythian origin of this people, he cannot decently reject his testimony in the present instance. — 'Testem quem quis inducit pro se — tenetur recipere contra se.'

As we are not writing the history of those ages, we shall content ourselves with observing that the Britons, after enduring the depredations of the barbarians for several years, at last derived courage from despair, and drove them back to their own territories. Gildas expressly states that, in his time, they were 'seated in the extremest parts of the island, occasionally emerging from thence for purposes of plunder and devastation;' and the whole tenor of Bede's history plainly shows that he knew of no[*] Pictish community to the

---

[*] Dr. Lingard — whose general perspicacity in questions of this sort we cheerfully acknowledge — is evidently mistaken in placing Candida Casa (or Whitherne in Galloway) in the Pictish territory, on the strength of its being the cathedral of St. Ninian, the apostle of the southern Picts. This, we think, will appear from the following considerations: — 1. In the time of Ninian, who died A. D. 432, the province of Valentia was, at least nominally, in the possession of the Romans, or Romanized Britons. 2. In the passage of Bede referred to by Dr. Lingard, Ninian is said to have

south of the friths, from the arrival of the Saxons to his own time.   Any one who bestows a moderate degree of attention on the early history of the island, will perceive that the conquests of Ida and his immediate successors in Bernicia were not made over Picts, but Britons of Cymric race; and that in the time of Oswy and Ecgfrid, the Saxons had not only military possession of a considerable tract of Pictish territory to the north of the Forth, but had even made some progress in colonizing it.   It is true that the battle of Drumnechtan, A. D. 685, re-established the independence of the Picts; but it is equally certain that they made no permanent conquest in the Northumbrian territory after that period.   This is decisively proved by the fact, that, at the time Bede wrote his history, A. D. 731, Abercorn, in Linlithgowshire, was within the Saxon limits, being described by him as situated 'in the Anglian territory, but adjoining the frith which separates the land of the Angles from that of the Picts.'   During the next 120 years, we find them engaged in a series of sanguinary conflicts with the western Britons, the Scots, and the Danes; and before A. D. 850, they ceased to exist as an independent nation.   We leave our readers to judge how probable it is that the Picts should plant a language, which it has never been proved that they spoke, in a district of which they never, as far as we know, had the civil administration for ten consecutive years.

We shall now bring an argument or two on the other side of the question, and leave our readers to judge which way the evidence seems to preponderate.

---

erected his church at Candida Casa of stone, 'insolito *Brittonibus* more.' 3. In a preceding passage (Eccl. Hist., l. i., c. l.), Bede expressly describes the frith of *Clyde* as the Boundary between the Britons and the Picts, 'sinus maris permaximus, qui antiquitus gentem Britonum a Pictis secernebat.' '*Antiquitus* secernebat' does not mean that the *Picts* afterwards gained a settlement to the southward, but refers to the subsequent occupation of Argyle by the *Scots*. 4. The population of Strath Clyde to the north, and of Cumberland to the south, was undoubtedly British. 5.   The writer of Ninian's life expressly says, that after ordaining bishops and priests among his Pictish converts, and putting all things in order, '*ad Ecclesiam suam est regressus*'—i. e. to his British cathedral at Candida Casa. In another instance, Dr. Lingard goes still more widely astray (vol. i., p. 278), when he places the Badecanwyllan of the Saxon chronicle in Lothian. It is undoubtedly — as Gibson supposes — Bakewell, called Bathequell as late as the 13th century; and *Peaceland*, where the chronicler places it, is not the land of the *Picts*, but the *Peak* in Derbyshire. The reference to Camden is nothing to the purpose.   He had no better authority for asserting that Lothian was called Pictland, than Hector Boethius — who contrived to extract the name out of the Pentland hills — as the Portuguese find Ulysses in Lisbon.

Let us first consult the Highlanders, who are universally allowed to be great genealogists, and to have excellent traditional memories. They were well acquainted with the Scandinavians, whom they, as well as the Irish and the Welsh, uniformly call Lochlinneach; and have also sundry traditions respecting the Cruithneach or Picts. But do they ever call the Lowland Scots, or their language, by either of those appellations? No such thing! they regularly apply to both the term Sassgunach* or Sassenach — the very word which they, as well as the Irish, Manks, Armoricans, and Welsh, also constantly employ to denote *English* and *Englishmen*. If Dr. Jamieson will clearly and satisfactorily explain how a people and tongue *not Saxon* came to be so styled by their Gaelic neighbours, we will *almost* promise to believe in his Pictish etymologies.

Our next appeal shall be to the language itself. The general drift of Dr. Jamieson's reasoning is, that the Picts were a Scandinavian people, speaking a language identical, or nearly so, with Icelandic. If this really were the case, we say with confidence that the Lowland Scotch cannot be its lineal descendant, for this plain reason, that it is not, as to its structure and basis, a Scandinavian dialect. A tongue of Norse extraction is distinguished from a German, Belgic, or Saxon one by several broadly marked and unequivocal peculiarities. In all the latter the definite article is a distinct prepositive term: — *e. g.*, Germ., der könig; Ang.-Sax., se cyning; Eng., the king. In the Scandinavian dialects it is uniformly postpositive and coalescing with its substantive, analogous to the *status emphaticus* of the Aramæan languages: *e. g.* — Icelandic, *konung*, king — *konunginn*, the king; Danish, *mand*, man — *manden*, the man. In Icelandic and its descendants there is a simple passive voice — *ek elska*, I love; *ek elskast*, I am loved: in all the German and Saxon languages the passive is formed by the perfect participle and the verb substantive, like the German *ich werde geliebet*. The above, as well as many peculiarities in the substance and form of the pronouns and numerals, are as conspicuous in Danish and Swedish, after five centuries of adulteration with Low German, as in the most ancient Icelandic monuments; and it is impossible for a person, even slightly acquainted with their structure, to read

---

* It may be objected they also call the Lowlanders, Dubh Gall — a name formerly given by the Irish to the Danes. This, however, is not a national appellation, but a term of contempt, denoting *black strangers*; also applied to Englishmen, but never to the *Picts*.

two consecutive sentences in one of those three languages, or any of their subordinate dialects, without perceiving to what family they belong. In Lowland Scotch, on the contrary, we meet with nothing of the kind. There we find not the smallest vestiges of a postpositive article or a passive voice; and the pronouns, numerals, and most of the particles, plainly belong to the Saxon family.

For the proof of those assertions we refer our readers to the grammars of Grimm and Rask; reserving to ourselves the privilege of saying a few words about Scottish *particles.* We shall preface our remarks with an extract from a work well known to Dr. Jamieson, in the hope that an argument founded on the principles there laid down will have some weight with him and his disciples.

'The particles, or winged words, as they have been denominated, are preferred in proof of the affinity between Greek and Gothic,* for several reasons. These are generally of the highest antiquity, most of them having received their established form and acceptation in ages prior to that of history. They are also more permanent than most other terms; being constantly in use, entering into the composition of many other words; constituting an essential part of every regular language, and determining the meaning of every phrase that is employed to express our thoughts. They are also least likely to be introduced into another language; because, from the various and nice shades of signification which they assume, they are far more unintelligible to foreigners than the mere names of things or of actions; and although the latter, from vicinity or occasional intercourse, are frequently adopted, this is rarely the case as to the particles; because the adoption of them would produce an important change in the very structure of a language which has been previously formed.' — *Jamieson, Hermes Scythicus,* p. 2.

All this is very excellent, and furnishes an infallible criterion for tracing the affinities of tongues. Whoever takes the trouble to compare the particles — especially the simple prepositions and conjunctions — in Icelandic and Anglo-Saxon — will find sufficient resemblance to prove that they are *kindred* tongues; and sufficient dissimilarity to show that they do not belong to the *same division* of the great *Germanic* family. Many particles in the two languages are identical, or nearly so, in sound and meaning — many are of cognate

---

* It seems rather an extraordinary instance of *nyctalopia* to see the affinity between Greek and Gothic, and not to see that between Lowland Scotch and Anglo-Saxon.

origin, but differ materially in form — and many others have nothing in common; proving clearly that the two tribes who spoke those languages must have been long and widely separated after branching off from the parent stock. The case is equally clear with respect to the derivative languages. Our English particles show a direct descent from Anglo-Saxon; while those of Denmark and Sweden are, with the exception of a few Lower Saxon terms, as unequivocally from the Icelandic. Every smatterer can see that the Danish preposition *imod* (contra) is not from Anglo-Saxon *ongean*, but from Icelandic *ámoti*, or *imoti*; and that this last cannot possibly be the parent of our English word *against*. Now, if the Lowland Scottish be tried by this criterion, the result will be anything but favourable to the theory of its Scandinavian origin. The presence or absence of a few Norse particles proves nothing decisive either way. Those which are wanting may have become obsolete, and those which actually occur might be introduced by the Danish invaders. But the existence of a large mass of words of this class, which never were Icelandic, but have their undoubted counterparts in Anglo-Saxon, fixes the character of the dialect beyond all controversy. We could furnish a long list of such terms; we will at present content ourselves with a few of the most ordinary and essential particles in AngloSaxon and Icelandic — leaving it to our readers ' ayont the Tweed' to decide whether the Scottish equivalents are more nearly allied to the former or the latter.

English.	Anglo-Saxon.	Icelandic
through	ðurh	ì gegnum
against	ongean	ì motï
by	bi, be	hìà (Dan. hos)
among	gemang	á medal
between*	betveonum	á milli
about	ymbutan, abutan	kringum
than	ðonne	enn
but	butan	enn, helldur
or	oððe	eda (Dan. eller)
neither	nauðer	hverki
and	and	ok
not	na	ecki
yet	gyt	ennthà
yesterday	gystrandag	ì gær

* The old Scottish form *atweesh* is clearly the Lower Saxon *twischen*. *Amell*, between, is found in Northumberland, but not in *Scotland*.

English.	Anglo-Saxon.	Icelandic.
soon	sona, suna	snart
when	hvænne	nær, er
how	hvu, hu	hversu.

We do not think it necessary to give the Northumbrian forms, as they are in general mere dialectical variations from southern English; ex. gr., *aboot* for about, *amang* for among; and generally identical, or nearly so, with the Lowland Scottish. We admit that a number of particles occur in this last-named dialect which are not found in modern English; nor can it surprise any one acquainted with the history of the British islands during the ninth and two following centuries, to find a few of Scandinavian descent, especially among the adverbs. But the number of ancient and radical particles derived from this source is much smaller than might have been expected. In fact, we doubt whether Dr. Jamieson's Dictionary furnishes six simple prepositions and conjunctions unequivocally of Norse origin.

The evidence furnished by the preposition *by* is so strong that we could be content to rest our case on it alone. There is not a vestige of the word in Scandinavian,* either as a separate particle or in composition. In Lowland Scottish it is extensively employed in both capacities, and enters intimately into the very structure of the language; often coalescing so closely with the fellow-members of a compound term as to be with difficulty distinguished. It is sufficient to allege the following vernacular terms in proof of this assertion: *aboon* (supra) — q. d., *á*, or *on*-be-ufan; *but* (sine), be-utan; *ben* (inner apartment), be-innan; *but* (outer apartment), of the same origin as *but* (without); to say nothing of *be–east*, *be–west*, *belive*, *bedene*, and a multitude of others. To sum up the matter in a small compass, we say, most confidently, that if the truly Christian sentiment ' let *by-ganes***' be *by-ganes*,' and the familiar household words *but* and *ben* are genuine Scottish phrases, Scottish is not and cannot be a Scandinavian dialect.

' But,' says Dr. Jamieson, ' it cannot be a dialect of the

---

* To those who allege the use of *be* as a prefix in Danish and Swedish, we reply with the following passage from Molbech's excellent Danish Dictionary: — 'The particle *be* is a mere borrowed word from the German; nearly all the words compounded with it are more recent than the *fourteenth* century, and a great part of them not older than the sixteenth, seventeenth and eighteenth.'

** We may just observe, that the auxiliary *be* (esse) is as foreign to the Scandinavian dialects as the preposition *by*. The Icelandic verb is *vera*; Danish *være*; Swedish *vara*.

Anglo-Saxon, as there is no good reason for supposing that it was ever *imported* from the *southern* part of the island.' Here we plainly perceive the fallacy which pervades every part of the Doctor's Dissertation. We know that the speech of Lothian was neither *imported* from the Thames, the Severn, nor the Trent; but we know too that it stands in the closest affinity to that used on the banks of the Tees and the Tyne; being, in fact — like that — Northumbrian Saxon, with a strong infusion of Danish and a small portion of Norman French: the very mixture which the known history of the district would lead us to expect. A careful grammatical analysis shows, moreover, that the Saxon forms the older portion or basis of the dialect; the two other component elements being demonstrably of more recent introduction. Clear as all this seems, Dr. Jamieson makes a bold attempt to bring the 'blue bonnets over the border.' He winds up an elaborate endeavour to prove that the term *Yule* must have been derived from the *Scandinavian Picts*, with the following observation: —

'The name *Yule* is, indeed, still used in England; but it is in the northern counties, which were possessed by a people originally the same with those who inhabited the Lowlands of Scotland.'

Valeat quantum! We happen to know that the term *Yule* is perfectly familiar throughout the *West Riding* of Yorkshire, south of the Wharf and Ouse, where a dialect prevails quite distinct from the Northumbrian, and where, nevertheless, every peasant burns his Yule-log and eats his Yule-cake, up to the present time. Did they learn all this from the *Picts*? — Certainly not, but from the *Danes*, who once constituted more than half the population in our eastern counties, from the Welland to the Forth; and of whom we find unequivocal traces, as well in the dialects as in the topographical appellations* of the district. The proposition that the northern counties were possessed by a people originally the same with those who inhabited the Lowlands of Scotland, being one of those commonly called *convertible*, we beg to state it in the following form: The Scottish Lowlands were possessed by a people originally the same with those who inhabited the north of England, — i. e., in the first instance, Northumbrian *Angles*, afterwards blended with Danes; and the Dano-Saxon dialect of this mixed race has

---

* A plain instance occurs in the present name of Whitby. In the time of Bede, and long after, it was called Streoneshalch; which the Danish occupants changed to Hvitby — q. d., the white town. All the *by*'s in our Anglian and Northumbrian provinces are of a similar origin.

in substance simultaneously descended to the present occupants of both districts. — Q. E. D.*

We recommend to Dr. Jamieson's consideration the following short passage from Wallingford, as, in our opinion, worth the whole of Pinkerton's Inquiry: —

'Sweyn, king of Denmark, and Olave, king of Norway, a short time before invaded Yorkshire, and reduced it to subjection. For there is, and long has been, a great admixture of people of Danish race in that province, and *a great similarity of language.*' — (*Chron. apud Gale,* p. 570.)

This concluding observation, equally applicable to Northumberland and Lothian, furnishes an easy and satisfactory solution of the entire question.

We have already observed that the works we have undertaken to review have different degrees of literary merit: some are necessarily meagre for want of materials; others, on account of the limited opportunities enjoyed by their compilers. In perusing their lucubrations we have frequently found cause to smile at their interpretations, and still more frequently at their etymologies; for every glossarist is, *ex officio,* an etymologist. We are not, however, disposed to scrutinize severely the defects of men who have done their best, but rather to thank them for preserving what might otherwise have been irretrievably lost. In the words of Wachter, 'Juvat hac obsoleta servari, aliquando profutura.' The spirit of scientific and rational etymology cannot fail to arise amongst us ere long, and whenever that happens these volumes will supply it with abundance of materials. Even Grose's 'Classical Dictionary of the Vulgar Tongue' furnishes matter on which a skilful and perspicacious critic might employ himself to good purpose.

Some of the compilations before us are in all respects too slight for any extended criticism. Among the smaller ones, the most respectable in point of execution is Mr. Wilbraham's 'Cheshire Glossary.' His words are well selected, and often judiciously illustrated; and his etymologies, though frequently defective, are seldom extravagant. The insertion of the South Lancashire words — which belong to the same dialect — would have added considerably to the value of

---

* Our readers can hardly need to be told that the Lowland Scotch poets of the Middle Age always call the language in which they composed, *Inglis* — English. For example, Dunbar in one of his controversial pieces says:
'I have on me a pair of Lothian hips
Sall fairer Inglis mak, and mair perfyte,
Than thou canst blabber with thy Carrick lips.'

the work. Many genuine Mercian terms might also be gleaned in Staffordshire, Shropshire, and Derbyshire: the sooner this is done the better, as every successive generation loses something of the speech of its forefathers.

The Norfolk and Craven Glossaries are on a larger scale, and both are highly creditable to the zeal and industry of the authors. They furnish the fullest view of the two principal branches of the Anglian dialect that has hitherto been given; and ought carefully to be consulted by every one who wishes to investigate the general analogies of our tongue. We would particularly recommend the perusal of the Craven Glossary to our dramatists and novelists, who, when they introduce a Yorkshire character, generally make him speak something much more like Hampshire — occasionally even broad Somersetshire. * They have, however, now the means of studying the purest form of the West Riding dialect, synthetically as well as analytically. The respectable author has embodied the speech of the romantic and interesting district where he resides, in a couple of dialogues, which, though not equal to Collier's in dramatic effect, are not destitute of merit. We can, at all events, vouch for the general accuracy of the dialect and idiom.

The most copious and best executed of our English vocabularies is undoubtedly Mr. Brockett's 'Glossary of North Country Words.' He had ample materials to work upon, and he has turned them to good account. His work, though the fullest of matter, exhibits by far the smallest proportion of corrupt forms; and his explanations, especially of Northumberland words, are generally correct and satisfactory. A few North Yorkshire words appear to have escaped his notice; and we have reason to believe that many provincial terms, current in Westmoreland and Cumberland, have never been collected by any glossarist. Most of these belong to the Northumbrian dialect, and ought to be embodied in Mr. Brockett's work. It is, of course, the business of the *natives* to collect and transmit them, and we hope that some of them will take the hint.

Dr. Jamieson's Dictionary has been so long before the public, and its merits are so well known, that any praise on our part would be superfluous. As we trust that another edition will be published ere long, incorporating both parts of the work in one regular series, we take the liberty of

---

* The little farce of the 'Register Office' is an exception. The Cleveland dialect is there given with perfect fidelity, and must have been copied from the life.

suggesting that it might be advantageously enlarged from the following sources: — 1. The Scottish Acts of Parliament, published by the Record Commission; especially the first volume — *if it ever appears.** 2. The ancient northern metrical romances; many of which are still in MS. 3. Mr. Brockett's Glossary; which is, in all essential points, in the same dialect as Dr. Jamieson's Dictionary, and furnishes valuable materials for its elucidation and correction.

We shall devote more space to the last book on our list — Boucher's 'Archaic and Provincial Glossary' — on account of the comprehensiveness of its plan, and our wish that a work which has long been a desideratum in our literature should be executed in a creditable and satisfactory manner. The first part was published in 1832, accompanied with a promise that the following portions should appear at intervals of two months. It is, however, so much easier to project than to execute, that the three years which have since elapsed have barely sufficed for the production of part the second.** We are without means to account for this extraordinary delay; and, to say the truth, we shall not much regret it, if it gives the conductors an opportunity of reforming the defects of their plan, and availing themselves of better sources of information than they at present seem to enjoy. We shall freely point out what we conceive to be the imperfections of the work, and sincerely hope that our observations — which are prompted by no hostile spirit of criticism — will be taken in good part.

In the first place, we cannot but regret that it has been thought expedient to publish the materials collected by Mr. Boucher, without any attempt at selection or discrimination. Mr. Boucher was a most worthy man, and exercised laudable zeal and industry in the prosecution of his favourite object. He has collected a multitude of words from a variety of sources, among which there is much that is valuable and well worthy of preservation. It is, however, easy to perceive that he was deficient in critical acumen, and imperfectly versed in the various branches of knowledge required for the scientific execution of a work of this sort. His Introduction shows that his ideas of the origin and affiliation of languages were singularly confused and erroneous.

---

* We ourselves rather despair of living to see either this volume — (which, considering the erudition and ability of its editor, could not fail to be of great importance) — or the 'Anglo-Saxon and Welsh Laws.' Everything interesting to the philologist and the general scholar seems to be studiously kept back to the very last. [Both have been published. ED.]

** No more was published. ED.

He regards (p. 2) all the European languages as derived from Celtic, and Celtic from Hebrew. In the next page he tells us that 'the languages of Europe may be traced to two sources — Celtic and Gothic; *if* indeed these two are radically different.' By and by, he informs us, that the Germans, Hungarians, and Turks, are of *Sclavonian* origin; and then, that the Sclavonian language is supposed to have been formed from a mixture of Grecian, Italian (!!!), and German. He discovers that the vocabulary of Icelandic is *scanty*; and that it is so nearly allied to Celtic that a Welshman or Bas-Breton could easily make himself understood in Iceland! It is not to be expected that a man with such confused and imperfect notions should be equal to a task that requires qualifications of no ordinary description; he might be useful as a pioneer, but he could never become a wise master-builder. The business of the present editors surely was not to cram down the throats of the public everything that Mr. Boucher had committed to paper, good or bad; but to proceed on a principle of rigorous selection and compression, and to adapt the work to the present advanced state of philological knowledge. Instead of this, they have given all Mr. Boucher's crudities, along with a good many of their own, and overloaded what is really valuable with a huge mass of useless and erroneous matter. The portion that has hitherto appeared is liable to the following exceptions.

1. One principle which ought to be strictly adhered to in works of this kind, is the rigid exclusion of mere modern words. The book before us professes to be supplementary to our ordinary dictionaries, and composed of different materials; it was, therefore, equally unnecessary and improper to encumber it with such every-day words as 'abeyance, abnegation, abstract, abut, acolyte, acquittance, action, admiral, admiralty, advocate, advowson, affianced, alcove, apprentice,' and a multitude of others of the like sort. The admission of them destroys all unity of plan, and makes an useless addition to the bulk and cost of the book. The prolixity with which they are treated makes the matter still worse: we have eight mortal columns about the game of *barley-break* — a word neither archaic nor provincial. It is no satisfaction to the public to be told that all this is derived from Mr. Boucher's MSS. The business of the editors of such works is to give us what we want, and not what we do not want.

2. It is of still greater importance to exhibit words in their genuine forms. Corruptions likely to create real difficulty may be briefly noticed, in order to refer them to their true

source; but those which involve no difficulty whatever should
be peremptorily rejected. In the unsettled orthography of
the middle ages, a word is often found in half a dozen different shapes — all erroneous, but easily intelligible. The
blending these and the genuine terms into one heteroge-
neous mass, as our editors have done, can only tend to
swell the work with useless matter, and to confuse the analogies of our tongue. Surely any schoolboy could discover
the meaning of *abhominable*, *anough*, *anudder*, *auncian*, without the aid of an archaical glossary; and the simple observation, that our provincials frequently omit the aspirate,
would have precluded all necessity for the incertion of such
words as *alpurth*, *alwes*, *arm*, *ash*, *awer*, and many more of
the same class. This indiscriminate heaping together of
every vicious form found in an old book or MS. necessarily
causes endless repetitions. After a good deal of prosing
about a corrupt word, we are referred to another distortion
of it, where we find nearly the same matter repeated — and
sometimes a word hardly worth giving at all occurs no less
than three times. What would our Greek and Latin lexicons be, if every error and corruption of the middle ages
had been registered with equal fidelity?

3. In Mr. Boucher's portion of the work, a number of
purely *Scottish* words occur. These, we conceive, ought to
have been omitted by the present editors, since as they now
stand they are positive blemishes. The book has clearly
no pretensions to the character of a *complete* Scottish dictionary — which it ought to be, if meant to be of any value
as a book of *reference* — and the little which is given is not
to be relied upon. The following may serve as a sample of
the care and skill bestowed on this department.

'BACHLE, BAUGH. To distort, reproach.'

This definition is backed by four quotations. In the first,
bachle means to put out of shape; in the second it is a substantive, denoting an old shoe or slipper; in the third, *bauchly*
is an adverb, meaning imperfectly, indifferently; and in the
fourth, *baugh* is an adjective, signifying poor, mean, inferior. Many other interpretations of Scottish words are
equally defective. There was no great harm in Mr. Boucher's collecting them and interpreting them as well as he
could; but there is now no excuse for giving mutilated and
erroneous accounts of terms fully and correctly explained by
Dr. Jamieson six-and twenty years ago.

We mention these defects, in the hope of their being
avoided in the remaining portion of the work; which, after

all drawbacks, contains much that is really of value. Two
of the conductors (Mr. Hunter and Mr. Stevenson) are known
as men of research, and well qualified to furnish materials
from sources to which few can have access. Many of Mr.
Stevenson's contributions from the MSS. in our public libraries are peculiarly important, and his Anglo – Saxon etymologies are generally correct. He does not succeed so well
in his illustrations from other languages, but *non omnia pos-
sumus omnes.* If he and his fellow-labourers will collect all
the *words* which deserve a place in an archaic and provincial glossary, accompanied with data for ascertaining their
meaning, they will be entitled to the thanks of the public —
whether their etymologies are right or wrong.

We think ourselves bound in fairness to give some specimens of the works which we have noticed, both for the
sake of justifying our criticisms, and of pointing out some
sources whence this part of our language may be illustrated,
that have hitherto been used imperfectly, or not at all. We
therefore warn our readers, that we are about to occupy a
number of pages with dry disquisitions about words and syllables, in order that those who have no relish for such matters may proceed *per saltum* to the next article. Our quotations are from Boucher's Glossary, when not otherwise
specified.

'Aandorn, orndorn, orn-dinner.'

This word appears in our glossaries in nine or ten different shapes, all equally corrupt. The true form is *undorn*,
or *undern*; Goth., *undaurn*; Ang.-Sax., *undern*; German, *un-
tern*. The word is sagaciously referred by Schmeller to the
preposition *unter*, anciently denoting *between* (compare Sanscrit, *antar*;* Lat., *inter*), q. d. the *intervening* period; which
accounts for its sometimes denoting a part of the forenoon,
or a meal taken at that time — and sometimes a period between noon and sunset. It occurs in the former sense in
Ulphilas, *undaurnimat*, ἄριστον (Luc. xiv. 12); in the latter,
in the Edda (Voluspà), where the gods are said to have divided the day into four parts — *myrgin*, morning; *mithean dag*,
noon; *undern*, afternoon; *aftan*, evening. The Lancashire
form *oandurth* approaches most nearly to the Welsh *anterth*,
forenoon; fancifully resolved, as we think, by Owen into
an tarth = without vapour. We rather suspect a connexion
with the Sanscrit *antar*.

---

* This is the true etymon of our *under* — not, as Tooke absurdly maintains, the Belgic *on neder*.

'ALDER. — A common expression in Somersetshire for cleaning the alleys in a potatoe-ground; i. e., for *ordering* them, or putting them into order.'

A most profound conjecture! We conceive the word means to *ridge* — an operation usually performed when potatoes are *hoed*. Bavarian *alden*, a furrow. — It is uncertain whether the Icelandic *allda*, a wave, is of kindred origin.

'ALLER.'

Mr. Boucher, misled by Keysler, describes the alder-tree as held in great veneration by our ancestors. Keysler's statement evidently belongs to the *elder*. The Danish peasantry believe this tree to be under the protection of a sort of goddess called Hyldemœr, who avenges every injury offered to it, and do not venture to cut an elder bough without falling on their knees and thrice asking permission. Several traditions on the subject are given in Thiele's 'Danske Folkesagen,' pp. 132-197. The resemblance of this hyperborean deity to a Grecian Hamadryad is not a little curious.

'AME, v. a.'

We are left by Mr. Boucher to choose among eight meanings affixed to this word by Hearne, four of which are certainly wrong. It is from the German *ahmen*; Bavarian, *amen, hämen*, properly to gauge a cask, also to fathom, *measure*. This is evidently the sense in his second quotation from Langtoft —

'A water in Snowden rennes, Auber is the name,
An arm of the sea men kennes, and depnes may none *ame*.'

We are not aware of its ever being used by the Germans to denote *compute, reckon*; as it seems to be in the passage first cited —

'Of men of armes bold, the number they *ame*.'

The connexion between the two ideas is however obvious enough. A diligent examination of our old writers would perhaps decide whether our *aim* comes immediately from this source, or more indirectly so through the medium of the French *esmer*. — Vide Ducange in Esmerare. An archer taking *aim, measures* or computes the *distance*.

'AMELCORN. — A species of *wild* wheat, no longer *cultivated*. There is little doubt that this word is deduced from that which follows it [*amell*, between], being so named from occupying a middle space between wheat and barley.' — *Stevenson*.

We doubt it greatly. It is simply the Upper German *amelkorn* — i. e., *triticum spelta*, more commonly *weisser–dinkel*, or *sommer dinkel*. It is rightly described by Cotgrave as *starch–corn*, being used for that purpose on account of the whiteness of the flour [compare Gr. ἄμυλον; Lat., *amylum*; Fr., *amidon*, starch]. The Scandinavian preposition *amilli* is unknown in Germany, and has moreover the tonic *accent* on the *second* syllable.

' AN; UNNE.—·To give, consent, wish well to. Saxon, *annan, unnan*.'

Lye's *anan*, dare, has led our etymologists grievously astray. The real infinitive is *unnan*, and the primary sense of the verb is not to give (dare), but to *favour, wish well* to; hence sometimes to *grant* as of favour, *concedere*. Dr. Jamieson's interpretations — to *owe*, and to *appropriate*, are totally inadmissible. The old German form *ge-unnan* is the parent of the modern verb *gönnen*, and *gunst*, favour. This leading sense of *indulgence, favour* — the prominent one in all the Germanic dialects — shows the improbability of Horne Tooke's etymology of *and*, q. d., *an ad, add* to the *heap*, in a forcible light.

' ANCOME, a small ulcerous swelling formed unexpectedly.'

None of our editors attempt an etymology of the word — nor would one be easily found — if hunted for in the usual way, *juxta seriem literarum*. A slight tincture of Icelandic grammar would however have taught them that the *accented* particle *à* is equivalent to our *on*; and pursuing this hint, they would have readily found in Haldorson's Lexicon *àkoma, vulnusculum, ulcusculum*, and have learnt at the same time that the genuine form is *oncome*. The Icelandic word also denotes a sudden shower, analogous to the Yorkshire and Scottish *down come*. We shall take occasion from this word to dwell a little on the importance of the *accents* of words in etymology. The Anglo-Saxon system of accentuation has been illustrated with accuracy and ability by Mr. Kemble, in a paper lately published in the 'Gentleman's Magazine' (July, 1835).* We shall therefore confine our remarks to Icelandic, to which the other ancient Germanic languages bear a general analogy.

Any one who looks into Haldorson's Lexicon, or a critical edition of any Icelandic author, will perceive many accentuated words, some of which are *monosyllables*. These accents do not so much denote the rhythmical *tone* of syl-

---

* We are happy, by the way, to see what fresh spirit and interest have recently been infused into the venerable and valuable Miscellany of Mr. Urban.

lables as the *quantity*; i. e., the presence of vowels long by nature, frequently convertible into diphthongs. These are radically and etymologically different from the short vowels, and must be carefully distinguished from them in tracing the origin and connexion of words. For example, *vin, friend*, is the old German *wini*; but *vin*, vinum, is the German *wein*. In like manner, *sál* is the German seele, Eng. *soul*; *mór*, ericetum, Eng. *moor*; *stó*, locus, Ang.-Sax. *stow*; *trú*, fides, German *treue*. A few practical applications of this observation to the branch of etymology that we are now treating will show the matter in a clearer light.

'FRAV, FREV, *from.*' — *Craven Glossary. Cumbrian.*

Barbarous corruptions! many of our readers will say. They are nevertheless genuine descendants of the Scandinavian *frá*, still pronounced *frav** in Iceland. As a corollary, we may add, that in the Icelandic lexicons we find *á* (*agna, ovis feminina*,) a word to all appearance utterly unlike any known synonym. But when we observe the accent, and learn that it is pronounced *aw* or *av* by natives, we immediately perceive its identity with the Sanscrit *avi*; Gr., ὄϊς (i. e., ὄϜις); Lat., *ovis*; provincial German, *auw*; and our own, *ewe*.

'LEAGH, or LEIGH, a scythe. It may be from *lea*, meadow, and *ag*, cut; or Swed., *lie*, a scythe.' — *Brockett.*

The first of these derivations, apparently borrowed from Willan, is downright naught; the second is something to the purpose. Both *leagh* and *lie* are from the Icelandic *liár, falx*. The terminating *gh* in the Northumbrian word, however pronounced, evidently originated in the *accented* vowel of *liár*.

'LOVER, LOOVER, a chimney, or rather an aperture in the roof of old houses, through which the smoke was emitted.' — *Craven Glossary.*

This word is used by Spenser and Langland. Our etymologists, not knowing what to make of it, derive it — *uno consensu* — from the French *l'ouverte*. It is plainly the Icelandic *lióri* (pronounced *liowri* or *liovri*); Norwegian, *liore*; West Gothland, *liura*; described in the statistical accounts of those countries as a sort of cupola with a trap-door, serving the two-fold purpose of a chimney and a sky-light.**

'DOVER, to slumber: Icelandic, *dofwa, stupere.*' — *Jamieson.*

Certainly not from *dofwa*, but from *dúra*, nearly equival-

---

* Compare the modern Greek pronunciation of ναῦς, βοῦς — *nafs, bofs*, &c.
** Lióri is evidently derived from *liós*, light — analogous to Fr. *lucarne*.

ent in sound to *duvra*, and meaning exactly the same thing as *dover*; viz., *per intervalla dormire*.

It would be easy to multiply similar instances: the above will show the power of the Scandinavian accents, and the necessity of attending to them in etymological researches. It is remarkable, that the Northumbrians and Scotch have in many cases preserved the ancient Norse pronunciation more faithfully than the Swedes and Norwegians. Respecting the *tonic* accent — it is sufficient to observe that, in ancient and dialectical words, it is almost invariably placed on the *radical* syllable. This short rule will enable our readers to demolish a multitude of etymologies — old and new.

' APPULMOY, a dish chiefly composed of apples.'

Mr. Stevenson's emendation, *appulmos*, and his derivation from the Old Saxon *muos* (food), though timidly proposed, are indubitable. *Muos, mues, moos*, and their compounds, are used extensively in Germany to denote preparations of *vegetables*. Bavarian, *melker–mues*, a sort of furmity; Bremish - Saxon, *kirschmoos*, a preparation of *cherries*; and, to come more immediately to the point, Lower Saxon, *appel-moos* (ap. Richey Idiot. Hamburg, and Schütz, Holsteinisches Idiotikon); Danish, *aeblemos*, and German, *apfelmuss*, all denote a sort of apple-sauce or marmalade. It is extraordinary that a man of Mr. Stevenson's research did not stumble on a word found in more than a dozen dictionaries and vocabularies.

' AREN, are. This *pleonastic* termination of the plural *are* is common in old writers.' — *Boucher*.

This final *n* or *en* is no *pleonasm*, but the regular grammatical plural, especially in the Mercian dialect. Every South Lancashire clown of genuine breed conjugates his verbs according to the following model: —

	Singular.	Plural.
1st person,	please,	pleasen,
2d ,,	pleases,	pleasen,
3d ,,	pleases,	pleasen.

It is remarkable that this Mercian plural resembles the German form *lieben, liebet, lieben*, much more nearly than the Anglo-Saxon *lufiath*. There are many reasons for believing that the written Anglo-Saxon, though perhaps generally *understood* by our ancestors, was by no means universally *spoken*.

' ASK, a newt or lizard.'

Mr. Boucher's idea of a connexion between this word and the Irish and Gaelic *iasg* (fish), *easg* (eel), is entitled to

some attention.   An affinity with the Greek ἀσπίς is possible,
but not easily proved.   We adduce the word chiefly for the
sake of pointing out a remarkable connexion between one
set of words denoting sharp or thorny objects, and a second
signifying fishes or reptiles, which runs through several
languages. The following, *inter alia*, may serve as a specimen: — Sanscrit, *ahi*, a serpent; Greek, ἔχις, ἔχιδνα, a viper — ἐχῖνος, a hedgehog — ἔγχελυς, an eel, (compare Latin
anguis, *anguilla* — Old German *unc*, a serpent;) Bavarian,
agel, a horse-fly or gadfly; German, *egel*, a leech — *igel*, a
hedgehog; Icelandic; *eglir*, a snake; — Gaelic, *asc** a serpent; *easg*, an eel; *iasg*, a fish: Welsh, *ball-asg*,** a porcupine; *ball-awg*, a hedgehog.   The German *igel*, hedgehog,
(Ang.-Sax. *igil*,) is undoubtedly so called from its sharp
thorns — (compare Teutonic *egida*, a harrow; Latin, *occa*;
Ang.-Sax., *eyla*, arista, carduus.) Ἐχῖνος is probably of
cognate signification. Ἔχις, ἔχιδνα, *egel*, a leech, and *agel*,
a gad-fly, seem to derive their names from the sharpness of
their bite; ἔγχελυς and *anguilla* from the *resemblance* to a
snake.   The ancient German *egidehsa*, a lizard; Ang. Sax.,
aδexe; modern German *eidechse*, is commonly resolved into
egi+dehsa.   The analogy of the preceding terms makes us
think that it is rather *egida + ahsa*, or *ehsa*.   The former
part of the word either includes the idea of *fear*, *disgust*, or
of something sharp or prickly.   In this latter case, the name,
though not applicable, as far as we know, to our European
lizards, would exactly suit the *lacerta stellio*.   It is very possible that the *Germans* may have brought the name from the
East, and applied it to the reptiles they found in Europe,
as the Ionians named the formidable Egyptian crocodile after
the lizards in their own hedges. — Vide *Herodot.*, ii. 69.

The tyro in etymology may exercise himself in tracing
the root *ac* or *ag*, through the various tongues in which it
occurs, and may observe how the idea of material sharpness
is transferred to bodily sensations, and then to mental emotions: ex. gr. — Ἀκω, ἄκανθα, ἀχίς, αἰχμή — *acuo*, *acus*, *acies*,
— Teut., *ekke* (edge), *ackes* (axe); Icel., *eggia* (acuere, hortari — Anglicè, to *egg on*); German, *ecke*, corner; Bavar.,
igeln, prurire, (compare Germ. *jucken*, Scott. *yeuk*, Eng. *itch*,)
— *acken* (to *ache*), ἄχος; Ang. Sax., *ege*, fear — *egeslich*, horrible — Eng. *ugly*; Icel., *ecki*, sorrow; Germ., *ekel*, disgust,
— cum plurimis aliis.   It is possible that Ang. Sax. *ege*, an

---

* Hallamshire people still sometimes call an *adder* an *asker*.   ED.
** *Asg*, a splinter; *awch*, *awg*, sharpness, keenness. — *Owen's Welsh Dictionary*.

eye, may be of the same family. Compare the Latin phrase *acies oculorum.*

'AWBELL.—A kind of tree, impossible to state the exact species — not observed in the *cognate languages.*—*Stevenson.*

Evidently the *abele* = poplar, [*] found in German and its dialects under the forms *alber, albboom, abelen, abelke, albe.* The *cognate languages* occupy a very large field, of which our etymologists have only explored a few corners; they should, therefore, be cautious how they make general assertions respecting them.

AWK,
ALOORKE,
ASKEW, } Oblique, awry, left, &c.
ASLET, ASLOWTE,
ASOSH,

We class these words, all of which convey the same radical idea, together; chiefly as a text for a long dissertation on *right* and *left.* Respecting Tooke's etymology of the former word, (that which is *ordered* or *commanded,*) we shall briefly observe that it is at once refuted by a comparison with the Greek ὀϱϑός, our own *upright,* and the Lower Saxon *comparative* form *rechter.* Apparently, Tooke was not aware that the phrase *right hand* was introduced into the Teutonic tongues at a comparatively recent period. It occurs once or twice in the Anglo-Saxon Gospel of Nicodemus, but is totally unknown in the Old German and Scandinavian languages. The common Anglo-Saxon term is *swithre,* q. d. manus *fortior* — but there is an older form in Cædmon, *teso,* the affinities of which are worth observing: Sanscrit, *dakshina*; Gr. δεξιός, δεξιτεϱός; Lat. *dexter*; Lithuanian, *deszine*; Gothic, *taihswo*; Old German, *zeso, zeswo*; Irish and Gaelic, *deas* (whence *deasil*); Welsh, *deheu*; words all indubitably of the same origin. That *right* simply means *straight, direct,* will, we think, appear from the application of its opposite *left,* which, we venture to affirm, never means the *remaining* hand. The following synonyms from the cognate languages may serve to exercise the ingenuity of our readers, and to show how boldly Tooke could draw a sweeping conclusion from very scanty premises.

Goth. *hleiduma*; Icelandic, Old German, and Ang.-Sax. *vinstri, winistar, winstar*; Swedish, *laetta*; Danish, *keit, kavet*; Belg. *lufte*; German and its dialects, *äbig, äbsch, affig, awech, gäbisch, glink, letz, link, lucht, luchter, lurk, lurz, schenk, slink,*

---

[*] The name is properly restricted to the *white* poplar (*populus alba.*) ED.

5

sluur, *schwude;* besides a multitude of minor variations.
Leaving some of the above terms to the disciples of Tooke,
we shall observe in general, that the numerous words denoting *left* may be classed under two leading ideas — *deficiency* and *deviation.* Of the first, we have a plain instance
in the Italian *mano manca.* The second is clearly perceptible in the Greek σχαιός, denoting *oblique,** left*, and also
by an obvious metaphor, foolish, awkward, rude; — compare
Lat. *scævus*, Icel. *skeifr*, oblique, Dan. *skiev*, Germ. *schief*,
and our own *askew*, together with the apparently collateral
forms σχέλλω, to warp; σχολιός, σχαληνός; Scot. and Yorksh.
skellered, warped by drought; Danish *skele*, to squint (Scoticè, to *skellie*); and perhaps *aslowte* and *asleet*. The ancient
gloss in Graff's Diutiska, *awikke*, *devia*, shows that the same
idea is contained in the provincial German *awech*, a dialectical variety of the forms *äbig*, *affig*, &c. The English counterpart *awk*, anciently, as appears from the Promptorium
Parvulorum, *left*, more generally denoted inversion or perversion; *awk* — end; *awk* — stroke, *i. e.* a *back* stroke (Ital.
un *riverso*); and the adjective *awkward*. With the prefix *ge*
it became *gawk*, *gawky*, left-handed, clumsy, evidently the
origin of *gauche*, a word which has greatly distressed the
French etymologists. The common German term *link* is apparently connected with *lenken*, to bend, turn; compare *lin-
quo*, *obliquus*, and perhaps λέχριος, λιχριφίς. The Bavarian
denk is remarkable as an instance of the interchange of *l*
with *d*, parallel with δάχρυ, *lacruma*; *dingua* (ap. Varro),
lingua. The Belgic and Lower Saxon *lufte*, *lucht*, *luchter*,
show that their English sister *left* is not from *leave*, at least
not its past participle. The true origin is *in nubibus* — if
any body can *honestly* connect it with λαιός and *lævus*,** or
with the root of the German *link* — we have no great objection. The Old German *lurk* furnishes an etymon not
only for *aloorke*, awry, but also for *lurk*, *latere*, *clam sub-
ducere se*, (compare Belg. *slink*, *left*, with our *slink away*,)
for *lurch*, the lateral heave of a ship, and *lurcher*. The Bavarian form *lurz* also denotes the loss of a double game at
cards, whence our term, *lose* one's *lurch* — *left* in the *lurch*.
The Gothic *hleiduma* is in the *superlative* form (compare
Lat. *dextimus*); it is apparently connected with the Gaelic
and Irish *cli*, *clith*; Armoric *cley*, *left*; the old German *kleif*,

---

* Passow, vir magnus, sed qui in etymologiâ parum videbat, makes *left*
the primary signification of σχαιός, and *oblique* the remotest, an evident
hysteron-proteron.
** Compare λαφός, left handed (ap. Hesychium).

oblique; and perhaps with *κλίνω*, *κλιτύς*, and *clivus*. The form *winistar*, with its kindred — by far the most prevalent in Old German, Anglo-Saxon, and Scandinavian — has been commonly referred to *van*, *defectus*. We suspect it to be the Sanscrit and Bengali *wam*, *left*, with a comparative suffix. *Asosh* may possibly be connected with the Welsh *asw*, *aswys* = *left*, or *osg* = oblique; but however this may be, we have little doubt that *asw* is legitimately descended from the Sanscrit *sanya*. *Schwude*, a term used by German waggoners, bears a strong resemblance to the Welsh *chwith*.

We have dwelt a little on this subject, in order to show the copiousness of the Germanic tongues, and the connexion between the different branches of the Indo-European family.

AUMBYR, AWMYR. — A measure of uncertain capacity, from *amphora*, *ἀμφορεύς*.

Though this etymon has the sanction of Ihre — a name never to be mentioned without respect — it is nevertheless erroneous. Awmyr is the German *eimer*, denoting a *bucket* — and a liquid measure varying in capacity according to the locality — anciently *einpar*, i. e., a vessel with a *single* handle; consequently, to deduce it from *ἀμφορεύς* — a vessel with *two* handles — is like identifying *solo* with *duet*. The real counterpart of *ἀμφορεύς* is *zwipar*; in modern German *zuber* or *zober*, a large double-handled vessel containing eight *eimers*; in Lower Saxon *töver* and *tubbe* — whence our *tub*. The above etymologies were unknown, even to Adelung, before the publication of the Old High German glosses.

BA, BOTH.

This remarkable word is made the vehicle for two very unfortunate guesses. The Latin *bis* is not a genitive absolute of the Gothic *ba*, both, but from the Sanscrit *dwis*; in Greek, dropping the labial, *δίς*; in Zend and Latin, dropping the dental, *bis*; the Icelandic, more faithful to its origin, exhibits *tois — var*; English, *twice*. The conjecture that our *both* is compounded of *ba+twa*, is instantly shown to be impossible by the German form *beide*, compared with *zwei*. The real genealogy of *both* is as follows: — Sanscrit *ub'ha*, *ub'hau*, (whence, inserting the liquid *ἄμφω*, *ambo*,) Lettish, *abbu*; Slavonic, *obo*, *oba*; Gothic, by aphæresis, *ba*, subsequently enlarged into *bajoths* (vid. Ulphilas, Matt. ix. 17, Luc. v. 38.); whence the Icelandic, *badir*; German, *beide*; Bavarian, *baid*, *bod*; English, *both*. The hypothesis of a Gothic origin of the Latin language, or any considerable portion of it, may be easily demonstrated to be a mere chimera: the languages are connected not by descent, but collaterally.

BAWSAND. — Streaked with white on the face, applied to horses and cattle.

Dr. Jamieson refers this word to Ital., *balzano, white-footed* ; while Mr. Stevenson laboriously endeavours to trace it to the ἵππος φαλίος of Belisarius. The readers of their lucubrations are likely to be in the same predicament as the Breton peasants mentioned by Madame de Sévigné, who thought their curé's new clock was the *gabelle*, until they were assured that it was the *jubilee*. The matter lies on the surface. *Brock* is a badger; *bawsin*, ditto; *brock-faced* (ap. Craven Glossary, and Brockett), marked with white on the face like a badger; *bawsin'd*, ditto. This simple analogy weighs more with us than five hundred pages from the Byzantine historians.

BLACK - CLOCK. — The common black-beetle. — *Hallamshire Glossary.*

The word *clock* — peculiar, we believe, in this sense, to the North-Anglian district — is used as a *generic* term for all coleopterous insects: ex. gr. *brown-clock*, the cock-chafer, *lady-clock*, the lady-bird (*coccinella septem punctata*), *bracken-clock*, a species of melolontha, *willow-clock*, and many others. This might seem a mere arbitrary designation, or local perversion of some more legitimate term. It is, however, a genuine Germanic word, and of remote antiquity, as is shown by the ancient gloss published by Gerbert — '*chuleich*, scarabæus.' It appears from Schmeller, that *kieleck* was the Bavarian appellation for the *scarabæus stercorarius*, late in the seventeenth century. The preservation of this term in a remote English province is a good illustration of Ihre's excellent aphorism — 'Non enim ut *fungi* nascuntur vocabula.'

Both Tacitus and Ptolemy describe the Angli as a tribe of *Suevi*, an account which we believe to be confirmed by the numerous coincidences between the Dialects of South Germany and those of our Anglian and Northumbrian counties. Indeed, we have our reasons for thinking that the language of the *Angles* was in many respects more a *German* than a *Saxon* dialect, and that it differed from the speech of Kent, Sussex, and Wessex, both in words and grammar.* We expect that the publication of the Durham and Rushworthian glosses will either confirm or disprove this conjecture.

---

* On the distinction between the Angles and the Saxons, see Dr. Donaldson's valuable contribution to the second volume of the Cambridge Essays. ED.

HELDER or ELDER, sooner (rather). — Perhaps from the word *older*. — *Halifax Glossary*, ap. *Hunter*.

Ἐτυμολογία γραωδεστάτη! The cognate languages show that *helder* is the true orthography, consequently the word has nothing to do with *old*. It might seem most obvious to refer it to the Icelandic *helldür*, *potius*, *proclivius*, with which it agrees pretty exactly both in form and meaning. But so few Scandinavian *particles* have become naturalized among us, that it is safer to have recourse to the Saxon form *gehældre*, absurdly derived by Lye from *hælan*, to heal. The true root is *hald* — acclivis; Icelandic *haldr*. Compare, Suabian, *halden*, a declivity, *halden*, to slope; Upper Austrian, *hälder*, *hälter*, rather, sooner; German, *hold*, *huld*, &c. The analogy between these words and the Latin *clivus*, *proclivis*, *proclivius*, is sufficiently evident, both in the primary sense of the terms as attributes of material objects, and their secondary application to denote operations or affections of the mind.

GAR. — To cause, make. — *Jamieson*, *Brockett*, *Craven Glossary*.

This word may be regarded as the Shibboleth of a language wholly or partially Scandinavian. The Germans and Saxons regularly employ *machen*, *macan*, which, in its turn, is unknown in pure Norse. *Garon*, to prepare, used by Otfried, has been long obsolete; a descendant, however, exists in *gerben*, to tan leather, formerly *garawen*. The root of the Icelandic verb *göra* appears to exist in the Sanscrit *kri*, facere; Persian, *kerden*; Greek, κραίνω; Latin, *creo*; and the gipsy *gerraf* — Imper. *gerr*. — undoubtedly of Oriental extraction. Mr. Boucher, in his remarks under 'bamboozle', confounds the gipsy language with the *flash* of our thieves and pickpockets, not knowing apparently that this remarkable race have a regularly constructed tongue, with eight cases to its nouns, and more inflections for its verbs than we ourselves can boast of. We are not going to digress into an analysis of it, but shall merely observe that the name by which they call themselves, *Sinte*, (*i. e.*, people of *Sind*,) bears an odd resemblance to that of the ancient inhabitants of Lemnos, the Σίντιες ἀγριοφώνοι of Homer, commonly supposed to be a tribe of Pelasgi. An intrepid antiquary, capable of seeing a long way into a millstone, might patch up a fraternity between the two, by some such process as the following. The Pelasgi were an Oriental race — the Σίντιες were Pelasgians — Lemnos, the place of their abode, was the workshop of *Vulcan* — the present Sinte, also Oriental, have from time immemorial exercised the trade of *tinkers*; ergo, &c.   As Cobbet used to say — *we* do not *vouch* for the fact.

LATE, or LEAT. — To search or seek; Icelandic, *leyta* [*leita*].—

Rectè! — This word will enable us to correct an erroneous interpretation of Sir Tristrem : —

> 'Wha wad lesinges *layt*
>   Tharf him ne further go' —

which *lait* Dr. Jamieson renders 'give heed to.' The meaning evidently is, 'He who would *seek* after falsehoods needs not to go any further.' The term *lait*, familiar to the inhabitants of the English northern counties, is, we believe, wholly unknown in Scotland proper; affording a presumptive argument, that the poem in which it occurs was written to the *south* of the Tweed. This we believe to have been the case with several other metrical romances usually claimed as Scottish. It is not sufficient for those who make this claim to show that they exhibit many words commonly employed in *Scotland*, unless they can also produce a number that were never used in *England*.

'LATHE, a barn.' — *Craven Glossary.*

From the Danish *lade*. It is well known that Chaucer puts this word in the mouth of one of his north country clerks in the 'Reeve's Tale,' who, as the narrator informs us, were of a town hight *Strother*. Dr. Jamieson, deceived by the Northumbrian words employed by the speakers, boldly claims them as Scots, and maintains that Strother is certainly Anstruther in Fife. We say, certainly not: but, as Dr. Whitaker long ago observed in his History of Craven, Long Strother in the West Riding of Yorkshire. This may be proved — *inter alia* — by the word *lathe*, common in Yorkshire and its immediate borders, but never heard in Scotland. Long Strother, or Longstroth* dale, is not a *town*, but a *district*, in the north-west part of the deanery of Craven, where the Northumbrian dialect rather preponderates over the Anglian. Chaucer undoubtedly copied the language of some native; and the general accuracy with which he gives

---

* This appellation exhibits a curious jumble of Celtic and Teutonic. Strother appears to have originally been *Strath-hir*, the *long* valley. The present form is a good example of the difference between the Celtic and Teutonic *idioms*. By the way the oddest specimen of the jumbling of those dialects that we know of occurs in the name of the mountain at the head of the Yarrow, — viz. *Mountbenjerlaw*. — *Ben-Yair*, or *Ben-Yarrow*, was no doubt the old Celtic name, and the Romanized Provincials and the Danes successively gave the *Mont* and the *Law*, both of which superfluities are now preserved *in cumulo*. [See also Brindon Hill in Somersetshire. Bryn, W. dùn, Sax. Hill, English, all meaning alike. N.]

it, shows that he was an attentive observer of all that passed around him.

We subjoin an extract from the poem, in order to give our readers an opportunity of comparing southern and northern English, as they co-existed in the fifteenth century. It is from a MS. that has never been collated; but which we believe to be well worthy the attention of any future editor of the Canterbury Tales. The italics denote variations from the printed text: —

'John highte that oon and Aleyn highte that other:
Of *oo* toun were thei born that highte Strother,
Ffer in the north I can not tellen where.
This Aleyn maketh redy al his gere —
And on an hors the sak he caste anoon.
Fforth goth Aleyn the clerk and also John,
With good swerde and bokeler by his side.
John knewe the weye — hym nedes no gide;
And atte melle the sak a down he layth.
Aleyn spak first: Al heyle, Symond — in fayth —
How fares thi fayre daughter and thi wyf?
Aleyn welcome — quod Symkyn — be my lyf —
And John also — how now, what do ye here?
By God, quod John — Symond, nede has *na* pere.
Hym bihoves *to* serve him self that has na swayn;
Or *ellis* he is a fool as clerkes sayn.
Oure maunciple I hope he wil be ded —
Swa *werkes hym* ay the wanges in his heed.
And therefore is I come and eek Aleyn —
To grynde oure corn, and carye it *ham* agayne.
I pray yow *spedes** us *hethen* that ye may.
It shal be done, quod Symkyn, by my fay !
What wol ye done while it is in hande?
By God, right by the hoper wol I stande,
Quod John, and see *how gates* the corn gas inne;
Fit saugh I never, by my fader kynne,
How that the hoper wagges till and fra !
Aleyn answerde — John wil *ye* swa?
Than wil I be bynethe, by my crown,
And se *how gates* the mele falles down
In til the trough — that sal be my disport.
Quod John — In faith, I is of youre sort —
I is as ille a meller as *are* ye.
* * * * *
And when the mele is sakked and ybounde,

---

* Apparently a *lapsus calami* for *spede*.

This John goth out and fynt his hors away —
And gan to crie, harrow, and wele away! —
Our hors is lost — Aleyn, for Godde's banes,
Stepe on thi feet — come of man attanes!
Allas, oure wardeyn has his palfrey lorn!
This Aleyn al forgat bothe mele and corn —
Al was out of his mynde, his,housbonderie.
What — whilke way is he goon? he gan to crie.
The wyf come lepynge *in* at a ren;
She saide — Allas, youre hors goth to the fen
With wylde mares, as faste as he may go.
Unthank come on his hand that *band* him so —
And he that *bet* sholde have knet the reyne.
Alas, quod John, Alayn, for Criste's peyne,
Lay down thi swerde, and I *wil* myn alswa;
I is ful *swift* — God wat — as is a ra —.
By Goddes *herte* he sal nougt scape us bathe.
Why ne hadde thou put the capel in the lathe?
Il hayl, by God, Aleyn, thou *is* fonne.'

Excepting the obsolete forms *hethen* (hence), *swa*, *lorn*,
whilke, *alswa*, *capel* — all the above provincialisms are still,
more or less, current in the north-west part of Yorkshire.
Na, *ham*(e), *fra*, *banes*, *attanes*, *ra*, *bathe*, are pure Northumbrian.   *Wang* (cheek or temple) is seldom heard, except
in the phrase *wang tooth*, *dens molaris*.   *Ill*, adj., for *bad* —
lathe (barn) — and *fond* (foolish) — are most frequently and
familiarly used in the West Riding, or its immediate borders.
Several of the *variæ lectiones* are preferable to the corresponding ones in the printed text, especially the line —

     ' I is as ill a meller as *are* ye.'

Now Tyrwhitt's reading, 'as *is* ye,' is a violation of idiom
which no Yorkshireman would be gnilty of.   The apparently
ungrammatical forms, *I is*, *thou is*, are in exact accordance
with the present practice of the Danes, who inflect their
verb substantive as follows:

Sing.	*Plur.*
Jeg er,	Vi ere,
Du er,	I ere,
Han er,	De ere.

In   Yorkshire.

Sing.	*Plur.*
I is,	We are,
Thou is,	Ye are,
He is,	They are.

It is worth observing, that the West Riding dialect exhibits, at least, as great a proportion of Scandinavian terms as the speech of the more northern districts. This we regard as a proof that Anglian and Northumbrian were distinct dialects prior to the Danish invasion. We subjoin a specimen of the Northumbrian dialect as it existed in the fifteenth century, extracted from a poem* written by a monk of Fountain's Abbey —

'In the bygynnyng of the lyf of man,
Nine hundreth wynteres he lyffed than.
Bot swa gret elde may nan now bere;
For sithen man's life become shorter;
And the complexion of ilka man
Is sithen febeler than was than.
Now is it alther febelest to se; .
Tharfor man's lyf behoves short be;
For ay, the langer that man may lyffe,
The mair his lyfe now sal him greve.
For als soon as a man is alde,
His complexion waxes wayk and calde:
Then waxes his herte herde and hevye,
And his heade grows febill and dyssie:
His gast then waxes sek and sair,
And his face rouches mair and mair.

*   *   *   *

Of na thing thar they sall have nede;
And without any manner of drede,
Thai sall noght fare as men fare here,
Who live evermair in drege and were.
For here baith king and emperour
Have drede to tyne thair honour;
And ilka ryche man has drede alswa
His gudes and riches to forgae.
Bot thai that sall gain heaven's blysse,
Sall never drede that joy to mysse:
For thai sall be syker ynoghe thare,
That thair joy sall last ever mare.'

A comparison of these lines with the extracts from Barbour and Wyntoun, in Ellis's 'Specimens,' will show the similarity of the language. The diction of the two Scottish writers is in several respects more *English* than that of the Yorkshireman.

---

* Clavis Scientiae, or Bretayne's Skyll-kay of Knowing, by John de Wageby — our specimen is from a publication by W. Jos. Walker, A. D. 1816.

The difference between the northern and midland dialects will most clearly appear on comparing with the above an extract from that lately recovered and highly curious piece of antiquity, 'Havelok the Dane' —

'The lond he token under fote,
Ne wisten he non other bote,
And helden ay the rithe [   ]*
Til he komen to Grimesby.
Thanne he komen there, thanne was Grimded,
Of him ne haveden he no red;
But hise children alle fyve
Alle weren yet on live;
That ful fayre ayen hem neme,
Hwan he wisten that he keme,
And maden ioie swithe mikel,
Ne weren he nevere ayen hem fikel.
On knes ful fayre he hem setten,
And Havelok swithe fayre gretten,
And seyden, "Welkome, loverd dere!
And welkome be thi fayre fere!
Blessed be that ilke thrawe,
That thou hire toke in Gode's lawe!
Wel is hus we sen the on lyve,
Thou mithe us bothe selle and yeve;
Thou mayt us bothe yeve and selle
With that thou wilt here dwelle.
We haven, loverd, alle gode,
Hors, and neth, and ship on flode,
Gold, and silver, and michel auchte,
That Grim ure fader us bitawchte.
Gold, and silver, and other fe,
Bad he us bitaken the.
We haven shep, we haven swin,
Bi leve her, loverd, and all be thin;
Tho shalt ben loverd, thou shalt ben syre,
And we sholen serven the and hire;
And hure sisters sholen do
Al that evere biddes sho;
He sholen hire clothen, washen, and wringen,
And to hondes water bringen;
He sholen bedden hire and the,

---

* Hiatus: Sir F. Madden conjectures '*wey*.' Perhaps '*sti*.' Comp. v.
2618, 19 —
        ' He foren softe bi the *sti*,
          Til he come ney at Grimesbi.'

For levedi wile we that she be.''
- Hwan he this ioie haveden maked,
Sithen stikes broken and kraked,
And the fir brouth on brenne;
Ne was ther spared gos ne henne,
Ne the hende, ne the drake;
Mete he deden plente make,
Ne wantede there no god mete;
Wyn and ale deden he fete,
And made hem glad and blithe;
Wesseyl ledden he fele sithe.' *

It would lead us to far to discuss all the dialectical peculiarities of this poem, which is on many accounts one of
the most remarkable productions of its class. It is easy to
see that it is written in a *mixed* dialect — more Mercian
than Manning's Chronicle — more Anglian than Peirs Plouhman — more northern than Gower's Confessio Amantis —
and more strongly impregnated with Danish than any known
work of the same period. This blending of different forms
renders it probable that the author was a native of East
Derbyshire or Leicestershire, where the Mercian and Middle
Anglian meet, and where there was a powerful Danish co-
lony during many years. The Scandinavian tincture appears, not only in individual words, but in various grammatical inflexions, and most remarkably in the dropping of
the final *d* after liquids — *shel, hel, hon, bihel* — which exactly
accords with the present pronunciation of the Danes. The
confusion between aspirates and non-aspirates, generally
reputed as a cockneyism — *hure* (our), *hende* (duck, Danish
aand, Germ. *ente*,) *eir, ether, is,* for *heir, hether, his* — is common to the vulgar throughout the midland counties. The mixture of dialects is sometimes exhibited in the same words; for
example, *carle* (husbandman) and *kist* (chest) are Anglian
forms, and the equivalents *cherle, chist,* Mercian.
We add a short specimen of the present vulgar dialect of
Cleveland; being Margery Moorpoot's reasons for leaving
Madam Shrillpipes' service: —

'Marry — because she ommost flyted an' scau'ded me oot o' my
wits. She war t' arrantest scau'd 'at ever I met wi' i' my boorn
days. She had sartainly sike a tongue as never war i' ony woman's heăd but her awn. It wad ring, ring, ring, like a larum,
frae morn to neet. Then she wad put hersel into sike flusters,
'at her feăce war as black as t' reckon creuke. Neă, for 't matter

* Havelok, pp. 66-68, vv. 1199-1246.

o' that, I war nobbut reetly sarra'd; for I war tell'd aforehand by some vara sponsible fowk, 'at she war a mere donnot.'*

The resemblance to Scotch is sufficiently obvious. The following is a short sample of the Craven dialect. The interlocutors are deploring the ignorance of some grouse-shooters, who did not know what to make of Yorkshire oatcakes: —

‘ *Giles.* — Thou sees plainly how th' girt fonlin didn't *ken* what havver cakes war.

‘ *Bridget.* — Noa, barn, he teuk 'em, as they laid o't fleăk, for round bis o' leather. I ax'd him to taste it; an *seea* taks up 't beesom start, potters *yan* down an' keps it i' my appron. He then nepp'd a lile wee nooken on't, not t' validum o' my thoum naal, an' splutterd it out ageean, gloaring *gin* he war puzzom'd, an' efter aw I could say, I cudnt counsel t' other to taste *ayther* it or some bannocks.'**

It will be perceived that the above is *North*-Craven, and slightly tinctured with Northumbrian. The proper Anglian terms for *ken, seea, yan, gin, ayther* — are *knaw*; sŏ̆ŏ; *one* (pron. *wūn*); *as if*; *awther*.

As a specimen of the Lancashire dialect, we give Collier's excellent apologue of the tailor and the hedgehog; just premising that the sage light of the village there pourtrayed is meant as an emblem of a *reviewer*.

‘ A tealyer i' Crummil's time, war thrung*** poo'ing turmets in his pingot, an' fund an urchou ith' had-lund reăn; he glender'd at 't lung, boh cou'd mey nowt on't. He whoav'd his whisket owr't, runs whŏăm, an' tells his neighbours he thowt in his guts 'at he'd fund a thing 'at God newer mede eawt; for it had nother heăd nor tele, hond nor hough, midst nor eend. Loath to believe this, hoave a dozen on 'em wou'd geaw t' see if they cou'd'n mey shift to gawm it; boh it capt 'em aw; for they newer a won on 'em e'er saigh th' like afore. Then they'dn a keawnsil, an' th' eend on 't wur, 'at tey'dn fotch a lawm, fawse, owd felly, het an elder, 'at cou'd tell oytch thing, for they look'nt on him as th' hammel scoance, an' theawt he'r fuller o' leet than a glow-worm's tele. When they'dn towd him th' kese, he stroak'd his beărd, sowghd an' order'd th' wheelbarrow wi' th' spon new trindle to be fotch't. 'Twur done, an' they beawld'n him awey to th' urchon in a crack. He gloărd at 't a good while, droyd his beărd

---

* From the farce of The Register Office.
** Craven Dialect, vol. ii. p. 300.
*** Pronounced *thrunk*. In this and the preceding specimens, we have occasionally adjusted the orthography to the English or Scottish standard, where the pronunciation does not materially differ.

deawn, an' wawted it ow'r wi' his crutch. "Wheel me abeawt agen o' th' tother side," said he, "for it sturs — an' by that it su'd be whick." Then he dons his spectacles, steared at 't agen, an' sowghing said, "Breether, its summot; boh feather Adam nother did nor cou'd kerson it — wheel me whoam agen."' *

This resembles Anglian more than Northumbrian — but is sufficiently distinct from both. The shibboleth of the three dialects is *house*, which the Northumbrian pronounces *hoose*, the North Anglian *häoose* — nearly like *au* in the Italian *flauto* — and the inhabitant of South Lancashire in a way *quod literis dicere non est* — but generally represented in print by *heawse*.

We know no better specimen of the genuine West of England dialect than Robert of Gloucester's Chronicle. The present Somersetshire and Devonshire are more barbarous and ungrammatical than the northern dialects — and their distinguishing peculiarities are well known.

We could extend our remarks on every branch of this copious subject to a much greater length, but the above may suffice *speciminis gratiâ*. We have perhaps already given our readers cause to twit us with the μηδὲν ἀγάν of the Grecian sage, and to tell us that our lucubrations on the barbarisms of our provinces are about as acceptable to the public, as the Antiquary's dissertation on Quicken's-bog was to the Earl of Glenallan. However greatly, therefore, we may long to prove that *dreigh* (tedious) is closely related to δολιχός, and that *leemers*, a north-country phrase for ripe nuts, profoundly referred by our glossarists to *les mûrs*, is more nearly akin to *leprosy*, we shall for the present be silent about these and other matters of similar importance. As Fontenelle observes, a man whose hand is full of truths, will, if he is discreet, often content himself with opening his little finger.

---

* View of the Lancashire Dialect, Introduction.

PRICHARD
ON THE CELTIC LANGUAGES.

[*Quarterly Review*, *September*, 1836.]

The Eastern Origin of the Celtic Nations proved by a comparison of their Dialects with the Sanscrit, Greek, Latin, and Teutonic Languages. By James Cowles Prichard, M.D., F.R.S., &c. Oxford. 8vo. 1831.

The Cimmerians, says Homer,* dwell at the extremity of the ocean, enveloped in clouds and utter darkness. Some of this darkness appears to have clung to all tribes bearing the name, whether related to each other or not. Were the ancient Cimmerians Celts? — were the Cimbri of kindred race? — do the modern Cymry derive their pedigree, and consequently their name and language, from the same source? These questions have been boldly answered in the affirmative; and the supporters of this hypothesis have expended a good deal of learning and ingenuity in tracing the march of the Cimmerii from the Euxine to the British channel — almost as minutely as Xenophon describes the advance and retreat of the Ten Thousand. We do not mean to say that the theory itself is either false or improbable; but we doubt whether any satisfactory evidence has been brought to prove it. Hitherto the matter rests on a few plausible conjectures and a similarity of names — a most fallacious argument in all cases. We know that our neighbours and fellow-subjects, the modern Cymry, are distinct from ourselves, both in race and language; but as to their origin and early history, they are still, like their namesakes of old, ἠέρι καὶ νεφέλῃ κεκαλυμμένοι — and likely to remain so.

Various attempts have been made to throw light upon the *primordia* of the people, by means of their language, which, excepting perhaps the Basque, appears to be the most ancient, the most singularly constructed, and the most true to its original form, of all European tongues. Most of those

---

* Odyssey, l. xi. verses 13 — 15.

attempts have signally failed, owing to the erroneous principle on which they were undertaken. It was argued that, as the Celts came from the east, they must have spoken an Oriental language; consequently one more or less related to Hebrew — the most ancient of Oriental tongues; a complete *non sequitur*! It must be admitted that a few remarkable coincidences have been pointed out, but the majority of alleged resemblances are altogether visionary. It is very possible that the Celts may have picked up a few* Semitic words in their progress through Asia, especially from the East Aramæan, or Chaldee, which has interchanged many vocables with Old Persian, and perhaps with other adjoining dialects; but it would be as easy to trace the bulk of the Celtic languages to Formosa or Madagascar, as to the land of Canaan.

These matters are, however, better understood than they were a century ago. It has been discovered that there are eastern languages of venerable antiquity, totally distinct from Hebrew, but bearing the closest affinity to the principal European tongues. It is now as certain that Greek, Gothic, and Slavonic are the descendants of some ancient dialect nearly related to Sanscrit, as that Portuguese is derived from Latin. The affinity of Celtic to this great family has been doubted, and even flatly denied. Colonel Vans Kennedy, in his elaborate 'Researches into the Origin and Affinity of the principal Languages of Asia and Europe,' goes so far as to affirm that 'the British or Celtic language has no connexion with the languages of the East, either in words or phrases, or the construction of sentences, or the pronunciation of letters.' This positive declaration, from a man of undoubted information and research, might seem decisive of the question. But when we find that he denies, in equally positive terms, the affinity between Sanscrit and Persian, which Sir William Jones and Professor Bopp have made as clear as the noon-day sun, we may be permitted to suspect that he has, in both cases, pronounced his verdict rather too hastily; and that Celtic may, in forensic language, be fairly entitled to a new trial. Dr. Prichard has under-

---

* Two coincidences are worth pointing out, on account of the extensive diffusion of the terms. Syriac גבינא (găbino), a ridge or summit; Welsh. *cefn*, a ridge, whence *Gebenna* mons — *hod.* les *Cevennes*; Chevin, or Shevin, a steep rocky ridge in Wharfdale. Syriac טוּרא (turo) mons; Welsh, *tor*, a protuberance; *twr*, a heap or pile. Compare Mount Taurus, in Asia — *die Tauren*, i. e., the higher Alps in the *Tyrol*, — and the numerous *tors* in Derbyshire and the West of England.

taken its cause, and as we think, with considerable success. He has not indeed exhausted the subject; nor has he dwelt upon the remarkable *difference* between Celtic and the languages more obviously related to Sanscrit, so much as he fairly might have done. But he has, to a certain extent, proved his point, and is entitled to the merit of being the first who has investigated the origin of the Celtic tongues in a rational and scientific manner. If we are not mistaken, one part of his researches throws a new and most important light on the formation of language. This we shall advert to more fully in the sequel, especially as the author himself does not seem fully aware of the consequences deducible from his statements.

The main strength of the Doctor's case seems to lie in the analogy which he has established between the numerals, the names of persons, and degrees of kindred, and of the most ordinary natural objects, in the Celtic dialects, and in the class of languages with which he compares them. Words of this description are of remote antiquity, and commonly of indigenous growth; since we cannot suppose that any people endued with the faculty of language could be long without them. Yet the coincidences between the two classes are too numerous and too striking to be the effect of accident; and, as Dr. Prichard well observes, the Celtic cognates appear under a peculiarity of *form*, which is the surest test of genuineness. For example : it is undisputable that the Sanscrit *swasurah* (father-in-law), Russian *svekor*, German *schwager*, Latin *socer*,* Greek ἑκυρός, and Welsh *chwegrwn*, are of common origin, and equally so that they are, in no instance, *borrowed* words, but formed, independently of each other, from the same primeval term, according to the genius and organic peculiarities of the respective tongues. Many of the adjectives and common verbal roots, adduced by Dr. Prichard, are undoubtedly akin to each other; but some of his examples, we fear, only resemble each other in sound. The proof derived from pronouns and particles would have been more complete, if they had been more minutely analysed; but perhaps the nature of those important words was not so well understood five or six years ago as it is at present. The Celtic personal terminations of verbs are undoubtedly formed on the same *principle* as the Sanscrit and Greek, as well as of *similar* materials. We think the perfect *identity* of the two classes is rather questionable; but we do not con-

---

* Terence's *Hecyra*, compared with *socrus*, is an obvious instance of the difference between an imported and a vernacular word.

sider the evidence supplied by the Celtic tongues less valuable, because it is of an *independent* nature. In one important point a real and fundamental difference seems to have been mistaken for a resemblance. The permutations of initial and final consonants in Welsh and Sanscrit are, upon the whole, correctly stated; but we fear the analogy attempted to be established between the two is hardly so good as Fluellen's parallel between Macedon and Monmouth. The case may be briefly stated as follows: — In Welsh, *initial* consonants are changed into others of the same organ, to denote a diversity of logical or grammatical relation: in Sanscrit, *finals* are changed exclusively for the sake of euphony; that is to say, the change is made in a different manner, and on a radically different principle. It is true that final consonants are occasionally commuted in Welsh, and initials, though in but few instances, in Sanscrit. These permutations are, however, in both cases, of little consequence, and depend upon partial, not general, laws. It is hardly fair or philosophical to deduce leading analogies from a few trivial exceptions.

In the statement of initial permutations in Erse, there appears to be a small oversight. Dr. Prichard observes that, in this language, each consonant appears in two forms only, termed the plain and the aspirated. Apparently he was not aware of a further modification produced by what the Irish grammarians call *eclipsis*, that is, by a prefixed consonant usurping, as it were, the office of the original one. Thus, *baile* (town) appears not only in the aspirated form bhaile (pronounced *vaile*), but also in the *eclipsed* form *mbaile*, pronounced *maile*, exactly analogous to *bara*, *vara*, *mara* (bread), in Welsh. Clumsy as this orthography seems, it has the advantage of showing the primary initial, which persons, imperfectly versed in Welsh, cannot always readily find. It might also have been observed that in Manks, commonly regarded as an Erse dialect, most of the initial consonants have three different forms.

In another instance Dr. Prichard seems disposed to adopt a conclusion not quite warranted by his premises. As it relates to a point of some consequence in tracing the analogy of languages, we shall quote the passage at length.

'It is to be observed that H never stands as the initial of a word in Erse in the primitive form, or is never, in fact, an independent radical letter. It is merely a secondary form, or representative, of some other initial, viz., F or S. It must likewise be noticed that the same words which begin with S or F, as their primitive initial in the Erse, taking H in their secondary form,

6

have, in Welsh, H as their primitive initial. This fact affords an instance exactly parallel to the substitution in Greek of the rough and soft breathings for the Æolic digamma, and in other words for the sigma. Οἶνῳ, as it is well known, stands for ϝοίνῳ, Ἕσπερος for ϝέσπερος, and ἑπτὰ probably replaced a more ancient form of the same word, viz., σεπτὰ; ἓξ stands for σὲξ; ὖς and ἕρπω for σῦς and σέρπω. These instances might lead us to suppose, as Edward Lhuyd had long ago observed, that the Greek language had originally a regular mutation of initial consonants, similar to that of the Celtic: though it was lost, except in these instances, or rather, as pointed out by these vestiges, previously to the invention of letters.' — pp. 31, 32.

Now, supposing that σεπτὰ and ἑπτὰ, ϝοίνος and οἶνος, were once *contemporary* forms in the *same dialect* of the Greek language, — a proposition which it might be rather difficult to prove — this would be far from amounting to 'a regular mutation of initial consonants, similar to the Celtic.' In Celtic the different forms are used, according to certain fixed rules, to denote different grammatical relations. In Manks, for example, *sooill* — (an eye) — in the vocative, and after certain prepositions, becomes *hooill*; and *shassoo* — (to stand) — is, in a variety of constructions, converted into *hassoo*. But do we find any such limitations in the employment of σῦς and ὖς? or have we any proof that certain tenses or moods of ἀνάσσω regularly had the digamma, while others as regularly wanted it? In Greek, and the languages allied to it, a mixture of forms either denotes a blending of dialects, or a transition-state of the language. Herodotus employs σῦς and ὖς indifferently; more recent prose-writers use only the latter. The classical language of Upper Saxony, chiefly derived from Southern or Upper German, has a number of duplicate forms from the Lower Saxon, and sometimes employs the two classes indiscriminately. But variations of this sort bear no analogy to permutations like *pen*, head; *ei ben*, his head; *ei phen*, her head; *vy mhen*, my head. The entire system is, as far as we know, peculiar to the Celtic tongues, and it exhibits a phenomenon as curious as it is difficult to account for. * In many

---

* We are persuaded that this Celtic process is essentially the Sanscrit Sandhi, the only difference being that in Sanscrit the final letter of a word is influenced by the initial of the next word, and in Celtic the initial is influenced by the final preceding. Instead of *tat murāri*, or *shat mama*, an Indian would write *tan murāri* and *shan mama*. A welshman says *Yn Nuw* instead of *yn Duw*, and *saith mlynedd* instead of *saith blynedd*. In the last example the influence of a nasal in *saith* (septem) remains, although the sound itself has disappeared. It would require a long dissertation to demonstrate the changes

cases these changes serve as substitutes for Greek and Latin *terminations*: — e. gr., in Irish, *geal* is *pulcher*, *gheal*, *pulchra*; *mor*, *magnus*; *mhor*, *magna*; masc., *crann mor*, great tree; fem., *cloch mhor*, great stone. A careful *comparative* analysis of the different Celtic dialects might, perhaps, furnish some clue to the mystery.

We could point out many discrepancies between the Cymric branch of the Celtic, and what the German philologists call the Indo-European family— viz. Sanscrit, Zend, Greek, Latin, Gothic, Slavonic, Lithuanian, with their descendants — we will, however, content ourselves with briefly indicating three of the most obvious.

1. In the latter* class of languages, substantives, adjectives, and pronouns, have a *neuter gender* —. a feature which, we believe, distinguishes them from all others. At least, there are no traces of any such thing in the Semitic, Celtic, Polynesian, or any other family of tongues which we have had an opportunity of examining.

2. They have also comparative and superlative degrees — not only parallel in signification — but of cognate origin, being all clearly connected with one or the other of the two leading forms in Greek — τεϱος — τατος (or Latin — *timus*); ιων — ιστος. The Welsh forms are equivalent in *signification*, but of totally different *structure*. Even Menage would hardly have ventured to class *du*, *duach*, *duaf* (*black*, *blacker*, *blackest*), with any Greek or Latin paradigm. The Erse dialects, which form their comparative and superlative by means of prefixed particles — (*e. gr.*, *geal*, white; *nios gile*, more white; *as gile*, most white) are still more remote.

3. In Welsh and Armoric, nouns and adjectives have, properly speaking, *no cases*, the different relations of words to each other being either denoted by the collocation, by a change of initials, or by the employment of particles. The few inflexions of Erse nouns bear no analogy to those of the Indo-European class, with the exception of the dative plural in *bh*, which, as Dr. Prichard observes, presents a remarkable resemblance to the Sanscrit *bhyam*, and Latin *bus*. The Doctor regards the Welsh as having lost its inflexions: we are inclined to think that it never had them, and that in this

---

to the sonant and aspirate, but it is believed that it would not be a very difficult task. N.

   * This, of course, does not apply to English, Italian, &c., which have lost their distinctive terminations. However, they still exhibit traces of it in the *pronouns*. It is remarkable that in Lithuanian — a language in many respects most closely allied to Sanscrit—the neuter gender is retained in adjectives and pronouns, but not in *substantives*.

and several other respects, it manifests a more primeval structure than the languages of the Erse family. *   There are some plausible grounds for conjecturing that most of the terminations in Greek and its kindred are of comparatively recent origin; and that, before these existed, grammatical relations were expressed in a way somewhat analogous to the Celtic process of modifying the sense of words by a change of their radical vowels.   This appears, *inter alia*, in the formation of particles from pronominal roots—*e. gr.*, Welsh *pa*, who, or what — *pe*, if — *po*, by how much — (*quo, quanto*) *pwy*, to.   This is not unlike the changes in the vowels of the Latin pronouns *hic* and *qui*, for which the German philologists account by supposing them to be formed from several distinct roots, *ha*, *hi*, *ho*, *hu*, &c.   We regard this supposition as both improbable and unnecessary, and think it much more likely that the vowels were changed to express a difference of grammatical relation.   It is possible, that the strong inflections in Greek and German verbs, σπείρω, σπερῶ, ἔσπαρον, ἔσπορα; Germ. pres. *finde*, pret. *fand*, part. *ge-funden*, &c., may have partly originated in a similar principle.   We say *partly*, as there is reason to believe that some of them are merely euphonic.

Upon the whole we are of opinion that the affinity between Celtic and the Indian family of languages is only partial, and that the ancestors of the Cymry in particular, must have been separated from the primeval stock, long before Sanscrit existed in anything like its present form.   Indeed, Dr. Prichard himself has made out a much stronger case for the Germanic and Slavonic tongues, than for those which he professedly treats of.   In one family, the affinity is chiefly in small classes of words, or individual terms; in the others, it pervades the whole structure of the respective languages.

* The enlarged acquaintance with ancient Celtic which we owe mainly to Zeuss enables us to reply to the objections in the three paragraphs here numbered. 1. The Celtic *had* a neuter gender. In Irish nouns its chief characteristic was the identity of the nominative, accusative and vocative cases singular, and the plural termination in *a*; this is like Latin and Greek. In Welsh the demonstrative *hyn* is neuter, as distinct from *hwn*, m. and *hon*, fem. 2. The old Irish comparative ended in *ithir* or *iu*, and the superlative in *em* or *emem*, as *isil*, *islin*, *islimem*, Zeuss p. 282; clearly analogous to Latin. The oldest Welsh superlative was *duam* from *du*, like Latin *facilimus*; *duach* probably came from *duas*, like the Gothic comparative. Zeuss p. 305. For the Irish cases yet in use, another, close connection with those of the Indo-Germanic tongues, see a paper by Hermann Ebel in Kuhn und Schleicher's Beiträge zur vergleichenden Sprachforschung, 1857, pp. 159—187. Of the Cymrii class the Cornish had the genitive case made by a change of *a* to *e*, or *e* to *y*; as *marh*, a horse, *merh*: *pen*, head, *pyn*. See Lhuyd's Archæologia Britannica. p. 242. N.

Nevertheless, though Dr. Prichard may have attempted to prove too much, he deserves praise for establishing a point which had eluded the researches of his predecessors, and which may eventually prove a valuable contribution towards the history of the human race. We feel no disposition to cavil at occasional errors of detail which we have noticed in the course of the work, especially as the data necessary for correcting them were in many instances unknown when he wrote it. In the case of another edition being called for, an attentive study of Bopp's 'Comparative Grammar,' and Pott's 'Etymological Researches,' would, as we think, induce him to alter or modify some of his conclusions, as well as enable him to supply some deficiencies. We cannot, however, refrain from expressing a wish that he had omitted the parallel between the Indo-European and the Semitic languages, in which, we fear, he succeeds no better than the multitudes who had made the same attempt before him. In nearly every instance the identity of the terms compared is questionable, and in many it is demonstrably imaginary. We will content ourselves with examining a couple of examples which, at first sight, appear very plausible. In Chaldee, חְלְתָי (tlithay) denotes *third* (tertius), and this, it must be allowed, looks and sounds very like the Sanscrit *tritaya*. But when we learn that, in the Chaldee word, the third consonant belongs to the *root* (חְלָת, three) — and in the Indian term to the *termination* — like the Greek τρι — ταῖος — we immediately discern a material difference between them. This becomes still more conspicuous upon comparing the Sanscrit *tri*, or Greek τρεῖς, with the Hebrew שָׁלֹש (shelosh), of which the Chaldee word is merely a dialectical form. Again: our English *wrong* is compared to the Hebrew רָע, evil. Supposing, for argument's sake, that the latter ought, as Dr. Prichard represents it, to be pronounced *rong*, and its original import to be *perverted*, *distorted*, still nothing is gained, unless it could be shown to be connected with the Anglo-Saxon verb *wringan — torquere*, from which our English adjective is notoriously derived. The following considerations are, we think, sufficient to show the futility of all attempts to establish a close affinity between the two classes. In the Semitic tongues, the great bulk of the roots are *triliteral*, independently of the *vowels* necessary for articulating them. They must in many cases be at least *disyllables*, and may, for aught we know, have been originally *trisyllabic*. The Sanscrit roots, on the other hand, are uniformly *monosyllables* — frequently a single consonant followed or preceded by a vowel, and rarely comprising more than a vowel and two consonants. They, therefore, who maintain that Sanscrit and Hebrew were originally identical, must either admit that the radical terms in the former language have been *mutilated* by wholesale, or that those of the latter have gained additional elements, *i. e.*, are in reality *compound words.* * Admitting the possibility of all this, still it is clear that nothing can be done in the way of comparative analysis, until it is shown *which* of the two suppositions is the true one. **

We now proceed, according to our promise, to consider the light which Dr. Prichard's researches appear to have thrown on the formation of language in general, at least of such languages as resemble the Indo - European and Celtic families in structure. The Semitic tongues furnish a few valuable analogies and general principles; and it is probable, that a *partial* connexion exists between them and the Japhetic class. A few names of natural objects are alike in each; and occasionally a resemblance, either real or apparent, may be traced in the pronouns and particles. Nearly all beyond this is mere conjecture, or assertion without proof; and we wish our readers to bear in mind that much of what we are going to say is inapplicable, or at best of doubtful application, to Hebrew and its cognates. To make our argument more intelligible, we shall begin with a few preliminary remarks on radical or primitive words. We do not profess, like Monboddo or Murray, to develope their *origin*, but merely to offer an opinion respecting their *nature*.

We observed, on a former occasion, that the manner in which philology has hitherto been studied, has proved one of the most serious obstacles to its advancement. This we believe to be signally the case with respect to what is commonly called *universal* grammar. Most of those who have undertaken to investigate its principles have gone the wrong way to work, and instead of carefully analyzing language to discover what it actually is, they set about demonstrating, *à priori*, what it ought to be. For example, we are told by reputable authors, that the mind of man is conscious of simple existence, whence the verb *to be*, 'the root of all other expression,' and that it is capable of sensations and emotions, to express which, men invented *verbs passive*. Again: mankind

---

* This composition must, if it ever took place at all, have been effected before the Assyrians, Hebrews, Arabs, and Ethiopians, became distinct peoples. Allowing for dialectical variations, all have the same triliteral roots.

** Semitic philologists have shown that a large number of the apparently triliteral roots are really biliteral; the so-called triliterals are not necessarily compound words, unless we would consider *stay*, *stand*, and *stop*, to be compounds. N.

have an active principle of *will*, or volition, the operations of which they denote by verbs active, manufactured for the purpose; and as an act implies an efficient *cause*, they found it necessary to represent that cause by a personal pronoun. Further: men are sensible of the existence of material objects, which they express by distinct terms called nouns substantive; and as these objects are possessed of certain distinguishing characteristics, another class of words, called adjectives, was invented to represent them. And finally: as persons and things stand in various relations towards each other of *time*, *place*, and many other modifications of their respective existences, it became necessary to describe those relations by several different classes of words, usually denominated adverbs, prepositions, and conjunctions.

All this sounds plausible enough; and we think it very possible that Psalmanazar fabricated his Formosan language on some such principles. The theory too, agrees, or seems to agree pretty well with the *existing state* of our own and many other tongues; but applied to the *elementary principles* of the class of languages which we are now considering, we believe it to be erroneous in almost every particular. A rigorous analysis of the Indo-European tongues shows, if we mistake not, that they are reducible to two very simple elements. 1. Abstract nouns, denoting the simple properties or attributes of things. 2. Pronouns, originally denoting the relations of *place*. All other descriptions of words are formed out of these two classes, either by composition, or symbolical application. As we are not aware that the matter has ever been represented in this point of view by any of our predecessors, it will be necessary to produce arguments and facts to justify it, and, in Jeanie Deans's phrase, to go to the root of the matter.

The common definition of a noun is that it is the name of a *thing* — and most philologists have proceeded on the apparently obvious conclusion, that the first step in language would be to give appellations to sensible objects. We maintain, on the contrary, that primitive nouns are not names of *things*, at least not of substances or material objects, but of their *qualities* or *attributes*.* There is, in this respect, a strict analogy between the operations of language and those of the mind. Our notions of matter are *conceptions* founded on *perception*; in other words, we judge of it by its properties, as they are discernible by our bodily senses. The profound-

---

* See, however, the modification of this view in the Essay on the Relative Import of Language. ED.

est philosophy and the most refined chemistry can carry us
no farther than this. The *words* expressive of those notions
are the earliest in language, and for a very good reason.
They are *simple conceptions*, and consequently may be ade-
quately denoted by *simple terms*. This is practically shown
by reference to the Sanscrit roots, to which the bulk of that,
and many other languages, may be traced. The Indian grammarians uniformly, and as we believe rightly, define them
by abstract nouns; and they will be found on examination
to express simple qualities, having no existence except as
predicated of some given subject. Some of them are employed as abstract nouns in their simplest form, many others
become so by the addition of a small suffix, apparently of
pronominal origin; and, as we shall hereafter show, they do
not lose this character when they become component parts
of other words.

But, it will be asked, what are names of things? We
answer, they are attributive nouns, used by a sort of synec-
doche, to express a substance by one or more of its distinctive *qualities*. A concrete noun, that is, the name of a
material object, stands for an aggregate of qualities, the full
import of which, as we observed on a former occasion, it is
clearly incapable of conveying. This may be instanced by
as simple an idea of the class as it is possible to conceive
— viz. *atom*. The original ἄτομος is a compound word selected by a distinguished philosopher, from the most expressive language in the universe, to denote the smallest possible modification of matter. Nevertheless, it says too much
and too little — too much, as being applicable to other things,
and consequently ambiguous — too little, because it does not
express all the properties even of an atom. The same is,
and ever must be, true of all concrete nouns: the only resource, therefore, is to fix on some prominent attribute, and
agree to let the word denoting it stand for the aggregate,
as we let an abbreviation stand for an entire word, or allow
a piece of paper not worth a farthing to pass current for
five or fifty pounds. We gave an instance of this kind in
a former article, relating to the word *fox*, and could adduce
some thousands of the like character if it were necessary.
We will content ourselves with a single additional example,
which may, perhaps, be new to many of our readers.

A Middlesex man would probably be much surprised to
hear a Norfolk farmer talk of the havoc made among game
and poultry by *lobsters*, and, on the matter being explained,
would doubtless think *lobster* a mighty absurd appellation for
the common stoat. But, in Katterfelto's phrase, there is a

reason for everything, if people only knew it. The same animal is, in Yorkshire. called a *clubster*, or *clubstart* — i. e. *clubtail*. The Norfolk and Yorkshire terms are evidently allied in origin, and both express the idea meant to be conveyed, viz. an animal with a thick tuft on its tail,* which is a true description as far as it goes. From this and many similar instances we may perceive that language is not so *arbitrary* a thing as many have supposed. Primary words may have been arbitrarily imposed, for anything we know — but, when it was once agreed that they should convey such and such meanings, the subsequent application of them became subject to certain definite rules, and we have no more right to pervert this established meaning, *ad libitum*, than we have to alter the received value of the Arabic numerals. For instance, to designate a stoat or a squirrel by an expression equivalent to *sine caudâ*, would defeat the purpose for which language was given to mankind.

Metaphysicians and philologists frequently talk of men *inventing* words to denote the operations of the understanding. We may be assured that they did no such thing; they only made new applications of those that already existed, according to some real or supposed analogy. The primitive elements of speech are demonstrably taken from the sensible properties of matter, and *nihil in oratione quod non prius in sensu* may be regarded as an incontrovertible axiom. Language has not even distinct terms for the functions of the different bodily senses, much less for those of the mind. The epithet ὀξύς, primarily meaning *sharp–pointed* or *edged*, is metaphorically applied to denote *acid*, *shrill*, *bright*, *nimble*, *passionate*, *perspicacious*, besides many minuter shades of signification. We may hence perceive the absurdity of those metaphysical theories which make language co-extensive with thought, and, as it were, identical with it — and the unavoidable imperfection of it as a medium of metaphysical investigation.

There has been much wrangling among grammarians as to the nature of adjectives, and their claim to be considered a distinct part of speech. Tooke's chapter on the subject is in many respects one of the best portions of his work. He has shown satisfactorily that *simple* adjectives only differ from substantives in their application, and that those with distinctive terminations are in reality compound words, having substantives for their basis. He does not indeed ex-

---

* Compare αἴλουρος, a cat, (according to Buttmann, αἴολουρος,) σκίουρος, a squirrel, &c. &c.

plain the nature of the additional elements very happily, when he resolves *en* , *ed* , and *ig* into his favourite *imperatives*, *give, add, join*; and he has, moreover, weakened his leading position by his loose and inaccurate method of stating it. He says —

'An adjective is the *name* of a *thing*, which is directed to be joined to some other name of a thing.'

Again —

'I maintain that the *adjective is equally and altogether as much the name of a thing as the noun substantive*. And so I say of *all* words whatever. For that is not a word which is not the name of a thing. Every word being a sound significant must be a sign, and if a sign, the name of a thing. But a noun substantive is the name of a thing and nothing more.

'If, indeed, it were true that adjectives were not the names of things, there could be no *attribution* by adjectives; for you cannot attribute *nothing*. How much more comprehensive would any term be by the attribution to it of *nothing*? Adjectives, therefore, as well as substantives, must equally denote substances; and substance is attributed to substance by the adjective contrivance of language.'

On being reminded of the distinction between *substance* and *essence*, Tooke replies —

'Well; I care not whether you call it substance, or essence, or accident, that is attributed. *Something* must be attributed, and therefore denoted by every adjective.'*

All this jangling might have been avoided if, instead of saying that words denote *things* or *substances*, terms at the best of ambiguous import, and open to endless cavil, it had been stated that they denote the *attributes* and *categories*, or *relations* of things. It might be difficult to prove that *space* is a *substance*, according to any legitimate meaning of the term; but there can be no doubt as to its being an *attribute* of every material substance, which must be more or less *extended*. We conceive that nouns may be defined as follows : — 1. abstract nouns, denoting qualities of things simply; 2. concrete nouns, in which a *single* attribute stands synecdochically for *many*; 3. adjectives, *i. e.* attributes used as descriptive epithets, being sometimes simple terms, *e. g. black, white, choice*; sometimes compound words, as *sorrowful, godlike, friendly, careless*, words which it is unnecessary to analyze. Simple adjectives only occur in particular lan-

---

* See *Diversions of Purley* , vol. ii. pp. 428—434; 438—439.

guages. In Sanscrit, Greek, Latin, and many others, all adjectives have distinctive *terminations*, which, as Tooke acutely remarks, were originally *separate words*. Most of these terminations have a *possessive* signification: for example, *barbatus* = barbâ præditus; others denote similarity, abundance, privation, analogous to our *like*, *ful*, *less*; and in all cases they do not so much belong to the *attribute* as to the *subject. Vir opulentus* is equivalent to *vir præditus divitiis*; and the termination *lentus*, undoubtedly significant, to borrow Tooke's phrase, puts the word in condition to be joined to some substantive.

It has been debated whether an adjective is equivalent to the circumlocution with the genitive case. This we apprehend may or may not be the case, according to circumstances. *Paternus amor* is potentially equivalent to *patris amor*, the ending *nus* having a *possessive* import; and it is actually so when spoken of a *father*, but not when applied to any other person. An uncle may feel an affection for his nephew *equal* to that of a parent, or even *greater*, and in this sense his attachment may be called *paternal*; nevertheless, it is not the affection *of a father*, but that of an *uncle*. In the latter case our own language furnishes a strictly proper term — *fatherly*, *i. e.*, vi termini, *fatherlike*. If a *bonâ fide* father were the subject of the discourse, *paternal* would be the more legitimate expression of the two; and it would be truly absurd to scout it on account of its Latin descent, when it adds so decidedly to the precision of our language.

We believe that no part of speech has been so completely misunderstoood as the verb. Tooke's dictum that a verb is *a noun and something more*, is true * as far as it goes; but he has not informed us *what* this something more is, nor has any one else, as far as we know, given a satisfactory account of the matter. Grammarians could not help seeing that a noun lies at the root of every verb: for example, that *dream* (*somnium*) is included in *I dream* (*somnio*); and they tell us that the difference consists in the enunciative or assertive power of the latter. But how did it acquire this power? or in what additional elements does it consist? Some say, in the verb substantive understood — a supposition logically impossible, as the phrase *ego* (*sum*) *somnium* proves on the face of it. Others, among whom is Harris, say that if we divest a verb of the accessaries of mood, tense, number, and person, a *participle* remains, so that γράφω is po-

---

* At least it is true of *finite* verbs; not however, as Tooke represents the matter, of the *roots* or *themes* of verbs.

tentially ἐγὼ (εἰμι) γράφων. This, indeed, is more in accordance with the principles of logic; but it is contradicted by the *form*, which, when the personal termination is removed, has no distinctive element of a participle in it. What do we discern in γραφ of the stubborn ων — οντος, the addition of which *constitutes* the participle; and which, in one form or other, has stood its ground for thousands of years, from the Sanscrit *tupan*, *tupantas* = τύπτων, τύπτοντος, down to the modern German *liebend*? In fine, what proof have we of the *transition* from γράφων ἐγὼ to γράφω, any more than for Menage's transmutation of *raposo* into *renard*? A verb divested of its paraphernalia may become an Irish participle, which is a mere abstract noun; but certainly not a Greek, Latin, or even an English one.

Some progress was made in ascertaining the nature of verbs, when it was shown that the personal terminations are in reality personal pronouns. Still the old difficulty remained as to the body of the word. Pott, whom we regard as one of the most acute of European philologists, observes that the verb is divisible into three constituent parts — root, connective vowel, and termination — [γραφ-ο-μεν, pet-i-mus] — answering to the predicate, copula, and subject, of a logical proposition. We do not clearly see how a mere euphonic syllable, often wanting, can constitute a legitimate logical copula; but supposing that *mus* is *nos*, and *i* a connective, meaning something or other — what is *pet*? In other words, what is a *verb* divested of its usual adjuncts? We answer boldly that there is no such thing in existence. Every verb includes in it a subject and predicate, or makes an assertion respecting some given person or thing. It must therefore *have a subject*, that is to say, it must be in some *person*. Take away this subject, and the verb becomes a *noun*, as the supines are in Latin, and the infinitives in all languages. The root of the verb is therefore a noun or attribute; and the personal terminations, as we have seen, are to be resolved into pronouns. It only remains to inquire what is the nature of the copula or connexion between them.

We have observed that Dr. Prichard's statements respecting the Celtic languages throw a new and important light on the formation of language; and this we hold to be particularly the case with respect to the verb. He has shown that the personal terminations in Welsh are pronouns, and that they are more clearly and unequivocally so than the corresponding endings in Sanscrit or its immediate descendants. However, he lays no stress upon a fact which we cannot but consider highly important: *viz.*, that they are evidently in *statu regiminis*, not in apposition or concord: in other words, they are not nominatives, but oblique cases, precisely such as are affixed to various prepositions. For example, the second person plural does not end with the nominative *chwi*, but with *ech*, *wch*, *och*, *ych*, which last three forms are also found coalescing with various *prepositions* — *iwch*, to you; *ynoch*, in you; *wrthych*, through you. Now the roots of Welsh verbs are confessedly nouns, generally of abstract signification; ex. gr. *dysg* is both *doctrina*, and the 2. pers. imperative, *doce*: *dysg* — *och* or — *wch*, is not, therefore, *docetis* or *docebitis vos*; but *doctrina vestrùm*, teaching *of* or *by* you. This leads to the important conclusion that a verb is nothing but *a noun*, combined with an *oblique case* of a personal pronoun, virtually including in it a connecting *preposition*. This is what constitutes the real *copula* between the subject and the attribute. *Doctrina ego* is a logical absurdity; but *doctrina mei*, teaching *of* me, necessarily includes in it the proposition *ego doceo*, enunciated in a strictly logical and unequivocal form.

If we mistake not, this view of the subject derives an important confirmation from a parallel construction in some of the Semitic languages. It is well known that this class of tongues has no simple present tense, for which various periphrastic forms are occasionally substituted. The present of the verb substantive is often denoted by an abstract noun denoting *being*, combined with the oblique cases of the different personal pronouns. The Hebrew word is יֵשׁ (yesh); but, as there might be some question as to the real nature and import of this word, we prefer adducing the Syriac form, אִית (ith), the plural of which is employed in *statu regiminis*, along with pronominal suffixes to express the various persons of the verb *to be*, according to the following paradigm: —

אִיתַי,	ithai,	literally existentiæ	mei	=	sum
אִיתַיךְ,	ithaich,	,,	tui	=	es
אִיתַרדִי,	ithau,	,,	sui	=	est
אִיתַין,	ithain,	,,	nostri	=	sumus
אִיתַיכוּן,	ithaichun,	,,	vestri	=	estis
אִיתַיהוּן,	ithaihun,	,,	illorum	=	sunt

We omit the feminine forms, which are exactly on the same principle. Compare the Welsh future* *byddav*, from the root *bod*, being, existence —

Sing. 1. byddav, ero   Pl. byddwn
       2. byddi   byddwch
       3. bydd   byddant

---

* The Welsh has no simple present tense, the future is occasionally employed instead of it.

There is another form, *oedd*,* commonly called an imperfect,
but seemingly an aorist —

Sing. 1. oeddwn, eram, fui   Pl. 1. oeddym
     2. oeddit   2. oeddych
     3. oedd   3. oeddynt

The analogy between the above Syriac construction and
those Celtic forms is striking, and there can be no mistake
respecting the precise nature of them, especially of the first.
אֵירֵי is unequivocally a noun plural; and the pronominal
suffixes are not nominatives in apposition or concord with
the noun, but oblique cases *sub regimine*. When participles
or adjectives are used with a pronoun to express the present
tense, as is frequently the case, the Syriac idiom invariably
requires nominatives in concord, analogous to the Latin
prior ille [*est*], *amantes nos* [*sumus*]. In this Aramæan construction, we see, if we are not deceived, the true primary
elements of a verb; and, among European languages, the
Welsh deserves the honour of having maintained them in
the greatest purity. It is not surprising that they cannot be
so clearly identified in Sanscrit, where so much has been
sacrificed to sound. There is, however, no doubt that the
Sanscrit personal terminations are pronouns, and it is equally
certain that they have not the forms of *nominatives*. *Mi* in
asmi (sum) *may* be a modification of the genitive *mē* = *ma-i*,
or of the locative *mayi*; but it cannot without violence be resolved into the nominative *aham*. More on this hereafter.

The following conspectus of the present indicative in five
branches of the Indo-European family will show the intimate connection between them, and the mutilation which our
own language has suffered : —

Sanscrit.

mānayāmi	mānayāmas
mānayasi	mānayat'ha
mānayati	mānayanti

Pracrit.

mānēmi	mānēmha
mānēsi	mānēd'ha
mānēdi	mānēnti

Doric.

τίθημι	τίθεμες
τίθης	τίθετε
τίθητι	τίθεντι

* With the leave of the Welsh grammarians, we are disposed to identify oedd with the noun oed, *time*, *age*, *duration*, so that *oedd-wn* is literally
duratio mei = fui.

Old High German.

varmanem	varmanemes
varmanes	varmanet
varmanet	varmanent

Latin.

moneo	monemus
mones	monetis ·
monet	monent.

The Welsh verb, though constructed on similar *principles*, seems, as we have already observed, to be composed of different *materials* from the rest. A minute analysis of the personal endings and other component parts of the Sanscrit and Greek verb would carry us far beyond our limits. We must, therefore, refer our reader to Bopp's 'Conjugations-System der Sanskrita-Sprache,' and to Pott's 'Etymologische Forschungen.' He may not perhaps assent to all the conclusions of these eminent philologists, but he will find abundant cause to admire their learning and ingenuity.

If our theory of a verb is correct, it follows that the usually received definitions of it are either erroneous or incomplete. It is said essentially to imply *action* or *motion*, and we are even gravely informed that such terms as *rest*, *lie*, *sleep*, are not less *actions* than *walk*, *fly*, *kill*. Are, then, *action* and *inaction* convertible terms? or when we say, 'the pyramids *stand* on the banks of the Nile,' do we assert that they either *act* or *move*? The truth is, that all those who fancy that verbs are distinguished from nouns, as animals are from plants, by a sort of *inherent* vitality, have proceeded on an utter misconception of their real nature. Motion or action is no more inherent in a verbal root than a meat-roasting quality is inherent in a smokejack, or the power of forging a horseshoe in a smith's hammer. Both these require an extrinsic moving power to make them efficient — and so do the themes of verbs. Their office is simply to denote the categories or predicaments of given subjects, which may either express existence, motion, action, sensation, or their opposites. The active power is in the *person* or *agent* — take away this, and there remains a mere imaginary quantity, or mental abstraction, ready indeed to become an attribute of any suitable subject, but no more capable of positive existence without one, than the whiteness of snow can remain after the snow is melted.

Our remarks can, of course, only be fully applicable to language in its original and genuine form. All language becomes merely mechanical in process of time in the mouths of the people, who seldom fail to corrupt what they do not

altogether understand. Bopp observes that when the force
of the pronominal suffixes of verbs was no longer felt, they
were replaced, or rather expounded, by detached pronouns
prefixed; and in some tongues, the comment has nearly
caused the disappearance of the text. The finite verb of
our remote ancestors, with its array of significant personal
ending, bore some analogy to a locomotive carriage, having
a propelling force within itself. We have allowed the wheels
and machinery to go to decay, but — to borrow an excellent
illustration of Tooke's — we still make a shift to drag the
body of the vehicle as a sledge. Such phenomena belong
to the corruptions of language, not to its legitimate operations.

We have thus endeavoured to show that nouns,* adjectives, and verbs are attributive words, either simply or in
combination with an additional element. We now proceed
to the second division of the subject.

Strictly speaking, pronouns may be called attributives, as
they express an attribute of a peculiar kind; but for practical purposes it is more convenient to consider them as a
separate class. When we describe them as a primitive part
of language, we speak of language in its known and visible
state, not as it *may* have existed at a period about which
we have no evidence. There is reason to believe that pronouns were, in reality, formed upon local particles, analogous to the ב, ל, מ, of the Hebrews; but the existence of
such is more a matter of probable inference than a positive
testimony. The Latin *is*, simple as it seems, includes three
distinct ideas — *person*, *masculine gender*, and *place*; but
though the portion of it denoting *place* may have once existed
separately, we cannot trace it with any certainty, while, on
the other hand, we find many prepositions, conjunctions,
and adverbs unequivocally formed from pronouns. The
number of pronominal roots in Sanscrit seems to have been
more considerable than it is at present. Some, which only
appear as particles, or portions of compound words, occur
as distinct pronouns in the cognate languages, and the
Celtic dialects help to supply several chasms. Professor
Bopp considers the monosyllabic forms as the only primitives;
and these are found to be chiefly demonstratives, or relatives.
We subjoin a list of them, with a few of the corresponding
forms in other languages: —

---

* For brevity's sake we omit all consideration of participles, which are
composed of the same materials as certain classes of adjectives, and are
often identical with them.

A, only found in composition in Sanscrit, but extensively employed in Celtic, both as a demonstrative and a relative.

I. (this) Lat. *is*; old German, ì-r.

K A. Lat. *quis*; Lettish, ka-s; Gothic, hva-s.

'T A. Gr. *τὸ*; Gothic, *thata*.

P A. Welsh, *pa*, who or what.

S A. fem sā; Zend. *ha*, *hā*; Dor. ὁ, ἁ; Gothic, *sa*, *so*; Ang. Sax. *se*, *seo*.

V A. ⎫
M A. ⎬ In oblique cases and compounds.
N A. ⎭

Y A. The Sanscrit relative.

The following may be probably deduced from Sanscrit particles and compounds, and cognate languages : —

D A. Sanscrit, *i-dam*, this; Gr. *δὲ*;·Irish, *da*, if.

R A. Sanscrit, *pa-ra*, alius; Gaelic, *ra*, *ro*, very, exceeding; Welsh, *rhy*, ditto.

Other monosyllabic forms occur, but they seem to be either deflected or compounded from the above: e. gr., *tya, this, that*, is considered by Bopp as compounded from ta + ya; and *ki, ku*, seem to be mere modifications of *ka*, according to the ancient principle of altering the radical vowels of words to denote a change of signification. Simple and insignificant as the above elements appear, they have exercised a most extensive influence upon language; and we believe that every tongue of what is called the Caucasian family is indebted to these, or at least to similar elements, for much of its organisation. It would require many volumes to discuss the subject in all its bearings; we shall, therefore, at present, confine ourselves to a brief sketch of a few of its principal features.

Most grammarians have regarded the personal pronouns as a kind of *substantives, intrinsically* denoting the person speaking, the person spoken to, and the person spoken of. We consider this theory to involve an utter impossibility. No word can *intrinsically* denote a person, that is, a being combining in itself a multitude of distinct qualities, known and unknown, still less any or every person. It can only express some characteristic attribute; and in the case of the words we are treating of, this attribute must be strictly applicable to every instance in which they are employed. *Ego*, for example, must denote some adjunct or relation of the person speaking, just as much as *triangle* expresses the most prominent characteristic of the mathematical figure so called. This relation, we conceive, can only be that of *place*; in other words, what we call personal pronouns are, at least

7

originally were, nothing more than *demonstratives*. The *possibility* of this is shown by reference to the Latin language.* *Hic, iste, ille*, are notoriously a sort of correlatives to *ego, tu, sui*, and, if the *custom* of the language allowed it, might, on every occasion, be substituted for them, without producing the smallest ambiguity. Instances of their being actually thus employed are not uncommon. Thus, ' Tu, si *hic* sis, aliter sentias.' — (Terence, Andr. 2, 1.) == ' If you were *I*, you would think differently;' and 'O *isti* qui ad deorum nos cultum invitatis.' — (Arnob., l. 1.) == 'O *you* who invite us to worship your gods!' besides the well-known formulæ of the Greek tragedians, οὗτος ἀνὴρ == ἐγώ, and ὢ οὗτος == σύ. We do not, indeed, perceive much resemblance between the demonstratives and the *nominative cases* of personal pronouns in Greek, Latin, or even in Sanscrit; but the coincidences in *oblique* forms, in the personal endings of verbs, and in particles, are so close and so numerous, as to render the affinity of the two classes more than probable. This will appear more clearly from the following paradigm of the Sanscrit 1st perfect; evidently an older form than the present, and the undoubted archetype of the Greek 2d aorist.

Sing.		Pl.	
1.	a-tuda-m.		a-tudā-ma.
2.	a-tuda-s.		a-tuda-ta.
3	a-tuda-t.		a-tuda-n.

We see no absurdity in supposing the above terminations to be relics of the demonstratives *ma, sa, ta*, == *hic, iste, ille*. *Sa* and *ta* actually exist in Sanscrit, and *ma*, as a proper demonstrative, may be deduced from *i-ma*, this — the ancient Greek form, μὶν — and a variety of particles. Its relation, in point of signification, to *hic*, may be inferred from the Greek μὲν, μετὰ, the Armoric pronominal suf-

---

* The same distinction is observed in many Asiatic languages. We request the attention of our readers to the following instances: —

        Armenian, *sa, ta, na;*
        Chinese, *che, na, nai;*
        Japanese, *kono, sono, ano*;
        Tagalian, *dini, dito, diyan.*

All the above forms correspond precisely to *hic, iste, ille*; and are systematically employed to distinguish objects connected with the first, second, and third persons. In the Tonga language, the particles *my, atoo, augi*, q. d. *hic, istuc, illuc*, are used, with great nicety of discrimination, to direct the action of the verb towards the first, second, and third persons, respectively. Many proofs might be adduced of the close connexion subsisting between the demonstrative and personal pronouns, as well as of the similarity of their component elements in nearly all the known Asiatic and European tongues.

fix *mâ* == Lat. ce, Fr. ci; e. gr., *an den mâ*, *this* man (cet homme - ci), and its employment in several* languages to form *datives* and *accusatives*, both including the idea of connexion or acquisition. Its affinity to the oblique cases of the pronoun *I*, in Sanscrit, Greek, Gothic, and some scores of tongues besides, will hardly be disputed.

The terminations of the Sanscrit present are, sing., *mi, si, ti*; pl., *mas, tha, nti*, almost exactly the Doric forms in μι. They are evidently composed of the same elements as the endings in the preceding paradigm, but are more fully developed. According to our theory of the verb, they were originally oblique, probably instrumental,** cases of pronouns, in construction with nouns, the preposition included in the case forming the *copula*.

We apprehend this view of the subject will help to explain an apparent anomaly in several languages, viz., the discrepance between the nominative of the pronoun of the first person and its oblique cases, and the absolute want of a nominative in the paradigms of οὐ and *sui*. Most grammarians regard the nominatives of the above words as *lost*; we are of opinion that they never existed — for this sufficient reason — that they were not wanted. The subject of the proposition was sufficiently pointed out by the personal *termination*, and the employment of a separate pronoun prefixed, appears to have been an innovation first introduced for the sake of emphasis, and even now but sparingly allowed in some languages. Had a nominative, corresponding in form to *mei*, ever been in current use, as the subject of the verb, as we employ the pronoun *I*, it is incredible that it should totally disappear, when it must have been one of the most common words in the language. The present Greek and Latin nominatives, ἐγώ (ἐγών), ego, and the German *ich*, anciently *ih*, may be traced to the Sanscrit *aham*. Professor Bopp regards *ah* as the root of this word == Germ. *ich*. We rather think, with Graff, that the terminating *m*, which appears in all the oblique cases, is the real root; and that *aha* is a particle prefixed for the sake of emphasis, perhaps related to *iha*==*here*, nearly analogous to the Italian *eccomi*.

Our readers will easily apply the above observations to the remaining personal pronouns, singular and plural; and

---

* *Mi, ma, mo*. occur in many languages as interrogative and indefinite pronouns, which are often closely connected with demonstratives and relatives.

** One strong ground for this supposition is, that the ancient Latin imperatives, *estod*—*vivitod*—and the analogous Veda imperative—*jiva-tût* ==*vivito* — are unequivocally in the *ablative* form.

7*

will not fail to observe the analogy between the first person of each in the verbal paradigm. The characteristic termination of the third person plural — Sanscrit, *nti*, Latin and old German, *nt* — has given grammarians a great deal of trouble. Dr. Prichard ingeniously suggests the Welsh *hwynt* (they) — in *regimine*, *ynt* — as the probable origin of it, and we have no doubt that there is a connexion between this pronoun and the *Welsh* verbal terminations, *ant*, *ent*, *ynt*. We do not, however, believe that the Sanscrit or Latin forms were *derived* from the Celtic, or that those languages ever had a separate pronoun resembling *hwynt* in form and meaning. We think it more probable that the similarity of the respective endings arises from their being formed by a *combination* of the same primeval elements, viz. the demonstrative roots *na* + *ta*. The Esthonian *need* (illi) may have been formed by a similar process.

We cannot help thinking it a strong confirmation of our theory, that the different pronouns and personal terminations are in many cases *commutable* with each other — *i. e.* the element which in one dialect stands for the first person, in another represents the second or third, and *vice versâ*. This will appear more evidently from the following conspectus of a few pronominal roots, with some of their ostensible derivations : —

MA. Esthonian, *ma*; Welsh, *mi*; Irish, *me*; Persian, *men*; Finnish, *mi-na*, I; Gr. μὶν, him; Hungarian, *ma-ga*, ipsemet. Plur. — Finnish, *me*; Lithuanian, *mes*; Slavonic, *my*; Gr. ἅμ-μες, we; ὑμ-μες, you.

VA. Gothic, *vit*; Slavon. *va*, *vje*, *we-two*; Sanscrit, 1st pers. dual, tuda — *vas*, *we-two* strike — plur. *vayam*; Zend. *vaem* (we); Goth. *veis*; Germ. *wir*; Ang. Sax. *we*.

Second Person. — Sanscr. acc. dual. *vām*; Zend. *vāo*; Slavon. (dative) *vama*, you-two. Plur. — Sanscr. acc. *vas*; Zend. *vō*; Lat. *vos*; Slavon. *vy*.

NA. (In the Finnish dialects *this* or *that*; Pali, *nam*, that; Gr. νὶν, him, her, them.) Sanscr. acc. dual, *nāu*, us-two; Gr. νῶϊ; Slavon. (dat.) *nama*. Plur. — Sanscr. acc. *nas*; Zend. *nō*; Lat. *nos*; Welsh, *ni*; Slav. (gen.) *nas*; Pali, *ne*, *nā*, those.

SA. (In Sanscrit and Armenian, *this*, Irish, *so*, ditto) Esthonian, *sa*, Finnish, *Si-nä*, Gr. συ, thou. Irish, *se*, he; *sinn*, we; *sibh*, you; *siad*, they. Germ. *sie*, she, they.

The above apparent anomalies and interchanges, capricious as they seem, are easily explained, if we suppose that the pronominal roots had primarily a *local* signification. Assuming, for the sake of argument, that VA was equivalent to the Greek οὗτος, it is easy to conceive that some tribes might use it in the dual and plural to express* *we* = Lat. *hi*, while others, with perfect propriety, applied it to denote *you* = isti. The same principle will serve to establish an affinity between the Greek pronominal forms — σφὲ, σφῶϊ, σφωέ, σφεῖς. Several of the German philologists have pointed out the probable connexion of σφὲ, σφωὲ, and σφεῖς with the Sanscrit *sva*, and Latin *sui*. However, not being able to divest their minds of the idea of a radical distinction between the second and third persons, they violently derive σφῶϊ from Sanscr. *tvam*, thou. We think it clear that all the above forms are from the *same root*, having primarily the force of αὐτος, or *ipse*, which, as every schoolboy knows, are of *all persons*. Otherwise, it is not easy to explain how Homer could use σφίσιν in the sense of *vobis* (Il. x. 398), or how the possessive σφέτερος could be employed indifferently to denote *his*, *our*, *your*, and *their*. Vide Hesiod, Opera et Dies, v. 2, Theocritus, Id. 22, v. 67.

We proceed to consider the affinity, or rather the identity, of pronouns and single particles, the establishment of which is, perhaps, the most important discovery·in modern philology. We shall preface our remarks with an extract from Sir Graves Haughton's Bengali Grammar, which, among some more than questionable positions and offensively audacious assumptions, contains several really ingenious and valuable observations.

'Prepositions were originally employed to contrast the relative positions of the different objects of nature; which were of course, in the infancy of society, the first things that required the employment of speech for their description. But, in proportion as the impressions received through the senses began to be comprehended, the operations of the intellect were developed, and man *became* (?) a reasoning being; and almost imperceptibly, a new application of language was required, to express the various relations of abstract ideas. And though there may seem to be no necessary connexion between the relations of material things and abstract notions, yet, as the comprehension of the latter gradually arises out of the consideration of the modes of material objects; so language, which had *resulted* from the necessity of describing whatever was within the scope of the senses, (?) came at last to be employed to denote the abstract conceptions of the mind; be-

---

* Bopp, who generally considers the personal pronouns as a sort of substantives, radically distinct from each other, admits that the Sanscrit *nas* (nos) is probably from the demonstrative root *na*; and originally had the import of the Latin *hi*. It does not seem to have occurred to him that f *hi* can denote *nos*, *hic* must be equally capable of denoting *ego*.

cause it was ready at hand, and saved the trouble of a new convention between the interlocutors. Hence, it must be purely metaphorical, as often as it is employed in the description of abstract ideas.

‘But the obvious distinction between language which had been[*] *invented* (?) to describe natural objects, and its figurative application to denote abstract ideas, must never be lost sight of in practice. Thus, when prepositions are employed for the purposes for which they were invented, they mark the relations of local position; as, “the bird flew *to, above, below, before, behind*, &c., the tree.” But, when the same prepositions are borrowed to express abstract conceptions, as, “fancy triumphs over reason,” or, “the mind revolts against oppression,” they imply nothing more than a mere mental contrast; and by convention we agree to think, that what we assimilate in our minds to *above* and *before*, &c., is better than what we designate by *below* and *behind*, &c., though there can be neither *up* nor *down, before* or *after*, in what is altogether intellectual.

‘From what has been remarked above, it will be evident that prepositions were, in the origin of language, almost as indispensable as verbs; for, without their aid, no verb except a neuter one could have conveyed a definite idea; as the prepositions alone denote the action of the verb. . . . . . And what may tend to prove their specific formation for their present use is, that they are almost universally the shortest words, and are incapable of being decompounded.’ — *Rudiments of Bengali Grammar*, pp. 106 — 8.

We refrain from meddling with the Monboddism of the above passage; but the observations on the primary and secondary applications of prepositions, and their importance in language, command our entire assent. We do not, however, regard prepositions and conjunctions, in *their existing form*, as primitive words, but as formed by inflection and composition from *pronouns*, chiefly demonstratives; at least, if any are entitled to be considered as original words, the simple forms μὲν, δὲ, ϱα, κε, τε, γε, ne, ve, ce, que, &c., many of which are also found in Sanscrit, are the most

---

[*] Theorists talk of the *invention* of words by savages, as if it were one of the easiest matters in the world. We beg to ask whether they *invent* any new words (i. e. *original* words) now-a-days; and if not — *when* the process ceased — and *why*? We believe it to be almost as easy to create a new particle of matter, as for a man — savage or civilized — to *invent* a fresh verbal root, and make it pass current as such. How many vocables have the Chinese added to their stock during the last three thousand years? or where do we find any recent terms not formed by derivation or composition from previously existing elements?

likely to be so. The pronominal origin of many particles is too obvious to be insisted upon. It will hardly be denied that *quò, quà, qui, quam, quum*, and our own *where, whence, why, whither*, &c., are mere modifications of *qui* and *who*, and that the Greek ὡς, ὅτε, and German *wie, wo, wenn*, &c. &c., are of similar origin. In like manner ἀλλά is merely a neuter plural of ἄλλος; ἀμφί, ἀμφίς, evidently connected with ἄμφω; and *sed, se* (without), as we formerly observed, are apparently ablatives of *sui*. We consider it as equally certain that *si* (if) is the ablative of the ancient demonstrative pronoun *sis*=*is*—q. d. **in this* [case], and *sic* the same word, with the addition of the enclitic *ce* — q. d. *in this* [manner]. Most of the Greek prepositions occur in Sanscrit under almost identical forms, and nearly all may be deduced, with more or less certainty, from Sanscrit pronominal roots. Sir G. Haughton observes that ἀπό, πρό, παρά, σύν, ὑπό, περί, ἐπί, ὑπέρ, are evidently identical with the Sanscrit and Bengali words *apa, pra, para, sam, upa, pari, api, upari*. He also refers πρός to *puras* (before); we think that *prati*, exactly the Homeric προτί, furnishes a more satisfactory etymology.

We refer our readers to Professor Bopp for a further investigation of the origin of the Sanscrit particles. Some of his etymologies are confessedly conjectural, others we conceive to be perfectly satisfactory. He appears to have established his leading positions — that pronouns and particles are closely related, and that they form a totally distinct class from nouns and verbs — on a firm basis. We have only space for two examples.

Grammarians are greatly puzzled to account for the various and seemingly conflicting meanings of the preposition παρά. We think they may be all satisfactorily deduced from its etymon, the Sanscrit indefinite pronoun *para* = *alius*, which is evidently capable of denoting addition, juxtaposition, approach, and similar relations, in which one thing is viewed in *conjunction with another*, and departure, deviation, distortion, change, &c., where a thing is considered as *distinct from another*. Παρέχω, πάρειμι, παραβάλλω, are examples of the former idea; and παρατρέχω, παρατρέπω, παραβαίνω, παρακούω, παροράω, and a multitude of similar expressions, — some literal and some metaphorical, but all including the idea of *difference* — belong to the latter. We

---

* Cf. Havelok, vv. 2119, 20 —
      'Thou mayt us bothe yeve and selle
      With that thou wilt here dwell:'
i. e. *if* thou wilt; a literal translation of *si*.

shall not at present discuss the probable affinity between
παρὰ and περὶ, πρὸ, περᾶν, præ, per, &c., respecting which
much might be said, but we think it important to observe
that the two leading significations which we have pointed
out in παρὰ, also appear in the German *ver* and its cognates. Thus *verschaffen*, to procure, *vergrössern*, to increase,
veralten, to grow old, *vernehmen*, to perceive, have a sort of
acquisitive sense; while *verachten*, to despise, *verderben*, to
destroy, *verführen*, to lead away, seduce, *verkaufen*, to sell,
and a multitude of others, convey an apparently opposite
idea. This latter idea of change, distortion, injury, &c., is
the more prevalent one in Anglo-Saxon and English words
compounded with *for* — *forego*, *foreswear*, *forget*, *for-
sake*, the Scottish *forspeak*, and many others. The editor
of the ‘Diversions of Purley’ (Mr. R. Taylor) well observes
that Tooke's etymology of *for* — viz. Gothic *fairina* (cause)
— does not apply to cases of this description*, and that
the various significations of *for* can only be studied to advantage by comparing the various Teutonic languages. The
Sanscrit etymon, which we have suggested for παρὰ, seems
equally capable of explaining the intensive and privative
acceptations of our *for* and the German *ver*.

Another family of words in the European languages — resembling in sound, but apparently different in signification
— seem to have the Sanscrit relative pronoun *ya* = *qui*, as
their common ancestor. In the Indian dialects a multitude
of particles are formed from this pronoun, analogous to the
derivatives of *qui* and its cognates — e. gr. Sanscr. *yat*, that,
quòd — *yatas*, whence, ὅθεν; *yadā*, when, ὅτε; *yadi*, if;
yadiwā, or, *si–ve*. The same element occurs in the particles of many other languages, in nearly the same significations, and they will generally be found to include the
force of a demonstrative or relative pronoun. For example,
Goth. *jah*, Old Germ. *ja*, *joh*, Finnish *ja* = *and*, may be
resolved into *in this* or *that* (*suppl. manner*), nearly equivalent to our *also*. The Greek τε, from the demonstrative
root TA, and Latin *que*, from the relative KA, are apparently of parallel import. We believe the same signification to be included in Goth. *jai*, *ja*, Germ. *ja*, Ang. Sax.

---

* Tooke's etymology is ludicrous enough when examined. *Fairina* is
itself a derivative word, and though it corresponds to αἰτία, it is not in
its sense of *cause* or *reason*, but always in that of *fault* or *crime*. The same
word is found in old German!— *vir-ina*, *scelus*. A little attention would
have shown that our preposition *for* stands for three different German
words, *für*, *vor*, and *ver*, and that our conjunction *for* is in all cases a corruption of the Anglo-Saxon *forthy* or *fortham* — exactly the Italian *perchè*.

gea, *gese*, Frisic *je*, Welsh and Armoric *je* = yes.* In the Scandinavian dialects *ja* is the answer to simple interrogations, and *ju*, *jo*, to questions including a negative. In all cases we conceive the particle simply means *in this* (manner), *thus* = Latin *ita*. The Sanscrit *yadi* appears to furnish a clue to the Gothic *jabai*, Frisic *jef*, Ang. Sax. *gif*, Old Germ. *ibu*, *ubi*, Lettish *ja*, Finnish *jos* = if ** — all denoting *in which* or *in that* [case or supposition] = Latin *si*. *Jabai* — from which the other Germanic forms are descended — appears to have originally been a dative or instrumental case of *ya*, analogous to *tubya* = Latin *tibi* (compare *ibi*, *ubi*, Gr. βίηφι, Slavonic *tebje* = tibi).

The *relative* import of the particle is most clearly discernible in the *distributive* phrases, Ang. Sax. *ge* sceap, *ge* oxan — both sheep and oxen, or, more familiarly, *what* sheep, *what* oxen; Latin *qua*** oves, *qua* boves; Ital. *che* piccoli, *che* grandi — both small and great; or in the comparative construction — Germ. *je* mehr, *je* besser, Lat. *quo* plus, *eo* melius; sometimes *je* mehr, *desto* besser, *quo* plus, *hoc* melius.

The above instances may serve to illustrate the manner in which adverbs and conjunctions are formed from pronouns. It will be observed that all those phrases, as well as all cases in which particles are formed from adjectives, are *elliptical*, requiring the words *place*, *time*, *manner*, v. t. q. to complete the sense — e. gr. ὧδε, *in this* [place]; *ibi* (from *is*) *in that* [place]; μακρὰν [ὁδὸν]; *primo* [loco]; *sero* [tempore]; *certo* [modo]. We do not stop to inquire whether such words are still adjectives and pronouns, or have become different parts of speech, our business being merely to show what they originally were. The process by which pronouns or pronominal adverbs might be converted into prepositions will be readily understood by considering the constructions *ubi* gentium, *quo* terrarum, *hic* loci, *eò* loci, and many others, where the relations of place, time, &c., are expressed in a manner closely analogous to government by a preposition. For example, *hic* might easily have been employed to denote *cis*, *juxta*, or any other relation of *prox-*

* Tooke's derivations of *yes* from *ay es*, *have that*, or the Fr. imperat. pl. a *yez*, are supremely absurd: it is as notorious as a matter of fact can be, that the Anglo-Saxon *gese* — the parent of our *yes* — existed long before the *modern* German *es* or the French *ayez* were heard of.

** We believe this to be the true etymology of *if*; not, as we formerly suggested, Sanscr. *i-va*, *sient*, or Germ. *iba*, doubt.

*** The German *je*, Dan. *jo*, Swed. *ju*, have the same distributive force in the phrase *je* zwei und zwei = two and two — Gr. ἀνὰ δύο. In many constructions they have a *restrictive* power, exactly equivalent to the Greek particle γε, which we believe to be of cognate origin.

imity; and *eò* was as capable of signifying *ultra*, *trans*, and similar ideas of remoteness as the words now sanctioned by custom. The Anglo-Saxon *geond*, beyond, is a mere demonstrative pronoun, expressing elliptically what the German *jenseits* describes more fully. Περᾶν is apparently a mere accusative feminine of Sanscr. *para*, q. d. *on the other* [side].

We must again refer our readers to Professor Bopp for a full exposition of the manner in which pronouns enter into the composition of words — the terminations and cases of nouns and participles — the formation of abstract substantives — and the suffixes of adverbs. A single example may serve to give our readers some idea of this part of the subject. The distinguishing termination of many Sanscrit genitives is *sya* — e. gr., ta-sya — *of this* ═ Gr. τοιο. This termination is apparently compounded from the demonstrative and relative pronouns — sa + ya — having in conjunction a *possessive* import. The same appears in *manushya*, man or human (compare Germ. *mensch*), from *manu*, and bears a remarkable resemblance to the ending of δημό — σιος — q. d., *belonging to* the people. The same explanation will serve for the Sanscrit participial suffixes — *tas*, *vas*, *nas* (Latin, *tus*, *vus*, *nus*), which are all apparently formed by the combination of pronominal roots, and have a sort of possessive signification. At least we regard this theory as much more probable and rational than that of Mr. A. W. Schlegel, who treats the formative syllables, producing such numerous and important modifications of the meaning of words, as in themselves destitute of signification. Speaking of the family of languages with inflections, he observes —

'Le merveilleux artifice de ces langues est, de former une immense variété de mots, et de marquer la liaison des idées que ces mots désignent, moyennant un assez petit nombre de syllabes qui, considérés séparément, *n'ont point de signification*, mais qui déterminent avec précision le sens du mot auquel elles sont jointes. . . . . . On décline les substantifs, les adjectifs, et les pronoms, par genres, par nombres, et par cas; on conjugue les verbes par voix, par modes, par temps, par nombres et par personnes, en employant de même des désinences et quelquefois des augments qui, séparément, *ne signifient rien*.' — *Observations sur la Langue et la Littérature Provençales.*

We consider this hypothesis as chimerical, and next to impossible. We believe that in language *ex nihilo nihil fit*; and we are at a loss to conceive how elements, originally destitute of signification, can determine the sense of anything with precision. To assume that they have no meaning, because we cannot always satisfactorily explain it, is only an *argumentum ad ignorantiam.* A mere Englishman sees no distinct meaning in the final syllables of man-*hood*, priest-*hood*, widow-*hood*, or of the German frei-*heit*, schön-*heit*, weis-*heit*. But a Bavarian, accustomed to talk of the ‘gute,’ or ‘schlechte *hait*,’ of things, can tell him at once that the termination in both languages denotes *quality*, *state*, *condition.** It is, therefore, lawful to conclude, from analogy, that the terminations in liber-*tas*, $\pi\varrho\alpha\acute{o}$-$\tau\eta\varsigma$, and many other abstract terms, have a distinct meaning, which was perfectly understood when they first began to be employed.

It is foreign to our present purpose to enter into a lengthened discussion respecting the *composition* of words — a feature which so remarkably distinguishes the Indo-European from the Semitic languages. We will, however, briefly advert to a species of composition of which traces appear in many languages. Grammarians have noticed the existence of words in cognate dialects, agreeing in all respects, except in possessing or wanting an initial *s*, — e. gr., $\mu\acute{\iota}\varkappa\varrho\varsigma$, $\sigma\mu\acute{\iota}\varkappa\varrho\varsigma$ — *fallo*, $\sigma\varphi\acute{\alpha}\lambda\lambda\omega$ — Goth., *ufar*** — Lat., *super*. This prosthetic *s* is of common occurrence in the Teutonic dialects; and Grimm sagaciously observes that it is in all probability a remnant of some ancient particle. We have reason to think that the remark was capable of a much more extensive application, and might be made to illustrate an important feature in the early formation of language. It will be found on examination that several other letters are employed in a similar manner. It is also remarkable that they are chiefly the same elements which form the basis of the pronominal roots, — as will appear from the examples which we are about to adduce. The most common prefixes are $\breve{a}$ (with its equivalents $\breve{e}$, $\breve{o}$), p (b, f, ph), *t* (d, th), k (c, q), &c., which are employed in a manner that can hardly be deemed arbitrary or accidental. We subjoin a few specimens of each out of many hundreds: —

A, &c. Lat. mulgeo; Ger. melken.		Gr. $\dot{\alpha}\mu\acute{\varepsilon}\lambda\gamma\omega$.
— ructo — —		$\dot{\varepsilon}\varrho\varepsilon\acute{v}\gamma\omega$.
Sanscr. danta; Lat. dens.		$\dot{o}$-$\delta o\grave{v}\varsigma$.
Sanscr. naman; Lat. nomen.		$\ddot{o}\nu o\mu\alpha$.
Sanscr. nak'ha; Germ. nagel.		$\grave{o}\nu\grave{v}\xi$.

* In old German, *heit* also denotes *person*. It occurs in the same sense in the ancient metrical version of the Athanasian Creed, published by Hickes. *Thesaurus*, vol. i. p. 233 — ‘Ne the *hodes* oht mengande’ — ‘neither aught confounding the *persons*.’

** Greek $\dot{v}\pi\grave{\varepsilon}\varrho$ is not a parallel case. The *spiritus asper* almost invariably becomes *s* in Latin — consequently $\dot{v}\pi\varepsilon\varrho$ and *super* are exactly equivalent.

To these we are disposed to add the copulative *a* in ἄλοχος, ἀτάλαντος, &c., and the syllabic augment — Sanscr. a — tudam, Gr. ἔτυπον, which we believe to be a *particle.*

P, &c.	Lat. rogo.	Sanscr. p-rach; Germ. f-ragen.
	Gr. ῥήγνυμι.	Icel. b-raka; Lat. f-rango.
	Lat. latus.	Gr. π-λατὺς; Germ. b-reit.
	Bavar. lukken.	Eng. pluck.
	Gael. iasg (fish).	Lat. piscis; Welsh. pysg.

T, &c.	Germ. reiben.	Gr. τρίβειν.
	Sanscr. asru; Lithu. aszara.	δάκρυ.
	Lat. ros.	δρόσος.
	Germ. rupfen.	δρέπω.

K, &c.	Lat. amo.	Sanscr. kam.
	Lettish. lobit (to flay).	Lat. g-lubo.
	Lat. lætus.	Iceland. g-lad.
	Lat. rapio.	Sanscr. grabh; Icel. gripa.
	Lat. nodus.	Icel. k-nut.
	Lat. aper; Germ. eber.	Gr. κ-άπρος.

S. The most common of all prefixes, especially in Erse and Lower Saxon. We add the following to the numerous instances adduced by Grimm. (Gram. ii. 701.)

Lat. memor.	Sanscr. s-mri (to remember).
Germ. link (left).	Belg. s-link.
Lat. nare (to swim).	Sanscr. s-na; Gael. s-namh.
Lat. nere (to spin).	Gael. sniomh.
Germ. reihe (row).	Ghel. sreadh.
Gr. κείρω.	Icel. skära.
Lat. limus.	Germ. schleim.

Many words seem to exhibit two or three gradations of this kind of composition, — e. gr., Sanscr. *lip,* to anoint (compare Homer's λίπ' ἔλαιον); Gr. ἀλείφω; Goth. s-a-lbon; Germ. rollen; Bavar. k-rollen; Eng. s-c-roll. We have actual evidence of the composition of many words bearing a considerable analogy to the above examples, especially in the Germanic dialects. Beichte (confession), bleiben, block, glaube, glied, gnade, flazan, fliesan, with many others, are known to be respectively compounded with the particles *be, ge, fra. Fret,* simple as it appears, consists of two distinct elements, — Goth. fra + itan = ex-edere; so that the modern German *ver-fressen* (to devour) is *twice* compounded with the same particle. Even many of the words usually regarded as Sanscrit roots are capable of being resolved into still simpler elements. For instance, the root *i* denotes *to go* (Lat. *i-re,* Gr. ιεναι); *ri,* also *to go,* may very possibly be a compound of ra + i = *pergere; tri* (to pass), ta + ri — q. d., go *thither; stri,* to strew, or spread, a further formation with

the particle *sa*, — and so of many others. Our readers will
find much ingenious speculation on this subject in Pott's
'Etymologische Forschungen.' We consider many of his
conclusions as highly deserving of attention; but we do not
feel disposed to agree with him in referring the above prefixes to the Sanscrit *prepositions*, in their *present form*, which
is evidently not their *primeval* one. We think, for example,
that *tri* is probably compounded, not, however, with the preposition *ati*, but with the pronominal or prepositional root
ta. We freely admit that all this is, in a great measure,
conjectural, and requires to be confirmed by a more copious
induction from cognate dialects. Could the fact be sufficiently established, it would afford scope for much curious discussion respecting the formation of language, and might perhaps serve as a clue in tracing the affinities of tongues, commonly supposed to be entirely unconnected. It is scarcely
possible for two languages to be more unlike than Sanscrit
and Chinese; but it is by no means improbable that both
were at a very early period much in the same condition and
partly composed of the same elements. Both consist of monosyllabic *roots;* and a few more pronouns and particles,
employed copiously in the connexion and composition of words,
might have made the latter not unlike the former. But
while the component elements of Greek and Sanscrit have,
as it were, crystallized into beautiful forms, Chinese, as an
oral language, has remained perfectly stationary, and is
still, as it was 3000 years ago, 'arena sine calce.'

We think one point satisfactorily established, — namely,
that pronouns and simple particles, instead of being, as Tooke
represents, comparatively modern contrivances, are in reality of the most remote antiquity, as well as of first-rate importance in language. The oldest dialects have invariably
more words of this class than the more recent ones, as may
be seen by comparing Homer with Sophocles, or the Gothic
of Ulphilas with the German of Luther. Their antiquity may
be further proved by a comparison of different families of
languages. Of all European tongues Finnish is perhaps the
most remote from Sanscrit. The numerals have nothing in
common, and there are very few coincidences in the names
of ordinary objects. Nevertheless the personal, demonstrative, and relative pronouns, and the terminations of the verbs,
are composed of nearly the same elements in both. It would
be as absurd to ascribe this coincidence to accident, as to
suppose that one race had borrowed terms of this sort from
the other; the only rational supposition is, that they are in
both languages derived from the same source, and conse-

quently existed long before Sanscrit and Finnish had assumed their present forms. Tooke's corollary proposition, that language, in its in-artificial state, was destitute of pronouns and particles, is the very reverse of truth; it being well known that the barbarous South-Sea islanders have many more than the most cultivated Europeans. An Englishman or a Frenchman has only one word for *we*, but a native of Hawaii or Tahiti has perfectly distinct terms for all the following combinations, — I + thou; I + he; I + you; I + they; I + my company. So unsafe is it to construct theories on insufficient evidence, or none at all!

We have thus endeavoured to convey our ideas of the primeval nature of language, and to exhibit a small portion of the evidence on which they appear to be founded. Had our limits allowed, we could have confirmed some of our positions by a much more extensive induction; but we trust we have said sufficient to excite investigation and discussion. Our object has not been to advance paradoxes, but to endeavour to throw light on the real elements of language, and to show what it is apart from the confessedly artificial divisions of grammarians. If our speculations are proved to be erroneous, we shall be ready to renounce them for something better; if they are sound, their truth will eventually be recognized. They at least represent language as a more simple thing than it is commonly supposed to be; and, if well-founded, may serve to elucidate some of the sciences more immediately dependent upon language. Whether they will help to settle the old quarrel between the nominalists and realists or not, is more than we will venture to affirm; but we are persuaded that the proving or disproving them would be of some consequence to universal grammar, and perhaps to logic and metaphysics.

ANTIQUARIAN CLUB-BOOKS.

[*Quarterly Review*, March, 1848.]

Publications of —

1. *The Cymmrodorion Society.* 1762, &c.
2. *The Society of Antiquaries.* 1770, &c. (Layamon, edited for the Society of Antiquaries by Sir F. Madden. 3 vols. 1847, 8vo.)
3. *The Commissioners on the Public Records of the Kingdom.* 1802, &c.
4. *The Roxburghe Club.* 1819, &c.
5. *The Surtees Society.* 1837, &c.
6. *The English Historical Society.* 1838, &c.
7. *The Camden Society.* 1838, &c.
8. *The Cambridge Camden Society.* 1841, &c.
9. *The Percy Society.* 1841, &c.
10. *The Welsh MSS. Society.* 1840, &c.
11. *The Chetham Society.* 1844, &c.
12. *The British Archæological Association.* 1845, &c.

It has been a frequent subject of complaint with the *laudatores temporis acti* that the present utilitarian age cares for nothing not immediately subservient to its own wants or enjoyments; that even knowledge is not sought after for its own sake, but only with a view of getting something by it. The titles at the head of the present article seem, however, to manifest a tolerably prevalent eagerness — real or affected — to learn something of what time has forgotten, without reference to the honour or profit to be derived from the study. We feel no disposition to quarrel with this spirit in any of its shapes. The information elicited is often interesting — even useful; and the speculations arising out of it, though frequently visionary, are harmless enough, when they do not lead to fierce disputes *de umbra asini*. We wish plenty of game and good success to the whole fraternity of archæologists, from the explorers of barrows to the excavators of Nineveh. Objects of little value in themselves may be of great importance in the hands of those who know how to make use of them. The coins of 'Ariana Antiqua' have

enabled Prinsep, Lassen, and Wilson to retrieve whole dynasties of Bactrian sovereigns; and, in our own country, the
arrow-head of flint, the brazen celt, the steel spear-head, and
the chased helmet tell their respective stories of different
states of civilization, and furnish their quota to the philosophic historian. Even what is simply curious is not to be
despised on that account. We like to learn the shape and
size of an Assyrian shield, even if we learn nothing else
relating to it; and we notice, by no means with indifference,
the resemblance between the head-gear of the Sacian chief
on the monument of Behistun and a modern Astrachan cap.

We nevertheless confess that there is one branch of antiquarian research which we regard as far superior to the rest.
Had the most skilful draughtsman furnished us with the most
accurate delineation of the last-mentioned relic of by-gone
ages, we should have felt that his merit was but small compared with that of the officer who has removed the veil of
more than twenty centuries from the inscriptions, thus enabling us not only to identify the personal representation of
Darius, but to trace the stirring events of his reign, and,
still more, to discern the impress of his mind. We need
not as yet give another lecture on this discovery; but we
may be just allowed to remark that the philosophical and
ethnological results of it are not the least interesting. We
have here a full confirmation of a point only imperfectly
known before, namely, that the Achæmenian sovereigns
spoke a language closely resembling the Vedic Sanscrit, both
in words and organization; and, consequently, were perhaps
as nearly connected in race with the Brahminic conquerors
of India as the Icelanders are with the South Germans.

A similar discovery of considerable interest, although the
interest is of a somewhat different nature, was made not
long ago in our own country. The stone cross at Ruthwell
had excited and baffled the curiosity of whole generations of
antiquaries. All could see that it was of ecclesiastic origin,
and of a period anterior to the Norman invasion; but the
Runic inscription, being mistaken for *Scandinavian*, served
to obscure the matter instead of clearing it up. It was not
till after repeated failures by the best foreign scholars that
the sagacity of Mr. J. Kemble* placed the matter in its true
light. He showed clearly that the verses are not Scandinavian, but *Anglo-Saxon* — the language that of the age and
province of Bede — and the inscription itself a portion of a

---

* *Vide* Archæologia, vol. xxviii. pp. 327—372; and vol. xxx. pp. 31—46.

spirited poem on the Crucifixion and Passion of our Lord. By a singular combination —

'——— quod optanti divûm promittere nemo
    Anderet' —   ,

the whole poem is discovered in a MS. long buried in a Vercelli library, the corresponding passages of which only differ in dialect from the lines engraved on the cross. Half-a-dozen ingenious explanations have been given of the beautiful design on the Portland vase, each perhaps possible in itself, but not one productive of conviction. The artistic merit of the monument is of course unaffected by our ignorance; but who does not feel that a single Greek or Latin distich, connecting it with a favourite classical subject, might have given it an interest far beyond what it now possesses? Such things are in themselves mere words; but, like the Spanish licentiate's epitaph, they are the clue to the *soul* that lies buried; and he who digs for it judiciously will, like the sagacious student, not fail of his reward. Thus we trust that Major Rawlinson will, ere long, evoke Nebuchadnezzar and Sennacherib as successfully as he has produced Darius. *

It will be said, perhaps, that all this has little relevancy to those who must confine their explorations within our own four seas. The chapter of ancient British inscriptions is an absolute blank, and the scanty amount of Roman and Runic Saxon is at length exhausted. What, therefore, remains but earth-work, stone-work, and the 'auld nick-nackets' of Captain Grose? We answer — a great deal — on paper and parchment. There is, perhaps, no nation in Europe that can compete with us in the number and value of our vernacular literary monuments — from the eighth to the fourteenth century: some of which — for example, the code of Anglo-Saxon laws, the poem of Beowulf, various pieces in the Vercelli and Exeter books, &c. &c. — are unique of their kind. The Icelandic Sagas, though superior as compositions, are of considerably later date; and the German literature prior to the twelfth century has little originality to boast of. Yet so incurious were we of our riches, that, till within a very recent period, the number of Anglo-Saxon works published averaged about three in a century, and of middle-English ones in their genuine form scarcely so many. It is well that something has been done of late to redeem us from this reproach; but still a great deal remains undone. We do not hesitate to say that there are valuable materials for the elucidation of national theology, hagiology, popular opinions,

---

* It is needless to remark how splendidly this hope has been realised. ED.

and particularly the origin and progress of our native language, which have not perhaps been seen by ten persons
now living, and whose very existence is unknown to the
great mass of our literary public.

The adventurers in this field may be classed something in
the same way as our money-dealers — individual discounters,
private firms of a few partners, and joint-stock associations
on a large scale. Some of the second division appear to
have acted on the principle that curious and recondite information, like money-profits, is too good a thing to be diffused among the multitude, and ought to be strictly confined
to their own fraternity. We are quite willing that family
documents, which not more than twenty people are likely to
care about, should be hoarded as cabinet curiosities; neither
do we quarrel with those who have restricted to five-and-
twenty copies re-impressions of uniques, of which there was
already one too many. But the case is different with works
possessing, not merely a British, but an European interest.
For example, take the Chronicle of Mailros, brought forth
for the first time in an accurate and complete form, by one
of the very few editors competent to such a task, under the
auspices of a Scottish Society. It is not so generally known
as it ought to be that this work is of the first importance
for the ethnological and civil history of our border counties,
completely refuting the crude theories propagated by Pinkerton and his disciples, which have met with too much acceptance both in Great Britain and on the continent. But
how are the majority of the literary world to know better?
A foreigner or a provincial student who inquires for the
Bannatyne book is told that it is not to be had for money;
his only resource is to take an expensive journey, or give
an extravagant price for an inaccurate and defective edition
in a voluminous collection of 'Scriptores.' We must say
that we more admire the system of certain English Societies,
who place a reasonable number of copies within reach of the
public, both to the satisfaction of the literary world, and to the
benefit of their own funds. We should be less inclined to complain of the close Clubs if they left a more free course of
action to other parties; but in more instances than one they
have shown themselves not a little sensitive about any apparent invasion of their supposed monopoly. It was notorious that a new and enlarged edition of 'Havelok the
Dane' was greatly wanted, and, as a matter of courtesy,
the Club under whose auspices the work came forth were
requested to allow of its re-impression, under the superintendence of the gentleman who is every way the best enti-

tled to the office.* This simple request was positively refused! and was only at length conceded with an indifferent
grace, on discovering that the execution was likely to get
into the hands of another party, little qualified to do justice
to the subject. Surely this is not the way to *diffuse* a taste
for our early language and literature! On another occasion
some influential members of the Roxburghe were told that
more than half their publications were wanting in our great
national repository. The reply was — 'We are glad to hear
it!' Doubtless a society has a right to be thus exclusive;
and so has a Duke to build a wall twenty feet high round
his park. We, however, prefer the taste and feeling of the
man who leaves an open paling.

This niggardly spirit is not confined to small literary coteries. One of the German editors of the 'Nibelungen Lied'
congratulates his readers that the oldest and best manuscript
of that noble poem was saved from 'the fate of being transferred to England — there to lie useless and unknown of in
some private collection.' This sarcasm does not apply to
all English owners of collections;** but more than one instance has come to our knowledge where permission to consult documents essential to the integrity of a published series,
was pointedly refused — though they are of high interest to
the European literary public, and not of the smallest personal consequence to the proprietor. Sometimes the existence, or, what amounts to the same thing, the locality of
a literary treasure is studiously concealed. The York Mysteries — the most curious and important collection of the
kind after the Townley — have disappeared for the third
time to an unknown 'limbus librorum,' where they will probably slumber as unprofitably as they did at Strawberry
Hill and at Bristol. Our next account of them may possibly
be that they are for ever lost, having been subjected to the
same fate which befel the Sebright, the Hafod, and so many
other private collections.

Our readers will not expect a detailed critique of all the
publications comprehended in our list. We say nothing of
many of the *Roxburghe* books, for reasons already intimated.
There are however good ones, as well as bad and indifferent. 'Havelok the Dane,' 'William and the Were Wolf,'
the 'Early English Gesta Romanorum,' and several others,
are valuable monuments of our early language and literature,
and ought to be rendered more generally accessible. Things

---

* Sir F. Madden. ED.
** The liberality of Sir Thomas Phillips is especially worthy of praise.

which have only a conventional worth might lose a portion of it if placed within everybody's reach; but we cannot conceive that either natural or intellectual products, if intrinsically good, are depreciated by their abundance. Who would now lay a heavy import-duty on oranges and pineapples, or venture to talk of editions of Don Quixote 'strictly limited to twenty-five copies'? Havelok the Dane would not in any case command so many readers as Guy Mannering; but there is no doubt that an edition of a few hundred copies would have been willingly received, and might have directed towards this branch of study the minds of many who only wanted an accidental impulse.

We have great pleasure in bearing our testimony not only to the superior liberality of the *English Historical* Society, but to the judicious choice and careful execution of their works themselves. Mr. Kemble's Anglo-Saxon Charters — equally important to the philologist and to the legal and constitutional antiquary — Mr. Stevenson's Ecclesiastical History and Opera Minora of Bede — Mr. Hardy's William of Malmsbury — Mr. Coxe's handsome and complete Roger of Wendover — in short, the Society's publications in general — form a series which any man may be glad to place in his library as satisfactory editions of intrinsically valuable books. Nennius would admit of further elucidation by a good Celtic scholar; but the text is a decided improvement, and the notes are sensible and useful as far as they go.

Next to the *English Historical* we feel disposed to rank the *Surtees*, both on account of the liberality of its constitution and the general value of its books. If a portion of these possess only a local interest, we must remember that the society was organized for local purposes and with a restricted sphere of action; and we are willing to connive at a few 'Wills,' 'Inventories,' and similar dry bones of ancient literature, in consideration of the sterling value of other publications. Not to dwell upon Reginald's account of St. Cuthbert, the collection of Durham historians, and other works the importance of which is obvious at once, we would specify the Townley Mysteries, the Durham Ritual, and the Anglo-Saxon and Northumbrian Psalters, as monuments, each unique in its kind, and furnishing materials for the elucidation of our northern dialects, both of the Saxon and mediæval period, which it would be vain to search for elsewhere. Even the 'Liber Vitæ, or list of benefactors to the shrine of St. Cuthbert,' possesses an interest far beyond what might have been expected from a mere catalogue of names. The initiated may there distinctly trace the changes of the original stock of Northern Angles caused by successive infusions of Scandinavian, West Saxon, and Norman blood, till all become blended in that current English nomenclature which to this very day bears the plain impress of all. On many accounts therefore we are wellwishers of the 'Surtees,' and would gladly see it organised on a broad basis and in the receipt of an income adequate to more extensive operations.

The *Camden* Society is undoubtedly the one which, from its numbers, the professed comprehensiveness of its plan, and the high literary character of many of its members, bids the fairest to supply a notorious deficiency in our literature, namely, in the departments of our early national history and the illustration of the early period of our language. With all our wealth and all our affectation of public spirit, not only the Germans, Danes, and Swedes, but even the Bohemians, have surpassed us in their well-directed, systematic, and successful cultivation of those fields. What have we to put in competition with the Monumenta Germanica of Pertz, the Scriptores Rerum Danicarum of Suhm and Langebek, the similar Swedish collection of Geijer and Afzelius, the long list of Icelandic Sagas, the Wybor Literatura Ceskè, and the numerous lexicographical, antiquarian, and historical labours of Jungmann, Schafarik, Hanka, and Palacky? Conscious of this unsatisfactory state of affairs, we could not but rejoice when twelve hundred men banded themselves together with the avowed purpose 'of perpetuating and rendering accessible whatever is valuable, but at present little known, amongst the materials for the civil, ecclesiastical, or literary history of the United Kingdom.' After a trial of nine years, we are constrained to say that the results do not precisely correspond with our expectations. Much of what has appeared is of comparatively limited interest, belonging rather to private biography than to general history, and being, moreover, of a period requiring little additional illustration. If works of this kind are to form the staple, it is impossible to foresee any end of them, since they may be found in our libraries by hundreds and thousands, quite equal in intrinsic merit to those that have already appeared. Among the few publications strictly historical, the value of the Chronicle of Joceline de Brakelonde is cheerfully acknowledged. We could also recommend the translation of Polydore Virgil to the careful study of the present race of tourists and travellers, in order that they may learn, if possible, to tell a plain story in plain words. Some of

the purely historical works appear to us undeserving of the
Society's patronage; others have been marred in the execution, of which more anon.   What we are most dissatisfied
with is the little that has been contributed towards the illustration of the progress of our vernacular language.   It was
understood at the commencement that this was to form one
of the Society's chief objects; and the most rational method
of promoting it would seem to be the publication of the remains of our early national writers — if not of the Anglo-
Saxon period, yet at all events of those from the twelfth
century to the end of the fourteenth.   Hitherto, however,
works of this class have hardly constituted one in ten of the
Society's publications; and we have reason to believe that
proposals to edit very valuable ones have been absolutely
discouraged by leading members of the Council, on the
ground that they would not suit the taste of the generality
of readers.   We thought that societies calling themselves
learned were not organized to pander to the corrupt taste of
a frivolous and novel-reading generation, but to try to direct
it into better channels.   Something, however, has been done
in this department, and a portion of it well.   Mr. Albert
Way's Promptorium Parvulorum is a truly valuable contribution, and we sincerely hope that he will shortly find leisure to give us the remaining portion of the work.   Dr. Todd's
Apology for the Lollards, and Mr. Robson's Three Metrical
Romances, are also creditable to the editors.   The Romances
have a special value, as being almost the only known specimens of the ancient North Lancashire dialect.   The Poems
on Richard II., edited by Mr. T. Wright, and the Thorn-
ton Romances, by Mr. J. O. Halliwell, would also come
within the category — but we have not had the means of
testing their accuracy, and we have our reasons for distrust-
ing everything done under the superintendence of those two
gentlemen, if the task demand the smallest possible amount
of critical skill or acumen.

Mr. Halliwell has been known some time as a dilettante
in the literature of the middle ages, and seems to possess a
pretty good opinion of his own qualifications.   In this we
are sorry that we cannot agree with him.   We are not going
to wade through the whole series of his publications, but
shall select one, which, as it was undertaken on the 'vo-
luntary principle,' may be fairly taken as a criterion.   Some
five or six years ago Mr. Halliwell and Mr. Wright edited,
conjunctis curis, a miscellany entitled 'Reliquiæ Antiquæ; or,
Scraps from Ancient Manuscripts.'   It did little credit to
their discrimination in selecting materials, or their skill in

editing them; but as they were under no obligation to attempt matters which they felt themselves unable to grapple with, it is at least an unobjectionable test of their capabilities. No one can cast a cursory glance over Mr. Halliwell's contributions without stumbling on many passages which have neither sense nor grammar; but as it might be alleged that he had faithfully copied his authorities, we will examine how far this is the case. In vol. i. pp. 287—291, he produces a Latin poem from a Lansdowne MS. of the fifteenth century, worthless enough at the best, but so full of stumbling-blocks of all sorts that we felt curious to ascertain who had actually perpetrated such nonsense. Our collation with the MS., which is not more difficult to read than the generality of the same period, gave a result of more than thirty gross errors of transcription, with as many false punctuations, in the course of two pages — many of them subversive of every shadow of meaning. If any reader has the courage to encounter pages 289 and 290 in their published form, we request that he will not impute to the scribe such grammar as ‘vox *iste* [est] jocunda,’ or such grammar and prosody united as ‘nulla premia sequitur,’ or ‘aguis’ for ‘ignis,’ or ‘male perire famæ’ for ‘malo perire fame.’ We also counsel him not to puzzle himself with ‘me retro *pingere* querit,’ ‘Jhesus *calamabat* Petrum,’ or ‘Emerunt *vagam*.’ These and many similar readings are entirely due to the editor, who might have found in MS. *pungere, clamabat*, and *vaccam*, if he had known how to look for them. ‘Stermito’ and ‘streo’ are blunders which an ounce of scholarship would enable any man to correct to *sternuto* and *screo*, particularly as the vernacular ‘snese’ and ‘spitte’ happen to be in their company. But ‘Arbor *Lencester*’ and ‘*cimliæ* quæ vendit omasum’ are awful bugbears, and calculated to cause deep musings. We therefore beg, in all charity, to inform the reader that ‘Lencester’ is neither the upas-tree nor the deadly night-shade, but *lentè stet;* and ‘cimliæ,’ — incredible as it may appear — nothing worse than *mulier*.

We think it will hardly be denied that an editor of this calibre miscalculated his powers when he undertook such a work as the ‘Chronicle of William de Rishanger.’ The only known copy was obviously made by an ignorant scribe, and swarms with corruptions of every kind and degree. This was a tolerable reason why it should not be undertaken by an editor morally certain to add as many more of his own. That he has done so will become speedily evident to any one who is able to compare the printed text with the MS., and, consequently, the edition is totally worthless in a critical and historical point of view. However, he had the prudence to avoid a rock upon which his coadjutor Mr. Wright sustained a most grievous wreck:—he refrained from giving a *translation* of his author. Indeed, that would have been a task beyond the powers of the best scholar in Europe.

It may be said that blunders of this sort are simply the fruits of ignorance and carelessness, such as a little experience might enable a man to avoid. We fear that in the case of Mr. Halliwell they are associated with a more incurable deficiency, namely, a total inability to enter into the true spirit of this species of study. There is sometimes as great a difference between persons enrolled in the nomenclature of the same erudite class, as there was between the author of the 'Antiquary,' who could enjoy the racy qualities and appreciate the knowledge of a Monkbarns, and the barber Caxon, whose business was with the *outside* of his honour's head. For example, — Percy, Warton, Ellis, and Price were something more than mere mechanical transcribers of ancient poetry. They had enlightened views of the true functions of editor in this department of literature, and we overlook their occasional inaccuracies and errors in consideration of the learning, the elegance, and good taste of their illustrations, and the originality of their remarks. Any one who is desirous to see a direct contrast to all this may find it in Mr. Halliwell's edition of the 'Harrowing of Hell, a Miracle Play, written in the reign of Edward II.' This, though no 'Miracle Play,' but simply a narrative poem, partly in dialogue, is extremely curious, and would have furnished an editor of a different stamp with materials for many interesting remarks respecting the dialect, the grammar and prosody, and the style and composition of the piece. Mr. Halliwell has, however, contrived to overlook everything of real interest, and his publication is only remarkable for the shallowness and irrelevancy of the preface, the farthing-candle style of the notes, and the slovenly inaccuracy of what he calls the translation. The only term that he attempts to explain, amidst a number of very unusual ones, is 'thridde half yer,' a phrase familiar to every reader of modern German; and his only effort at criticism is to pronounce the contest between Jesus and Satan to be 'miserable doggrel.' Such things are matters of taste; we for our part think it much superior to the editor's version of the whole piece, both in force and propriety of expression. There are indeed some ludicrous deviations from modern ideas of congruity, as well as some curious special pleading. If honest Sancho Panza had taken cognizance of the piece, he

would doubtless have remarked on the oddity of making
the devil swear 'Par ma fey,' like a good Old Christian,
and putting a metaphor taken from the game of hazard in
the mouth of the Saviour. A professed editor might lawfully enough have made the same observation, but all that
Mr. Halliwell has done is to obscure the matter as much as
possible. Thus : —

> 'Still be thou, Satanas!
> The is fallen *ambes-aas*' —

i. e. ames–ace, the lowest throw on the dice. This he has
chosen to render —

> 'Be quiet, Satan!
> Thou art defeated.'

But observe how he can pervert the sense of the very plain-
est passages : —

> 'When thou bilevest [*i. e.* losest, renouncest] all thine one,
> Thenne myght thou grede and grone.'

Halliwell. — 'When thou hast none but thine own left,
Then mayst thou weep and groan' —

the precise contrary of the sense meant to be conveyed.
Again —

> 'Habraham, ych wot ful wel
> Wet thou seidest everuchdel,
> That mi leve moder wes
> Boren and shaped of thi fleyhs [flesh].'

Halliwell. — 'Abraham, I well know
Everything thou sayest,
That my beloved mother was
Born and formed of *thine!*'

Here the plain declaration that the Virgin was of the seed
of Abraham is distorted to something which the author never
dreamt of. Such are the fruits of people meddling with
matters which they have neither learning to understand nor
wit to guess at.

Mr. Wright, the coadjutor in the 'Reliquiæ,' and one of
the chief working members of the Camden and some other
societies, has employed himself during a pretty long period
with the literature of the middle ages, and has had considerable practice in extracting and editing MSS. reliques of
various sorts. On the strength of this he has in a manner
constituted himself editor-general in Anglo-Saxon, Anglo-
Norman, Middle-English, and Middle-Latin, and seems to be
regarded by a certain clique as a supreme authority in all

departments of archæology. He has indeed some requisites
for making himself useful in a field where industrious workmen are greatly wanted. But his activity is so counterba-
lanced by want of scholarship and acumen, that he can never
be more than a third or fourth rate personage, bearing about
the same relationship to a scientific philologist and antiquarian
that a law-stationer does to a barrister, or a country druggist
to a physician.

We have stated that we have had no means of testing the
accuracy of Mr. Wright's first Camden publication — the
'Poems on Richard II.' The second, entitled 'Political
Songs of England, from John to Edward II.,' swarms with
errors of transcription and interpretation equally gross; we
need not hesitate to assert that no work more fatal to all
claims of editorial competency has appeared since Hartshorne's
'Ancient Metrical Tales.' A single page will justify this
assertion. One piece (pp. 44—46) is a song levelled against
simoniacal prelates. The poem is perfectly easy to any one
who understands the most ordinary classical and scriptural
allusions; but a man who understands neither, and whose
acquaintance with Latin idiom and syntax is matter of history
or romance, may very possibly make sad havoc of it. Passing over the memorable 'fungar vice totis'* — an enormity

---

* P. 44, 1. 3, of the poem — 'Fungar tamen vice totis,' appropriately
rendered 'I will assume all characters in turn.' It is hardly necessary to
say that 'cotis' stands as plainly in the MS. as in any black-letter Horace.
We subjoin a few random specimens of the editor's happy perception of
the sense of his originals, when he has succeeded in reading them rightly.
P. 11: Noah, David, and Daniel — 'morum vigore nobiles' — are compli-
mented on being 'noble in the vigour of *good breeding.*' Again, p. 14 —

> 'Vitium est in opere, virtus est in ore.'
> 'While vice is in the *work*, virtue is in the *face.*'

P. 32 —   'Calcant archipræsules colla cleri prona,
              Et extorquent lacrimas ut emungant dona.'

'The archbishops tread under foot the necks of the clergy, and extort
tears, *that they may be dried by gifts.*' We imagine that 'emungere dona'
would be more likely to empty the pockets of the inferior clergy than to
dry up their tears. With equal felicity, 'opum metuenda facultas' (p. 34)
is rendered, 'the *revered* possession of riches;' and 'rerum mersus in ar-
dorem' [absorbed in the passion for wealth], 'immersed in the heat of
temporary [temporal?] affairs.' It will not avail to say that all or any of
the above blunders originated in typographical errors. A hardworked
man might possibly overlook even such a misprint as 'totis' for 'cotis;'
but when he ventures on translation he volunteers the measure of his foot.
We may add from the Appendix, p. 344, a pleasant example of skill in the
language of the middle ages: — 'Pride hath in his paunter [*net*; *panthera*
— Fr. *pantière*] kauht the heie and the lowe;' the said *paunter* being gravely expounded in a glossarial note by 'pantry.' We presume the editor

which only *one* graduate of five years' standing was capable of perpetrating — we request attention to the following stanza: —

> 'Donum Dei non donatur
> Nisi gratis conferatur;
> Quod qui vendit vel mercatur,
> Lepra Syri vulneratur;
>> Quem sic ambit ambitus
>> Ydolorum servitus
>> Templo sancti spiritus
>> Non compaginatur.'

Here the satirist, who has just been complaining of the scandalous trafficking in sacramental ordinances, proceeds to declare that the man who sells or buys the gift of God is infected with the leprosy of (Naaman) the Syrian (transferred to Gehazi as a punishment for his covetousness); and adds — alluding to well known passages in the Epistles of St. Paul — that he whom pecuniary corruption, *which is idolatry,* thus influences, is no member of the temple of the Holy Spirit. We beg the reader to observe how admirably this has been understood by the translator: —

'God's gift is not given if it be not conferred gratis; and he who sells and makes merchandize of it, is, in so doing, struck with the leprosy of *Syrus*: the service of idols, *at which* — [head of Priscian! servitus — *quem*!] — his ambition thus aims, *may not be engrafted on* the temple of the Holy Spirit.'

Translated indeed! The rendering of the concluding stanza of the poem is equally absurd; but we have not space for it. Partridge, or Hugh Strap, would have shown himself a Bentley in comparison. We proceed to examine his quafications in two departments in which he has made himself tolerably prominent — Anglo-Saxon and Early English. The first piece we had occasion to bring to the test was a metrical fragment on the Virgin Mary, apparently a production of the thirteenth century, printed in 'Reliquiæ Antiquæ,' vol. i. p. 104. In this, consisting of just six lines, there are five false readings, three of them destructive to the sense — *on* for *hu, oaweth* for *haweth,* and *owre* for *ewre*; — to say nothing of two obvious corruptions, unintelligible as they now stand, but removable by two monosyllables in

---

had heard of people 'eaten up with pride,' and concluded that this voracious personage must needs have a larder for his provender. Not a bad parallel to Le Roux de Lincy's transmutation of 'Bran the Blessed' into 'Bran le Blessé.'

brackets. We were next startled, in a metrical version of the 'Ave Maria' of the same period (p. 22), at the totally unknown formula 'the lavird *thich* the,' which turned out, as everybody can foresee, to be a blunder for 'the lavird *with* the' — (Dominus tecum!) One of the few really good things in the volume is an elegant and spirited paraphrase of the 'Gloria in excelsis' (p. 34), evidently of the best age of Anglo-Saxon poetry. On inquiring whether this had fared any better than the rest, we found, besides minor errors, the following gross corruptions; — *sigerœst* for *sigefœst* (victorious), *dretunes* for *dreames* (joy), and *ge-meredes* for *generedes* (salvasti) — words not even Anglo-Saxon, and totally unauthorized by the MS., which, like all of that period (ninth century), is perfectly easy to read. Nor is this all; the editor has contrived to expose himself still more glaringly in a passage where he has preserved the letters of the original. The well-known expression of the Vulgate, 'et in terra pax hominibus *bonœ voluntatis*,' is almost literally reproduced in the paraphrase —

> 'And on eorthan sibb
> gumena ge-hwileum
> gódes willan' —

which last line is actually printed in the Reliquiæ 'Godes willan' — voluntate *Dei!* On the very next page is a prose version of the Pater Noster, apparently of the tenth century. Hoping that this had surely escaped, we soon found that we had supposed too fast — *alyf*, permit, staring us in the face instead of *alys*, deliver! Thus we have a phenomenon reserved for the present age — an editor of large pretensions who not only tramples on the most ordinary rules of Latin syntax, but has shown himself totally ignorant of the most hackneyed phrase of Horace, the story of Naaman, the words of one of the most familiar Psalms, the 'Gloria in excelsis,' the Angelical Salutation, and the Pater Noster!

A performer capable of blundering so dreadfully where everything is easy and straightforward, cannot be expected to succeed very well where there is a little scope for criticism. Among the pieces contributed by Mr. Wright to the 'Reliquiæ Antiquæ' is a collection of Middle-English (and Anglo-Norman) Glosses by Walter de Bibblesworth. It has been observed on a former occasion in this journal (vol. liv. p. 329) that ancient glossaries, though highly valuable in themselves, are better let alone by novices, as it requires considerable knowledge of languages, and a certain skill in conjectural criticism, to use them to any good purpose. For example, with regard to 'honde, *aleine*,' it is necessary not only to be aware of the capricious employment and omission of the aspirate, but to know 'onde, *breath*,' — a very uncommon word in that sense — in order to restore the gloss to its true form, 'onde, *haleine*.' We therefore find no fault with Mr. Wright for not having grappled with the numerous difficulties of the above piece, some of which might baffle a scholar; but we cannot help saying that he has displayed an absolutely astounding degree of ignorance with respect to some of the easiest and most common terms in both languages. Thus it requires no great conjuration to see that 'tharine' and 'henete' are not even English words, and that the corresponding 'bouele' and 'lezart' absolutely require 'tharme' [A. S. thearm; Germ. darm] and 'hevete' [evet or eft]. Should any inquisitive German or Dane attempt to sift this vocabulary for etymological materials, we beg to inform him that 'szynere, *une lesche*,' is not a guinea — called in flash language a *shiner* — but a *shiver* or slice of bread; and that *segle* is neither rick nor rice, which 'ric' might be conjectured to stand for, but what gods call *secale cereale*, and mortals *rye*. We would also hint that there is no such English plant as 'sarnel,' nor any French one known by the unpronounceable name of 'le necl,' but that *darnel*, Fr. ivraie, and *néele*—hodiè *nielle*—Anglicè *cockle*, are better known than liked in both countries. We trust to his own sagacity for discovering that 'tode, *crapant*,' should be crapaut, and that neither a 'feldefare,' nor any other member of the genus Turdus, was ever called 'grue,' — a fowl which, if it were carnivorously disposed, could eat a dozen fieldfares to breakfast, — but very possibly 'grive.' Some of the articles are quite as enigmatical as Mr. Halliwell's 'Arbor Lencester;' for example, we find, p. 79, col. 1, 'bore, tru — of a nalkin, de fubiloun.' A great bore indeed! — in its present shape — but reducible to reasonable dimensions by substituting, from one of the editor's own authorities, 'tru de *subiloun* — bore of an *alsene, i. e.* awl,' — a good old-fashioned name for that classical implement — and still preserved in the *elsin* of our northern counties. Occasionally the editor has the grace to manifest a little misgiving that all is not right, sometimes with reason and sometimes without. For instance, he boggles at 'suluuard, *putois?* and 'brocke, *thelson?*' — as well he may, they being phantoms of his own conjuring up for *fulmard* and *thessoun*, alias *tessoun*, a well-known old French word for a badger. Once more, p. 80, col. 2: —

'Avenes eyles (?) des arestez.'

To be sure this does look rather odd; but a *tant soit peu*
Norman-Saxon scholar, or anybody more disposed for inquiry
than helpless wonderment, could readily have produced from
Cotgrave —

'Areste — the eyle,* awne, or beard of an eare of corne.'

Our readers may judge from the above samples, which
are capable of being multiplied *ad infinitum*, how well qualified Mr. Wright is to edit Chaucer's Canterbury Tales —
a task requiring, above all others, a combination of scrupulous accuracy, sound learning, critical discernment, and
classical taste — which he nevertheless has had the modesty
to undertake. They may also perceive with what singular
grace and propriety he vituperates his predecessor Tyrwhitt
for *philological deficiencies!* Tyrwhitt had only a moderate
knowledge of Early English, which there were few means
for studying scientifically in his day. But he was, in the
comprehensive sense of the terms, a sound and elegant
scholar and a judicious critic; and though he may be now
and then caught tripping, he never exposes himself so egre-
giously as Mr. Wright does — and will continue to do if he
is left to himself. We would by no means be understood
to affirm that all his publications are as irredeemably bad as
the portions that we have specified. When his way is quite
plain and smooth, when his MSS. are legible, and the sense
cannot be mistaken, he sometimes gets on pretty well; but
he almost infallibly stumbles over a difficulty of the size of
a pebble. His place in this department of literature ought
to be the secondary one of purveying the raw material for
more skilful editors; and, if he is wise, he will confine himself to this office, in which, we allow, he may make himself tolerably useful.

Half-learned smatterers, who never swarmed more than
they do at this time, are the very plague and pestilence of
our literature; and everything to which they give a permanent shape becomes a permanent injury. Much of what has
been lately put forth had better have rested on the shelves
of our great libraries; the publications, as we now have
them, are much worse than the very worst MS. exemplars.
The errors of these are comparatively harmless as long as
they are let alone, and often furnish the means for their
own rectification; but when wafted on the wings of a thousand printed copies, there is no foreseeing what mischief
they may do. We will give a couple of instances. Some

---

* From Anglo-Saxon eȝle, arista.

fifty or sixty years ago, Pinkerton took upon himself to edit a series of metrical romances and other pieces under the title 'Ancient Scottish Poems.' Dr. Jamieson, believing all these to be Scottish, which several of them are not, and committing the still greater mistake of supposing them to be reasonably accurate, industriously transferred all the words which seemed to need explanation to the pages of his Dictionary. This he did in perfect good faith; but it is now notorious that many of them are no words at all, and never were, but mere blunders of Pinkerton, who, being neither palæographer nor philologist, has, as might be expected, perpetuated in print all sorts of monstrosities. However, they remain embodied in Dr. Jamieson's work, and are frequently appealed to by British and foreign philologists, particularly if they happen to countenance some blunder or crotchet of more recent sciolists. Again, in 'The Arrival of Edward IV. in England,' a narrative of the fifteenth century, printed for the Camden Society about eight years ago, we have these words, without note or comment appended: —

'Wherefore the Kynge may say, as Julius Cæsar sayde, he that is not agaynst me is with me.' — p. 7.

We fear it would be difficult to find this in Cæsar's Commentaries, but most people may remember something like it in the Gospels. We believe that this truly astounding *text* originated in the following manner. The earlier copies had in all probability 'J. C. sayde,' an abbreviation of which there are numberless instances. Honest John Stow, the writer of the Harleian transcript, or the scribe whom he followed, being laudably desirous of making everything quite plain and clear to his readers, filled up the blank in his own way by enlarging J. C. into *Julius Cæsar*. After the lapse of two centuries and a half Julius Cæsar is roused from his repose in the Harleian collection to be duly installed in a thousand copies of the Camden Society's maiden publication, there to remain as a monument of the wisdom of our ancestors and ourselves, and as a puzzle to future generations of mole-and-bat critics. It might appear incredible that men who have read and written so much should have learnt so little. But persons of his class are often like the country foot-post, who travels more miles in a year than anybody, but only knows the road from Weston to Norton, and sees very little even of that. His object is to earn his weekly wages, not to study the flowers which spring by his path, or the birds which cross it, or to know the hills and spires which break the monotony of the distant horizon. But let us not be too hard on these lettered culprits. The stream of shallow and frothy literature would not flow along and spread itself as it does, if the minds of readers were not in a 'concatenation accordingly.' The facilities for acquiring knowledge multiply every day, but we doubt whether there ever was a period exhibiting such a dearth of solid general information among persons presumed to be well educated. Such knowledge is little sought after, because it requires habits of attention and observation which most of the present generation find it troublesome to acquire. They see objects without observing them, and learn things without knowing them. Thus, shallow and ignorant writers are safe while they are sure of readers of the same quality. When Mr. Thomas Wright, in his Glossary to 'Piers Ploughman,' gravely expounds *brok* by 'an animal of the badger kind,' the downright silliness of the remark is not so obvious to those who do not know that the species of badgers in the world known to Langland amount to just one; and, consequently, 'donkey, an animal of the ass kind,' would be a less gratuitous piece of information. But enough for the present of Zoology.

We are not unaware of the important undertakings of the University of Oxford in this department of literature, especially Wicliffe's Bible and Orm's Paraphrase and Exposition of the Gospels; and when those works are properly before the public, as we trust they shortly will be, we may possibly direct the attention of our readers towards them in a more special manner. * We rejoice, meanwhile, that we have at length the means of dwelling a little upon a highly important publication of the Society of Antiquaries, namely, a complete edition of Layamon's 'Brut, or Chronicle of Britain,' in two texts, under the superintendence of Sir F. Madden. This poem had been partially known for the last fifty years by the remarks and extracts of Tyrwhitt, Ellis, Sharon Turner, Conybeare, and others. But the specimens furnished by those scholars were brief, and neither their readings nor their interpretations were always to be relied upon. It was subsequently treated in a more satisfactory manner by two gentlemen who have made this branch of literature their especial study. Mr. Kemble furnished a valuable paper on the grammar and dialect in the 'Philo-

---

* Wicliffe's Bible was published in 1850 by the Rev. J. Forshall and Sir F. Madden, and the Ormulum made its appearance in 1852 under the auspices of the Rev. R. M. White. The proof-sheets had been previously submitted to Mr. Garnett's inspection, and his services were handsomely acknowledged by the accomplished editor. ED.

logical Museum;' and Mr. Guest gave an able analysis of
Layamon's Metrical System, together with a long extract
from one of the texts, accompanied by a translation, in his
'History of English Rhythms.' But the great point was to
place the entire poem within reach of those who have neither
opportunity nor inclination to grapple with the obscurities
of MSS.; and this has now been done under a very careful
eye, and with a rich accompaniment of elucidations.

Our readers do not require to be told that a poem of more
than thirty thousand lines, of the transition period of our
language — embodying a greater amount of a peculiar form
of that language than can be collected from all other known
reliques of the same century — must be of no small importance for the grammar and history of the vernacular tongue.
The changes that gradually made English something different from Anglo-Saxon are neither to be vaguely attributed
to a supposed Norman influence, which was a mere trifle
as regards its vocabulary, and absolutely nothing as to grammar and idiom, nor to be guessed at *per saltum*, but to be
traced by a careful historical induction through all the stages
of which we possess written documents. No one can hence-
forth attempt such a task without a careful study of Layamon, any more than a man, knowing nothing of Homer and
Herodotus, ought to dogmatize about early and later Ionic.
Sir Frederick Madden well observes, that a composition of
such great length must assist us in forming a better notion
of the state of our language at the end of the twelfth and
the beginning of the thirteenth centuries, than could be obtained from the short and scattered specimens already in
print; and that, by the aid of the second text, composed
long after the former, though immediately founded upon it,
we are enabled to perceive at once the still further change
that the language had undergone during the interval, and
note to what extent the diction and forms of the earlier text
had become obsolete or unintelligible.

The Spectator remarks that there exists a natural curiosity
to know something of the personal circumstances and history
of an author newly brought under our notice. With respect
to Layamon our curiosity must, in a great measure, remain
at fault. He cannot, indeed, be asserted to be a non-entity,
or mere verbal abstraction, as certain new-light critics predicate of Homer. However, we know hardly as much of
him as we do of Hesiod, and that little is entirely communicated by himself — his own age, and four or five succeeding ones, observing a provoking silence respecting one who
underwent no small amount of mental and bodily toil for

9

their amusement. He informs us that his father's name was Leovenath; that he exercised the profession of a priest at Erneley-on-Severn, adjoining to Radstone; 'ther he bock radde;' and that he conceived the happy thought of recording the 'Origines Britanniæ' — confining himself, with more moderation than some Irish antiquaries, to the period *after* the flood. As the libraries, public and private, of his own district were but scantily supplied with the necessary authorities, our zealous priest made a pilgrimage 'wide through the land' in search of materials. Having succeeded in procuring the English book made by St. Bede, the Latin one of St. Albin and St. Austin, and the 'Brut d'Angleterre' of Wace, he thus graphically describes the good account to which he turned them: —

> 'Laȝamon leide theos boc,
> & tha leaf wende.
> he heom leofliche bi-heold,
> lithe him beo drihten.
> fetheren he nom mid fingren,
> & fiede on boc-felle,
> & tha sothe word
> sette to-gadere:
> & tha thre boc
> thrumde to ane.' — vol. i. p. 3.

'Layamon laid before him these books, and turned over the leaves; lovingly he beheld them. May the Lord be merciful to him! Pen he took with fingers, and wrote on book-skin, and the true words set together, and the three books compressed into one.'

We suspect that the art of *thrumming* three or more old books into one new one is by no means obsolete among *original* authors of the present day; though, perhaps, few of them would avow it so frankly as the good Priest of Erneleye. It would, however, be great injustice to consider Layamon as a mere compiler. He availed himself, as he needs must, of the facts and legends recorded by his predecessors; but he often made them his own by his method of treating them. Respecting his obligations to Wace's version of Geoffrey of Monmouth, Sir F. Madden says: —

'This is the work to which Layamon is mainly indebted, and upon which his own is founded throughout, although he has exercised more than the usual licence of amplifying and adding to his original. The extent of such additions may be readily understood from the fact, that Wace's *Brut* is comprised in 15,300 lines, whilst the poem of the English versifier extends to nearly 32,250, or more than double. These additions and amplifications, as well as the more direct variations from the original, are all pointed out in the notes to the present edition; but their general character, as well as some of the more remarkable instances, may be properly noticed here. In the earlier part of the work they consist principally of the speeches placed in the mouths of different personages, which are often given with quite a dramatic effect. The dream of Arthur, as related by himself to his companions in arms, is the creation of a mind of a higher order than is apparent in the creeping rhymes of more recent chroniclers, and has a title, as Turner remarks, to be considered really poetry, because entirely a fiction of the imagination. The text of Wace is enlarged throughout, and in many passages to such an extent, particularly after the birth of Arthur, that one line is dilated into twenty; names of persons and localities are constantly supplied, and not unfrequently interpolations occur of entirely new matter, to the extent of more than a hundred lines. Layamon often embellishes and improves on his copy, and the meagre narrative of the French poet is heightened by graphic touches and details, which give him a just claim to be considered, not as a mere translator, but as an original writer.'

After giving a minute account of the more remarkable additions to Wace, Sir Frederick observes, —

.'That Layamon was indebted for some of these legends to Welsh traditions not recorded in Geoffrey of Monmouth or Wace, is scarcely to be questioned; and they supply an additional argument in support of the opinion that the former was not a mere inventor. Many circumstances incidentally mentioned by Layamon are to be traced to a British origin — as, for instance, the notice of Queen Judon's death; the mention of Taliesin and his conference with Kimbelin; the traditionary legends relative to Arthur; the allusions to several prophecies of Merlin; and the names of various personages which do not appear in the Latin or French writers. References are occasionally made to works extant in the time of Layamon, but which are not now to be recognised. . . . . From these and other passages, it may be reasonable to conclude that the author of the poem had a mind richly stored with legendary lore, and had availed himself, to a considerable extent, of the information to be derived from written sources. We know that he understood both French and Latin; and when we consider that these varied branches of knowledge were combined in the person of an humble priest of a small church in one of the midland counties, it would seem to be no unfair inference that the body of the clergy, and perhaps the upper classes of the laity, were not in so low a state of ignorance at the period when Layamon wrote, as some writers have represented.' — *Preface*, vol. i. pp. xiii.—xvii.

After showing that the date of the composition of the poem

9 *

may with great probability be fixed about A. D. 1205, and
that the influence of Norman models, though considerable as
to the external form of the work, was insignificant with relation to its phraseology, the editor observes, —

'It is a remarkable circumstance, that we find preserved in
many passages of Layamon's poem the spirit and style of the
earlier Anglo-Saxon writers. No one can read his descriptions of
battles and scenes of strife without being reminded of the Ode
on Æthlestan's victory at Brunan-burh. The ancient mythological
genders of the sun and moon are still unchanged, the memory of
the *witena-gemot* has not yet become extinct, and the neigh of the
hœngest still seems to resound in our ears. Very many phrases are
purely Anglo-Saxon, and, with slight change, might have been
used in Cædmon or Ælfric. A foreign scholar and poet (Grundt-
vig), versed both in Anglo-Saxon and Scandinavian literature,
has declared that, tolerably well read as he is in the rhyming
chronicles of his own country and of others, he has found Layamon's beyond comparison the most lofty and animated in its style,
at every moment reminding the reader of the splendid phraseology
of Anglo-Saxon verse. It may also be added, that the colloquial
character of much of the work renders it peculiarly valuable as a
monument of language, since it serves to convey to us, in all probability, the current speech of the writer's time as it passed from
mouth to mouth.' — pp. xxiii., xxiv.

The justice of the above criticism will be manifest to any
one who, with a competent knowledge of Layamon's language,
compares his orations and descriptions of battles with the
corresponding passages of Wace or Robert of Gloucester.
In the latter everything is flat and tame, many degrees
below Geoffrey of Monmouth's prose in point of graphic
power and animation; but Layamon often shows considerable
skill and discrimination in selecting those parts of the narrative most capable of poetic embellishment; and, though he
had to struggle with a language which was ceasing to be
Anglo-Saxon but had not yet become English, he not unfrequently manifests great felicity of diction, and a ready
command of words suitable to the subject. Much of this
must be necessarily lost on the mere English scholar, as
the proper appreciation of it depends upon the perception of
the true force and import of the Saxon and semi-Saxon terms
that constitute the chief staple of the poem. We therefore
recommend those who wish to form a judgment of the merits
of our early English epic to devote a little attention to the
language of Alfred and his predecessors; and, whatever they
may think of the 'Brut,' they may at all events acquire a
kind of knowledge creditable to an Englishman, and capable

of becoming useful in a variety of ways. Those who are unwilling to pass this ordeal must consent themselves with Sir Frederick Madden's translation.

We cannot conclude our remarks on the original sources and character of Layamon's work without a few words on the obligations of our own literature and that of all Western Europe to a writer whom it has been greatly the fashion to abuse — Geoffrey of Monmouth. We leave entirely out of the question the truth or falsehood of his narrative. Scarcely a Welshman of the old school could now be found to vouch for Brutus's colonization of Britain; though we dare say it is to the full as true as the settlement of Italy by Æneas, and many other things gravely recorded by Livy and Dionysius of Halicarnassus. The merit of Geoffrey consists in having collected a body of legends highly susceptible of poetic embellishment, which, without his intervention, might have utterly perished, and interwoven them in a narrative calculated to exercise a powerful influence on national feelings and national literature. The popularity of the work is proved by the successive adaptations of Wace, Layamon, Robert of Gloucester, Mannyng, and others; and its influence on the literature of Europe is too notorious to be dwelt upon. * It became, as Mr. Ellis well observes, one of the corner-stones of romance; and there is scarcely a tale of chivalry down to the sixteenth century which has not directly or indirectly received from it much of its colouring. Some matter-of-fact people, who would have mercilessly committed the whole of Don Quixote's library to the flames, Palmerin of England included, may perhaps think this particular effect of its influence rather mischievous than beneficial. We are far from sympathizing with such a feeling. Whatever might be the blemishes of this species of literature, it was suited to the taste and requirements of the age, and tended to keep up a high and honourable tone of feeling that often manifested itself in corresponding actions. Above all, we must not forget that it is to the previous existence of this class of compositions that we are indebted for some of the noblest productions of human intellect. If it were to be conceded that Wace, Layamon, and the whole cycle of romances of the Round Table might have been con-

* See particularly Mr. Panizzi's remarks on the influence of Celtic legends, in the Essay on the Romantic Narrative Poetry of the Italians, prefixed to his edition of the Orlando Innamorato and Orlando Furioso, vol. i. pp. 34 —46, 390—92, &c. Mr. Beresford Hope has made an amusing attempt to show that Geoffrey's story of Brutus and his descendants may be substantially true. — *Essays*, pp. 95—141.

signed to oblivion without any serious injury to the cause
of literature, we may be reminded that Don Quixote certainly, and Ariosto's Orlando most probably, arose out of
them. Perhaps Gorboduc, and Ferrex and Porrex, might
not be much missed from the dramatic literature of Europe;
but what should we think of the loss of Lear and Cymbe-
line? Let us, then, thankfully remember Geoffrey of Monmouth, to whom Shakespeare was indebted for the groundwork of those marvellous productions, and without whose
'Historia Britonum' we should probably never have had them.
A spark is but a small matter in itself; but it may serve to
kindle a 'light for all nations.'

   The metre of Layamon is remarkable for its constant fluctuation between two perfectly distinct systems, — the alliterative distich of the Anglo-Saxons, and the more recent
rhymed couplet partially employed by the early Welsh bards,
and on a still more extensive scale by the Norman trouvè-
res.   Supposing that we have the poem nearly as the author
left it, this irregularity is a strong indication of the rudimentary and unsettled state of our language and literature
at the commencement of the thirteenth century. The remarks
of the editor will place the matter in a clearer light: —

   'The structure of Layamon's poem consists partly of lines in
which the alliterative system is preserved, and partly of couplets
of unequal length rhyming together. Many couplets indeed occur
which have both of these forms, whilst others are often met with
which possess neither. The latter, therefore, must have depended
wholly on accentuation, or have been corrupted in transcription.
The relative proportion of each of these forms is not to be ascertained without extreme difficulty, since the author uses them everywhere intermixed, and slides from alliteration to rhyme, or from
rhyme to alliteration, in a manner perfectly arbitrary. The alliterative portion, however, predominates on the whole greatly over
the lines rhyming together, even including the imperfect or asso-
nant terminations, which are very frequent.   In the structure of
Layamon's rhyme, Tyrwhitt thought he could perceive occasionally an imitation of the octo-syllabic measure of the French original, while Mitford finds in it the identical triple measure of Piers
Ploughman. The subject, however, has been discussed more fully,
and with greater learning, by Mr. Guest in his "History of English Rhythms," in which he shows that the rhyming couplets of
Layamon are founded on the models of accentuated Anglo-Saxon
rhythms of four, five, six, or seven accents. A long specimen is
given by him in vol. ii. pp. 114—124, with the accents marked
both of the alliterative and rhyming couplets, by which it is seen

that those of six and five accents are used most frequently, but that the poet changes at will from the shortest to the longest measure, without the adoption of any consecutive principle. In the later text, as might be expected, both the alliteration and rhyme are often neglected; but these faults may probably be often attributed to the errors of the scribe.' — pp. xxiv., xxv.

This is perhaps all that, in the present state of our information, can be safely advanced on the subject of Layamon's metrical system. The rhythmical irregularities here adverted to are the more remarkable when contrasted with Langland, who, though a century and a half later, adheres with the utmost strictness to the alliterative system of the Anglo-Saxons; and with Orm, who, in a work of about the same extent, employs scrupulously throughout the fifteen-syllable couplet, without either rhyme or alliteration, but modulated with an exactness of rhythm which shows that he had no contemptible ear for the melody of versification. It is true that in this instance we have the rare advantage of possessing the author's autograph, a circumstance which cannot with confidence be predicated of any other considerable work of the same period. The author was, moreover, as Mr. Thorpe observes, a kind of critic in his own language; and we therefore find in his work a regularity of orthography, grammar, and metre, hardly to be paralleled in the same age. All this might in a great measure disappear in the very next copy; for fidelity of transcription was no virtue of the thirteenth or the fourteenth century, at least with respect to vernacular works. It becomes, therefore, in many cases a problem of no small complication to decide with certainty respecting the original metre or language of a given mediæval composition, with such data as we now possess. As the general subject, and its particular application to the work of Layamon, present several points of considerable interest, we shall devote a little space to the discussion of them. Sir F. Madden says: —

'With respect to the dialect in which Layamon's work is written, we can have little difficulty in assuming it to be that of North Worcestershire, the locality in which he lived; but as both the texts of the poem in their present state exhibit the forms of a strong western idiom, the following interesting question immediately arises — how such a dialect should have been current in one of the chief counties of the kingdom of Mercia? The origin of this kingdom, as Sir Francis Palgrave has remarked, is very obscure; but there is reason to believe that a mixed race of people contributed to form and to occupy it. We may therefore conclude, either that the Hwiccas were of Saxon rather than Angle origin, or that, subsequent to the union of Mercia with the kingdom of Wessex, the western dialect gradually extended itself from the south of the Thames, as far as the courses of the Severn, the Wye, the Tame, and the Avon, and more or less pervaded the counties of Gloucester, Worcester, Hereford, Warwick, and Oxford.

'That this western dialect extended throughout the Channel counties from east to west, and was really the same as the southern, appears from a remarkable passage in Giraldus Cambrensis (written in 1204), in which he says, "As in the *southern* parts of England, and chiefly about *Devonshire*, the language now appears more unpolished (*incomposita*), yet in a far greater degree savouring of antiquity — the northern parts of the island being much corrupted by the frequent incursions of the Danes and Norwegians — so it observes more the propriety of the original tongue, and the ancient mode of speaking. Of this you have not only an argument but a certainty, from the circumstance that all the English books of Bede, Rabanus, King Alfred, or any others, will be found written in the forms proper to this idiom." It is difficult at present to understand how far Giraldus meant to assimilate together the *spoken* language of Devonshire and the written works of Alfred and others, but in all probability the chief difference must have consisted in pronunciation, and in the disregard of certain grammatical forms, which would not of themselves constitute a separate dialect. There can be no doubt that the written language, previous to the Conquest, was more stable in its character, and more observant of orthographical and grammatical accuracy, than the spoken; but it is impossible to collate together Anglo-Saxon manuscripts without being struck with the occasional use of anomalous forms, which are termed by grammarians, rather too arbitrarily perhaps, corruptions. Without therefore going so far as Ritson (whose opinion of itself was little worth), that "the vulgar English of the period was *essentially different* from the Saxon used in the charters of the Conqueror;" or Sir Francis Palgrave, who thinks "that a colloquial language, *approaching nearly to modern English*, seems to have existed concurrently with the more cultivated language which we call Anglo-Saxon," — there are many reasons to induce us to believe that the spoken language in the reign of Edward the Confessor did not materially differ from that which is found in manuscripts a century later.

'That the dialects of the western, southern, and midland counties contributed together to form the language of the twelfth and thirteenth centuries, and consequently to lay the foundation of modern English, seems unquestionable; and it is remarkable that the same period is pointed out by philologists for the origin of Italian from the ancient and varied dialects of that country.' — *Pref.*, pp. xxv. — xxviii.

The above statement furnishes a very probable view of the subject, and we are by no means prepared to say that it is not the correct one. However, we would observe that there are few matters more difficult than to determine, *à priori*, in what precise form a vernacular composition of the thirteenth century might be written, or what form it might assume in a very short period. Among the Anglo-Saxon charters of the eleventh and twelfth centuries, many are modelled upon the literary Anglo-Saxon, with a few slight changes of orthography and inflection, while others abound with dialectical peculiarities of various sorts. Those peculiarities may generally be accounted for from local causes. An East Anglian scribe does not employ broad Western forms, nor a West-of-England man East-Anglian ones, though each might keep his provincial peculiarities out of sight, and produce something not materially different from the language of Ælfric. It is not very easy to affirm what course was taken by Layamon. It is not improbable that he might write in the dialect of his district, or, at all events, that traces of it might be found in his work. If we assume this, which is not absolutely certain, two questions of no very easy solution arise — whether those broad Western forms, so prominent in the poem, actually emanated from the author, and whether they really belonged to the North Worcester district? To decide the first point, it would be necessary to have access either to the priest's autograph or to a more faithful copy of it than it was the practice to make either in his age or the succeeding one. A transcriber of an Early English composition followed his own ideas of language, grammar, and orthography; and if he did not entirely obliterate the characteristic peculiarities of his original, he was pretty sure, like the Conde de Olivares, '*d'y mettre beaucoup du sien.*' The practical proof of this is to be found in the existing copies of those works, almost every one of which exhibits some peculiarity of features. We have Trevisa and Robert of Gloucester in two distinct forms — 'Piers Ploughman' in at least three — and Hampole's 'Pricke of Conscience' in half a dozen, without any absolute certainty which approximates most to what the authors wrote. With regard to Layamon, it might be supposed that the older copy is the more likely to represent the original; but we have internal evidence that it is not the priest's autograph, and it is impossible to know what alterations it may have undergone in the course of one or more transcriptions. Again, assuming that he would write in the dialect of his district, it may be doubted whether the Western peculiarities in question really belonged to that district. The most prominent ones occur pretty frequently in charters and other documents of the Channel counties, - and those immediately adjoining, from the twelfth century downwards; but we have not been able to trace similar ones in Worcestershire documents, which are pretty numerous, and of much the same period. We should rather expect, in the locality of Arley-Regis, a dialect resembling that of 'Piers Ploughman,' as edited by Dr. Whitaker; and if we could suppose that a transcriber south of the Avon substituted *v* for initial *f*, and *eth* for final *en* in plural indicatives, it would be no more than has actually been done in other instances. Sir F. Madden observes that forms belonging more properly to the Mercian and Anglian dialects occasionally present themselves, and though they are too few to ground any positive conclusion on, it is by no means impossible that they may be vestiges of a more original type of the poem. Questions of this sort are to be decided by evidence, and we must be content to let the present one remain in abeyance till we meet with the author's own copy, or find direct proof of the prevalence of a Western dialect in North Worcestershire. As the poem now stands, the preponderance of forms belongs to the literary Anglo-Saxon, or may be directly deduced from it: the numerous provincialisms are those of the southern and south - western counties, and might easily be introduced by transcribers of that district.

Though in the present, and various other instances, it is difficult to arrive at a positive conclusion respecting the original form of a mediæval composition, there are certain criteria which will frequently enable us to determine approximatively in what district a given copy of it was made. Much misapprehension prevails on this subject, and many grievous mistakes have been made by editors and commentators in assigning MSS. to localities to which they could not possibly belong. It may not, therefore, be inexpedient to point out a few characteristics that may serve to guide us in a great number of cases.

The whole body of our Anglo-Saxon literary monuments, from the eighth century downwards, is reducible to two great divisions, West-Saxon and Anglian. Political events gave a decided preponderance to the former, so that, towards the end of the ninth century, we perceive its influence on the *written* language in almost every part of England. It also appears to have acted powerfully upon the spoken dialect of the Western Mercians, who were originally Ang-

les, but who seem to have gradually adopted various peculiarities of the West-Saxon speech. The Anglian branch,
including the Northumbrian division of it, once boasted of
a flourishing and extensive literature; but civil commotions
and the ravages of foreign invaders gradually caused the
bulk of it to disappear. A few fragments fortunately escaped the general wreck. Besides the verses uttered by
Bede on his death-bed, the inscription on the Ruthwell Cross,
and the fragment of Caedmon printed in Wanley's Catalogue,
we have in the Durham Ritual, published by the Surtees
Society, and in the celebrated Gospels, Cott. MS. Nero, D.
4, undoubted specimens of the language of Northumbria in
the tenth century. A portion of the Gloss to the Rushworth
Gospels in the Bodleian Library, supposed to have been
written in Yorkshire, is in the same dialect. The Glosses
to the Psalter, Cott. MS. Vesp. A. 1, also printed by the
Surtees Society, though more southern, are of the same
generic character, that is to say, Anglian as distinct from
West-Saxon, — and, on account of the antiquity and purity
of the language, they are the most valuable monument of
the class. Those pieces present a form of language differing in many important points from the West-Saxon, and
approximating in some degree to the Old-Saxon and the
Westphalian dialect of Old-German. The dialects descended
from this were, in the eleventh century, and perhaps still
earlier, distinguished from those of the south and west by
the greater simplicity of their grammatical forms; by the
preference of simple vowels to diphthongs, and of hard gutturals to palatals; by the frequent and eventually almost universal
rejection of the formative prefix *ge*; and by the recurrence
of peculiar words and forms, never found in pure West-
Saxon. Another characteristic is the infusion of Scandinavian
words, of which there are slight traces in monuments of the
tenth century, and strong and unequivocal ones in those of
the thirteenth and fourteenth. Some of the above criteria
may be verified by a simple and obvious process, namely,
a reference to the topographical nomenclature of our provinces. Whoever takes the trouble to consult the Gazetteer
of England will find, that of our numerous 'Carltons' not
one is to be met with north of the Mersey, west of the
Staffordshire Tame, or south of the Thames; and that 'Fis-
kertons,' 'Skiptons,' 'Skelbrookes,'* and a whole host of

---

* The only exception as to words beginning with *Sk* appears to be Skil-
gate, in Somersetshire. Skenfreth, in Monmouthshire, is of Celtic origin.
Two remarkable words are Skephouse (Sheephouse)-Pool, near Bolton Abbey.

similar names, are equally *introuvables* in the same district. They are, with scarcely a single exception, Northern or Eastern; and we know, from Aelfric's Glossary, from Domesday and the Chartularies, that this distinction of pronunciation was established as early as the eleventh century. 'Kirby,' or 'Kirkby,' is a specimen of joint Anglian and Scandinavian influence, furnishing a clue to the ethnology of the district wherever it occurs. The converse of this rule does not hold with equal universality, various causes having gradually introduced soft palatal sounds into districts to which they did not properly belong. Such are, however, of very partial occurrence, and form the exception rather than the rule.

If we apply the above criteria to the concluding portion of the Saxon Chronicle, comprising the reign of Stephen, we find a systematic omission of the prefix *ge* in all participles except * *gehaten* (called); *muneces* (monks), for *munecan*; the definite article *the* of all genders, numbers, and cases; forms such as *carlamen*, *scort*, *scæ* (she), a word ucknown in the West-Saxon. We have internal evidence that this portion of the Chronicle was written at Peterborough. Again, in the Suffolk charters of the twelfth and thirteenth centuries, in Kemble's Codex Diplomaticus, vol. iv., and Brit. Mus. Add. MS. 14847, we meet with *kirke*, *ekelike* (eternal), *alke* (each), *unnen* (granted) for *geunnen*, *sal* (shall), and *aren* (sunt), itself a sufficient indication of an Anglian dialect at that period. The above peculiarities, and many similar ones, are those of the northern and eastern district already specified; and they may serve as tests of other productions of the same locality. We have no direct evidence where Orm's Paraphrase of the Gospels was written; but, when we find the same systematic omission of the formative *ge*, the same predilection for hard gutturals — e. gr. *cwennkenn* for quenchen — a definite article nearly indeclinable, the33r (their) for *heora*, the plural verb substantive *arrn*, and moreover a strong infusion of Scandinavian words and phrases, we see at once that it is neither Southern nor Western, but Eastern Midland, and most probably penned within fifty miles of Northampton.

The language of the Southern district, of which the Thames

---

and Skutterskelf═Shivering-Self or Cliff, near Stokesley, in Cleveland. The only Charltons in this northern and eastern district are four hamlets in Northumberland, sectional divisions of the same township, and therefore reducible to one.

* It is singular that this word retained the prefix in the Northumbrian dialect, after every other had lost it.

and the Gloucestershire Avon may be broadly assumed as the northern boundaries, is easily distinguished from that of the eastern and northern divisions. Not to mention the topographical nomenclature, such as Charlton or Chorlton, Shipton or Shepton, Fisherton, &c. &c., instead of the hard forms above specified, we find, from the twelfth century downwards, *chirche*, *muchel*, *thincke*, *worche*, *eche* (eternal), *hwiche*,* or *hwuche*, with a multitude of similar forms, not accidentally or partially, but systematically employed. Provincialized monuments of this branch also exhibit initial *v* for *f*, *ss* for *sh*, and in Kent, *z* for *s*, — and all that properly belong to it are remarkably tenacious of Saxon forms, which all but disappeared in some other districts before the middle of the thirteenth century. The prefix *ge* (*y*, *i.*) is rarely dropped; the inflections of nouns, pronouns, and verbs are West-Saxon, with slight modifications; and the archaic idioms and inversions contrast strongly with the perspicuity and simplicity of more northern compositions. Those peculiarities, and the gradual manner in which they arose, are exemplified in various charters and other documents, as may be seen, for example, in Kemble's Codex Diplomaticus, vol. iv. Chart. 773 and 799. The former of these, dated A. D. 1044, is tolerable West-Saxon; the version of the thirteenth century annexed to it shows a pretty copious sprinkling of provincial forms; also the second, written about 1300; but a mutation of a grant of 1053 is still broader; while all three, with all of the same class, retain numerous forms and inflections, which it would be vain to search for in the Chronicle of King Stephen or Orm's Paraphrase.

The Western Mercian bears a general resemblance to the Southern class in its adoption of soft palatal forms and the partial retention of archaic inflections. The shibboleth of it, as a distinct dialect from Northumbrian and North-Anglian on the one hand, and Southern and South-Western on the other, is the indicative plural in *en* — we — ye — they lov-*en* — still current in South-Lancashire. This form also appears to have been popularly known, if not in East-Anglia proper, at all events in the district immediately to the westward, since we find it in Orm, in an Eastern-Midland copy of the Rule of Nuns, sæc. xiii., and in process of time in Suffolk. Various conjectures have been advanced as to the origin of this form, of which we have no certain examples

---

* It is curious to trace the gradual retreat of *whilk* before *which*, from Kent to Berwickshire.

before the thirteenth century.* We believe the true state
of the case to have been as follows:—It is well known that
the Saxon dialects differ from the Gothic, Old-German, &c.
in the form of the present indicative plural — making all
three persons to end in aþ or ad;— we — ȝe — hi — lufi-aþ
(ad). Schmeller and other German philologists observe
that a nasal has been here elided, the true ancient form
being *and*, *ant*, or *ent*. Traces of this termination are found
in the Cotton MS. of the Old Saxon Evangelical Harmony,
and still more abundantly in the popular dialects of the
Middle-Rhenish district, from Cologne to the borders of
Switzerland. These not only exhibit the full termination *ent*,
but also two modifications of it, one dropping the nasal and
the other the dental. *E. g.*: —

> Pres. Indic. Plur. 1, 2, 3 liebent;
> „ lieb-et;
> „ lieb-en; .

— the last exactly corresponding with the Mercian. It is
remarkable that none of the above forms appear in classical
German compositions, while they abound in the Miracle-
plays, vernacular sermons, and similar productions of the
thirteenth and fourteenth centuries, specially addressed to
the uneducated classes. We may, therefore, reasonably conclude from analogy that similar forms were popularly current
in our midland counties, gradually insinuating themselves
into the written language. We have plenty of examples of
similar phenomena. It would be difficult to find written instances of the pronouns *scho*, or *she, their, you*, the auxiliaries *sal, suld*, &c. &c., before the twelfth century; but their
extensive prevalence in the thirteenth proves that they must
have been popularly employed somewhere even in times which
have left us no documentary evidence of their existence.

Compositions more or less Mercian are pretty numerous:
—the difficulty of arranging them arises from the rarity of
pure, undoubted specimens. Many of our present copies
have passed through the hands of several transcribers, each
of whom has altered something; while others are notoriously
adaptations of Northumbrian or Southern compositions to a
Midland dialect. The systematic employment of verbal
plurals in *en* is the most certain proof of Mercian influence.
It is a question of fact, not always of easy determination,
whether that influence is original or secondary. From its
central position this dialect was liable to be acted upon by
its neighbours on all sides, and to act upon them in its turn,

---

* *Sceolon, aron*, and a few similar words, are no real exceptions, being
in structure not present tenses but preterites.

on which account Midland compositions appear under innumerable modifications, and are extremely difficult to classify.

Though the above rules prove nothing positive respecting the original dialect of Layamon, they may serve to show where the two existing copies were *not* written. No such composition at that period could be penned in Northumbria, in Yorkshire, or eastward of the direct line from London to Sheffield. Our own opinion is that both were transcribed to the south of the Avon, and that the priest of Ernley's original language — though retained in substance — agreed more closely with the literary Anglo-Saxon than either text does at present. We would further observe that it is not from this form that our present English is directly descended. A language agreeing much more closely with our standard speech in words, in idiom, and in grammatical forms, existed in the Eastern Midland district before Layamon's 'Brut' was written. This form, which we may, for the sake of distinction, call Anglo-Mercian, was adopted by influential writers and by the cultivated classes of the metropolis — becoming, by gradual modifications, the language of Spenser and Shakspeare. Whoever takes the trouble to compare Chaucer with Orm's Paraphrase and Mannyng's Chronicle — making allowance for the provincialisms of the latter — will at once perceive their strong resemblance in grammar and idiom; and this resemblance will be rendered still more evident by contrasting all three with Layamon or Robert of Gloucester. Sir Francis Palgrave's theory of a colloquial language, nearly approaching to modern English, concurrently existing with Anglo-Saxon — may be partially true as to certain northern and north-eastern counties; but it is totally erroneous with respect to the southern and south-western districts. Orm's Paraphrase is more English than Anglo-Saxon, while Layamon's 'Brut' of the same period is more Anglo-Saxon than English. Contemporary Kentish and Hampshire documents follow still more closely the analogy of the ancient speech of Wessex. Particular words were admitted into the standard speech from those extreme southern dialects; but their general influence upon it during the thirteenth and fourteenth centuries was very inconsiderable. After the fourteenth century the cultivated language began to act powerfully upon all provincial forms, and it is still daily reducing them within narrower limits. The adoption of the speech of Leicestershire* and Northamptonshire

---

* We believe Mr. Guest was the first to point out the analogy between the Leicestershire dialect and classical English. 'History of English Rhythms,' vol. ii. p. 193.

as the standard form, in preference to that of Kent and Surrey, is one of the many phenomena which we can perceive, but cannot account for otherwise than conjecturally. It is possible that Chaucer and Wickliffe may have exercised something of the same influence in England as Dante and Boccaccio did in Italy, and Luther in Germany.

As a specimen of the work and a text for the application of the foregoing rules and remarks, we shall select some lines from the account of the flight of Childric and the death of Colgrim, being the continuation of the extract given by Mr. Guest, 'History of English Rhythms,' vol. ii. pp. 114—123.

FIRST TEXT. MS. COTT. Calig. A. ix.	SECOND TEXT. MS. COTT. Otho. C. xiii.
ʿTha ƷeT cleopede Arthur: atheleʃt kingen. Ʒurʃtendæi wæs Baldulf: cnihten alre baldeʃt. nu he ʃtand on hulle: & Avene bi-haldeth. hu ligeth i than ʃtræme: ʃtelene fiʃces. mid ʃweorde bi-georede; heore ʃund is awemmed. heore ʃcalen wleoteth: ʃwulc gold-faƷe ʃceldes. ther fleoteth heore ʃpiten: ʃwulc hit ʃpæren weoren.	ʿZet him ʃpeketh Arthur: baldeʃt alre kinge. zorʃtendai was Baldolf: cniht alre baldeʃt. nou he ʃtond on hulle: and Avene bi-holdeth. hu liggeth in than ʃtreme: ʃtelene fiʃces.
Efne than worde: tha the kȳg ʃeide. he bræid hæƷe his ʃceld: forn to his breoʃten. he igrap his ʃpere longe: his hors he gon ʃpurie. Neh al ʃwa ʃwi[the]: ʃwa the fuƷel flizeth. fuleden than kinge: fif and twenti thuʃend. whitere monnen: wode under wepnen.	Efne than worde that the king ʃaide. he breid hehƷe his ʃcelde: up to his breoʃte. he grop his ʃpere longe: and gan his hors ʃporie. Neh al ʃo ʃwithe: ʃo the fowel flieth. folwede than kinge: fif and twenti thouʃand.
Tha iʃeh Colgrim: wær Arthur com touward him. ne mihte Colgrȳ for than wæle: fleon a nare ʃide. ther fæht Baldulf: bi-ʃiden his brother.	Tho iʃeh Colgrȳ: war Arthur com toward him. ne mihte he fliht makie: in nevere one ʃide.
tha cleopede Arthur: ludere ʃtefne. Her ich cume Colgrim: to cuththen wit ʃcullen ræchen. nu wit ʃcullen this lond dalen; ʃwa the bith alre laththeʃt.	tho ʃaide Arthur: to Colgrim than kene. Nou we ʃolle this kinelond: deale ous bi-twine.

Æfne than worde:
tha the king saide.
his brode swœrd he up ahof:
and hærdliche adun sloh.
and smat Colgrimes hælm:
that he amidde to-clæf.
and there burë hod:
that hit at the breoste at-stod.
And he sweinde touward Baldulfe:
mit his swithre hŏde.
& swipte that hæfved of:
forth mid than helme.
tha loh Arthur:
the althele [athele] king.
and thus geddien agon:
mid gomenfulle worden.
Lien nu there Colgrim:
thu were iclumben haze.
and Baldulf thi brother:
lith bi thire side.
nu ich al this kine-lond:
sette an eorwer [eower] abȝere hond.
dales & dunes:
& al mi drihtliche volc.
thu clumbe a thissen hulle:
wunder ane hæȝe.
swulc thu woldest to hævene:
nu thu scalt to hælle.
ther thu miht kenne:
much of thine cunne. '

Efne than word:
that the kinge saide.
his brode sweord he ut droh:

and uppe Colgrim his helm smot.

and to-cleof thane brunie hod:
that hit at the breoste a-stod.
And he a wither sweyncde:
to Baldolf his brother.
and swipte that heved of
forth mid than helme.
tho loh Arthur the king:

and thes worde saide.

Li nou thar Colgrym:
the [thou] were iclemde to heze.
and Baldolf thin brother:
lith bi thine side.
nou ich al this kinelond:
sette in zoure tweire hond.

ze clemde to hehze:
uppen thisse hulle.
ase theh ze wolde to hevene:
ac nou ze mote to helle.
and thare zeo mawe kenne:
moche of zoure cunne. '

— *Layamon's Brut*, vol. ii., pp. 471–6.

Admidst the rudeness of its versification and language, the reader who is capable of picking out the meaning will not fail to discern in this episode — (which is too long for us to give *in extenso*) — a considerable portion of rough vigour, occasionally enlivened with graphic touches. In the lines now quoted, the comparison of the Saxons submersed in the Avon to dead fishes, though somewhat fanciful, presents a striking picture to the mind's eye. The addresses of Arthur are, as a general's should be, brief and energetic; and the author shows his natural good taste in not dwelling upon minute details of slaughter. In this respect he presents an advantageous contrast to some Italian epic-writers, who are often so long in killing or half-killing a champion that the reader feels tempted to skip a leaf or close the book. Arthur's sarcasm respecting Colgrim's share of the kingdom will remind the classical scholar of Marius's reply to the ambassadors of the Cimbri, and the reader of 'Ivanhoe' of Harold's answer to Tosti. We must also bear in mind that this episode, with many similar ones, is no servile copy. As the editor observes in his note, 'This long and highly poetic narrative

10

is due to the imagination of our English poet; for in his original, the conclusion of the battle, the death of Baldulf and Colgrim, and the flight of Cheldric, are described in four lines.'

A comparison of the two texts will show the numerous liberties taken by the more recent transcriber, in transposing, altering, and abridging those passages which he did not like or could not understand. Several parallel cases might be pointed out; and this shows how unsafe it frequently is to speculate on the original form of a mediæval composition from such copies as we happen to possess. Both our existing MSS. of the 'Brut' are of the same age — the second probably not fifty years later than the first; yet we find a visible change in language, and, what is still worse, a strong propensity to tamper with the integrity of the matter. If the older MS. has undergone a similar ordeal, which is by no means unlikely, it must be difficult indeed to fix the original readings. Each, however, may be taken as an evidence, more or less exact, of the grammar and dialect of the period and locality to which it belongs. The analyses of the grammatical peculiarities of the work, furnished by Mr. Kemble, Mr. Guest, and Sir Frederick Madden, save us the trouble of entering into further detail respecting them; and we cannot do better than refer our readers to what they have said. Those who wish to trace the literary history of the poem, and its connexion with the legends of contemporary and succeeding writers, will find ample satisfaction in the notes of the editor. With a full sense how heavily the task must have pressed on a gentleman not a little burdened already with official duties, we cannot but thank him for his labours, and congratulate him on their successful termination. It would certainly be no charity to wish to bind him again to a similar undertaking: but we cannot refrain from expressing a hope that when the inedited portion of Robert of Brunne's Chronicle makes its way to the press, he may have an opportunity of contributing to its illustration. The value of that work as a monument of language, and a repository of early traditions, is not sufficiently known; and the incidental observations of Sir Frederick Madden, in his notes on Layamon, show that he is fully qualified to do justice to the subject.

ON THE LANGUAGES AND DIALECTS OF THE BRITISH ISLANDS.

[*Proceedings of the Philological Society, Vols I & II.*]

The author believes that many members of the Society feel a particular interest in the investigation of the languages and dialects now or formerly current in the British islands; and he proposes to submit a few remarks on such points connected with them as appear most worthy of notice.

The Celtic dialects have obviously the first claim on our attention on the ground of priority: and it is, moreover, a matter of curiosity to inquire what influence they have exercised upon our present forms of speech. It is also of some importance to the general philologist to ascertain what place they occupy in the European and Asiatic families of languages. Till lately they were supposed by various eminent scholars to form a class apart, and to have no connexion whatever with the great Indo-European stock. This was strongly asserted by Col. Vans Kennedy, and also maintained, though in rather more guarded terms, by Bopp, Pott and Schlegel. The researches of Dr. Prichard in 'The Eastern Origin of the Celtic Nations,' and of Professor Pictet of Geneva, in his truly able work, '*Sur l'Affinité des langues Celtiques avec le Sanscrit,*' may be considered as having settled the question the other way; and as proving satisfactorily that the assertions of the philologists above-mentioned were those of persons who had never properly investigated the matter, and were consequently incompetent to decide upon it. The demonstration of Pictet is so complete, that the German scholars who had previously denied the connexion, now fully admit it; and several of them have written elaborate treatises, showing more affinities between Celtic and Sanscrit than perhaps really exist. This may serve to show the danger of dogmatizing in philology upon insufficient data.

It is but justice to the memory of a meritorious Celtic scholar, Edward Lhuyd, to observe that he clearly pointed

10 *

out the affinity between the Celtic dialects and such Indo-European languages as were then known, nearly a century and a half ago. Sanscrit had at that period scarcely been heard of in Great Britain; but the many coincidences which Lhuyd incidentally shows between Welsh, Gaelic, &c. and the Greek, Latin and Teutonic tongues, prove that he was well aware of the affinity between them. One instance which he gives is so creditable to his sagacity, and withal so instructive, that we may be permitted to dwell a few moments upon it.

No German or English philologer has, as far as the author knows, given a satisfactory etymology of the term *summer*. Lhuyd justly observes that it is, etymologically speaking, the same word as the Welsh *hav*; and that the proof of this may be found in the Irish forms *samh* and *samradh*, the Gaelic *s* answering to the Cymric *h*. Professor Pictet has observed the affinity between the Sanscrit root *'sam* and the Irish *samh*, both involving the idea of *mild*, *soft*, *gentle*; *samhradh* being literally the mild or genial quarter. The Sanscrit term is recognised by the German philologists as the root of the ancient Teutonic *samft* = English *soft*: and the author thinks it afforded a more likely etymology for the Greek adjective ἥμερος, *mild*, *tame*, and for ἡμέρα, *day*, than has hitherto been offered. It would seem very unlikely, *à priori*, that *day* and *night* could be derived from the same root; yet there is reason to believe that such is the case in one instance. *'Samanī*, confessedly from *'sam*, is a Sanscrit term for *night*, apparently on account of its *stillness*; as *summer*, and ἡμέρα, supposing them to be from the same root, convay the idea of a mild genial *temperature*. An analogy of this kind between such apparently remote languages as Welsh, German, Greek and Sanscrit, is calculated to suggest a variety of important reflections.

It is scarcely necessary to adduce the testimonies of Cæsar and Tacitus as to the similarity between the ancient British and the Celtic of Gaul. The declaration of Cæsar that the language of the Belgæ differed from that of the other Gauls, is explained by Strabo, who describes the different tribes as μικρὸν παραλλάττοντες ταῖς γλώσσαις, — slightly diverging in language; in other words, the difference was merely dialectical. Several elaborate attempts have been made to show that the language of the Gauls and other continental Celts, and consequently that of a majority of the Britons, was in fact Gaelic; the Armoric and Cymric dialects being peculiar to the Picts. Though our materials for deciding this question are not very copious, it is believed that, if fairly examined and used, they will be found sufficient. Besides many proper names, Greek and Latin authors have preserved several hundred Gallic words, many of them appellations of plants and other common objects. A considerable proportion may be identified as still subsisting, or capable of explanation in living Celtic tongues; but, as far as they go, they do not afford much countenance to the Gaelic hypothesis. Some of them are undoubtedly found in Gaelic, but very few *exclusively* so; and what may be considered as decisive of the question is, that the *forms* of the most remarkable words cannot be reconciled to the peculiarities of the Gaelic dialects.

The following instances, to which many others might be added, may perhaps be regarded as affording some countenance to this assertion: —

Petorritum, a four-wheeled carriage; adduced as a Gallic word by Cicero, Quintilian and others: Welsh, *peder*, four, and *rhod*, a wheel.

Pempedula, according to Dioscorides, Apuleius, and other ancient medical writers, the Gallic name of the *Quinquefolium*, or cinquefoil. In Welsh, *pumdalen*; from *pump*, five, and *dalen*, a leaf. We may here observe the analogies of the Æolic πέμπε, five and the Sanscrit *dala*, leaf.

Candetum, according to Columella, a Gallic measure of 100 feet. Welsh, *cant*, a hundred.

The above etymologies may be considered as certain; and it is equally certain that words including those elements cannot be Gaelic, to the genius and structure of which they are totally foreign. The Gaelic terms for *four*, *five*, *hundred*, are respectively *ceathair*, *cuig*, *cead*; it is therefore as impossible that the words we have adduced should be Gaelic, as that τετραφύλλον, πενταφύλλον, and ἑκατόμπεδον should be pure Latin.

Again, *Epona*, a deity said to be adopted from the Gauls, was the goddess of *horses*; Eporedia, now Ivrea in Piedmont, and its inhabitants, the *Eporedices*, were so called from their devotion to horse-racing and skill in horse-breaking. *Ep.* is not extant in Welsh as a simple term for a horse, but Pelletier gives it as ancient Armorican, and it still subsists in compounds and derivatives: *ebran*, horse-provender; *ebol*, a colt (*equuleus*), and some others. *Rhedu* and *rhedeg* are the common Welsh terms for *to run* or *to race*. The Gaelic word for *horse* is *each*; whence we may infer that the Eporedices did not employ that dialect, but one analogous to that of the Cymru or Armoricans.

Further, *Halle* and *Hallein* are names of various places in Southern and Middle Germany possessing *salt-works*; and in some localities *Hall* is used as a simple appellative, denoting any place where salt is manufactured. It is well known that Southern Germany was long occupied by Celtic tribes, many of them emigrants from Gaul, and this at once points out the Cymric and Armorican *hal, halen*, salt, as the etymology of such places. The Gaelic *sal-ann*, and the German *salz*, are equally out of the question.

A great mass of collateral evidence might be adduced from continental proper names, ancient and modern; such as *Nantuates, Nantouin, Nanteuil*, and many others, — obviously from *nant*, a valley, a word unknown in Gaelic: from words still current in France, *ex. gr. goelan*, a gull, Breton *gwelen*, Welsh *gwylan*, Gaelic *faelan*; *goemon*, sea-weed, Welsh *gwymon*, Gaelic *feaman*; and from the fact that most of the words preserved by ancient authors agree more nearly with the Welsh or Armorican equivalents than with the corresponding terms in the Irish or Highland dialects. *Velarus*, water-cress, would appear at first sight to come nearer the Gaelic *biolar* than the Welsh *berwr*. But the truth is, that *biorar* (from *bior*, water) is the ancient and genuine Gaelic form; *velarus* and *biolar* being mere euphonic modifications to avoid the unpleasant concourse of two *r*'s. At all events, the Armorican form *beler* comes as near as the Gaelic.

It is right to observe, that there is one ancient Gallic term which, as far as our present information goes, can only be explained from the Gaelic, namely, *carbidolupon*, the *Plantago major*, or broad-leaved plantain. The plant in question had the credit of possessing vulnerary properties; and, supposing *carbidolupon* to mean *wound-wort*, it readily resolves itself into the Gaelic *cearbadh*, wound or cut, and *lubh* or *luibh* herb, — a term not found in Welsh. *Beliocanda, Achillæa millefolium*, or yarrow, might bear either the interpretation of *hundred flowers* or *hundred-leaves*. In the former case, the first portion of the word would appear to be the Gaelic *billeog*, leaf; in the latter, the Welsh *bloen*, flower, would come as near as any Gaelic word; but in every case, the latter half, *canda*, hundred, would be non-Gaelic. *Scobiis*, the elder-tree, is plainly the Breton *skao* and Welsh *ysgaw*. The Gaelic word is *droman*. One of the most remarkable among the few relics of ancient Gaulish that we possess, occurs on a tablet found at Paris A. D. 1711, representing a bull, with three birds, and bearing the inscription TARWOS TRIGARANOS. The monument is supposed to have reference to the mythology of the ancient Gauls: the words of the inscription are (bating the terminations *os*) Welsh to a letter; *tarw*, bull, *tri*, three, and *garan*, crane.

In Gaelic, *tarbh*, bull, and *tri*, three, agree pretty well; but *corr*, or *corr-mhonadh*, is a totally different word from *gāran*. We may here observe the obvious analogy between *gāran* and the Greek γέρανος, and may also remark that the Celtic word is *significant*, being derived from *gār*, a shank, and consequently is not a borrowed word, though the Greek term possibly may be.

If we have succeeded in establishing the point that the language of the ancient Gauls bore a general analogy to the dialects of Wales and Armorica, it will follow, as a corollary, that the same analogy extended to the language of South Britain. It has already been observed that attempts have been made to deny this, and to show that the ancient South Britons were Gael, and that the Welsh language was, before and during the Roman period, confined to the provinces north of the Forth and Clyde. Much stress has been laid on the testimony of E. Lhuyd, who thought he could detect in the names of rivers and other local appellations in South Britain, traces of an older Gaelic population. It may here be observed, that by those ancient Gael (or Gwyddel as he calls them) Lhuyd neither means the *Scoti* nor the Britons of the Roman period, but a primitive race whom he supposes to have preceded the Cymru in Britain and the Milesians in Ireland, and whose existence in the former country, though possible enough, is purely hypothetical. It is more to the point to observe that Lhuyd's premises do not bear out his conclusions, scarcely one of the terms which he alleges being exclusively Gaelic. One on which he lays great stress is *Wisk*, the name of several British rivers, which he observes is the Gaelic *uisge*, water. But though *wysg* in Welsh does not now precisely mean *water*, it means a stream or current, and, metaphorically, *course*, *career*; an analogy of import sufficiently close to justify the belief of its being of the same origin as the Gaelic word. It would be easy to show that all the other words which he alleges are known to the Welsh or Armorican dialects, either as simple terms or in compounds and derivatives; consequently the hypothesis attempted to be founded on them falls of itself to the ground.

It is not meant to be asserted that the language of the Southern Britons was, strictly speaking, Welsh. The Cymric or Welsh was not the whole British language, but a particular dialect, chiefly prevalent in certain northern and western provinces. Cæsar informs us that many Belgæ were established in the southern parts of the island, and the Welsh themselves make a distinction between the Lloegrians and the Cymru. Giraldus Cambrensis, speaking of the Welsh and Cornish languages, expresses an opinion that the latter bore the most analogy to the speech of the ancient Southern Britons; and there are plausible reasons for believing that idea to be well-founded. That the ancient South British could not be Gaelic, is shown abundantly by the topographical nomenclature of the country, both ancient and modern. The non-Gaelic terms, *pen*, *pant*, *nant*, *comb* (W. cwm), a valley, *chevin* (W. cefn), a ridge, and many similar ones, occur in almost every country; while, on the other hand, peculiar Gaelic terms found in almost every barony in Ireland, such as *cluain*, plain, *sliabh*, mountain, are totally unknown in England. Another argument may be deduced from Celtic terms still current, especially in provincial dialects, which it is believed are more numerous than is commonly supposed.

The pointing out of particular instances will belong to a subsequent branch of our inquiry; at present it may be observed, that though the Cornish and Breton regularly corresponding with the Welsh in forms (which is the most certain proof of affinity), it is not to be denied that they not unfrequently agree with the Irish in particular words. For example, Ir. *athair*, serpent; Bret. *aer*. Ir. *alacht*, with young; Bret. *ala*, to calve, yean. Ir. *boabhalta*, simple, stupid; Bret. *bavedik*. Ir. *bochd*, poor; Corn. *bochodoc*. Ir. *faobhar*, edge of a sharp instrument; Corn. *fyvar*; with many others. We are not, however, to regard such words as *borrowed* from the Gaelic (of which there is no proof), but as collaterally descended in both classes from the ancient Celtic. The Breton *asrech*, Corn. *edrak*, *edrege*, Ir. *aithrighe*, repentance, are remarkable for their resemblance to the Gothic *idreigon*, to repent, which the Teutonic philologists know not well how to analyse. Another word of unknown origin used by Ulphilas, viz. *aibr*, gift or offering, bears a strong likeness to the Welsh *aberth*, sacrifice. These instances might almost lead one to suspect that our present text of the Gothic Gospels was revised in some locality where Celtic theological terms were current: but it would be unsafe to erect a theory upon so slender a foundation.

Some eminent scholars, particularly Adelung, and Price (the editor of Warton's 'History of Poetry'), have expressed an opinion that Welsh was, in fact, the language of the Belgic Gauls, and state as a proof of this, that it exhibits strong symptoms of admixture with Teutonic. There appears to be no solid foundation for this hypothesis. There are undoubtedly a number of Teutonic words in the Armorican dialects, and still more in the Irish, which *may* have been derived from the Belgæ of Gaul or Britain, or the Firbolg, said to have preceded the Scoti in Ireland. But the Cymru proper were, of all known Celtic tribes, the most remote from Germanic influence. It is not to be supposed that Belgic immigrants in Hampshire and Wiltshire could influence the language of Strath Clyde, Cumberland, or North Wales; and excepting a few terms adopted at a comparatively recent period from the Anglo-Saxon or English, there is nothing in the whole compass of the language that can be proved to be *borrowed* from the Teutonic. Words with Germanic prefixes and affixes are totally unknown; and where the terms are cognate, the peculiarity of form proves the Welsh ones to be genuine. For instance, *cas*, to hate, is not borrowed from the German *hassen*, nor *hal*, salt, from *salz,* any more than the Greek ἅλς is borrowed from *sal*, or ἕρπω from *serpo*, or *vice versâ*. One observation appears to be nearly conclusive as to this point. It is a well-known peculiarity of the Germanic tongues, that they abound in words beginning with *s*, followed by one or more consonants; and similar combinations are also admissible in Gaelic and Armorican. But no such union would be tolerated in Welsh. An initial *s* is invariable followed by a vowel; and when the etymology would require the concurrence of a consonant, it is either elided, as in *seren*, star, Armorican *steren*; or the pronunciation is softened by prefixing a vowel, as *ysnoden*, a band or fillet, Lowland Scotch *snood*. This remarkable peculiarity is scarcely to be reconciled to the idea of a strong admixture of German blood and German language. The fact is, that Adelung set out with a preconceived idea of the radical non-affinity of the two classes of tongues; and whenever he met with a Celtic word resembling a German one, directly concluded that it must have been borrowed. For example, he takes it for granted that the Celtic *abhall* (*afall*) *apple*, was borrowed from the German *apfel*, though the word is found in all the Celtic, Teutonic and Sclavonic dialects, and does not in reality belong to one more than another, having descended to all from some common source.

These remarks on the Celtic languages have been made partly with the view of stating some of the apparent grounds for considering them as branches of that great family of tongues which has spread itself from Central Asia to the extreme west of Europe. One of the latest writers on the subject, Mr. Johnes, though he regards Asia as the cradle of the race, thinks it probable that the Celts did not, as is commonly supposed, pass by the Euxine and the Danube in their progress westward, but by Syria and Africa into Spain, and afterwards into Gaul. The serious objections to this hypothesis are: — 1. There is no mention whatever in ancient history of Celts either in Syria, Egypt, or Mauritania. 2. Ancient writers uniformly represent the Celts as intruders from the *eastward* upon the Iberians. 3. There is no positive trace of Celticism in any known African language; while every Indo-European dialect, from Hindostan to Portugal, shows unequivocal proofs either of admixture with Celtic elements or of a community of origin, and not unfrequently of both. In the Romance languages, and some of the Germanic dialects, this phenomenon may be easily explained on historical and geographical data; but there are languages extensively prevalent, spoken by tribes remote, as far as we know, from all direct Celtic influence, that nevertheless exhibit many remarkable correspondences with that class of tongues, some of which are apparently too close to be explained by a remote collateral affinity. It will be sufficient to give a few select instances from the Armenian and the Slavonic, both of which differ as strongly from Celtic in their organization and general characteristics as any members of the Indo-European family differ from each other: —

ARMENIAN.			CELTIC.
dsiern	hand	G*. & W.	dourn, dorn, *fist*.
khuir	sister	W.	chwaer.
djur	water	W.	dwr.
ardj	bear	W.	arth.
dzarr	tree	—	derw, *oak*.
mis	flesh	—	mes, *dish*, *meal*.
datel	to judge	—	dadlen, *to litigate*
bari	good	Bret.	brao; G. breagh.
Pag-anel	to salute	W. G.	pog, *a kiss*.
tun	house	G.	dun, *a fort*; W. din.
phait	wood	G.	fiadh; W. gwydd.
am	year	G. W.	am, *time*.
oskr	bone	W.	asgwrn.
gloukh	head	W.	clog, in pen-glog; G. cloghan, *skull*.
sir	love	W. G.	serch.
air	man	G.	fear; W. gwr.
amis	month	W.	mis.
lousin	moon	—	lloer.
khoz	swine	—	hwch.
arjat	silver	G.	airgiod.
amarn	summer	—	samhradh.
boun	trunk, stock	W.	bon; G. bun.

* *G*. Gaelic; *W*. Welsh; *Bret*. Breton.

ARMENIAN.			CELTIC.
I werah.... *over, upon*.....		W.	gwor, gor; G. for.
kin........ *woman*........		G.	coinne.
ter, *lord; gen.* tearan.......		W.	teyrn.
khagzr .... *sweet*........		—	chweg.
ail........ *but*..........		G.	ail, *other.* (Cf. Gr. ἀλλά.)

The coincidences with the Slavonic dialects are much too numerous to be here given at length. In the following list an attempt is made to point out some of the most remarkable: —

SLAVONIC.			CELTIC.
baba .... *an old woman*........		Ir.	badhbh, *sorceress.*
blag...... *good*		—	breagh; Bret. brav.
blesk....... *brightness*		—	blosg, *light.*
blejat (Rus.) *to bleat*		W.	bloeddiaw, *to cry out.*
blato....... *mud*...............		—	llaid.
bodat (Rus.) { *to prick, to butt with the horns* .... }		—	pwtiaw, *to butt, poke.*
borju ...... *I fight*		Ir.	borr, *victory;* borras, *soldier.*
bran .... *battle*		—	braine, *chaptain, chief.*
briju....... *I shave*		W.	byrrau, *to crop.*
*Br'z...... *quick*		—	pies; Ir. brise; E. *brisk.*
briag ...... *bank, shore*..........		G.	{ braighe; W. bre, *high ground;* Sc. brae.
vitaz....... *conqueror*...........		W.	buddyg.
vlaga ...... *moisture*		—	gwlych; Ir. fliuch.
vladuika ... *ruler*		—	gwledig; Ir. flaith.
vlas ...... *hair*		—	gwallt; Ir. folt.
vl'k........ *wolf*..............		Ir.	breach.
vl'na....... *wool*		W.	gwlan; Ir. ollan.
vran .... *raven, black*..........		Ir.	{ bran, *raven, black;* W. bran, *raven.*
vriema, *gen.* vriemene, *time*........		Bret.	breman, *now.*
varit (Rus.). *to boil*		W.	berwi.
voz........ *upwards;* vuisok, *high.*.		Ir.	uas, *up;* uasal, *high noble.*
v'rt .... *garden*		—	gort.
viera ...... *faith*		W.	gwir; Ir. fior, *true.*
glava...... *head*		—	pen-glog; Ir. clogan, *skull.*
glas ...... *voice*		W.	llais.
gor'kui .... *bitter*		Ir.	geur, *sour, sharp.*
grom ...... *thunder*		Bret.	kurun (κεραυνός).
debel ...... *thick*..............		W.	tew.
dlani ...... *palm of the hand*		W. G.	dourn.
dl'g .... *debt*		Ir.	dlighe; W. dyled.
dol........ *valley*		W.	dol.
drozd, drozg *thrush*		—	tresglen.
dibri ...... *valley*		—	dyffryn.
zima ...... *winter*		—	grauav, *anciently* gaem.
kash'li .... *cough*		G.	cas; W. pas.
kobuila ... *mare*		—	capull; W. keffyl, *horse.*

* The medial comma represents the hard *jerr.* A soft jerr is denoted by (ĭ).

SLAVONIC.			CELTIC.
kolieno	*knee* ....:.............	G.	glun; W. glin.
kovatz	*smith*	W.	gov.
kradu	*I steal*	G.	creachaim.
kr'vï	*blood*	W.	crau. (Lat. cruor).
krag (Polish)	*circle*	—	crwn, *round*.
liek	*medicine*	Ir.	leigheachd.
lag	*grove*	W.	llwyn (Rom. λόγγος).
mal	*little*	—	mal, *small, light*.
minu	*I pass*	—	myned, *to go*.
ml'zu	*I milk*	Ir.	blighim.
more	*sea*	W. G.	mor.
mas........	*flesh*	W.	mes, *a meal*; E. mess.
rad	*willing*	—	rhad, *free, gratuitous*.
pani (Illyr.) .	*trunk of a tree*	—	bon; Ir. bun.
rouno	*fleece*	W.	rhawn; Ir. ron, *hair of animals*
salo........	*fat*	Ir.	saill.
slob........	*weak, infirm*	W.	clov.
slava.......	*glory*	Ir.	cliu (Gr. κλέος).
slug	*servant*	—	sgolog (Ger. schalk).
slied	*footsteep*	—	sliocyt (E. slot).
snieg	*snow*	—	sneacht.
soloma(Rus.)	*straw*	W.	calav.
son (Russ.) .	*sleep*	G.	suain.
such	*dry*	W.	sych.
srzde	*heart*	G.	cridhe.
srieda	*middle*	W.	craidd.
tuin	*hedge*	G.	dun, *fort*.
cherv	*worm*	—	crumh.
shirok	*broad*	—	sïr, long.
shui	*left, sinister*	W.	aswy.

Many of the above terms have undoubtedly only a collateral affinity, as they co-exist in Sanscrit and other languages; but others are, as far as is at present known, peculiar to Celtic and Slavonic, and exhibit an absolute identity of form and meaning such as we should hardly expect, *à priori*, to find in languages so remote from each other. Among the former class may be noticed the root *cas* (cough), as a good example of the agreement as well as of the difference of the various members of the great Indo-European family of tongues. The Sanscrit *kās*, Gaelic *cas*, Lithuanian *kosulys*, a cough, *kostu*, I cough, and Slavonic *kushell*, exhibit the guttural initial; the German *husten*, Lowland Scotch *host*, Armenian *huz*, the aspirate; the Welsh and Armoric *pās*, and Greek *βήξ*, the labial; and the Latin *tussis*, the dental. The Kurdish *goka* bears a singular resemblance, not only to the upper German *kauchen* and the English *cough*, but also to several Finnish dialects; Finnish proper, *köhkä, kökhä*; Esthonian *köhhä*; Hungarian *köhe*; Lappish *kossas*. We may here remark, by the way, that this and a variety of similar instances would lead one to suspect that the Finnish and commonly so-called Indo-European languages may be more nearly related to each other than the generality of philologists seem willing to allow. Another word, appearing in both lists; Armenian *tun*, house, Slavonic *tuin*, a hedge, is deserving of notice for its probable identity, not only with the Celtic *dun*, *din*, but also with the German *zaun*, a hedge; Anglo-Saxon *tun*, a hamlet; and lowland Scotch *town*, a homestead. The radical idea is that of *inclosure*, as is proved by the primary verbs; Anglo-Saxon *tynan* (still extant in the Lancashire *tyne*, to shut), and Irish *dunaim*, I shut, inclose, barricade. Another remarkable word is — Russian *son*, Gaelic *suain*, sleep. Though these words are undoubtedly cognate with the Sanscrit *swapna*, it is worthy of notice that they agree closely in *form* with the Pracrit *suna*, produced, agreeably to the genius of that dialect, by the elision of the medial consonants. The Greek and Welsh have *duplicate* forms: Gr. ὕπνος, W. *hep*, from *swapna*; and Gr. εὐνη, W. *hun*, from *suna*. A similar phænomenon may be observed in the Pali and Pracrit *pati*, Doric ποτί, Armenian *pat*; compared with Sanscr. *prati*, Ionic πρότι, ordinary Hellenic πρός. It is possible that a careful analysis of Pali and Pracrit forms, for which there are unfortunately few facilities at present, might lead to the discovery of analogies between Sanscrit and the languages of Europe which have not hitherto been suspected.

The extensive affinities of *worm*, which is found in one form or other in nearly all languages of the class, have been repeatedly noticed by German philologists as examples of the interchange of the guttural initial (Sanscrit *krimi*, Lithuanian *krimis*) with the palatal (Slavonic *cherv*) and the labial (Latin *vermis*, Engl: *worm*, Welsh *pryv*). They appear to have overlooked our *grub*, which has a decidedly Celtic aspect, and, rather an unusual phænomenon in English words, agrees more closely with the Gaelic form *crumh* than the Welsh-*pryv*. This however does not prove it to be adopted from the Gaelic, since, though the Welsh prefers the labial form to the guttural, it has in many cases duplicate forms, e. g. *crys* and *pres*, haste. *Cruv* may therefore have existed in the Lloegrian British though not now found in Welsh.

With respect to the second class of terms, namely those apparently peculiar to Slavonic and Celtic, the resemblance of such terms as *vran* and *bran*, raven; *kovatz* and *gof*, smith; *vladuika* and *gwledig*, chief, illustrious; is too obvious to be here insisted on. It is difficult to say how far they may or may not be *borrowed*, as we have scarcely any data for ascertaining the ancient juxtaposition or absolute separation of the tribes. Tacitus informs us that the language of the Æstii * approximated to that of the Britons. If that were really the case, it might be conjectured that there is at least one relic of their speech in the Lithuanian *merga,* maiden (Welsh *merch*), a term which has not a little puzzled the native etymologists. Generally speaking, however, the Lithuanian and Lettish languages show fewer correspondences with Celtic than are found in the ecclesiastical dialect, or ancient Slavonic. This, there is reason to believe, was the language of the Pannonian provinces, where it is possible those who spoke it might have more or less intercourse with Celtic tribes.

A remarkable word found in all the Slavonic dialects, but admitting of no etymological explanation within their limits, is *bolvan,* an idol or statue. Pott, in his 'Dissertation on the Lithuanian Language,' after giving the forms of it in the different dialects, adds — "Mihi etymon vocis ignotum." Grimm also points it out as a very peculiar word in the last edition of the 'Deutsche Mythologie' without attempting to account for it. An etymology, appearing at least plausible, is furnished by the Armorican *peulvan,* of which Pelletier gives the following account in his 'Dictionnaire de la Langue Bretonne': — "PEULVAN: a long stone, erected perpendicularly in the form of a pillar or post; a rough unwrought column. This word is current in Basse Cornouaille, towards Audierne, where several of those stones occur on the high roads and in waste places. It is a compound of *peul* — post or pillar — and *man,* figure, personage, appearance; signifying perhaps the appearance of a man standing upright; the form of the first plural (*peulvanet*) denoting beings that are animated, or reputed to be so. May not our ancestors have placed those stones as objects of some sort of worship or religious ceremony, and as a kind of idol?" The idea that those monuments were objects of religious reverence in the Druidical times is generally adopted by the antiquaries of Britany, and it is stated that the peasantry have still some vague superstitions respecting them. We may here remark, that the Wallachian *balavanu,* evidently the same as the Slavonic word, simply means a large stone, thereby approximating more to the Celtic *peulvan* in material import. If we admit the identity of the terms, it would follow that the Slavonians have been the borrowers in this

* The name of *Aestii* may have been given to some of the neighbouring tribes, as well as to the Finnish race, which is represented by the modern Ests.

instance, the component parts of the word being significant in Celtic but not in Slavonian; nor, it is believed, in any other Indo-European language. This might lead to an interesting inquiry whether, and to what extent, the mythologies of the two races appear to be connected. The setting-up a pillar of stone or wood as a rude symbol of some deity appears to have been a practice almost universal with pagan nations.

The occurrence of Celtic words in the Albanian language may be easily accounted for, as we know that Celtic tribes were intermixed with the Thracians as late as the time of Trajan. One of the most remarkable coincidences is the term for *egg*: Albanian βεì (pronounced *vi*), Cymric *wy*. Here again the Gaelic *ubh* is more remote, though it accords very well with the Latin *ovum* and Greek ὠόν (Æolic ὠϝόν). *Groua*, woman, may be referred either to the Gaelic *gruag* or Welsh *gwraig*. *Dovre*, hand, is more analogous to the Welsh or Gaelic *dourn* than to the Slavonic *dlani*. Most of the words common to Celtic and Albanian are however identical with those already pointed out in the Slavonic dialects, and may have been introduced from that quarter.

We now come to the portion of the subject most immediately interesting to ourselves, — the inquiry how far the Celtic dialects appear to have influenced the current language of England. Though this at first sight appears a simple question, it is not without its difficulties; at least, there are many points on which we cannot arrive at absolute certainty. Our parent language, the Anglo-Saxon, is, as a whole, very distinct from Welsh, or any other Celtic dialect; still there is a certain affinity between them, and it is necessary to distinguish carefully between what has been derived from what is merely collateral. Again, where terms have been actually adopted, it is not always clear which was the borrowing party. When different races are in contact there is generally some interchange of vocables, and after a lapse of many centuries it is not in every case practicable to ascertain the original proprietorship. Moreover, Welsh and Armorican are partially *Romanized* languages, yet having many original roots closely cognate with the Latin; so that, in attempting to eliminate mere Latinized words, it is often difficult to know where to stop. Adelung, the author of 'Mithridates,' appears to have regarded the Germanic and Celtic languages as radically unconnected with each other; and, in pursuance of this idea, gives a long list of terms ostensibly borrowed by the Celts from their neighbours. On this one of his countrymen, much his superior as a comparative philologist, makes the following judicious remarks: —

" Adelung's comparison of modern Celtic words with Latin and German is very far from satisfactorily establishing the point which among others he attempts to deduce from it, namely, that the Cymru are undoubted descendants of the Belgæ, who are described by Cæsar as much intermixed with Germans; and who consequently, on their emigration to Britain, brought with them many terms adopted from the Low German. Now many of the words alleged by him are not borrowed at all; and respecting others, it may be questioned whether they were not, on the contrary, borrowed by the German from the Celts. To answer such nice questions properly requires a more profound and comprehensive investigation than has hitherto fallen to the lot of this class of languages. In some words the determination is easy; in others, perhaps, absolutely impossible. In future it will be necessary carefully to separate what is really extraneous from the Celtic tongues before they can be safely employed for ethnographical or philological purposes. Little attention has hitherto been paid to this matter, and consequently a helpless confusion has arisen with respect to these languages and their genealogical relation to other branches, which it will cost endless trouble to unravel *."

It is not our present purpose to enter upon the comprehensive field here pointed out, though we may furnish a few hints and data towards its fuller exploration. The inquiry with which we are more immediately concerned is, whether the Germanic tribes, and more particularly the Anglo-Saxons, adopted words of Celtic origin, and to what extent? That some such process did take place is probable in itself and confirmed by the experience of many parallel cases. The Romans themselves adopted various Gallic words; and our intercourse with the East has served to introduce a number of Persian, Indian and even Chinese terms into our own language. It is, moreover, evident from the account given by Cæsar and others, that the Gauls, though inferior to the Greeks and Romans in civilization, were more advanced than the Germans; and we know that the colonial Britons, prior to the breaking up of the Romans Empire, had acquired all the useful and ornamental arts of the Romans. The invading Franks and Anglo-Saxons consequently found many implements, processes and artificial productions, of

---

* Pott. (ap. Ersch and Gruber's Encyclopædia); Art. INDOGERMANISCHER SPRACHSTAMM.

which they previously knew little or nothing; and what is more likely than that they should partially adopt the names by which they were designated? We may also easily conceive that they would be occasionally struck by the apparent oddity of the words current among the conquered race, and employ them themselves in a familiar or ludicrous sense, in the same way that *flash* terms are frequently used by educated Englishmen. An instance of each description will help to illustrate our meaning. We know from Martial that *bascauda* was a British word in the time of Domitian; and there is not the smallest reason to doubt that the Welsh *basgawd* and our own *basket* are perfectly identical with it in origin. Again, the verb *to bother* is seldom used by ourselves except in the comic or familiar style: but in the Irish, from which we originally adopted it, it is a perfectly serious word, and occurs repeatedly in the Scriptures in the sense of *mente affligi* or *conturbari*. The same observations might be extended to other classes of words; but to proceed to our immediate object of showing how far those influences have operated upon our current speech, we shall first produce a select list of terms relating to the ordinary arts of life, such as agriculture, masonry, carpentry, cookery, needlework, &c. &c., which appear to be of Celtic origin. A few French, Italian and Germanic terms will be given for the sake of illustration, as also some apparently of Latin origin, when there appears reason to believe that they were adopted from the Celtic inhabitants of the island, and not from the Latin or Anglo-Norman.

Welsh.

*basgawd	basket.
berfa	barrow.
botwm	button, Fr. bouton from bouter to push.
brag, *malt, whence*	brasium, Lat. barb.
bragodlyn, *spiced wort*	bragget.
bràn, *skin of wheat*	bran.
brat, *clout, rag*	brat, *a child's pinafore*, Yorksh.
brodiaw, *to darn, embroider*	broder, Fr. broider, E. prod, a point.
brywes, *bread dipt in dripping,* &c.	brewis, Yorksh.
bwyell, *hatchet*	Ger. beil; E. bill.

* The Celtic terms in the following lists are Welsh, except when otherwise specified. Ff represents the ordinary f. Single f is pronounced like *v*. Abbreviations: — W. Welsh; G. Gaelic; Br. Breton; Fr. French; Ital. Italian; Ger. German; Sc. Lowland Scotch; Prov. Provincial. [For some additions to the original list, the Editor is indebted to H. Wedgwood, Esq.]

11

Welsh.

cab, caban, *hut*	cabin.
cae, *enclosure, hedge*	quay. Port. cazo Dkade.
caman, *road*	Ital. camino; Fr. chemin.
càn, *white*	{ caned, *applied to vinegar*, &c. *full of white flakes.*
cawg, *cup*	coggie, Sc.
ceubal, *boat*	cobble.
clwt, *patch*; clytiaw, *to patch* . .	clout.
cnap, *button* . . . . }	knob.
cnwb, *knob*. . . . . }	
craff, *claps, brace*	cramp-iron; Fr. agraffe.
crampoez, Br.(Corn. crampothan)	crumpet.
crochan, *a pot*	crock, crockery.
crog, *a hook*	crook.
crogi, *to hang, suspend*	Fr. crocher, accrocher.
crwt, *a crust*	Fr. crouste.
cwch, *boat*	cock-boat.
cwysed (from cwys, *ridge, furrow*)	gusset. gousset a pocket.
cyllell, *a knife*.	Sc. gully.
cyl, cylyn	kill, Prov.; kiln, Eng.
chwiogen, *cake, manchet*	whig, Yorksh., *a sweetened cake.*
dantaeth, *choice morsel*	dainty.
darn, *a patch*.	darn.
deintur, *frame for stretching cloth*	tenter.
dref, *bundle*; drefa, 24 *sheaves* .	threave.
ffasg, *a bundle*	fadge, Yorksh.
fflaim, *cattle-lancet*	fleam. Du. vlieme.
fflasged, *large wicker vessel* . . .	flasket, Yorksh., *a pail.*
fflaw, *shiver, splinter*	flaw.
ffris, *nap of cloth*	frieze.
ffynel, *air-hole, chimney*	funnel.
gaflach, *fork*	gavelock, *iron crow*.
gardas (gar, *shank*, tas, *tie*) . .	garter, jarretière.
gefyn, *fetter*	gyve.
greidell, *iron baking-plate*	griddle.
grual	gruel.
gwain, *a carriage*	wain.
gwall, *rampart*.	wall.
gwald, *hem, border*	welt.
gwdyn, *a with*	woodie, Sc.
gwialen, *a rod*	gaule, Fr.
gwiced, *little door*	wicket.
gwlanen (from gwlan, *wool*). . .	flannel; Heref. flannen.
gwlyb, *liquor*.	flip.
gwn, *robe*	gown.

Welsh.

gwyfr	wire.
gwyntell, *basket*	windle, *measure of capacity*, Lancashire.
gwyth, *channel, water-course* . .	goit, *a mill-course*; also a river in Cheshire.
heislan, heisyllt, *instrument to dress flax*	hatchell, hackle.
hem, *a border*	hem.
hob, *measure of capacity*	hoop, *qr. of a peck*, N. Yorksh.
hws, *a covering*; hwsan, *a hood* .	housing, nouper to sweep.
hwff, *a hood*	howve, O. Eng.
kadak, Br. (G. adhag) *shock of corn*	hattock, Yorksh.
llath, *rod*	lath.
llogell, *drawer, partition*	locker.
llwyar, *a spoon*	löffel, Germ.
llymry, *jelly made with oatmeal* .	flummery.
masg, *stitch in netting*	mesh.
magl, *stitch in knitting*	maille, Fr.
matog	mattock.
mop, mopa, *maukin*, &c.	mop.
mwrthwyl, *hammer*	martello, Ital.
paeol, *a pail or pot*	pail.
pan, *cup, bowl*	pan.
parc, *field, inclosure*	park.
parsel, *shooting-butt*	bersaglio, Ital.
peg, peged, *a measure*	peck.
peled, *little ball, bullet*	pellet.
picyn, *a small hooped vessel* . .	piggin.
piser, *a jug* (Bret. picher) . . .	pitcher, pitsen Du. to draw water.
potes, *a cooked mess*	pottage.
plymwriaeth, *lead-work*	bloomery, *melting furnace, foundery*. No.
posned, *saucepan*	posnet, Yorksh.
rhail, *a fence, mound*	rail.
rhasg, *a slice*	rasher.
rhasgliaw, *to slice off, rasp* . .	râcler, Fr.
rhic, rhig, *notch, groove*	ridge.
rhigol, *trench, drain*	rigole, Fr.
rhill, *a row*	drill.
rhim, *raised edge or border* . . .	rim.
rhuwch, *rough garment*	rug.
sawduriaw, *to join, cement* . . .	solder.
saim, *grease*	seam, *lard*, Prov.
soch, *sink, drain*	sough.

11*

Welsh.

sopen, *lump, bunch*	sop, Prov. *lump of hay.*
swmer, *a beam*	summer-tree.
syth, *stiffening, glue,* &c.	size.
tacl, *instrument, tool*	tackle.
taradr, *an auger*	tarrière, Fr.
tasel, *fringe, tuft*	tassel.
teddu, *to spread*	ted, *to spread hay.*
tincerdd, literally, *tail-trade, low-est craft* . . . . }	tinker; cf. Sc. caird.
torth, *loaf*; Br. tartez, *cake* . .	tart; Fr. tourte.
tres, *chain or strap for drawing* .	trace.
trul, *a borer* . . } truliaw, *to bore* }	drill; Ital. trivella.
ystwc, *shock of corn*	stook, N. Eng.

Some thousands of familiar terms, to all appearance Celtic, might be collected from the various Romance and Germanic languages, especially from the provincial dialects. The following list, selected from a much larger one, may serve as a specimen: —

anterth, *forenoon*	oandurth, } Lancashire.
enderv, Br., *afternoon*	yeandurth, }
asbri, *trick, mischief*	spree?
baldorddus, *prating*	balderdash.
bas, *low, shallow*	bas, Fr.; base?
bamein, Br., *to bewitch, cheat* . .	bam, *imposition.*
blew, *hair of animals*	flew, O. Eng.; *fur.*
blod, Br., *soft, tender*	blöd, Dan., *soft* (metaph., *soft, timid*; Sc. blate).
bourd, Br, *trick, jest*	bourd, Sc.
braoued, Br.; *potio cocta*	brodo, Ital.; broth.
broud, Br., *goad, point*	prod, Prov.
burel, Br., *coarse cloth.*	borel, O. Eng.
bwg, *hobgoblin*	bug, bugbear.
bwgwl, *ditto*	bogle, Sc.
bygylu, *to threaten.*	bully.
byrdew, *short and thick, squabby* .	purdy, Durham.
carawl (*properly love-song*) . . .	carol.
cebyr, *rafter* (Bret. kebr, *a couple*)	chevron.
cecys, *hemlock*	kex.
cefn (Br. kein), *back.*	chine.
ceitlen, *smock-frock*	kittel, Ger.
cic, *foot*; ciciaw, *strike with the foot.* . . . . }	kick.
cil, *recess.*	gill, N. Eng., *a ravine.*

Welsh.

cluder, *heap, pile* . . . . . . cludeiriaw, *gather in a heap* } . .	cluther, Yorksh.
cnipws, *a fillip*	nawp, Yorksh.
cnoc, *a rap*	knock.
cnòl, *round summit hillock*	knoll.
cnul, cnull, *passing bell*	knell; knoll, Yorksh.
cob, *a thump*	cob, cobbing.
coblyn, *a sprite*	goblin; cf. Ger. kobold.
cocru, *to indulge*	cocker.
cog, *truncheon*; cogel, *short staff*.	cudgel.
crim, *crimp, ridge* . . . . } crimpiaw, *to raise in ridges* } . .	crimp.
cris, *scale, crust*; crisb, *crisp casting*; crisblu, *crumbling*. . . . . }	crisp.
crwth, *fiddle* . } crythwr, *fiddler* }	crowd, crowder.
crwcan, *to bend*; crwcwd, *squatting*; cwrc, cwrcwd, *id* . . . . }	crouch.
cwrian, *to squat*	cower.
cwta, *short*	cutty, Sc.
cwtws, *a lot*.	cut (*draw cuts*).
cwll, *separation*; cyllu, *separate* .	cull.
chwant, *desire*	want.
chwap, *smart stroke*	whap.
chwedleua, *to prate, gossip* . . .	twaddle.
dwn, *dusky* (Gael. don, *brown*) .	dun.
elv, Bret., *white poplar*	alb, Ger.
esmwyth, *even, soft*	smooth.
fagl, *blaze, flame*	fackel, Ger. *torch.*
filawg (*properly starting, skittish*), } *a young mare* . . . . }	filly.
foriwr, *explorer, scout*	foriere, Ital.
fug, *deception*	fudge.
fwg, *dry grass*	fog; Yorksh. *eddish*; Sc. moss.
fwrw, fwrwr, *down*	fur. Joder.
fwtog, *scut, short tail*.	fud; Prov. Ger. and Sc.
gil, *fermentation*	gyle-fat, Yorksh.; *wort-tub.*
glwth, *voracious*	glouton, Fr.; glutton.
glyn, *valley*	glen.
grawn, *roe of fishes*	rawn, N. Eng.
grymialu, *to murmur*	grumble.
gwammalu, *to waver*	wamble, wabble.
gwastel, Bret., *cake*	wastel; O. Fr. gastel.
gwariaw, *to spend*	ware, Yorksh.

Welsh.

gwas, *youth servant* . . . . } vassus, vassallus, Lat. barb.;
gwasawl, *serving* . . . . } vassal.
gweddu, *to yoke, unite, marry* . . wed.
gwica, *to carry about for sale* } . . hawk, hawker.
gwicawr, *pedlar* . . . . }
gwichyn, *a pole-cat* . . . . . . fitch, fitchet.
gwyal, *mark* . . . . goal.
gwychr, *valiant* . . . . wacker, Ger.
gwylaw, *to weep* . . . . wail.
hebog, *accipiter* . . . . hawk.
hecian, *to halt, limp* . . . . . . hitch.
herlawd, *a youth* . . . . harlot, O. Eng.; *a man-servant.*
herlodes, *a hoyden* . . . . harlot, *meretrix.*
hochi, *to expectorate* . . . . . . hawk.
hoeden, *a flirt* . . . . hoyden.
hwch, *a swine* . . . . hog.
llachiaw, *to cudgel* . . . . lick.
llaw, *hand*; llawf, *palm* . . . . lofi, Isl.; loof, Sc.
llawd, *youth* . . . . lad.
llodes, *a girl* . . . . lass.
llithraw, *to glide, slip* . . . . . . slidder, Prov.
llug, *partial*; in comp. e. gr. } . . lukewarm.
llugdwym, *tepid* . . . . . . }
llumon, *chimney* . . . . lum, Sc.
loumber, Br. *ditto* . . . . loover, Prov. l'ouvre.
madredd, *pus* . . . . matter.
mollt, *a wether* . . . . { moulton, O. Fr.; montone, Ital.; ram; mutton.
mwygl, *tepid, sultry* . . . . muggy.
nugiaw, *to shake* . . . . nudge.
osi, *to attempt, venture* . . . . . oss, Lancash.
pan, *down, four, nap* . . . . . . pane, O. Eng.
paneg, penygen, *entrails* . . . . paunch.
piciaw, *to throw* . . . . pitch.
pigwn, *turret, alarm-tower, &c.* . . beacon.
pinc, *smart, gay* . . . . pink, *to adorn*, &c.
posiaw, *to interrogate, embarrass* . posc, puzzle.
priawd, *possessed, owned, spouse* . } bride.
priodas, *marriage*; priodi, *to marry* }
pwea, *hobgoblin* . . . . puck.
pwmp, *round mass*; dim. pwmpl, } bump, pimple.
   knob, &c. . . . . }
pwtian, *to thrust, butt* . . . . . put, pote, Prov.; *to poke, butt.*
rhawd, *a drove, heap* . . . . . . rout, O. Eng., *a crowd.*
ruth, Corn., *ditto* . . . . routh, Sc., *abundance.*

Welsh.

rhwyb , *to tear, snatch*	rive.
rhwyg , *ditto*	rug, Sc. *to tear.*
skor, Br., *prop*, *stay*	shore.
skourjez (fr. skourr, branch, &c.)	scourge.
sil , Br., *strainer*	sile, Yorksh.
souba , Br., *to dip*	sop , soup.
soegi , *to steep*	soak.
stanka, Br., *to dam up , obstruct* .	stanch.
tal , *lofty, of high stature*	tall.
tariaw, *to loiter, stay*	tarry.
tasg, *a job, piece-work*	task.
tociaw, *to cut short*	dock.
topyn , *a crest*.	toppin , Yorksh.
tosiaw , *to jerk, throw*	toss.
tripiaw , *to stumble*	trip; cf. Fr. trebucher.
troddi , *move forward, progress* .	trudge.
trwyn , *a snout*	trogne, Fr.
wyna, oena, *to bear lambs.* . . .	yean.

The above examples, which are not a twentieth part of what might be alleged, will, it is presumed, show how necessary it is for the etymologist to take the Celtic element into consideration in the investigation of the languages of Western Europe. It is believed that most of the above terms are genuine Celtic, though it is possible that in a few cases the counterparts given may not be *derived* from them, but only collateral. It may, however, be observed, that the finding an isolated term in an Anglo-Saxon or German vocabulary by no means proves it to be *vernacular* to that language. Many words occur in 'Lye's Dictionary,' for instance, derived from the glossaries of the eleventh century, which are notoriously not genuine Anglo-Saxon, and cannot be traced to any known roots in the Germanic tongues. For instance, we find *comb*, a valley, which is not Saxon nor ever was, being evidently the Welsh *cwm*. It is obvious that many other terms may be in the same predicament; even the presence of a word in a number of ancient dialects does not prove it to belong to that class of languages. It will be sufficient for the present to adduce a single example.

The word *leather*, in one form or other, occurs in all the Celtic and most of the Teutonic dialects; the question, therefore, is to determine in which it is most likely to be vernacular. It is to be observed in the first place, that the manufacture of leather was undoubtedly more extensively practised by the Gauls than by the Germanic tribes, as described by Tacitus. Secondly, the word is of ancient currency among the Celts, as is shown by its appearing in all the dialects, and in the earliest known compositions; for example, in the poems of Taliesin, believed to be of the sixth century. Moreover, there is a strong evidence that it never was a *vernacular* Anglo-Saxon term. It scarcely ever appears as a distinct word, its occurrence being nearly confined to a few compound names of manufactured articles, for which Ælfric's glossary is almost the sole authority. Finally, it is important to observe that it is *significant* in Celtic, being derived from W. *lled;* G. *leathan*, broad, flat; while in the Germanic dialects it has no known etymology. Should all these considerations lead us to conclude that the Germans borrowed the word from the Celts, it is obvious to infer that the same process might take place with respect to many other terms of similar import.

The various speculations connected with general philology deducible from the subject which we have been considering, would lead us into too wide a field at present. Some of them may perhaps afford matter for a subsequent paper; it will be sufficient on this occasion to advert briefly to a single class of words, which appears to present some interesting phenomena.

Words with initial *gw* in Welsh or Breton generally correspond with the Sanscrit and German initial *w*, Latin *v*, Italian *gu*, French *g.*, and Gaelic *f*: e. gr. W. *gwéu*, to weave; Sansc. *wē*; Bret. *gwasta*, to ravage; Lat. *vastare*; Ital. *guastare*; O. Fr. *gaster*; Eng. *waste*; Gael. *fàsaich*. Some words of this class deserve to be more particularly adverted to. It is well known that a number of vocables in the Teutonic dialects begin with *qu*, or some equivalent combination; and it is remarkable that a great proportion of them correspond to Cymric terms with initial *gw* or *cw*. The Mœso-Gothic, the oldest Germanic language, exhibits in its present state eleven leading words of this class, eight of which may be referred with great probability to Cymric or Armorican counterparts.

qväinon (or in Gabelentz's orthography, qainon, *to whine;* Du. kwynen)	W. cwyno.
qairnus, *quern or hand-mill;* in Holstein, quarr	gwyraw, *to revolve.* (cf. North Frisic, querdel, *a weathercock.*)
qairrus, *placid, mild;* Swed. qvar.	gwar, *id.*
qal (u. v. *subjugation*); A. S. cwaele, *destruction,* &c.; cwellan, *to quell, kill*	gwalla, *to injure, destroy.*

qens, *a woman* . . . . gwen (*properly a fair one*), *female.*
qithan (O. Germ. quedan, *to say*) gwedyd.
qivs, *alive* (vivus) . . . . gwio, Br., *vivacious.*
qistjan, *to destroy* . . . . gwasta, Br., *id.*

The three remaining terms *qiman*, to come, *qithus*, the womb, and *qramms*, wet (Dan. klam, Eng. clammy), may possibly be connected with W. *camu*, to step; *ceudawd*, the womb or inside; and *gwlyb*, moisture, Bret. *gleb*; but they do not manifest the strict parallelism of form which appears in the other words.

The following coincidences with Anglo-Saxon and the Low German dialects may also be noticed: —

cwacian, *to quake*, A. S. . . . . gwegiaw, *to totter.*
cwartern (*custodiæ domus*), *prison* gwared, *to guard*
cwanian, *to pine, languish* . . . . gwàn, *weak, feeble.*
quad, Low Germ., *bad* . . . . . gwaeth, *worse.*
quaddern, *to prate* . . . . chwedleua, *id.*
quarke, *the throat* . . . . gwar, *the neck.*
quinka, *to flutter, start* . . . . . gwinka, Br., *to wince.*
quide, *to complain* (A. S. cwythan) gwyth, *wrath, indignation.*
quasse, Prov. Dan., *to squeeze* . gwasga, *id.*
quakka, *to croak, quack* . . . . . gwacha, Br., *to croak.*
cuthe, A. S., *known* . . . . . . gwydd, *knowledge.*
quaint(O. Fr. coint), *smart, spruce,* } &c.; N. Yorksh., whent, *strange* } gwaint (Br. koant), *neat, trim.*
quip, *sarcasm*, &c. { gwib, *sudden course*; chwipyn, { *quick turn.*
quibble, *verbal evasion*, &c. . . . gwibl, *a turn, quirk.*
quer, Germ. *athwart.* . . . . . . gyyr, *oblique, awry.*
quarl, Low Germ., *pustule, blister* { { gwerbel, Bret., *a tumour*; cf. { warble, *a swelling in cattle* { *caused by insects.*
quäll, Swed., *evening* . . . . . . gwyll, *darkness,*
queelder, Du., *low ground outside* } the dikes . . . . } gwaelawd, *low ground, a bottom*; gwaelder, *lowness.*

The above and similar words may furnish a useful clue for tracing the origin of many French and Italian words commencing with *g* and *gu*. For example, the comparison of *galopper* and *gualoppare*, shows that *u* or *w* was an original portion of the word; and this directs us to W. *gwil-hobain*, literally to make quick jumps, an excellent analysis of the meaning of the term. The Scottish *wallop* is the same word with the loss of the guttural.

Many more coincidences might be produced, particularly

from the Romance and provincial German dialects; but the above are sufficient to establish the analogy. Commonly the above initials correspond to a simple *w* in Sanscrit: for instance, *wad*, to speak, is the root agreeing with the W. *gwedyd*, and O. Germ. *quedan*; but sometimes a different characteristic appears: e. gr. *jiva* is the Sanscrit representative of Goth. *qivs*; *hansa* (goose) of Bret. *gwaz* and *harit* (green) of W. *gwerdd*. It may, therefore, be suspected that those and similar words have emanated from primitive forms resembling the Celtic, and that the prototype of *harit*, for example, was more like W. *gwerdd* than the Latin *viridis*. Something analogous appears to have existed in some of the older German dialects; at least Paulus Diaconus assures us that Woden was called Gwoden by the Langobardi. The resemblance of the Langobardic form to the Gwydion of Welsh mythology is not unworthy of notice. O'Brien's etymology of Dia Ceadaoine, the Irish name of Wednesday, q. d. the day of Gwodan, is specious enough, but will not bear examination. It is merely cead, or ceud aoine, the *former fast*; Friday, simply called aoine, *the fast*, being regarded as the more considerable one.

The initial *chw* in Welsh words is in some cases a mere mutation of *gw*, but in general it corresponds to the Sanscrit and German *sw*, *swasri*, sister, W. *chwaer*; *swadu*, sweet, W. *chweg; swid*, to sweat, W. *chwysu*. The W. *chwech*, six, in conjunction with the remarkable Pushtoo *spash*, would imply that the Sanscrit *shash* was originally *swash*, or something like it. The Gaelic generally preserves the sibilant and drops the labial; e. gr. *sior*, tister, *sant*, desire (W. *chwant*), which again would suggest a suspicion that a similar process may have taken place with the Sanscrit *s'ans*, desiderare. A root *swans*, supposing it to have ever existed, would exactly harmonize with W. *chwant*, desire, *chwennych* to wish, according to the usual law of permutation. The Germanic dialects, it is well known, agree most faithfully with the Sanscrit in this combination. The Slavonic ones, including Lithuanian and Lettish, stand in the next degree of proximity, but occasionally manifest a disposition to drop the labial. The other cognate languages either substitute a guttural or an aspirate, harden the *w* into *p*, vocalize it, or drop it altogether, as will be rendered manifest by tracing the Sanscrit *swid*, to sweat, and *swid*, white, through their various affiliations. Pictet refers the Gaelic *speur*, sky, firmament, to Sanscrit *swar*; if it really is of that origin, and not, as there is room to suspect, a mere disfigurement of *sphæra*, it is a remarkable instance of the hard or Median form in a western dialect. *Piuthar*, G., sister, in which the sibilant appears to be dropt, seems to give some countenance to its genuineness. Compare W. *yspyddyn*, the white thorn; Armenian *spid*, white; Pers. *sipid*, &c. &c.

There are some remarkable coincidences between Welsh and Armorican words commencing with *gw*, and Sanscrit roots with initial *s'w* (*palatal s*), which it would exceed our present limits to discuss more particularly.

In concluding, for the present, the Celtic portion of our subject, a few miscellaneous observations will be offered on such points as appear most interesting to the general philologist. As a preliminary to this, it may be advisable to make a few further remarks on the *genuineness* of the Celtic terms, placed in comparison with those of other European languages, and the means by which that genuineness may be tested. There are cases in which it is difficult to arrive at any absolute certainty: — for example, the resemblance of the Welsh *celu* (to conceal) with the Latin *celo* would create a suspicion that the former was borrowed from the latter; while on the other hand, the way in which it branches out into derivatives and compounds is strongly in favour of its originality. The safest principle in this investigation is, to regard that language as having the best claim to originality which furnishes the most satisfactory explanation of the original roots, or component elements of words. Most persons, for example, would be apt to suppose that the familiar term *funnel* was undoubtedly a vernacular English word, and to repudiate all idea of a Celtic origin for it. Nevertheless it will be found, on examination, to have neither etymology nor intrinsic meaning in Teutonic; while the Welsh *ffynel* (air-hole) is demonstrably derived from *ffwn*, breath, referred with great probability by Pictet to Sanscrit *pavana*, and exactly equivalent to Latin *spiraculum*. *Coble*, a boat, admits of no satisfactory explanation from Anglo-Saxon or German sources; but the Welsh *ceubal* may be resolved into *hallow shaft* or *trunk*: thus showing both the antiquity and genuineness of the term. The word *bride* occurs indeed in all the Germanic dialects, Gothic included, but it is in all a perfectly isolated term, without intrinsic meaning. Some German philologists have indeed referred it to Sanscrit *prī*, amare; an etymology which violates the established laws of permutation of letters. In all known Teutonic cognates of this root, we regularly find *f* instead of *p*: *frion*, to love; *freyen*, to woo; *freund*, friend, &c. &c. It would have been more to the purpose to compare Greek πρίαμαι, to obtain by purchase; which is strictly cognate with Welsh *priawd* (proprius), possessed, owned, a spouse; the stem of *priodi*, to marry; *priodus*, marriage; and many words of allied import. The allusion is to the custom, almost universal among semi-civilized nations, of purchasing a bride from her parents. The Germanic term has every appearance of having been borrowed; the Celtic words are undoubtedly original. Another remarkable instance occurs in the word *travail*, labour, sorrow, &c.; French *travail*; the origin of which is nowhere to be found, except in Welsh *trafael*, a compound of the prefix *tra*, exceeding, and *mael*, work, labour; consequently not borrowed from the French or English. The word undoubtedly came to us through the medium of the Norman French: but we have another form of it deduced more directly from the original; viz. *turmoil*, stir, bustle; and moreover the simple form *moil*, to labour; a word common in our older writers.

Another important criterion for determining the genuineness of words, is the observation of the *forms* peculiar to the various languages and dialects. It is well known, for example, that the *spiritus asper* in Greek does not in general correspond with *h* in Latin, but is a representative of a more ancient sibilant or digamma; and the same aspirate in the Germanic tongues is a modification of a more primitive guttural, *k* or *g*. It has already been observed by Lhuyd and others, that where the Greek and Latin differ, the Welsh generally corresponds with the former and the Gaelic with the latter; and that the Teutonic tongues bear a greater analogy to the Gaelic than the Cymric, especially in the sibilants, as may be instanced in Greek ἅλς; Welsh *halen* (salt); Latin *sal*; Gaelic *salann*; German *salz*. When therefore we find words current in the Teutonic dialects in which this analogy is not observed, we may suspect them not to be original. The term *hawk* (Old German *happuc*) is found in one form or other in all the dialects; but instead of following, as it regularly ought to do, the analogy of Gaelic *seabhog*, it agrees with Welsh *hebbog*, and was therefore probably borrowed from a Cymric dialect. The Welsh *hafyn*, a haven or harbour, seems to be significant in the sense of a *still, calm place*; and if it be original, the German *hafen* is evidently not. In like manner the Gaelic *seiceal* (flax-comb) shows the Welsh *heislan, heisyllt*, to be genuine words, and our *hackle* or *hatchel* most probably adopted ones. *Hem* and *seam* are radically the same word; but the latter is the only legitimate Germanic form. Pursuing the same analogy with respect to the gutturals, we may feel pretty confident that our *corner* is not of Teutonic origin, but from the Welsh or Bret. *cornel*; the true Anglo-Saxon form being *hyrn*. *Cyrm*, cry or clamour; *cyrman*, to cry, though of ancient standing in Anglo-Saxon, are suspicious from their agreement with the Celtic *garm*, and are probably not so genuine as the other form *hryman*.

Words adopted by the Celtic tribes from the Latin occasionally furnish interesting data respecting the ancient pronunciation of particular letters; for example, *ysgeler*, wickedness, Latin *scelus*, must have been adopted by the colonial Britons from the Romans, as it was never current among the Anglo-Saxons or Normans; and serves as an evidence at the present day that *c* before *e* had the hard sound, not the soft palatal or sibilant one now given to it by most modern Europeans. From the description given by Quinctilian and others of the harsh sound of the Latin *f*, it is conjectured to have partaken in some degree of the nature of a sibilant. This idea receives some countenance from a singular phænomenon in Irish; namely, that certain words obviously borrowed from the Latin do not commence with *f*, but with *s*. A few instances are, Irish *sorn*, oven, Welsh *ffwrn*, Latin *furnus*; Irish *suist*, a flail, Welsh *ffust*, Latin *fustis*; Irish *srian*, a bridle, Latin *frænum*; Irish *scinister*, a window, Latin *fenestra*. It is difficult to assign any cause for this discrepancy, except we suppose a marked distinction between the pronunciation of the Latin element and the ordinary *f*, which is a very common constituent of Irish words.

The insertion or omission of a nasal element, something analogous to the Sanscrit *anuswara*, is very common in the Celtic dialects. The general tendency of the Gaelic, as compared with Welsh, is to -drop the nasal sound; for example, Welsh *cainc*, branch, Gaelic *geug*; Welsh *dant*, tooth, Gaelic *deud*; Welsh *cant*, hundred, Gaelic *cead*; with many others. The employment of this element in the Cymric dialects sometimes appears a little capricious: for instance we have *lleipr*, flaccid, English limber; *lleiprog* muræna, English lamprey; *tampyr*, a wax-light, English taper; and *llimp*, smooth, soft, agreeing closely with English limp. An attention to this phenomenon will frequently enable us to detect analogies which otherwise would not be very obvious: for instance, the Anglo-Saxon *sið*, M. G. *sinth* semita, does not bear a very close resemblance to Welsh *hynt*, way, path, journey. But when we learn, by comparing the other Teutonic dialects, that the original form is *sind*, and remember that the Cymric *h* regularly answers to the Teutonic *s*, we have less difficulty in admitting an original affinity between the two. It is even possible that *semita* may be the same

word, with the insertion of a vowel. The Gaelic *saod*,
track, journey, agrees with the Anglo-Saxon in the omission
of the nasal.

Pott, treating of the remarkable propensity of the Pali
and Pracrit dialects to reject a liquid following a mute, observes that a similar phenomenon sometimes presents itself
in other languages, instancing the Low German *bost*, English *boast*, as probably identical with High German *sich
brüsten*. The Welsh *ffrost*, bragging, boasting, appears to
give some countenance to this idea. Other instances of the
same phenomenon occur in Anglo-Saxon *spaecan*, English
speak, compared with German *sprechen*; and Anglo-Saxon
specca, English *speck*, *speckle*, compared with the Yorkshire
spreckle and the South German *spreckeln*. The Welsh forms
brych, variegated, *ysbrychu*, to speckle, show that the *r* is
original. By the same analogy, *to pat* may very well be
from the Welsh *pràtiaw*, to stroke or fondle; and *to fume*,
from Welsh *ffromi*, to chafe, be indignant. Many similar
instances might be given from a great variety of languages.

A number of interesting examples might be produced of
the manner in which labials and gutturals are interchanged
in the Celtic dialects, and in words which other languages
appear to have adopted from them. Thus we have in Welsh
ceru and *bicru*, to wrangle, English *bicker*; Gaelic *seasg*,
dry, Bret. *hesk*, Welsh *hysp*; Welsh *llac*, *ys–lac*, slack, German *schlaff*; Gaelic *sgolt*, to split or cleave, German *spalten*;
with a multitude of others. The keeping this peculiarity
in mind will render many etymologies very obvious which
have hitherto been little known. Sometimes a dental appears
as the substitute of the labial· or guttural: as Gaelic *cas*,
cough, Latin *tussis*; Gaelic *ceathair*, four, Greek τέσσαρες.
This permutation is however comparatively infrequent.

It has been frequently observed by philologists, that new
words appear to have been formed in various languages by
prefixing a consonant to the simple root. Many curious illustrations of this process may be derived from the Celtic
dialects. If, for example, we take a number of simple words
commencing with *l*, we shall find that the corresponding
terms in other languages, and even in the same language,
frequently prefix a guttural, palatal, or sibilant element.
Thus Welsh *llab*, stroke or blow, appears in the augmented
forms *clap*, *flap*, *slap*; Welsh *llac*, laxus, *slack*; Welsh *llag*,
segnis, remussus, *lag*, *laggard*, *flag*, *slug*, *sluggard*; Welsh
llavar, loquela, Danish *klavre*, to prate, Sc. *claver*, Sp. *palabra*, word, speech; Welsh *llawr*, area, also in the enlarged
form *clawr*, Gaelic *clàr*, *blàr*, a flat surface, plain, English

floor. A comparison of the different Welsh and English forms will show that the words *rib*, *ridge*, *brim*, *brink*, *crimp*, *stripe*, all include the same radical, modified according to the processes already pointed out; viz. by the interchange of labials and gutturals; the insertion of a nasal, or the prefixing of one or more consonants.

One of these preformatives, if they are to be regarded as such, is deserving of more especial notice. Grimm, in his 'Deutsche Grammatik,' observes that the initial *s* frequently appears to have originally been a distinct component element, probably a particle; and that the root of the Anglo-Saxon *smael*, English *small*, for example, appears to exist in the Slavonic *mal*, little. This sagacious conjecture is excellently confirmed by the co-existence of the simple and the augmented forms in Welsh; *mal*, light, fickle, *ys-mal*, light, small; *ys* being a common prefix, apparently answering to the Latin *ex* in its intensive signification. A knowledge of this phenomenon enables us to establish a connexion between a multitude of words in all the Indo-European languages, especially between the Celtic and Teutonic branches. The following list, which is capable of being greatly enlarged, may serve as a specimen: —

Welsh.

Welsh	English
pawd, *shank*	ys-bawd(*blade-bone*); spawd,Prov.
brig, *shoot*	ys-brig; sprig.
brych, *variegated*	ys-brych; spreckled, Yorksh.
garm, *cry*	ys-garmes, *conflict*; skirmish.
cawd, *covering*	ys-gawd,*shadow*; schatten,Germ.
cin, *skin*	ys-gin, *fur-robe*; skin.
gogi, *shake, jog*	ys-gogi; shog, Sc.
crafu, *scratch*	ys-grafu; scrape.
cre, *cry*	ys-gre; schrey, Germ.
crech, *cry*	ys-grech; shriek, screech.
cub, *bundle*	ys-gub, *sheaf, broom*; sceaf, A.-S.; scopa, Lat.
— —	ys-gubor, *carn*; scheure, Germ.
cud, *motion*	ys-gudaw, *move hastily*; scud, scuttle.
cwta, *short*	ys-gwt, *short-tail*; scut.
llac, *lax*	ys-lac; slack.
llaif, *cutting-off*	ys-leifiaw, *slice*; sliver, Prov.
llwch, *stagnum*	ys-lwch, *quagmire*; slough.
mal, light	ys-mal; small.
mwg, *smoke*	ys-mwcach, *puff of smoke*; smoke.
noden, *thread*	ys-noden, *filled*; snood, Sc.

Welsh.

par, *spear*	ys-par; spear.
paith, *prospect*	ys-peithiaw, *explore*; spy.
pig, *point*	ys-pig; spike.
— —	ys-pigawd; spigot.
pin, *sharp point, pin*	ys-pin, *thorn*; spina, Lat.
pinc, *chaffinch*	ys-bincyn; spink, bull-spink, Yorksh.
plyg, *fold*	ys-plyg; splice.
twc, *cut*	ys-twc, *shock of corn*; stook, Prov.
gwain, *service*	ys-wain, *esquire*; swain.

It will be seen from the following instances that the Gaelic frequently agrees with the Teutonic and other dialects in prefixing the sibilant, when the corresponding words in Welsh want it.

Welsh.

llai, *mud*	G. laib, slaib; slab, slabby.
llifu, *grind, polish*	sliob; schleifen, Germ.
llimp, *soft*	sliom, *smooth, slender*; slim.
llyngcu, *swallow*	sluig; *schlucken*, Germ.
mèr, *marrow*	smior; smior, Isl., *butter*, &c.
naddu, *to cut*	snaidh; schneiden, Germ.
nofio, *to swim*	snamh; snā, Sanscr.
nyf, *snow*	sneachd; snieg, Slav.
bar, *rail, shaft*	sparr, *beam*; spar.
colpo, Ital, *blow*	sgeilp, *stroke*; skelp, Yorksh.
calidus, Lat.	sgald; scald.
kel, Bret. *narration*	sgeul; spell? A.-S.

Sometimes the Teutonic dialects, as well as the Latin, omit the initial *s* of the analogous Gaelic words:—

Gaelic.

slad, *steal*	W. lladratta; latro, Lat.
slat, *rod*	llath; lath.
snàthad, *needle*	nydell; nädel, Germ.
sniomh, *spin*	nyddu; nere, Lat.
sneedd, *larva pediculi*	nedd; nit.
spadal, { *plough-staff*	pattle, Sc.
{ *short oar*	paddle.
spairt, *plaster*	parge.
stang, *pool*	tank.
streup, *altercation*	threap, Prov.

Generally speaking, however, the Teutonic, especially the Belgic and Low German dialects, agree with the Gaelic more frequently than with the Welsh.

The following Anglo-Saxon words with the sibilant initial may be referred, with more or less probability, to the annexed simple forms in Celtic: —

Anglo-Saxon.	Welsh.
scearfan, *to cut in pieces*	cerfio, *to cut.*
scen, *bright, clean, sheen*	cain, *bright.*
scop, *stem, trunk*	cyff.
scriðan, *to wander*	crwydraw.
scrob, *shrub*	craobh; Gael. *tree.*
scycels, *mantle*	kougoul; Bret. *cloak.*
slican, *to strike*	llaciaw, *to beat.*
slið, *smooth, mild*	llaidd.
sliw, *dyed, coloured*	lliw, *colour.*
slog, *slough*	llwch.
smaeðe, *smooth*	mwyth, esmwyth; Gael. maoth.
sparran, *to shut, fasten*	bar.
spearca, *spark*	gwraich.
straede, *step*	troed, *foot.*
straegan, *strew*	traff, ys-traff, *spreading.*
strec, *brave, stout*	trech.
swaec, *savour*	chweg, *sweet.*
swaeð, *footstep*	gwadn, *sole.*
sweard, *sward, turf*	gweryd.
sweor, *neck*	gwar.

The following miscellaneous words are of similar character: —

Welsh.	
glafoerio	slaver.
grill, *sharp, creaking*	shrill.
gwegiaw, *to totter*	swag.
gwichiaw, *cry sharply*	squeak.
pwcca, *hobgoblin*	spuken, Germ., *to be haunted.*
tarpare, Ital. *to prune*	sterp, Bret., *pruning-hook.*
ramper, Fr. *to creep*	skrampa, Bret.
grin. Eng.	skriña, Bret.
troule, O. F. *trollop*	stroulen, Bret.

Much light would be thrown on the science of comparative etymology, if we could positively ascertain in every case whether the simpler or the fuller form ought to be regarded as the original. For example, have the Sanscrit *snā*, to bathe, Gaelic *snamh*, to swim, gained a prefix; or have the Latin *na—re*, Welsh *nofio*, lost a primitive initial? This inquiry is beset with numerous difficulties, and many specious arguments might be alleged on both sides of the question. The Welsh prefix *ys* may be plausibly accounted for as a *significant* element, modifying in many instances the import of

12

more simple roots, which therefore may be reasonably presumed to have had a distinct previous existence. The comparison of a number of languages is also generally in favour of the simple form. The ostensible root *mal*, denoting comminution, diminution, *v. t. q.*, occurs in a multitude of tongues, Semitic included; while *ys-mal* and *small* are exceptional forms, and very probably compounds. On the other hand, it must be remembered that certain combinations of letters admissible in one language are not tolerated in others. No Welsh word can commence with *s* followed by a consonant; nor can a liquid or a medial mute follow an initial *s* in Latin. If therefore original words, differently constituted, existed at all, they must necessarily undergo some modification to adapt them to Roman or Cymric organs. Supposing the Latins to adopt the Sanscrit root *smrĭ*, to remember, it is very likely that they would drop the sibilant, especially in a reduplicate form like *memor*. It is true that the objectionable sound might be and actually was got rid of in a variety of ways : by inserting or prefixing a vowel; by vocalizing the second consonant, especially if a labial; by substituting a tenuis for a medial; or by dropping the second consonant instead of the first. Thus we find the German *schwester*, which comparatively few nations in the world could utter with facility, under the various modifications of *sister*, *soror*, *sior*, *piuthar*, *chwaer*, *hor*, and *kho*; and our own *star*, as *ἀστηρ*, *ser*, and *sitarah*; while the Sanscrit *tāra* may possibly have lost its initial. It has been remarked on a former occasion that the Welsh often overcomes the difficult articulation by prefixing a vowel, *e. g. ysgeler*, from Latin *scelus*; but there are some remarkable instances of an elision of the second consonant which do not appear to be generally known.

	Welsh.
stan, O. Germ., Lat. *stare* . . .	safu.
staff	saffwn, *beam, shaft*.
staunen, Germ., *to wonder* . . .	sànu.
sterno, Lat., *to spread*	sarnu.
στέργω, *to love*	serch.
stoppel, Germ, *stubble*	sofl.
stimulus, *a goad*	swmwl.
stun	sỳnu, *to be stunned* or *amazed*.
stürzen, Germ., *to fall*	syrthiaw.
stið, A.-S., *stiff*	syth.

A little examination would probably bring to light many others, and help to establish analogies scarcely suspected. For instance, Gaelic *sil*, to drop, distil, Welsh *hidlu*, may possibly be cognate with Latin *stillo*. Thus the Latin *limus*, mud, appears to be related to our *slime*, and *limus*, askance, to the Low German *slim*; and as a Latin word cannot commence with *sl*, it is very likely that the sibilant may have been rejected. Many similar phænomena might be pointed out, some of which may perhaps become the subject of a separate paper. At present we shall conclude this division of our subject with observing, that an accurate knowledge of the permutations of sound in cognate languages is the very foundation of all rational etymology. Much has been undoubtedly accomplished in this department, but large fields still remain comparatively unnexplored. It is believed that the light which might be thrown on this subject by a careful study of the peculiarities of the Celtic languages, renders them eminently worthy of the attention of philologists.

In proceeding to give some account of the dialects which immediately succeeded, and to a considerable extent supplanted the British Celtic, it is proposed to commence with those peculiar to our Northern provinces, not as being necessarily first in order, but as those which upon the whole are the most susceptible of classification and illustration.

As the invading Saxons consisted of several different tribes, it is reasonable to presume, from known analogies, that diversities of dialect already prevailed among them; and this presumption is confirmed by incidental expressions of Bede and other early writers. The Mercians of the midland provinces, the three divisions of East, Middle and North Angles, and the Northumbrians, extending from the Humber to the Forth, are distinctly stated to have been descendants of the Angli, who were a powerful tribe on the continent as early as the time of Tacitus. We know that those northern tribes had their popular and religious poetry, and, in process of time, vernacular translations from the Scriptures and other devotional works, entirely or chiefly in their own dialect. For example: the poems of Cædmon, a native of the north-east of Yorkshire, were not, we may presume, originally in the ordinary West-Saxon dialect, in which we now have them, but in the form exhibited in the specimen, unfortunately very brief, printed by Wanley from an ancient manuscript. An elaborate analysis of the peculiarities of this fragment, by Professor Halbertsma, will be found in the introduction to Dr. Bosworth's Anglo-Saxon Dictionary. The Runic inscription on the Ruthwell Cross, illustrated by Mr. Kemble, and the verses said to have been pronounced by Bede on his death-bed, as given in the St. Gallen manuscript of Cuthbert's letter, relating his last moments, present the same peculiarities of form and orthography, but they are too scanty to afford us anything approaching to

12*

a view of the dialect as a whole. Some monuments have however survived the general wreck of the Northumbrian and Anglian literature, of considerable value in a philological point of view. The first in time and importance, but which has not hitherto met with the attention that it deserves, is the Cotton MS. in the British Museum, Vespasian A. I., a Latin Psalter of the seventh century, with an interlineary Anglo-Saxon gloss, apparently of the ninth century, or possibly still earlier. A short comparison of this gloss with the Psalter published by Spelman, or any other of the ordinary West-Saxon texts, will show that it differs from them considerably in orthography, in grammatical forms, and, not unfrequently, in its vocabulary also. In short, it is not West-Saxon, but belonging to the Anglian class of dialects; and its general correspondence with other known monuments, to be noticed hereafter, renders it highly probable that it emanated either from Northumbria or some adjoining locality. A regular specification of all its peculiarities would occupy too much space, and would require a fuller examination of the MS. than it has hitherto received. Occasionally too the MS. fluctuates between common West-Saxon and Anglian forms; but the latter have such a preponderance as to give a decided character to the text. Among orthographical peculiarities, the most prominent is the regular substitution, of *oe* for the broad *e* of the West-Saxon, corresponding to *uo* in Old High-German and the accented *ó*, and occasionally *ae* in Icelandic: e. gr.

boen, *prayer;* West-Saxon, bén.
boec, *books;*   ,,   béc.
coelan, *to cool;*   ,,   célan.
doeman, *to judge;*   ,,   déman.
foedan, *to feed;*   ,,   fédan.
spoed, *fortune;*   ,,   spéd.
swoet, *sweet;*   ,,   swét.
woenan, *to think;*   ,,   wénan.

The analogy of the cognate dialects shows that the Anglian is the more original form.

Other variations in vowels and diphthongs, though pretty frequent, are not so constant as the above. There is a general tendency to substitute simple sounds for complex ones: e. gr. *a* for the West-Saxon *ea: all*, omnis, W.-S. *eall: e* for *æ: deg*, day, W.-S. *dæg*; *fet*, vessel, W.-S. *fæt;* also for *eo: leht*, light, W.-S. *leoht:* occasionally *o* for *u: thorh*, through, W.-S. *thurh*. A thorough examination of the MS. might perhaps enable us to discover and classify other peculiar forms.

The grammatical inflexions also present noticeable variations from the ordinary type. The plural of feminine nouns in the sixth form of Rask commonly ends in *e: theode*, populi, W.-S. *theoda*. Feminines in *u* preserve that vowel throughout the singular: e. gr. *gifu*, gift; gen. dat. acc. *gifu*, instead of W.-S. *gife*. The same vowel occurs in many adjectives and participles feminine, where the ordinary dialect has more frequently *e:* as *micclu*, magna, W.-S. *mycle*. In the personal pronouns, the accusatives *mec, thec, usic, eowic*, answering to the German *mich, dich, euch*, are of regular occurrence. In the demonstrative pronoun or article, the nom. fem. is generally *sie* instead of *seo*, and in the oblique cases *e* takes place of *æ:* e. gr. gen. *thes, there*, W.-S. *thæs, thære*. The dative masc. and neut. in both numbers is uniformly *thæn*, a form deserving of notice for its correspondence with the Mœso-Gothic *thaim*. Passing over a number of other minute variations in nouns and pronouns, we may observe that the most marked characteristic of the dialect appears in the first person singular of the present indicative of regular verbs, which uniformly terminates in *u* or *o*, presenting a close analogy to the Old Saxon and Lithuanian, but long obsolete in the West-Saxon. Thus *getreowu*, I believe; *cleopiu*, I call; *sellu*, I give; *ondredu*, I fear; *sitto*, I sit; *drinco*, I drink; *ageldu*, I pay or yield, where a later hand has added l'. [vel] *offrige*; *getimbru*, instruam; gloss *a secunda manu*, l'. *lacre*; according to the ordinary dialect. The second person generally ends in *s* instead of *st*, both in the present and imperfect: *neosas*, thou visitest; *acerres*, thou turnest away; *gesettes*, thou placest; *lufedes*, thou lovedst; *gewonades*, thou diminishedst; *neasades*, thou visitedst; *smiredes*, thou didst anoint; where it will be observed that *edes* or *ades* is substituted for the ordinary ending of the second person imperf. *odest*. The third pers. pl. imperf. also frequently ends in *un — fuledun*, they became corrupt, W.-S. *fu!odon*, — another point of agreement with the Old-Saxon. The verb substantive has also several peculiarities, the most remarkable of which is the plural of the present indicative *earun* (sumus, estis, sunt), the original of the English *are*, but totally unknown in West-Saxon. Another important characteristic of the dialect is the frequent omission of the prefix *ge* in past participles: *hered*, praised, W.-S. *geherod*; *bledsad*, blessed, W.-S. *gebletsod*; *soth*, sought, W.-S. *gesoht*; thus approximating in some degree to the Norse tongues. The importance of this characteristic will appear when we come to classify the more recent dialects.

The documents which we have next to consider belong to

a period when lapse of time and external causes appear to
have affected in some degree the purity of the dialect; but,
in recompense, we have the advantage of knowing pretty
accurately to what locality and what age they are to be referred.   We here allude to the gloss of the celebrated Durham Gospels (Cotton MS. Nero, D. 4.), and that of the
'Rituale Ecclesiæ Dunelmensis,' lately edited for the Surtees Society by Mr. Stevenson.   A chronological note in
the latter document fixes the date of a portion of the MS.
in A. D. 970, and the identity of the dialect, and it is also
believed of the hand-writing in both, conspire with all the
external evidence which we posses, to induce us to refer
the whole Anglo-Saxon portion to Durham or its vicinity, in
the tenth century.   These texts agree with that of the Psalter in the general cast of the orthography: e. gr. in substituting *a* for the West-Saxon *ea: all*, omnis; *arm*, brachium:
e for *æ*: *feger*, pulcher; and for *eo*: *lcht*, lumen: *oe* for *é*:
doema, judicare.   On the other hand, there are various peculiarities sufficient to give a distinct character to the text;
one of the most remarkable of which is the frequent substitution of *i* for *e* both in simple syllables and diphthongs:
gilef for *gelef*, *mægi* for *mægc*, *thiostrum* for *theostrum*, *hiara* for
heara [W.-S. *heora*], *iwer* for *eower*.   The differences in grammatical forms may be attributed partly to the effect of time
and partly to extraneous influences.   In the first person of
verbs, *o* is much more frequent than *u*: *fehto*, pugno; *beto*,
castigo; *wuldrigo*, glorior.   The plural ð is commonly softened down to *s*: *biddas*, precamur; *giwoedes*, induite; *wyrcas*,
facite.   The final *n* is generally dropped in infinitives: *gi-
mersiga*, celebrare; *cuoetha*, dicere; *inngeonga*, intrare.   The
oblique cases and plurals of weak nouns (Rask's 1st class)
drop the final *n* in all genders: *hearta*, corda; *earthe* (dat.),
terrâ; *nome* (W.-S. noman), nominis; and not unfrequently
an is converted into *o* or *u*: *ego*, oculi; *witgo* and *witgu*, pro-
phetæ (gen. sing. and nom. plur.).   The last two peculiarities
approximate to the Icelandic, which also drops the final *n*,
and as they do not occur in the older text of the Psalter,
they may possibly be the results of an intermixture with
the Northmen.   The writer has not met with purely Scandinavian *words*, either in the Gospels or the Ritual; but a
friend, well acquainted with the former MS., informs him
that *by*, a town or village, and *at*, the prefix to the Norse
infinitive, occur once or twice.   It is proper to observe that two
of the above supposed indications of a more recent age also
occur on the Ruthwell Cross, namely the infinitive in *a*:
halda for *hyldan*, or *healdjan*; and the termination of weak

nouns in *u* for *an*: *an galgu* for *on gealgan*. If therefore this
monument is to be referred to the ante-Danish period, which
the history of the district would rather incline us to suppose,
those peculiarities, and perhaps some others, must be considered as belonging to this particular subdivision of the
dialect. Possibly the Ruthwell and Durham texts may be
Northumbrian, in the strict sense of the word, and the
Psalter, Anglian or Mercian.

The last considerable text of this class is the gloss to the
Bodleian MS., commonly called the Rushworth Gospels, respecting the locality of which we can form at least a probable presumption. The gloss was the work of two scribes,
Owen and Farmenn, the latter of whom describes himself as
priest at *Harawuda* or Harewood. The only Harewood specified in the Domesday survey is the well-known place of
that name in Wharfdale in Yorkshire; and the analogy of
the dialect to that of the Durham texts enables us to fix the
origin of it with tolerable certainty in a northern county,
as likely York as any other. Wanley, who was a good
judge of the age of MSS., refers the Saxon portion of it to
the end of the ninth or the beginning of the tenth century.
It appears indeed, from the grammatical forms, to be somewhat older than the Durham Gospels, but in all material
points the dialect is the same. A connected specimen, in
which the discrepancies from the ordinary West-Saxon are
specified, will show the nature of the text more satisfactorily
than the enumeration of isolated words. It is observable
that the earlier portion of the gloss, executed by Farmenn,
approximates in several points to the ordinary dialect, where
that of his coadjutor Owen agrees closely with the Durham
texts. For example, in the Gospel of St. Matthew, the present indicative commonly ends in *e* and the infinitive in *an*:
sprece, loquor; *sprecan*, loqui. Phenomena of this kind may
be attributed to the political and literary preponderance of
the West-Saxon branch in the ninth and tenth centuries.

The result of the foregoing investigation is, that there
exists a class of documents exhibiting a marked difference
in orthography and grammatical forms from the ordinary
West-Saxon tongue. Two of these, the Durham Gospels and
the Ritual, may be referred with certainty to the heart of
Northumbria; and another with great probability to the West
Riding of Yorkshire, in a locality where, at this day, a
river forms the boundary between the Northumbrian and
North-Anglian dialects. The remaining one, the Cotton
Psalter, cannot with certainty be proved to be of Northum-
brian origin, geographically speaking; but the general agree-

ment of its forms with those of the other monuments enables us to pronounce with tolerable confidence, that it belongs to that Anglian division of which the Northumbrian was a branch. It is moreover the oldest and purest considerable specimen of that class, and therefore occupies an important place among the Teutonic dialects, to the general grammar and analogies of which it affords many valuable illustrations. It is hardly necessary to say that all the documents of which we have been treating are of the highest importance for the study and elucidation of our vernacular dialects; and we may be allowed to express a hope that they will ere long be rendered more * available to the public than they have hitherto been.

Our Lord's dialogue with the woman of Samaria is given as a specimen of the Rushworth text, from which it will be seen to agree more generally with the Durham monuments than with the Psalter. A comparison of the corresponding passage from the Hatton Gospels will show that the latter text, though upwards of two centuries later, preserves, with but slight deviations, the grammatical forms of the West-Saxon; thus proving that the leading peculiarities of the glosses are inherent in the dialect, and not the corruptions of a more recent period.

John iv. 1—26. Want of access to the Rushworth and Hatton MSS. has made it necessary to trust to a transcript, occasionally, it is feared, of doubtful accuracy. The Hatton text is that of the ordinary Anglo-Saxon Gospels, with slight verbal and orthographical variations. The Rushworth gloss, like all others of the same character, adheres servilely to the order and phraseology of the Latin, of which it frequently mistakes the true sense. Consequently it is totally subversive of the vernacular idiom, and is chiefly valuable for its grammatical forms.

RUSHWORTH GOSPELS.	HATTON GOSPELS.
John, chap. iv.	John, chap. iv.
Thæt forthon [the hælend] ongætt [thætte] giberdon tha *alde* wearas thætte *the* hæl[end]monige thegnas wyrceth and *fulwath* thonne loh' [annes]: *thch* the, I' swa he, *the* hæl' ne *fulwade* ah thegnas his: forleort Judeam cor-	Tha se hælend wiste thæt tha Pharisei ge hyrden thæt he hæfde ema [ma] lcorning-cnihta thonne Johannes: theah se hælend ne fullode ac hys leorning-cnihtas: Tha forlet he Judea land and for eft on Galilea. hym gebyrede thæt

---

* The writer may be allowed to state that the Psalter is now printing for the Surtees Society, under the superintendence of the Rev. Joseph Stevenson.

tho and *foerde* efter sona in Galileam. wæs *gi* dæfendlic wutudl' [ice] hine thætte of' [er] *foerde therh* tha burig [Samaria]. com forthon in tha cæstre Samar', *thio* is gicweden Sichar, neh *thær byrig* thætte *salde* Jacob Josepes suno his. wæs wutudl' ther wælla Jacobes. The hæl' forthon *woerig* wæs of gonge, sitende wæs, l' sat, swa ofer thæm *woella*: tid wæs swelce *thio* sexta. wif [com] of *thær byrig* to hladanne thæt wæter, cwæth him *the* hæl'; *sel* me *drinca.* thegnas wutudl'. *foerdun* in cæstre thætte mete *bohtun* him. cwæth f' thon to him thæt wif *thio* Samaritanesca, hu thu Judesc mith thy *arth* drincende from me *giowes* tu tha the mith thy wif's [sio?] Samaritanesc? ne for thon *gibyrelic* bith Judea to Samaritaniscum. giondswarade *the* hæl' and cwæth him, gif thu *wistes* hus [*domum*, Lat.] Godes and hwelc were se the cwæth the *sel* me *drinca* thu wutudl'. l' woenis mara, gif thu *georwades* [giowades?] from him and [he] *gisalde* the wæter cwic welle. cwæth to him thæt wif, driht [en] ne m [in?] hwon tha hlado hæfest thu, and the pytt neh is: hwona, l' hwer, forthon hæfest thu wæter cwic welle? ah ne *arthu* mara feder usum Jacobe sethe *salde* us *thiosne* pytt, l' *wælla*, and he of him dranc and suno his and feothor fota, l' neæno [netenu], his? giondsworade the hæl' and cwæth, eghwelc sethe drinceth of wætre this [* thæt ic *seld*] [selo?] in ecnisse: sethe wutudl' drinceth of wætre thæt ic seld him ne thyrstæ in ecnisse. ah wæter thæt ic

he scolde faran thurh Samaria land. witelice he com on Samarian cestre the ys genemned Sichar neah tham tune the Jacob sealde Josepe his sune. thær wæs Jacobes wylle. se hælend sæt æt tham welle, tha he wæs werige gan: and hyt wæs mid-dayg. tha com thær an wif of Samaria wolde water feccan. Tha cwæth se hælend to hyre, gyf me drincan. hys leorning-cnihtes ferdon tha to thare ceastre woldon heom mete beggen. Tha cwæth thæt Samaritanisse wif to hym, hu mete bydst thu ad me drinken thonne thu ert Judeisc and ic em Samaritanisc wyf? ne brucath Judeas and Samaritanisce metes ætgadere. Tha answerede se hælend and cwæth to hyre, gif thu wistes Godes gyfe and hwæt se ys he cwæth to the, sele me drinken, witodlice thu bede hyne thæt he sealde the lyfes wæter. tha cwæth thæt wif to hym, leofne, thu nafst nan thing mid to hladene, and thes pett ys deop: hwanen hafst thu lyfes wæter? cwest thu thæt thu mare sy thonne ure fader Jacob se the us thisne pyt scalde, and he and hys bearn and hys nytanu of tham druncan? Tha andswerede se hæl' and cwæth to hyre, ælc thare therst eft the of thisse wætere drinketh; witodlice ælc thare the drincth of tham watere the ic hym sylle beoth on him wylla forth færendes wæteres on ece lyf. tha cwæth thæt wif to him, hlaford sele me thæt me ne therste, ne ic ne thurfe her water fecchan. tha cwæth sa [se] halend to hyre, ga and clype

---

* A blunder for *thyrsteth.*

seld him bith in *thœm* wælla wætres *saltes* in life ecum. cwæth him thæt wif, drih' sel me this wæter thæt ic ne thyrste, ne ic ne *cymo* hider to hladanne, l' to fyllanne. cwæth him *the* h' [ælend], ceig were thinum and cym hither. ondsworade thæt wif and cwæth him ne *hafo* ic wer. cwæth to hir *the* hæl' wel thu cwede thætte ic ne *hafo* wer. fife forthon weoras thu *hæfdes* and nu thonne *hæfes* ne is thin wer. this sothlice thu cwede. cwæth him thæt wif drih' ic *gisiom* forthon *witgu arth* thy [thu]. fædres ures on more thissum *giworthadun* and gie *cweothas* thætte in hierus' [alem] is *thio* stow ther *giworthade* ge *gidæfnath* is. cwæth hire the hæl' la wif *gilef* mé forthon com *thio* tid thonne ne on morum thissum ne in hierusal' to worth*adun* thone fæder. gie *worthigas* thætte we [gie] ne *wutun*. we wordigath thætte we *wutun* we; thætte f' thon hælo of Judeum. ah com *thio* tid and nu is thone sothlice weorthigas ge-worthadun thon fæder in gaste and mith sothfæst' [nisse]. f' thon and the fæder hiæ *soeceth thuslico* f'thon geworthigas hine. in gaste and sothfæstnisse us *gidæfnath* to worthanne. cwæth to him thæt wif, ic wat thætte the *gicorna* com * * * * * *gisægeth alle.* cwæth hir the hæl' ic *am* sethe ic *spreco thec* mith.

thinne cheorl and cum hider. tha hym answerede thus thæt wif and cwæth, nabbe is nænne cheorl. tha cwæth se halend to hyre, wel thu cwethe thæt thu næfst ceorl. witodlice thu hafst fif cheorles, and se the thu nu hafst nis thin ceorl: æt tham thu segdest soth. Tha cwæth thæt wif to hym, leof, thas me thincth thu ert witega. ure faderes hyo gebeden on thissene dune and ge secgeth thæt on Jerusalem syo stow the thæt man on gebydde. Tha cwæth se halend to hyre; la wif, gelef me thæt seo tid cymth thonne ge ne hiddeth tham fader ne on thisse dune ne on Jerusalem. ge gebiddeth thæt ge nyten. we gebiddeth thæt we witon; for tham the hale is of Judeum. ac seo tid cymth and nu ys thonne sothe ge-bedmen biddeth thonne father on gaste and on sothfæstnysse. witodlice se fader secth swilce the hyne gebiddeth. gast ys God and tham the hine biddeth gebyreth thæt hyo gebidden on gaste and on sothfæstnysse. Thæt wif cwæth to him, ic wat thæt Messias cymth, thæt ys ge-nemned Crist, thonne he cymth he cyth us ealle thing. se hælend cwæth to hyre, ic hyt em the with the sprece.

Unfortunately there is a complete chasm of several centuries in the literary history and monuments of the Northumbrian dialects; no considerable specimen being extant exhibiting their state in the eleventh, twelfth, or thirteenth centuries.

In the fourteenth we find abundant remains, and such as entitle the Northumbrian to rank as a leading literary dialect. It may be questioned indeed whether the productions of the northern bards did not exceed those of their brethren in the south in number and merit, prior to the appearance of Gower and Chaucer. Our present business however is with their language, which, when compared with that of the Durham Gospels, will be found to have undergone a considerable change. Of the Saxon declensions of nouns little remains except the genitive singular; the definite or emphatic form of the adjective has totally disappeared; the article (*se, sie,* þæt) appears in the form *the* in all genders; the feminine pronoun of the third person (*hie* or *hyo*) becomes *she* or *scho*; the genitive plural *heara* or *hiara* (*eorum, earum*) is superseded by the possessive *their*; and the first person of the present indicative in *o* or *u,* the most remarkable characteristic of the ancient dialect, is attenuated to *e.* The plurals of verbs in *s,* which in the Durham and Rushworth texts appear along with the more ancient form in *th,* are generally retained, especially in the imperative mood; while the prefix *ge,* which there was already a tendency to omit in Northumbrian Saxon as early as the days of Bede, is scarcely to be met with in the fourteenth century, except in the single participle *ihaten* (called or named). Many words are also found which do not occur in the earlier texts, or in the West-Saxon dialect. Some of these were in all probability current among the Angles, but there are many others which do not appear to have ever been Saxon, in the strict sense of the term. The history of the district would lead us *à priori* to attribute the introduction of them to the Northmen ; and we have both external and internal evidence that such a process actually took place. Giraldus Cambrensis and John of Wallingford assert in direct terms that there was a strong infusion of Danish in the population and the language of our northern provinces; and, if confirmation of their testimony were needed, it would be abundantly supplied by the names of landed proprietors preserved in the Domesday Survey, by the present topographical nomenclature of the district, and by a multitude of words,-unequivocally of Norse origin. The change of the local name Streoneshalch to Hvitby or Whitby, consequent on the Danish occupation of the district, is well-ascertained, and it is believed that all the names of towns and villages in *by* in the north and east of England are of similar origin. Derby, for example, did not receive its present name till the ninth or tenth century, its original Saxon appellation being Northweorthig.

A remarkable coeval monument, both of the state of the population and of the language, which there are good reasons for attributing to the age of Edward the Confessor, is

still extant in Aldburgh church, Holderness, in the East
Riding of Yorkshire; it is an inscription commemorating the
foundation of the edifice, or more probably of a preceding
one, in the following terms:

Ulf het aræan cyrice for *hanum* and for Gunthara saula*.

Ulf bid erect the church for him and for the soul of Gunthar.

Waving the consideration of those points which more immediately concern the historian and the antiquary, it will be
sufficient for us to observe that the name of the founder
Ulf is unequivocally Norse, the Anglo-Saxon form being
Wulf; and that the form of the dative pronoun *hanum* is
unknown in all Saxon dialects, being in fact identical with
the Old-Norse *hanum*,** Swedish *honom*. A comparison of
the Icelandic Landnama Bok or Roll of Proprietors with the
Domesday Survey of Yorkshire would furnish many coincidences of names of general occurrence in the Scandinavian
provinces, but not known as Anglo-Saxon or German.

It appears that this admixture of the Northmen in the
population of the Northumbrian provinces had not produced
its full effect upon the language in the tenth century; as,
with the exception of one or two isolated words, there is
nothing that can be satisfactorily referred to that class of
dialects, either in the Durham texts or the Rushworth Gospels. In the fourteenth century the traces of this influence
become much stronger. The 'Cursor Mundi' and the Northumbrian metrical version of the Psalms abound with words
totally unknown in the Saxon dialects, but of regular occurrence in Icelandic, Danish and Swedish. One of the most
remarkable of these is the Scandinavian prefix to infinitives,
at think, *at do*, instead of *to think*, *to do;* which, as Mr. Stevenson justly observes,*** is an unequivocal criterion of a
purely northern dialect, and an equally certain one of the
Scandinavian influence whereby that dialect has been modified. Its retention in the present local speech of Westmoreland † is a sufficient proof of its being truly vernacular.
Another remarkable Scandinavianism is the particle *sum* in

---

* Archæologia, vol. vi. p. 40. There is some doubt whether the second
name should be read Gunthar or Gunwar. Brooke, the author of the paper
in the 'Archæologia,' translates *"for hanum"* *"pro Hano"* as if it were a
proper name, contrary to all grammar.

** As extant in Runic inscriptions. The present Icelandic form is *hönum*.

*** Boucher's Glossary, *v. at.*

† Vide Wheeler's Dialogues, first published in 1794. The first para-
graph of the prefatory discourse furnishes the two following examples: —
"I hed lile *et* dea," "I had little to do;" "A wark ets fit for nin but parson
et dea," "A work that's fit for none but a parson to do."

the sense of *as*, Danish *som*: e. g. "swa sum we forgive oure detturs," so as we forgive our debtors. This form appears to be now obsolete; but *war* for *was*, Dan. *var; war*, worse, Dan. *raerre;* and the apparently ungrammatical inflexions of the present tense singular, *I, thou, he thinks*, perfectly analogous to the Danish *jeg, du, han taenker*, are still regularly current in North Yorkshire. Besides these we find, both in ancient and modern times, *braid* to resemble, Swedish *bråas;* "han bräas på sin fader;" in Yorkshire, "he *braids* on his father," *i. e.* takes after or resembles him; *eldin* firing, Dan. *eld* fire; *force* waterfall, Isl. *fors; gar* make or cause, Isl. *göra; gill* ravine, narrow valley, Isl. *gil; greet* weep, Isl. *gråta; ket* carrion, Dan. *kiöd* flesh; *lait* seek, Dan. *lede; lathe* barn, Dan. *lade; lite* little, Dan. *lille;* with innumerable others, either totally unknown in Anglo-Saxon or found under perfectly distinct forms. It is proper to observe that some of those words and forms are not peculiar to the Northumbrian district, but are also current in the North-Anglian dialect of the West Riding of Yorkshire, where they were equally introduced by the Danes.

It would lead us too far to discuss the distinctive peculiarities of the different subdivisions of the Northumbrian dialect. A form of speech, extending at one time from the Humber to the Forth, and from the German Ocean to the Irish Channel, could hardly be expected to preserve a perfect uniformity under the various influences, both social and political, to which it has been subjected during eight or nine centuries. At present we find the Northumbrian proper, including North and East Yorkshire, the lowland Scottish of the Lothians, the Cumberland and Westmoreland dialects, and the North Lancashire, all to exhibit their respective features of difference; chiefly consisting in minutiæ that it would be difficult to make intelligible in a small compass. A little knowledge of those characteristics would however have proved very serviceable to our editors of ancient poetry and compilers of glossaries, who have created no small confusion by assuming many compositions to be Scottish which were in all probability written between the Humber and the Tyne, certainly to the south of the Tweed. Thus Jamieson cites as Scotch at least a dozen works which have no real claim to that character; and Sir Walter Scott has grounded a variety of theories respecting the composition of Sir Tristrem on the supposed fact of its having been produced within the Scottish border. The writer has elsewhere* given his rea-

* Warton's History of English Poetry, vol. i. p. 109. ed. 1840.

sons at length for believing it to have been a Northumbrian poem, the only existing copy of which was transcribed and considerably altered in a midland county. The 'Proces of the Sevyn Sages' was edited by Weber from the Auchinleck MS. under the gratuitous idea that it afforded the purest and most original text. He speaks disparagingly of the Cotton MS. (Galba, E. 9.), pronouncing it to have been altered by a Scottish transcriber. The truth is, that the Cotton text is not Scottish but pure Northumbrian; and a careful comparison of the two will, it is believed, furnish abundant evidence that the Auchinleck copy is a *rifaccimento* or adaptation of the original Northumbrian text to the dialect of the midland counties, not always very skilfully executed. The same process appears to have been exercised on 'Havelock the Dane,' though more of the northern character has been preserved; and there are also copies of the 'Cursor Mundi' in Midland English, though it can be easily proved it was originally written in Northumbrian. This was in fact the literary dialect of the whole North of England, and no native of that district would have written anything in Southern English which he meant to have currency among his immediate neighbours. A short extract from the 'Cursor Mundi' will place this point in a clear light. Speaking of a legend of „our Levedi and Saint John," the author states: —

> "In a writte this ilke I fand;
> Himself it wroght I understand.
> In suthrin Englys was it drawn,
> And I have turnid it til ur awn
> Langage of the northern lede
> That can non other Englis rede."

The number of the literary monuments of Northumbria, from the fourteenth to the sixteenth century, precludes us from giving anything like a general view of them, or attempting to specify the changes which gradually took place in the language. As it may not however be uninteresting to compare its earlier with its declining state, a specimen of each is exhibited for that purpose. The first is taken from the Northumbrian Metrical Psalter, Cotton MSS., Vespasian, D. 7.

TWENTY-THIRD [TWENTY-FOURTH] PSALM.

> Of Laverd is land & fulhed his;
> Erþeli werld & alle par in is.
> For over sees it grounded he,

And over stremes graiþed it to be.
Wha sal stegh in hille of Laverd wiuli,
Or wha sal stand in his stede hali?
Underand of hend bidene,
And þat of his hert es clene;
In unnait þat his saule noght nam,
Ne sware to his neghburgh in swikedam.
He sal fang of Laverd blissinge,
And mercy of God his helinge.
Þis is the strend of him sekand,
Pe face of God Jacob laitand.
Oppenes your yates wide,
Ye þat princes ere in pride,
And yhates of ai uphefen be yhe,
And king of blisse income sal he.
Wha es he king of blisse? Laverd strang,
And mightand to fight, Laverd mightand lang.

Oppenes, &c.
Wha es he king of blisse at isse?
Laverd of mightes es king of blisse.

It is worth while to observe how many pure Saxon and Norse terms occur in this short piece, most of them now supplanted by words of Latin origin: viz. *graithed* prepared, *stegh* ascended, *winli* gracious, *underand* innocent, *unnait* vanity, *swikedam* deceitfulness, *fang* receive, *strend* generation, *laitand* inquiring, *uphefen* elevated. Many of these terms have a singular emphasis to those who understand the etymology of them; *underand*, for example, is the precise counterpart of Lat. *innocens*. A careful study of the remains of our language, as written and spoken in the thirteenth and fourteenth centuries, will indeed show that a vast number of Latin and Romance words have been since introduced without being absolutely needed.

Our next specimen is from the York Mysteries, formerly in the library of Lord Orford and afterwards in the possession of Mr. Bright. This collection is interesting on many accounts, and not the least so as being an undoubted and authentic specimen of the language of the city of York during the latter part of the fourteenth century. At that time the speech of the southern parts of the island had begun to make considerable inroads upon that of the more cultivated classes in the north, and a great portion of the Mysteries is almost as much metropolitan as Northumbrian. Fortunately an older copy of the play describing the creation of our first parents, has been preserved along with the more recent revision. Though this, as compared with the 'Cursor Mundi' or the Psalter, is much softened down, it still retains strong traces of its original Northumbrian character. The various readings are from the more recent copy.

YORK MYSTERIES.

CARDMAKER'S PLAY.

Deus. In hevyn and erthe duly bedene,
Of v. days werke evyn on to ende,
I have complete by curssis clene;
Me thynke ye space of yame well spende.

In hevyn er angels fayre and brighte,
Sternes and planetis yar curssis to ga[1].
Ye mone servis on to ye nyght,
The son to lyghte ye day alswa[2].

In erthe is treys and gres to springe;
Bestis and foulys bothe gret and smalle;
Fysschis in flode; alle othyr thyng
Thryffe and have my blyssyng alle.

This werke is wroght now at my wille;
But ȝet can I no best see
Yat acordys be kynde and skyll,
And for my werke myght worschippe me.

For perfytte werke ne ware it nane[3],
But ought ware made y^t myght it ȝeme.
For love mad I yis warlde[4] alane[5]:
Therfor my loffe sall[6] in it seme.

To kepe this warlde[4] bothe mare[7] and lesse,
A skylfulle best yane wille I make
Eftyr my schape and my lyknes,
The wilke salle[6] worschippe to my [me] take.

Off ye symplest part of erthe y^t is here
I sall[6] make man, and for yis skylle,
For to abate his hauttande chere,
Bothe his gret pride and other ille.

---

[1] B. goo.   [2] also.   [3] none.   [4] worlde.   [5] alone.   [6] shalle.   [7] more.

OF THE BRITISH ISLANDS.

And also for to have in mynde
How simpylle he is at hys makyng.
For als febylle I sall[6] fynde hym
Qwen he is dede at his endynge.

For yis reson and skylle alane[8],
I sall[6] make man lyke on to me.
Ryse up y^u erthe in blode and bane[9],
In schape of man I commaunde the.

A female sall[10] y^u have to fere;
Her sall[6] I make of y^i lyft[11] rybe:
Alane[8] so sall[6] y^u nought be here
Withoutyn faythefull frende and sybe.

Takys now here ye gast[12] of lyffe
And ressayve bothe youre saules[13] of me.
The femalle take y^u to y^i wyffe;
Adam and Eve your names salle[6] be.

Adam. A lorde! full mekyll is y^i mighte;
And yat is sene in ilke a syde.
For now his here a joyfull syght,
To se yis worlde so lange[14] and wyde.

Mony[15] divers thyngis now here es
Off bestis and foulis bothe wylde and tame:
Ʒet is nan made to y^e [y^i] liknes,
But we alone; a lovyd by y^i name!

Eve. To swylke a lorde in all ye degre
Be evirmore lastande lovynge,
Yat tyll[16] us swylke[17] a dyngnite
Has gyffyne before alle othyr thynge.

And selcouth thyngis may we se here
Of yis ilke warlde, so lange[14] and brade[18],
With bestis and fowlis so many and sere:
Blessid be he y^t [hase] us made!

---

[8] allone.   [9] bone.   [10] shalte.   [11] lefte.   [12] goste.   [13] soules.
[14] longe.   [15] many.   [16] to.   [17] suche.   [18] broode.

Adam. A blyssid lorde! now at y^i wille
    Syne [19] we er wroght, woche saff to telle,
    And also say us two un tylle
    Qwate [20] we sall [6] do and whare [21] to dwelle.

Deus. For yis skyl made I ȝow yis day
    My name to worschip ay whare [21].
    Lovys me for y^i and lovys me ay
    For my makyng, — I axke no mare [22].

    Bothe wys and witty sall [6] y^u be,
    Als man y^t I have made of noght.
    Lordschippe in erthe yan graunt I the;
    Alle thynge to serve the y^t I have wroghte.

    In paradyse salle [6] ȝe same wone:
    Of erthely thyng get ȝe no nede:
    Ille and gude [23] both salle [6] ȝe kone:
    I salle [6] ȝou lerne ȝoure lyve to lede.

Adam. A lorde! sene we salle [6] do no thyng,
    But louffe y^e for y^i gret gudnesse [24],
    We sall [6] ay bay to y^i byddyng,
    And fulfill it both more and less.

Eve. His syng sone he has on us sette
    Beforne alle othre thyng certayne.
    Hem for to love we sall [6] noght lett,
    And worschip hym with myght and mayne.

Deus. At hevyne and erth first I begane,
    And vi days wroghte or I walde [25] ryst.
    My warke is endyde now at mane;
    Alle lykes me welle, but yis is beste.

    My blyssyng have yai ever and ay!
    The seveynte day sall [6] my restyng be:
    Yus wille I sese, sothely to say,
    Of my doyng in y^is degre.

---

[19] sethen.   [20] whatte.   [21] where.   [22] more.   [23] goode.   [24] goodnesse.
[25] wolde.

To blys I salle[6] ȝow bryng:
Comys forth ȝe tow with me!
Ȝe salle[6] lyffe in lykyng;
My blyssyng wyth ȝow be. — Amen.

Here, besides a gradual approximation of the orthography to the southern standard, it will be observed that the forms *nane*, *alane*, *warlde*, *lange*, *brade*, &c. become in the later copy *none*, *alone*, *world*, *long*, *broad*; and that the Northumbrianisms *swa*, *gude*, *sall*, *swilke*, *til*, have respectively become *so*, *good*, *shall*, *such*, *to*. The present participle in *and*, a certain criterion of a northern dialect subsequent to the thirteenth century, and the imperative plural in *s*, with a few other peculiarities, are preserved in both copies.

ON THE PROBABLE RELATIONS OF THE PICTS AND GAEL

WITH

THE OTHER TRIBES OF GREAT BRITAIN.

[*Proceedings of the Philological Society. Vol. I.*]

It is scarcely necessary to observe, that there are few points of ethnology on which historians and antiquaries have been more at variance with each other, than respecting the real race of those inhabitants of a portion of Caledonia popularly known by the designation of Picts. The difficulty arising from this discrepancy of opinion is increased by the scanty and unsatisfactory nature of the materials now available to those who wish to form an independent judgement. No connected specimen of the Pictish language has been preserved; nor has any ancient author who knew them from personal observation, stated in direct terms that they approximated to one adjoining tribe more than another. They are indeed associated with the Scots or Irish as joint plunderers of the colonial Britons; and the expression of Gildas that they differed in some degree from the Scots in their customs, might seem to imply that they *did* bear an analogy to that nation in certain respects. Of course, where there is such a lack of direct evidence, there is more scope for conjecture; and the Picts are pronounced by different investigators of their history to have been Germans, Scandinavians, Welsh, Gael, or something distinct from all the four. The advocates of the German hypothesis rest chiefly on Tacitus's description of their physical conformation. Dr. Jamieson, assuming that the present Lowland Scotch dialect was derived from them, sets them down as Scandinavians; Bishop Lloyd and Camden conceive them to have been of Celtic race, probably related to the Britons; Chalmers, the author of 'Caledonia,' regards them as nothing more than a tribe of Cambrians or Welsh; while Skene, one of the latest authors on the subject, thinks he has proved that they were the ancestors of the present race of Scottish Highlanders.

There is no reason to doubt that there was *some* point of distinction between the Picts and the adjoining tribes. Nennius describes them as one of the four nations then inhabiting Britain; and Bede represents them as distinct from the Britons and the Scots, both in nationality and language. Innes, who was almost the first to throw a little light upon the chaos of ancient Scottish history, considers them to have been those ancient Caledonian tribes who retained their independence; and that their language differed from that of the colonial Britons in having remained unmixed; while that of the latter was partially Romanized. This supposition is probably not far from the truth. That the Picts were actually Celts, and not of Teutonic race, is proved to a demonstration by the names of their kings; of whom a list, undoubtedly genuine from the fifth century downwards, was published by Innes, from a manuscript in the Colbertine library. Some of those appellations are, as far as we know at present, confined to the Pictish sovereigns; but others are well-known Welsh and Gaelic names. They differ, however, slightly in their forms from their Cymric equivalents; and more decidedly so from the Gaelic ones; and, as far as they go, lead to the supposition that those who bore them spoke a language bearing a remote analogy to the Irish with its cognates, but a pretty close one to the Welsh.

In the list furnished by Innes the names *Maelcon*, *Elpin*, *Taran* (i. e. thunder), *Uven* (Owen), *Bargoit*, are those of personages well known in British history or tradition. *Wrgust*, which appears as Fergus in the Irish annals, is the Welsh *Gwrgust*. *Talorg*, *Talorgan*, evidently contain the British word *Tal* forehead, a common element in proper names; ex. gr. *Talhaiarn*, Iron Forehead; *Taliesin*, splendid forehead, &c. *Taleurgain* would signify in Welsh golden or splendid front. Three kings are represented as sons of *Wid*, in the Irish annals *Foit* or *Foith*. In Welsh orthography it would be *Gwydd*, wild; a common name in Brittany at the present day, under the form of *Gwez*. The names *Drust*, *Drostan*, *Wrad*, *Necton* (in Bede *Naitan*), closely resemble the Welsh *Trwst*, *Trwstan*, *Gwriad*, *Nwython*. It will be sufficient to compare the entire list with the Irish or Highland genealogies, to be convinced that there must have been a material distinction betweeen the two branches. Most of the Pictish names are totally unknown in Irish or Highland history, and the few that are equivalent, such as Angus and Fergus, generally differ in form. The Irish annalists have rather obscured the matter, by transforming those names according to their national system of orthography; but it is remarkable that a list in the 'Book of Ballymote,' partly given by Lynch in his 'Cambrensis Eversus,' agrees closely with Innes, even preserving the initial *w* or *u* where the Gaelic would require *f*. This, by the way, is an independdent testimony of the authenticity of the Colbertine list, which, there is reason to believe, was compiled at or near Abernethy, in the very heart of the Pictish territory, and consequently from *original* materials.

The philological inferences to be deduced from this document may be thus briefly summed up; — 1. The names of the Pictish kings are not Gaelic, the majority of them being totally unknown both in the Irish and Highland districts, while the few which have Gaelic equivalents decidedly differ from them in form. Cineod (Kenneth) and Domhnall or Donnel, appear to be the only exceptions. 2. Some of them cannot be identified as Welsh; but the greater number are either identical with or resemble known Cymric names; or approach more nearly to Welsh in structure and orthography than to any other known language. 3. There appears nevertheless to have been a distinction, amounting at all events to a difference in dialect. The Pictish names beginning with *w* would in Welsh have *gw*, as *Gwrgust* for *Wrgust*, and so of the rest. There may have been other differences, sufficient to justify Bede's statement that the Pictish language was distinct from the British, which it might very well be without any impeachment of its claim to be reckoned as closely cognate.

The remaining direct evidence as to the character of the Pictish language unfortunately lies in a very small compass. Almost the only Pictish word given as such by an ancient writer is the wellknown *Pen val* (or, as it appears in the oldest MSS of Beede, *Peann fahel*), the name given by the Picts to the *Wall's End*, or eastern termination of the Vallum of Antoninus. It is scarcely necessary to say the first part of the word is decidedly Cymric; *pen*, head, being contrary to all Gaelic analogy. The latter half might be plausibly claimed as the Gaelic *fal; gwall* being the more common term in Welsh for a wall or rampart, *Fal*, however, does occur in Welsh in the sense of *inclosure*, a signification not very remote.

There is a collateral evidence on this subject which does not appear to have been sufficiently attended to. In the Durham MSS of Nennius, apparently written in the twelfth century, there is an interpolated passage, stating that the spot in question was in the Scottish or Gaelic language called *Cenail*. Innes and others have remarked the resemblance between this appellation and the present Kinneil; but no one appears to have noticed that *Cenail* accurately represents the *pronunciation* of the Gaelic *cean fhail*, literally *head* of *wall*, *f* being quiescent in construction. A remarkable instance of the same suppression occurs in *Athole*, as now written, compared with the *Ath-fothla* of the Irish annalists. Supposing then that *Cenail* was substituted for *Pean fahel* by the Gaelic conquerors of the district, it would follow that the older appellation was *not* Gaelic, and the inference would be obvious. It is proper to observe that the terminus of the wall of Antoninus is commonly placed at Carriden, several miles to the eastward. There are, however, strong reasons for believing that Kinneil was the real termination, which it would be foreign to our particular province to discuss.

Another evidence, and a decisive one if admitted in its literal import, is that the Irish missionary St. Columba was obliged to employ an interpreter when preaching to the Northern Picts. Skene, who regards the Picts as Gael, endeavours to get rid of this by making the interpretation refer to the Latin Bible, not to the saint's discourse; and quotes Adamnanus as saying merely "verbum Dei per interpretatorem recepto." The entire passage, as it stands in Colganus, is as follows: — "Alio in tempore quo Sanctus Columba in Pictorum provincia per aliquot demorabatur dies, quidam cum tota plebeius familia, verbum *vitæ* per interpretatorem, *Sancto prædicante viro*, audiens credidit, credensque baptizatus est." — *Adamn. ap. Colganum*, l. ii. c. 32. Here it will be observed, Adamnanus does not say "verbum Dei" which might have been construed to mean the Scripture, but "verbum *vitæ*, *sancto prædicante viro*," which can hardly mean any thing but "the word of life, as it was preached by the saint." A subsequent biographer will inform us how he understood the passage. There is a voluminous Irish life of St. Columba by Magnus O'Donnel, who states that he diligently consulted all sources of information then extant (*i. e.* about A. D. 1500), among which were some very ancient vernacular biographies. In the abstract of O'Donnel's work given by the Bollandists, the transaction already referred to is described in the following terms: — "Demorante viro Sancto in prædicta Pictorum regione, ac verbum vitæ gentili populo annunciante, inter alios adfuit quidam plebeius percupidus intelligere quæ prædicabantur. Et quia idiomatis, in quo verba salutis proponebantur, erat ignarus, accivit interpretem per cujus expositionem mysteria fidei a Sancto prædicata attente intelligens, ac aure ac animo devota excipiens, ipse cum uxore, liberis ac tota familia fidem Christi amplexus, salutari lavacro a viro Sancto regeneratus est." — *O'Donnel*, l. ii. c. 75. Here the biographer plainly asserts that the plebeian Pict did not understand St. Columba's language, "idiomatis erat ignarus," consequently his vernacular language was not Gaelic.

Chalmers, who perhaps maintains the absolute identity of the Picts with the Welsh rather too strongly, observes that the ancient topographical appellations of the Pictish territory can in general only be explained by the Cymric dialects, giving as one strong point the number of local names beginning with the Welsh prefix *aber*, which he remarks was in several instances subsequently changed by the Gael into *inver*; *Inverin*, previously *Aberin*; *Invernethy*, formerly *Abernethy*. Skene, who felt the force of this argument, tries to get rid of it by maintaining that *aber* is essentially a Gaelic word, being compounded of *ath*, ford, and *bior*, water; and intimating that it cannot be similarly resolved in Welsh. We shall not stop to remark on the utterly gratuitous nature of this etymology, nor to inquire whetter the estuary of a large river is a suitable place for a ford; but shall merely observe that the term may be much more satisfactorily accounted for by a different process. There are three words in Welsh denoting a meeting of waters; *aber*, *cynver* and *ynver*; respectively compounded of the particles *a*, denoting juxtaposition, *cyn* (Lat. *con*), and *yn*, with the root *ber* flowing, preserved in the Breton verb *beri* to flow, and all virtually equivalent to our word *confluence*. *Inver* is the only term known in any Gaelic dialect, either as an appellative or in proper names; and not a single local appellation with the prefix *aber* occurs either in Ireland, or the Hebrides, or on the west coast of Scotland. Indeed, the fact that *inver* was substituted for it after the Gaelic occupation of the Pictish territories, is decisive evidence on the point; for, if *aber* was a term familiar to the Gael, why should they change it?

It will be sufficient to mention two more local appellations which can only be explained from the Cymric, viz. the *Ochil* Hills in Perthshire, Welsh *uchel*, high; Gael, *uasal*; and *Brun Albain*, according to the author of the tract ' De Situ Albaniæ ' (supposed to be Giraldus Cambrensis), the name of the Dorsum Britanniæ, or ridge dividing the Picts from the Scots; Welsh *bryn*, a ridge. The wellknown Gaelic appellation is *Drum Albain*. *Ochiltree* in Ayrshire, within the limits of the Strath-Clyde Britons, is easily resolved into *uchel*, high, and *tref* or *tre*, hamlet or habitation; and is only mentioned here for the sake of the analogy. *Bryneich* was the British name of the province of Bernicia, quasi *regio montana*.

The Celtic terms adduced by Chalmers from the old Scottish laws are not so conclusive; most of them admitting of explanation from the Gaelic. Those from the Lowland Scotch dialect would be of some weight, if we knew precisely in what part of Scotland they originated; respecting which there is a lack of information. A sufficient number of Cymric words proper to the district between the Forth and the Frith of Murray, would go a great way towards determining the points in dispute; and it is believed that such might be found, if properly sought for.

Respecting the territorial limits of the Picts, we may observe that much confusion has arisen from regarding Galloway as one of their ancient provinces. It is certain that in the age of Bede, and long after, there were no Picts in Galloway, which is uniformly represented as a British province (occasionally encroached upon by the Northumbrian Saxons), from the fifth to the ninth century. It is believed that Jocelin, abbot of Furness in the tenth century, is the earliest author who describes it as a Pictish territory; and subsequently, the Picts of Galloway are mentioned by several authors, down to the twelfth century. Innes supposes them to have been refugees from the Scottish invasion; and Chalmers regards them as emigrants from Ireland, where there were several tribes of Cruithne, of whom little is known except that they were regarded as distinct from the Irish proper. We have now no materials for deciding this question, any further than by remarking that in this later period the term *Picts* was applied with some laxity of signification. After Kenneth Mac Alpin's conquest, the Scottish kings are often called Pictish kings, and kings of the Picts, because they then ruled over the Pictish territory; and their subjects in Lothian are sometimes called Picts, though the majority of them were probably Saxons. It is therefore possible that the inhabitants of Galloway might be called Picts, though they were not properly such; as the English are popularly called Britons from inhabiting Great Britain.

There has been some dispute respecting the import of the various terms by which the Picts have been designated. The idea that they were called *Cruithneach* by the Gael, because they were eaters of wheat, appears to have no sufficient foundation. Both Lhuyd and O'Brien concur in regarding the word as equivalent to *brithneach*, variegated, from their custom of staining their bodies. Chalmers ingeniously suggests that the Brython, mentioned in the Welsh Archæology as a tribe distinct from the Lloegrians and the Cymru, were no other than the Picts; and that *Cruithne* is merely the Gaelic form of *Brython*, substituting as usual the guttural for the labial. Cruithneach may however be regularly derived from *cruth*, figure or shape, and in this case both terms, as well as the present name of the Bretons, *Brezounek*, from *Brez*, Welsh *brith*, variegated, woule be synonymous with the Latin *Picti*. This appears more probable than Owen's interpretation, *Peithwyr*, quasi, *inhabitants of the plains*, which we know many of them were not; but, on the contrary, tenants of the most rugged mountain districts in all Britain.

It will be easily understood from the preceding remarks, that the writer considers Skene's hypothesis of the substantial identity of the Picts with the present Highlanders as totally ungrounded. There are, probably enough, descendants of the Picts both in the Highlands and the Lowlands; but that the Scoto-Irish race gained the predominance in the former district, is demonstrated by the language, which does not differ in any essential point from that of the opposite coast of Leinster and Ulster; bearing, in fact, a closer resemblance than Low German does to High German, or Danish to Swedish. The Albanic Duan, of the twelfth century, follows the analogy of the Irish grammar throughout, and a recent Gaelic grammarian (Munro), observes that Knox's Liturgy and other compositions of the sixteenth century do not differ from the Irish of the same period. It is believed that no instance exists of a similar identity of speech between tribes of different origin, as the Picts are allowed to have been, separated by their geographical position and living for centuries under a distinct government. If we suppose the Dalriadic Scots, whose migration from Ireland to the west coast of Scotland in the fifth century is a well-ascertained historical fact, to have eventually become superior in numbers to the Picts, as we know they did in military and political power, the final prevalence of their language is easily accounted for.

The subject of the general relation of the Irish or Gaelic to the other Celtic tongues, is too copious and difficult to be fully discussed at present. It resembles the Welsh in many points of grammatical structure, in a considerable proportion of its vocabulary, and in that remarkable system of initial mutations of consonants which distinguishes the Celtic languages from all others in Europe. On the other hand, it differs in several material points, particularly in having a distinct genitive and dative case; the latter, in the plural number, bearing an evident analogy to the Sanscrit and Latin, to which languages it also approximates in many affixes and other formatives, unknown in Welsh. To de-

termine its exact place in the Indo-European family is perhaps the most difficult problem in philology.   When all has
been separated which can be fairly considered as analogous
to the Cymric and Armorican, there still remains a great
preponderance of terms which cannot be satisfactorily referred to any one race known to have inhabited Europe.
Some are found in Finnish; many more in Slavonic and the
Romance dialects; while those corresponding to Sanscrit vocables are perhaps the most numerous and remarkable of
any.   Some philologists have expressed an opinion that the
Scoti or Milesians were of Germanic race; or at all events
had been subjected to Germanic admixture; and the language,
as we now find it, certainly gives some countenance to that
hypothesis.   For example, *teanga* is the only word current
for *tongue*, totally different from the Welsh *tavod;* and *leighis*,
to heal, *leagh*, physical, are evident counterparts of our Saxon
term *leech*.   The following words, constituting a very small
proportion of what might be produced, may serve as further
specimens of the class: —

> Beit, both.
> Coinne, woman, quean.
> Daor, dear.
> Dorcha, dark.
> Dream, company, people; A S. truma; O. E. trome.
> Drong, throng.
> Faigh, to get, obtain; *Dan.* faae.
> Feacht, fight.
> Frag, woman, wife; *Germ.* frau.
> Lairè, thigh; *Dan.* laar.
> Lagh, law.
> Lab, lip.
> Laoidh, poem, lay; *Germ.* lied.
> Lasd, loading, ballast; *Germ.* last.
> Leos, light; *Isl.* lios.
> Lumhan, lamb.
> Sàr, very exceeding; *Germ.* sehr.
> Seadha, saw.
> Seal, a while, space of time; A. S. sael, sel.
> Seam, a peg or pin; *Dan.* söm, nail.
> Sgad, loss, misfortune; *Dan.* skade.
> Sgaoil, separate, disperse; *Sw.* skala.
> Sgeir, rock in the sea, skerry; *Isl.* skèr.
> Sgarbh, a cormorant; *Isl.* skarfr.
> Snaig, creep, *sneak*.
> Sneachd, snow.
> Sliochd, family, race; *Germ.* geschlecht.

Slug, swallow; *Germ.* schlucken.
Smachd, power, authority; *Germ.* macht.
Smeoraich, smear.
Snaidh, cut; *Germ.* schneiden.
Spaisdrich, walk; *Germ.* spazieren.
Spàr, a beam or joist.
Streang, a string.
Sreamh, a current, stream.
Steagaim, parch, fry; *Sw.* steka, to roast, fry, broil.
Strith, strife; *Germ.* streit.
Trath, time, season; A. S. thrag; O. E. throw.

Some of the above terms may have been introduced in the ninth and following centuries by the Northmen; but many of them occur in the oldest known monuments of the language; they are also accompanied by many compounds and derivatives, which is commonly regarded as a proof of long naturalization; and are moreover current in Connaught, where the Danes never had any permanent settlement. One of the most remarkable indications of a Teutonic affinity is the termination *nas*, or *nis*, exactly corresponding to our *ness* in *greatness, goodness; ex. gr.* breitheam*nas*, judgment, fiadh*nis*, witness, &c.* This affix is too completely incorporated in the language to be a borrowed term, and it moreover appears to be *significant*, in the sense of *state, condition*, in Irish, though not in German. As far as the writer knows, it is confined to the Gaelic and Teutonic dialects. The Irish *sealbh*, property, possession; *adj. sealbhach, proprius*, would also furnish a plausible origin for the German *selber, self*, a word which has no known Teutonic etymology. These approximations and various others which might be pointed out, not only to German but to Latin, Sanscrit, and other languages of their class, seem to show that the distinctive portion of the Gaelic tongues is of comparatively later introduction into the west of Europe, and that the Cymric and Armorican have more faithfully preserved the peculiarities of the ancient Celtic. For instance, the entire want of *cases* in Welsh, Cornish and Breton, is a mark of antiquity exhibited by no other European tongue, in its original condition.

Respecting the affinity of the Gaelic dialects to each other, it will be sufficient to say that Irish is the parent tongue; that Scottish Gaelic is Irish stripped of a few inflections; and that Manks is merely Gaelic with a few peculiar words and disguised by a corrupt system of orthography.

---

* A writer in the "Saturday Review" has pointed out that this remark is incorrect. ED.

ON THE ORIGIN AND IMPORT OF THE AUGMENT IN SANSCRIT AND GREEK.

[Proceedings of the Philological Society. Vol. I.]

It has long been suspected that the vowel-prefix to certain past tenses (Sanscr. *a*, Gr. *ε*) was originally a distinct element, potentially modifying the signification of the verb in its expression of the various relations of *time*. Not to dwell upon its restriction to particular tenses, it may be briefly observed, that in the older compositions in Sanscrit it is sometimes omitted, and sometimes separated from the verbal theme and placed between two prepositions. In Greek, the Ionic and Æolic dialect frequently reject it altogether; and in certain verbs compounded with prepositions it is not unfrequently prefixed to the preposition instead of the radical portion of the verb. All these phenomena seem totally inconsistent with the idea of its being any integral part of the verbs to which it is joined; as it is notorious, that though the constituent parts of compound terms may be disjoined by tmesis, the elements of truly simple words never are. Various theories have been advanced by grammarians to account for the origin and ascertain the precise force of this prefix. Some, confining their views to the Greek language, suppose it to have originated in the imperfect of the verb substantive, $ἦν$ or $ἦ$, *was;* an hypothesis involving a gross solecism, and subversive of all the established analogies of the Indo-European languages. Buttmann conjectures it to be nothing more than a mutilation of the reduplicate prefix of the perfect, so that $ἔτυπτον$ was originally $τέτυπτον$. Though this idea might appear to derive some countenance from the epic forms of the second aorist, in which the syllabic augment and the reduplication appear to be employed almost indifferently, a slight comparison with the analogous forms in Sanscrit will show it to be totally untenable. Pott also regards the augment as a sort of imitation of the reduplication, but does not adduce any arguments in support of his position that appear of much cogency. Bopp has advanced an hypothesis, which has, at all events, the merit of originality — not to say singularity. He supposes the augment to be identical with the negation prefix *a* or *an* (Gr. $ἀ$, $ἀν$), so that $ἔλεγον$ for instance is to be resolved into $ἀ$-

λεγον, *I say no longer* = *I said*; the prefix not conveying a negation of the action, but simply of its *present occurrence*. In the last published part of his 'Vergleichende Grammatik,' Bopp labours to vindicate his theory against some severe and cogent remarks of Lassen in the 'Indische Bibliothek;' but his defence is more remarkable for its learning and ingenuity than for its success in convincing the reader. He himself, indeed, seems to have some misgivings respecting the soundness of his hypothesis, since he admits that the prefix in question may be only collaterally related to the negative particle, as being derived from the same demonstrative pronominal root; and that, instead of denying the actual presence of the action, it may merely affirm its remoteness. He affects indeed to consider the two solutions as virtually identical; to which it is sufficient to reply, that the latter hypothesis is completely subversive of the former, and that the same element could hardly signify *that, there, yonder, then,* affirmatively, and express, *vi termini*, a negative proposition at the same moment. The object of the present paper is to show that the explanation which Bopp himself allows to be admissible, — namely, that the augment may be regarded as a demonstrative particle, primarily expressing *remote place*, and secondarily *remote time*, — is the one which unites the most probabilities in its favour. One cannot help feeling some surprise at the extremely limited view which has hitherto been taken of this question. Some have confined their investigations to the Greek, which gives absolutely no data for deciding the point: others have gone no further than the Sanscrit, which does not furnish any very satisfactory ones. The most rational and philosophical method of proceeding would have been to inquire how the same modification of time is expressed in other languages, especially those cognate with Greek and Sanskrit. If we find that any of those distinguish the past from the present by means of prefixes, and further, that those prefixes have a distinct meaning, suitable to the functions which they discharge, it is, *à priori*, very possible that the augment in Greek and Sanscrit may be of similar origin and similar import.

The Latin language will not afford us any assistance in this investigation; since, though it has partially retained the reduplication, it exhibits in its present state no distinct traces of a syllabic augment, or substitute for one. If we proceed to the Celtic, we shall find that all the dialects regularly form the preterite by the aid of prefixes, some of which are plainly significant. These preformatives are pretty numerous in Welsh, especially in ancient poetical compositions; but the one most commonly employed is *a*; *e. gr.* *canu*, to sing; *a ganodd*, cecinit; *caru*, to love; *a garodd*, amavit. In old manuscripts the particle is regularly joined to the verb in writing; *aorug*, he made, or did; *aganodd*, he sung; so that, had this orthography been persisted in, the prefix would have appeared as integral a part of the verb as *a* in Sanscr., *atudat*, or *e* in Gr., ἔτυπτε.

The precise force of the Welsh element in this combination can only be inferred by analogical reasoning. As a pronoun, *a* denotes *who, which, that;* as a preposition, *with*; and as a conjunction, *and.* Reasons will be produced in the course of the present paper for believing that its original import was *there*, or *then;* denoting with greater precision the *time* of the action expressed by the verb. That it had a distinct meaning may be inferred from its changing the initial of the verb to which it is joined: *a ganodd* from *canu; a dorrodd*, broke, from *torri.* This phænomenon in the Celtic languages almost invariably denotes a grammatical or logical relation; namely, government, concord, composition or other modification of a word by something in immediate conjunction with it. It would be contrary to the analogy of the language to suppose that this effect could be produced by a *verbum otiosum*, or mere expletive.

Though *a* is sometimes used in Irish as a sign of the preterite tense, it is of comparatively unfrequent occurrence. The particle most commonly employed is *do*, which is seldom omitted, except when the verb precedes its subject. As a particle, *do* signifies *to*, and is employed as the sign of the dative and the infinitive. In ancient Irish we find greater variety of particles, and sometimes a combination of them, employed for the same purpose. *At, ad, no, ro, ad no, do no*, and *do ro* seem to be used indiscriminately, except that sometimes the compound forms may have the idea of greater precision or emphasis annexed to them. *No* and *do no* are interpreted by the lexicographers to signify *then,* which we believe to be the real import of most of those formative particles, the Greek and Sanscrit augment included. The prefix *ro* has its exact counterpart in the Welsh *rhy*, often used by old writers to form the perfect, pluperfect and future tenses. The element is significant in both languages as a particle implying *excess, what is over and above,* or *further*; and appears, when joined with verbs, to answer pretty accurately to our *moreover.* We may here remark the similarity of the Homeric particle ῥὰ, so frequently used in transitions. The common idea, that this word was formed by aphæresis from ἄρα, is both gratuitous and contrary to analogy. We believe the opinion of Mr. Donaldson in the 'New Cratylus,' who regards it as an independent term, implying *addition*, *excess*, *remoteness*, both alone and in composition, to be much better founded. It is indeed just as easy to affirm that ἄρα is a compound, as that ῥά is an abbreviation.

The Gothic language exhibits a few instances of reduplication in preterites; but, with the exception of the particle *ga*, which will be noticed hereafter, neither it nor any other Germanic dialect has any thing formally corresponding to the augment. There is, however, a curious analogy in Upper German, which, if it had occurred to Bopp, might possibly have made him doubt the soundness of his theory respecting the negative import of the augment. Both in Old and Middle High German we find the particles *tho*, *do*, *ther*, *der*, prefixed to verbs in the past tense, without any special reference to the idea of *then* or *there*, but simply, as it would seem, to denote the completion of the action. In translations from the Latin it frequently corresponds to the preterite in that language, unaccompanied by any particle. Thus in Tatian's 'Evangelical Harmony,' we find "quad *tho* Maria" = dixit Maria; "*tho* ward gitruobit" = turbatus est; "tho *ther* stigun sine bruoder" = ut autem ascenderunt fratres ejus. In the writings of the middle ages we find *do* and *der* employed nearly in the same manner. In the first edition of the Upper German Bible, A. D. 1462, are twenty examples of this construction in the first chapter of Genesis; as for example, ver. 3—4, "Un Got *der* sprach (dixit) liecht werde gemacht. Und das liecht ward gemacht; un Got *der* sache (vidit) daz liecht das es ward gut." So *der* rieff = vocavit; *der* macht = fecit; *der* beschuoff = creavit, &c. &c. Not only *der*, but also *hin* and *her* are frequently joined to verbs and participles in Middle High German to increase the emphasis and show that the action is done thoroughly.

The verb in the Slavonic languages presents some remarkable phenomena, well worthy the consideration of the philologist. It is known that in this class of tongues a regular, perfectly philosophical distinction is made between perfective and imperfective verbs, that is, between those expressing an action completed at once and not repeated, and those denoting continuance or reiteration. Thus *to dig*, implying a continued action, is regarded as imperfective; but *to bury*, which is done only once to the same subject, is a proper perfective. Sometimes this distinction is inherent in the form of the verb; but in many cases, verbs naturally imperfective, become perfective in the preterite by prefixing a preposition. What particular preposition may be employed with individual verbs depends on the custom of the language; those denoting *out*, *from*, *by*, *with*, *after*, are most commonly in use. Thus kropliù, I besprinkle, might denote a *habit* of so doing; to express a single definite act of it, already accomplished, would require *po* or *na* (after) to be prefixed to the simple preterite. The future perfect is formed in a similar manner by prefixing some one of the above-mentioned particles to the present tense. In all those compound phrases a sort of feeling appears to prevail, that the particle is necessary to convey the idea of completeness of action or precision of time, and in a great many cases the Slavonic preterite perfective would correspond pretty accurately with the Greek or Sanscrit aorist, used definitely.

The only remaining European language which seems to offer any analogy is the Albanian, which forms the future by prefixing *do te* to the present: e. gr. *thom*, I say, *do te thom*, I shall say. As a particle of place *do* signifies *where*; if transferred to express the idea of *time*, it would naturally denote *when* or *then*, which may be employed with equal propriety in a future or a past acceptation. Thus the Irish *ro* = moreover, is used with preterites, and its counterpart, the Welsh *rhy*, both with the preterite and future.

The languages of Central Asia also present a few analogies. The ancient Armenian prefixes *e* to the preterite, exactly like the Greek: but this formation is confined to the third person of one particular conjugation. The Kurdish also employs several particles in the formation of past tenses; as *che kiria*, fecit, from the root *ken*, make, &c. We have no means of ascertaining whether those particles have a distinct meaning, or what it is. In Persian the particle *be* or *bu*, prefixed to the present, converts it to a future: *pursem*, I ask, *bupursem*, I shall or will ask. The Georgian also employs a variety of preformative particles in conjugation, but the precise analysis of them has not hitherto been made known.

In the Coptic language the system of verbal preformatives is more fully developed than in any of the Indo-European. Every tense has its appropriate particle, apparently meant to express the particular modification of time supposed to be included in the entire phrase. Thus *e* is the sign of the present tense; *na* of the imperfect; *a* of the preterite definite; *sha* of the preterite indefinite; *ne a* and *ne sha* of the pluperfect; *e-na* the future; *ta* or *ta-re* the future indefi-

14

nite, &c. It is true that several grammarians regard those prefixes as auxiliary verbs; but there are reasons, which we cannot here discuss at length, for believing that most of them are of pronominal origin. The particle *ent* or *et*, used in one of the preterite formations, is confessedly identical with the relative pronoun in form; and Benfey admits that they are, in all probability, of common origin.

In the languages of Southern India the system of verbal formatives expressing the time of the action is carried to a great extent. Thus Anderson observes (Rudiments of Tamul Grammar, page 44), 'The Tamul grammarians resolve most of the derivative forms of a verb into three parts; viz. *paghudi* the root, *vighudi* the form of termination [distinguishing the persons], and *ideimilei* the intermediate argument, which is generally employed as the formative of the different tenses.' MacKerrell also remarks (Grammar of the Carnātaca Language, p. 85), 'Verbs in the Carnātaca language, whether possessing an intransitive or a transitive meaning, are conjugated by adding to their roots, in three of the tenses (viz. present, past and future), certain affixes expressive of *time;* and to these the affixes denoting persons being attached, the inflexion is complete.' The particles thus employed are pretty numerous, and the rules for the application of them are rather intricate; but it is obvious that they are all regulated by the same general principle, of specifying the *time* of the action more precisely than could be done by merely using the verbal root with its personal affixes.

The Polynesian languages, especially those of the eastern division, furnish copious and valuable materials for the illustration of the point in question. The whole conjugation of the verb — as far as distinction of tense is concerned — depends on the employment of certain particles, which, allowing for the difference of dialect and pronunciation, are nearly common to the great body of the east insular Polynesians, properly so called. A minute account of them will be found in Humboldt and Buschmann's great work, 'Ueber die Kawi Sprache:' it will be sufficient for us to observe, by way of specimen, that in Tahitian the present is generally distinguished by the particle *nei* and the preterite by *na.* The original import of *nei*, as a local particle, is *here*, and its derivative one, as an adverb of time, *now*; which shows at once its force as a formative of the present tense. *Na* in like manner signifies, as a separate particle, *there* and *then*, and is employed to express the preterite tense in a way exactly analogous to the '*der* sprach' of the Middle High

German. In Kawi and Tagala this prefix is regularly incorporated with the verb. Kawi, *hem*, assemble; pret. *nahem*, assembled: Tagala, *pinta*, demand; pret. *naminta*, demanded — *p* being converted into *m* by an euphonic process well known to Malay scholars. It is obvious that the circumstance of the prefix being incorporated in writing in these latter dialects, is one of the accidents of language, or a mere orthographical fashion, and makes no difference as to the actual force of the particle, which we may safely conclude to convey the sense of *then* in all cases where it is used to denote an action that is past.

Passing over other languages of this family, we shall briefly observe, that the most western one, the Malagasy, forms its tenses with remarkable neatness and precision by prefixing the particle *mi* for the present, *ni* for the preterite, and *hi* for the future; e. gr. solo (verbal root) = substitution; *mi*solo (aho), I substitute; *ni*solo, I substituted; *hi*solo, I shall substitute. When we take into consideration the undoubted affinity of the languages, there can be little question that these particles have the same force as the Tahitian, Philippine and Javanese prefixes already specified. The idea of precision of *time* is carried so far by the Malagasy, that they even combine it with local particles. Respecting this peculiarity Mr. Freeman observes, "The want of a substantive verb, corresponding with the *esse* of the Latins, and to be employed in the same manner, is compensated in many cases by a mode of structure which prevails extensively in the Malagasy language, and which constitutes one of its marked peculiarities; namely, that of making adverbs and prepositions susceptible of tense or time, by distinguishing the past from the present*." Thus *amy* and *tamy* both have the general signification of *at*, *with*, *by*; but to express the idea of *present* time, "*is* with," *amy* would be employed; while *tamy* would include the category of *past* time, "*was* with:" e. gr. "ny mazava mahazava ao *amy* ny maizina," the light *shineth* in darkness; but with a past signification, "ny Teny *tamy* n'Andriamanitra," the Word *was* with God. This may serve as an instance, among innumerable others, that languages commonly reputed barbarous may not be without their refinements.

It would far exceed our limits to attempt anything like an individual discussion of the numerous languages of the American continent. It will be sufficient to observe that

---

* Observations on the Malagasy Language, ap. Ellis. History of Madagascar, vol. i. p. 409.

14*

most of those respecting which we possess definite information bear a general analogy to the Polynesian family and the languages of the Deccan, in their methods of distinguishing the various modifications of time. In the Araucanian *che* is the sign of the second present; *bu* of the imperfect; *uye* of the imperfect; *a* of the future, and *abu* of the aorist. In many cases those formative particles have a determinate signification; e. gr. in Guarani, *bià* or *bihà* = afterwards, forms the imperfect, and *raco* = already, or *naco* = certainly, the perfect, provided it speaks of a circumstance which the narrator has seen. In some instances those distinctive particles are interposed between the verbal root and the personal termination, and sometimes those three constituents are so thoroughly incorporated that it requires a careful analysis to separate them. We may, however, venture to assert in general terms, that a South American verb is constituted precisely on the same principle as those in the Tamul and other languages of Southern India; consisting like them of a verbal root, a second element defining the time of the action, and a third denoting the subject or person.

The object of the foregoing remarks is to endeavour to establish the point of a frequent employment of particles determining more or less precisely the *time* of the action expressed by verbs, in a great variety of languages. In many cases those particles, though no original part of the verbal root, are essential to the integrity of the verbal phrase, which could not predicate time or completed action without them. Some of them, for instance the Celtic and Coptic *a*, agree exactly in form with the Sanscrit augment, there being no external difference between Sanscr. *as'ranshit* = Gr. ἔκλυε and the Welsh *aglywai* or *aglybu*, audivit, written as it was once the practice to write them. The identity of the Celtic element with the Sanscrit one cannot perhaps be proved by any direct evidence now within our reach. We are aware that the Indian grammarians represent the augment as being destitute of signification in itself; and arguments from the analogy of other languages are all that we have to oppose to this assertion. Those which we have adduced are not, it is presumed, entirely destitute of weight; and they form only a small portion of the evidence bearing upon this point which might be collected. It would be easy to affirm that the Gothic particle *ga*, Germ. *ge*, which never appears out of composition, has no original independent meaning: but it is imagined that no one would persist in that opinion after carefully comparing the different dialects, and observing how frequently it modifies the sense and the circumstances of propositions. One of its functions is exactly equivalent to that of the Greek augment, there being a number of verbs exhibiting simple forms in the present, but regularly prefixing *ga* or *ge* to form the preterite and the past participle. The actual import of this particle can only be inferred from analogy. Grimm has adduced strong reasons for believing it to be cognate with the Latin *cum*, to which it is clearly equivalent in *ga*-sintha, companion, coitinerant, from *sinthan*, to go or travel, and many similar compounds. As a formative of the preterite, it may be presumed to be parallel with the Slavonic *s* = with, employed much in the same way: e. gr. *beregu*, I am considering; perf. *sbereg*, I have (fully) considered.

After all, the strongest argument in favour of the theory now advocated is, that the great majority of prefixes in all known languages are evidently significant; and that our being unable to trace the derivation or meaning of a few only proves our want of information. It may be said that many of the analogies that have been adduced are from barbarous languages, and consequently of little weight. To this it is easy to reply, that the ancestors of the Greeks were at one period much more barbarous than the Malays or Javanese of the present day, and that the languages of uncivilized races are not necessarily deficient in regularity of structure or propriety of expression. And if, as there is good reason to believe, such languages often show the original force of the component parts of words more clearly than those which have been subject to a long process of refinement, that very circumstance shows that the philosopher and the comparative etymologist may profitably include them in the compass of their researches.

ON THE ORIGIN AND IMPORT
OF THE GENITIVE CASE.

[Proceedings of the Philological Society. Vol. II.]

To constitute connected and intelligible language, it is not sufficient to place words in juxtaposition; it is also of paramount necessity that the *relations* of the words with each other should be correctly indicated. In the Indo-European languages, the relations of verbs are denoted by personal terminations, elements implying time, contingency — v. t. q. — and those of nouns by changes of form called *cases*. It has been common among grammarians to regard those terminational changes as evolved by some unknown process from the body of the noun, as the branches of a tree spring from the stem; or as elements unmeaning in themselves, but employed arbitrarily or conventionally to modify the meanings of words. This latter theory is countenanced by A. W. Schlegel, in a well-known passage in his work, 'Observations sur la Langue et la Littérature Provençales,' the following extract from which will sufficiently explain the author's views. After dividing all known languages into three classes; — languages destitute of grammatical structure, languages employing affixes, and languages with inflexions, he observes, respecting the class last-mentioned: —

'I am of opinion, nevertheless, that the first rank must be assigned to languages with inflexions. They might be denominated the organic languages, because they include a living principle of development and increase, and alone possess, if I may so express myself, a fruitful and abundant vegetation. The wonderful mechanism of these languages consists in forming an immense variety of words, and in marking the connexion of the ideas expressed by those words by the help of an inconsiderable number of syllables, which, viewed separately, have no signification, but which determine with precision the sense of the words to which they are attached. By modifying radical letters, and by adding derivative syllables to the roots, derivative words of various sorts are formed, and derivatives from those derivatives. Words are compounded from several roots to express complex ideas. Finally, substantives, adjectives and pronouns are declined, with gender, number and case; verbs are conjugated throughout voices, moods, tenses, numbers and persons, by employing, in like manner, terminations, and sometimes augments, which by themselves signify nothing. This method is attended with the advantage of enunciating in a single word the principal idea, frequently greatly modified and extremely complex already, with its whole array of accessory ideas and mutable relations."*

The writer having already stated his objections against this theory of Schlegel, in an article in a well-known periodical, does not need to repeat them at present. It is doubtless known to those acquainted with the modern school of German philology, that several distinguished contemporaries of Schlegel have espoused a doctrine diametrically opposite to his. Not to mention W. Humboldt and Pott, Professor Franz Bopp has, in his 'Comparative Grammar,' instituted an elaborate analysis of all the grammatical terminations, with a view of identifying them with pronouns or pronominal roots. We shall not now inquire whether all his assumptions are to be implicitly relied upon: but no one acquainted with his works will refuse him the credit of great learning, research and ingenuity, or deny that he has made out a *primâ facie* case for his leading position deserving at least an attentive consideration.

The object of the present paper is chiefly to discuss a single point of the general subject; namely, the probable origin and import of the termination of the genitive case, especially in Sanscrit masculine nouns in *a*, which if they do not constitute the bulk of the language, form at all events a considerable proportion of it. The termination in question is *sya;* nom. *vrĭkas*, a wolf; gen. *vrĭkasya;* which Bopp identifies with the Vedic pronoun *sya;* observing that this pronoun is evidently compounded from the demonstrative *sa* = this, and the relative *ya* = who. Bopp does not attempt to give the rationale of the combination; nor has he, or any other German author, as far as we know, shown by an extensive induction from other languages, that there is any proper or usual connexion between the functions of the relative pronoun and those of the genitive case.

It would be rash to assert that the genitive always and necessarily includes a relative pronoun, since there is no doubt that this modification of the sense of a noun may be, and in fact frequently is, expressed in other ways. Evidence will however be produced to show that it *can be* so expressed; and that there is ground for inquiring whether

* P. 14 *et seq.*

the principle may not operate in cases which have not hitherto been supposed to include this element.

The Semitic languages, which, generally speaking, have no cases, employ various contrivances for expressing the relation of possession or qualification, usually denoted by the genitive of the Indo-Europeans. The most common method in the older languages is the so-called *status constructus*. In this, as is well known, the modified word is not, as with us, the predicate or qualifying noun, but the subject or leading one. For example, in the Hebrew phrase *father of the king* (äbi-melech), *äb*, father, shortens its vowel and is augmented by a terminal syllable; while *melech*, king, remains unaffected: much as if we were to say *patris rex*, instead of *pater regis*. Some remarks on the supposed analysis of this construction will be given hereafter: at present it is more properly connected with the leading object of the present essay to observe, that besides this method of expressing the genitive case, there is a periphrasis with the relative pronoun, of most common occurrence in the Aramean languages, but not unknown in Hebrew.

Thus, Hebr. shir *asher* lĕ Shelomoh, the song of Solomon, literally, the song *which* to Solomon. Syriac, nauso *d*-simo, chest of silver = chest *which* silver. Frequently this construction is rendered more precise, particularly in Chaldee and Syriac, by connecting with it a pronominal suffix: em-*he. d*-Jeshua = the mother *of him—who* Jesus, *i. e.* the mother of Jesus; barth-*ho-d*-Herodia, the daughter of her who Herodias. As this form furnishes a complete and intelligible resolution of the phrase, it is possible that there may be an ellipsis of the personal pronoun in those cases where the relative alone is employed; a supposition which may not be without its use when we come to consider parallel cases from other languages.

The Samaritan *d*, the Ethiopic *za* and the Amharic *ya* are, in like manner, at once relative pronouns and signs of the genitive case, as will be shown by subsequent examples. The last-mentioned is remarkable for its external identity with the Sanscrit relative *ya*, which however in all probability is purely accidental. The vulgar Arabic has several analogous methods of expressing the genitive, as may be seen in Dombay's 'Grammatica Mauro-Arabica.' One of these signs of possession, *dsa*, appears to be closely cognate with the Ethiopic *za*, originally a relative pronoun. Of the various prefixes indicating the genitive given in Professor Newman's contribution to our knowledge of the Berber language, lately published in the 'Zeitschrift für die Kunde des Morgenlandes,' several are clearly identical with forms of the relative pronoun, as we shall have a future opportunity of pointing out more fully. This, by the way, may serve as a further confirmation of the true Semitic character of the Berber.

It is true that most grammarians regard the Aramean prepositive *dolath*, when it is the sign of the genitive case, not as a relative, but a preposition or particle, equivalent to the Latin *de*. We have however a decisive proof to the contrary in the Ethiopic. When the leading noun is masculine, *za*, the masculine relative, is employed as the sign of the genitive; but when the governing noun is feminine, the connective is not *za*, but *enta*, the *feminine* form of the relative. It is hardly necessary to say that a mere particle could not be affected in this way, the feminine gender of a preposition being something difficult to conceive.

Several other African languages present results perfectly analogous. The forms of the Coptic have not been sufficiently studied to justify the expression of a positive opinion as to their nature. Several however of the signs of the genitive case correspond so closely in form with various demonstrative and relative pronouns, as to excite a strong suspicion of the community of their origin. Leaving this point for further investigation, we proceed to observe, that in the Galla language *kan* is both the relative pronoun and the sign of the genitive case: *e. gr.* eni *kan* duffu, he that comes; kitāba *kan* dalota, *kan* Jāsus Christos, the book of the generation of Jesus Christ: *lit.* the book *which* the generation *who* Jesus Christ. The Yoruba language, spoken on the western coast, exhibits precisely the same phenomenon, except that *ti* supplies the place of *kan*: ille *ti* mo wo, the house *which* I pulled down; ille *ti* babba, house *of* father. The similarity of the Yoruba *ti* to the Syriac *d* and the Ethiopic *za* is probably accidental, but the functions of each are precisely the same.

Some of the Polynesian languages express the relation of possession by the mere juxtaposition of the terms, and consequently throw no light on the point which we are discussing. The greater part of them however employ prefixes, many of which are identical with forms of demonstrative or relative pronouns, or so similar as to encourage the belief that they are of kindred origin. Thus, in Malagasy, *ny* is both demonstrative pronoun or definite article, and the sign of the genitive case: *ny* filazany *ny* razany *ny* Jaisosy Kraisty, *the* book *of* the generation *of* Jesus Christ. In the Marquesan, the Hawaiian and the New Zealand languages, *na* is equally the pronoun of the third person $=$ *he*, *that*, &c. and the prefix denoting the genitive. Respecting the last-mentioned language, Dr. Dieffenbach observes in the sketch of New Zealand Grammar appended to his 'Travels,' that the relative is expressed by the *genitive* of the personal pronoun: *e. gr.* the man *who* showed, te tangata *nana* e waka-kite, *lit.* the man *of him* showed. This resolution of the phrase appears so much at variance with the principles of logic that there is great room to question its soundness. The analogy of other languages would rather lead us to believe, that for the sake of greater precision, the demonstrative element *na* is doubled to form a relative, much as in Norse and Anglo-Saxon: *sa-er*; *se-þe* $=$ who, *lit.* the-the, or the-that. The object of this duplication appears to be to establish a more precise connexion between the antecedent and the relative clauses, a portion of the complex expression being referred to each.

The forms which we have hitherto considered are strictly analytic, and in some of them, especially the Aramean and the Ethiopic, the identity of the genitival prefixes with the relative pronoun does not admit of a doubt. Now, though synthetic forms are not necessarily strictly parallel with the analytic ones of the same import, it is clearly possible that they *may* be so. No one disputes that the Latin *mecum* is in all respects equivalent to σὺν ἐμοὶ, or that the Spanish future *cantaré*, I will sing, is a mere transposition of *hé de cantar*, I have to sing. In like manner, when we find in Sanscrit or any similar language a termination potentially equivalent to a prefix in a Semitic tongue, or to a significant postfix in a Tartarian or American one, there is at least an ostensible ground for inquiring whether all may not virtually be different shapes of the same thing.

We can indeed have no direct evidence respecting such forms as the Sanscrit *vrĭkasya*, since we know too little of the earliest state of the language to pronounce positively respecting the precise force and composition of its numerous affixes. But we can perceive that the termination of the word in question is to the eye and the ear the same as the relative pronoun *ya*; and we may argue without imputation of any great rashness, that if *which wolf* can mean *of a wolf* in Syriac or Ethiopic, *wolf which* may have precisely the same import in another tongue. This view may be strengthened by further analogies, some of which we shall briefly notice.

In the popular dialects of India related to Sanscrit, and commonly supposed to be descendants of it, the genitive is in most cases formed by affixes, commonly *kā, kī, kē,* which exhibit the remarkable peculiarity of always agreeing in gender with the governing noun. Thus in the phrase "the *brother* of Jesus" the genitive would be Jesu*kā*; but "the *mother* of Jesus" would require a different form, Jesu*kī*. Here, we may observe in the first instance that this phæ-nomenon proves clearly that the affix does not belong to the noun to which it is attached, but to the one which governs it, and with which it is in grammatical concord. Secondly, the termination is in the majority of instances identical with the Sanscrit interrogative pronoun, which in many languages is notoriously closely connected with the relative in import, and frequently in form, and may in fact become a substitute for it in propositions where doubt or contingency is implied. We shall probably therefore not greatly err if we resolve the expression into the component parts — brother *who* Jesus, mother *who* Jesus, i. e. *of* Jesus, analogous to the con-structions which we have been considering in analytic lan-guages. It may be also worth inquiring whether the same solution is not applicable to the numerous Sanscrit attribu-tives in *ka* and *ya,* which are generally equivalent to the ge-nitive of the noun from which they are formed, and are compounded with an element externally not differing from the interrogative and relative pronouns. In Slavonic there is a general disinclination to the employment of the genitive case, the place of which is supplied by possessive adjectives. One leading form of those in *ii,* fem. *iya,* is identical with the emphatic or definite form of ordinary adjectives, which in the cognate Lithuanian are visibly formed by affixing the demonstrative pronoun *jis.* Bopp, in his 'Comparative Grammar,' refers this element to the Sanscrit relative *ya,* and argues with great probability that the definite forms of adjectives in all the ancient Teutonic languages are of the same origin. Supposing this point to be established, it is obvious that a genitive case, equivalent in import and similar in form, may include the same element within it.

Here again the analytic languages serve to aid our theory. By prefixing the relative, the Syriac, Ethiopic, and other tongues form adjectives from substantives, ordinal numbers from cardinals, and possessive pronouns from personal suf-fixes, and there seems nothing extravagant in supposing that a relative or any other pronoun may exercise the same func-tions at the end of a word that it does at the beginning. It would indeed be easy to point out many instances where the postfixes of older languages have become prefixes or distinct prepositive words in more recent ones.

We may here properly consider the Afghan or Pushtu, both on account of its local position and its general affinity to the dialects of India Proper. Some of its forms are remarkable, and it is conceived of great importance for the elucidation of the present inquiry. Respecting the genitive case, Professor Dorn in his valuable Memoir on the Pushtu* makes the following observations : —

"The genitive is formed by prefixing the word *da*, which however is not to be regarded as a proof of affinity between Pushtu and Semitic (inasmuch as in Chaldee also, *d* serves to form the genitive). This *d* [in Pushtu] is evidently of the same origin as the German *der*, *die*, *das*; and we shall hereafter find it again among the pronouns. I conceive indeed that this *da* was originally written *dah*, and that it is nothing more than the pronoun demonstrative. This idea is confirmed by our finding *dah* in Pushtu works employed as a sign of the genitive case, as for example *dah du kum*, of both worlds."

Professor Ewald takes the same view of the matter in his paper on the Afghan language published in the 'Zeitschrift für die Kunde des Morgenlandes,' some time before the appearance of Dorn's Memoir, where he observes that the genitival prefix *da* is a demonstrative with the force of a relative. Neither Dorn nor Ewald gives any analysis of another remarkable prefix of the genitive, viz. *tsa*, restricted in that particular form to the pronoun of the first person, but probably identical in origin with *sa*, the prefix of the second person: e. gr. *mā*, I; *tsa-mā*, of me; *tā*, thou; *sa-tā*, of thee. Here we may observe, that the consonant *tsa*, peculiar to the Afghan language, is not related to the dentals or sibilants, but to the *palatals*, being in fact frequently commutable with *cha* $=$ Pers. چ ; and we may therefore reasonably suspect from known analogies, that, as a formative of the genitive case, it is a mere mutation of the relative pronoun *chah*.

The above phenomena are the more important from the circumstance that the Pushtu is confessedly an Indo-European dialect, occupying a medium place between the Persian and the dialects of India. If, as we have great reason to believe, its genitival prefixes are equivalent in import and cognate in origin to the postfixes of the Hindee dialects, and those again may be traced to the Sanscrit relative or

---

* Mémoires de l'Académie Impériale des Sciences de St. Pétersbourg, 1840.

interrogative pronoun, various interesting conclusions, too obvious to be insisted upon, would be deducible from the fact. It is remarkable that the postfix to the genitive case in Sikh or Punjābī is *dā*, identical in form with the Afghan prefix; and that there are traces of *da* as a demonstrative root in various Indian languages: e. gr. Sanscr. *idam*, this; Zend, *dem*, *dim* = Sanscr. *tam*, Gr. τόν: accusative of the demonstrative pronoun *ho* = Sanscr. *sa*. It is possible indeed that this form may be only a modification of the more original root *ta*; but it is found in so many languages, that it may at all events be regarded as very ancient.

With respect to the languages of Southern India not related to Sanscrit, the Tamul, of which the others are only sub-dialects, presents no direct analogy, since in it the relative pronoun is entirely wanting, being usually supplied by the participle. There is however a construction in the higher dialect, or Shem Tamul, which seems to deserve a little notice. A class of participial words called *vineiyech-chams* is used extensively to supply the place of conjunctions and other connectives. Thus *enaru*, the past vineiyechcham of *enakiratu*, to say, to call, performs the functions of *that* (*quod* or *ut*) and its future *ennum* serves to denote a general relation between the terms which it connects, equivalent to a genitive case. Thus, *puyal–ennum–vāri*, the water of the clouds, literally, the water which may be, or is to be, called clouds; in other words, water respecting which clouds may be predicated, or more concisely, *cloud-water*. It is obvious that the word *which*, or *that*, supposing it to exist in Tamul, might exercise precisely the same office, *quod* being potentially equivalent to τὸ λεγόμενον; and thus it appears that the above construction bears a close analogy to the bulk of those which we have already analysed.

The Tartarian class of languages also furnishes a valuable confirmation of this theory, which cannot be better stated than in the words of Dr. W. Schott (Versuch über die Tatarischen Sprachen, pp. 52, 53): — "The Turco-Tartarians denote the genitive by the form *ning*, which may be recognized as the Manchu *ni* with a nasal increment. This nasal addition answers [in sound] with the Turco-Tartarians to the German *ng*; with the Osmanlis however it is softened to *ñ*. The *ning* of the Turkish dialects may be regarded as the full form of the genitive of the higher Asiatics, or at least most nearly approaching it: and we actually find in the Manchu itself a postpositive particle *ningge*, which does not indeed become a genitive in that language *, but expresses a relation, or stands for the relative pronoun. The agreement in form of both is too striking to be explained as merely casual; and as to the transition of the relative into a genitival particle, we find examples of it in other languages. Several Chinese elements, which originally only expressed a relation to something preceding,—a sort of relative pronoun or *articulus postpositivus*, become also exponents of a genitival relation. This transition is shown in a remarkably unequivocal manner by the particle *ti*, peculiar to the modern style, which is as frequently a sign of the genitive as a relative**: e. gr. *ngo—ti*, mine, from *ngo*, I: thus, *ngo—ti hiung*, my (older) brother, and on the same principle, *ngo-ti* phung-yeu *ti* hiung-*ti*, my friend's brother. The word governed becomes connected with the governing one, as a sort of possessive adjective."

Schott's remarks on the extension of the principle to the Finnish languages are curious and instructive, but cannot be conveniently abridged so as to find a place in the present paper.

We may here briefly notice the Semitic construct form mentioned at the commencement of the present paper. In Hebrew masculines singular, the governing noun does not alter its termination, except in a few instances; but in Ethiopic, the syllable *a* is regularly affixed: e. gr. *wald*, son; wald*a* Māryām, the son of Mary. A probable explanation of this form may be found in languages where the governing noun is regularly accompanied by a pronominal affix denoting *his*, *her*, *its*: v. t. q. as in Hungarian, where "the birth of Jesus," Jesus, or Jesusnak születtes-*e*, is literally "Jesus," or "to Jesus, birth — *his*." If therefore we suppose that the termination *a* in Ethiopic construct nouns, -*i* and *u* in Hebrew and Arabic ones, and *t* or *th* in feminines, are derived from pronominal affixes, which they are not unlike in form, we shall have, at all events, a plausible solution of the matter.

In the Albanian language, the governing noun, if masculine, regularly subjoins *i*, but if feminine, *e*, which are in fact a demonstrative pronoun of the third person. Similar to this is the *izafet* construction of the Persians, where an *i*, written in certain cases, but more generally in unpointed

---

* It appears however as the formative of the absolute possessive pronoun, which is notoriously allied to the genitive in many languages: e. gr. *mi ni-nggę = le mien.*

** The identity of this Chinese particle with the *ti* of the Yorubas in form and functions is not a little curious.

texts only perceptible in the pronunciation, is subjoined to the governing noun: *dost-ĭ puser*, the friend of the boy; *puser-ĭ dost*, the boy of the friend. Pott in his remarks on the Belúchi language ingeniously suggests, that this syllable is in fact a relative pronoun, cognate with the Sanscrit *ya*. Supposing this to be the case, it would be exactly analogous to the Semitic constructions with the relative prefix, but would differ in the order of its arrangement from the Sanscrit, assuming the latter to include the relative in the termination of the genitive.

According to Lassen, the same formation of the genitive occurs in Pehlĕvi: *kup-i-Fars*, mountain of Persia; it is also employed as a connective between the substantive and the qualifying adjective: *andarvai ĭ rushan*, the bright atmosphere. Respecting these constructions, Lassen observes, "I believe that this is in both cases to be explained from the relative *ji* [yi] for *ja* [ya]. Constructions in Zend like *gâum jim Sughdŏ sajanem* = regionem quam Sughdae situm; *puthrĕm jat Aurvat aspahē* = filium quod (quem) Aurvataspis, in which the relative denotes the connexion of a qualifying word with a preceding noun, lead to this assumption." This Zend construction is remarkable for its similarity to the analytic forms employed in Semitic.

The above is only a small part of the evidence which might be adduced in support of the assumed connection between the termination or prefixed sign of the genitive case and the relative, or occasionally, the interrogative or demonstrative pronoun. Even languages which have no distinct relative, but express it synthetically, help to confirm the theory; as for instance, in Basque the relative postfix is *an*, and a common termination of the genitive *en*. Similar phænomena are presented by several American languages, if the analyses in Adelung's 'Mithridates' are to be relied on.

In conclusion we briefly observe, that the object of all the different forms of the genitive case is to establish the same sort of connexion between *words*, that the relative does between *clauses*; namely, to show that one of them may be *predicated* of the other; thus serving as a kind of logical copula. It is in fact of the very essence of human intellect to perceive the relations of things, and of human language to enunciate them; and if we could not refer those relations to their proper subjects and objects, we should not be able to make our ideas intelligible. The particular point which we have been discussing is still open to further investigation; since many of the phenomena connected with it have not even been adverted to. Could the view we have taken of it be finally established, it would lead to the presumption that Schlegel's theory of the non-significance of grammatical inflexions must be radically unsound, since it is clear that if one termination be originally significant, all others may be equally so; and it is reasonable to suppose that the languages of the Indo-European class, which Schlegel had principally in view, are organized throughout on the same general system. Arguing *à priori*, it seems more rational to presume that the human mind would employ means obviously adapted to a definite end, than that it would be guided by blind chance or mere caprice in its operations. It would also, be difficult to give a plausible reason why the barbarous Finns, Tartars, and similar tribes should express logical and grammatical relations by significant postfixes, and that the most cultivated and intellectual races in the world should employ mere jargon for the same purpose. Such theories appear too nearly related to the exploded doctrine of occult causes in natural philosophy; and if they are to be admitted, they ought at all events to be more satisfactorily proved than has hitherto been done.

A few select examples of the principal constructions alluded to in the preceding inquiry are here subjoined.

Hebrew, *Asher*. Relative: *asher* lo hayyam, cujus est mare; *lit.* who to him [is] the sea.

    Sign of Genitive: haggibborim *asher* le-David, the warriors of David.

Contracted form, *sh*. *She*-l-i, of me; *lit.* which to me.

    mittatho *she*-le Shelomo, the couch of Solomon; *lit.* the couch *of him*, who, or which, to Solomon.

Chaldee, *di*. Rel.: *di* medar-*hon*, whose habitation; *lit.* who habitation of them.

    Gen.: nehar *di* nur, river of fire.

Syriac, *d*. Rel.: *d*-bar David, who [was] the son of David.

    Gen.: cthobo *d*-musiqi, book of music.

    —— br-*e-d*-Chakim, the son of Hakim; *lit.* son of him who Hakim.

Samaritan, *d*. Rel.: cul *d*-ramach, all which creepeth.

    Gen.: baraha *d*-Pharan, the wilderness of Pharan.

Ethiopic, *za*, *enta*. Rel.: wald *za*-rakab-o, the son who found him. *enta* atmaq-o, [she] who baptized him.

    Gen.: Mazmor *za* Dáwith, psalm of David.

    —— Anqatz *enta* samāy, the gate of heaven.

Amharic, *ya*. Rel. and Gen.: *ya*nabara *ya*-Heli lĕdsh, *who* was the son *of* Heli.

Vulgar Arabic, *dsa**, *dse*. Gen.: el sifr *dse* 'l kitab, the volume of the book.

The Berber forms are so peculiar, and withal so important that they appear to deserve a more detailed examination. The first thing which strikes us is the variety of forms, greatly exceeding that of any other Semitic dialect. Some of these are evidently compound, others abbreviated, and some apparently mere dialectical variations. It is difficult to determine the original forms with certainty; but as far as may be judged from a comparison of the cognate dialects, the following appears to be an approximation to the real state of the case. There is one set of forms consisting of a consonant followed by a simple vowel: *wa*; *tha* or *ta*, *gha* or *ya*; *na*; *da* or *dsa*; *ka*; or of a consonant preceded by a vowel: *aw*; *ath*; *agh* or *ay*; *an*; *al*; *ads* or *ad*; *ak*.

These are sometimes combined into such forms as *awwi*; *aghi* or *ayyi*; *akka*; *anni*; *wayyi*; *sayyi*; *winna*; *widsa*; *widsak*; *anwa; anta*; *natta, nyawmi*; or abbreviated into the simple prefixes: *w*; *u*; *ds* or *d*; *gh* or *y*; *n*; *k*.

In their primitive acceptation, they appear for the most part, if not altogether, to have been *demonstratives*; but they are also extensively employed in the following capacities: 1. personal pronouns; 2. relatives and interrogatives; 3. particles, especially prepositions and conjunctions; 4. genitival prefixes; 5. formatives of verbs and abstract nouns. To enter into all the details of the above divisions would amount to an analysis of the entire structure of the Semitic languages, on which, it is believed, they are calculated to throw considerable light. It may be sufficient for our present purpose to observe that the shorter forms *an*, *am*, *al*, *ay*, *aw*, *ghi* or *yi, ni*, *n*, *w*, *u*, are preferred as signs of the genitive case; being at the same time occasionally used as relatives, though not so frequently as the longer forms. A few examples may suffice for the present.

Relative. *wi* ikhza Rabbi, whom God cursed.

ur illi *w*-araykishnan, there is not [any] who enters.

Genitive. akadum *aw* warghaz, the face of the man.

The form most commonly employed is *an* (relative and demonstrative *anni*), especially with substantives and pronominal suffixes.

baba, father; gen. *an*-baba.

thakli, female slave; gen. *an*-thakli.

an-nagh, of us.

---

* The same element appears to be included in the relative pronoun *elledsi*, q d. the—who. *Dsu* is also said to be used as a relative by the Tajjite Arabs.

15

> *an*-wan, of you.
> *an*-san, of them.

Sometimes, as in Aramaic, the pronominal suffix is also inserted: *e. gr.*

> ammi-*s an* baba, son of the father;
> *lit.* son *of him — who* father.

Examples of the remaining forms, too numerous to be here specified, will be found in Newman's Grammar, and Venture's French and Berber Dictionary, lately published by the Société de Géographie at Paris.

Galla, *kan*.   Rel.: eni *kan* duffu, he that comes.
>   Gen.: *kan* Judaia bosonáti, in the wilderness of Judea.

Yoruba, *ti*.   Rel.: ille *ti* mo wo, the house which I pulled down.
>   Gen.: ille *ti* babba, house of father.

Malagassy, *ny*. Demonstr. and gen.: *ny* mpanjaky *ny* Jiosy, the king of the Jews.

Hawaiian, *na*. [Pronoun of third person, *he*, *it*.]
>   Gen.: parau *na* te Atua, the word of God.

Sanscrit, *ya*. [Relative.] Gen.: vrikas-*ya*, of a wolf.
>   *ka-s* [Interrogative.] Gen.: asma-*kam*, of us. [Compare the possessive forms — mama*ka*, meus; tava*ka*, tuus; asma*ka* (in the Vedas), noster.]

Hindostani. Gen. masc. form, Kudā-*kā* betá, son of God.
>   Gen. fem. form, Yisu-*kī* mā, mother of Jesus.

Guzerati, *nō*. [Pali demonstr. *na*?]
>   Gen.: chokara-*nō*, of a boy. Fem.: Yisu*nī* mā, mother of Jesus.

Punjābī, *dā*. [Zend. demonstr. *da*?]
>   Gen. kavi *dā*, of a poet. Fem.: Yisu*dī* mātā, mother of Jesus. [Compare the Pushtū genitival *prefix*, *da*-bādi-shah, of a king, &c., and the demonstrative pronoun *dā* saray, this man.]

In other dialects we find *chō*, *chī*, *jō*, *jī*, as terminations of the genitives. These may be probably regarded as modifications of the Sanscrit interrogative and relative pronouns, *ka-s*, *ya*. *Jō*, *jē*, are relatives in Haroti, Guzerati, and it is believed also in other dialects.

Persian, Pehlĕvi, Beluchī, *i*. Gen.: kup-i-Fars, mountain of Persia.

Albanian, *i. e.* [Definite article, *the*.]
>   Gen.: Pirri *i* Abrahamit, son of Abraham. Fem.: emma *e* Jesuit, mother of Jesus.

The Manchu postfixed relative *ningge*, *ngge*, of which *jingge* is a collateral form, has a variety of functions, serving, *inter alia*, to form — 1. Participles, active and passive: aracha-*ngge* = ὁ γράψας and τὸ γραφόμενον. 2. Possessive adjectives, often resolvable into a genitive: niyalma-i-*ngge*, human, q. d. characteristic *of* man. 3. Possessive pronouns: mini-*ngge*, mine, q. d. *quod mei* (est). This is with great probability identified by Schott with the Turco-Tartarian and Finnish forms of the genitive.

Uighur, Jaghatai. &c., *ning*, at-*ning*, of a horse.

Osmanli, *uñ*, *nuñ*: adem-*uñ*, of man; cheshmeh-*nuñ*, of a fountain.

Finnish, Lappish, &c., *n*, *en*: cala-*n*, of a fish; kabmak-*en*, of a boat.

Hungarian, *nek*, *en**: á-tenger-*nek*, of or to the sea; á-hegy-*en*-tal, on the other side of the mountain.

The hypothesis of Bopp, that the possessive terminations of Indo-European adjectives, numerals, &c., and the formatives of many abstract nouns were originally pronouns, seems to derive some support from the following analytic constructions in Semitic.

Syriac, *ruch*, spirit, *d*-ruch [*lit.* which spirit = πνευματικός].

Cardinals: trēn, 2; tloth, 3.
Ordinals: *da*-trēn, second; *da*-tloth, third. [Compare Sanscr. dwiti*ya*, triti*ya*, &c.]

Ethiopic, *tzarq*, rag; *za*-tzarq, ragged: lamtz, leprosy; *za*-lamtz, leprosus: Maryam, Mary; *za*-Maryam, Marianus.

Cardinal: selus, three.
Ordinal: menbāka *za*-selus, lectio feriæ tertiæ.

---

* The variety of functions exercised by the element *na* and its modifications in languages of almost every part of the world is not a little remarkable. Compare New. Zeal. *nana*, Lazian *nam* = qui; Gael. *nan*, *nam*, plur. gen. article; Sanscr. *nãm*, termination of gen. plur.; Pali and Armenian *na* = hic, iste, &c. Other examples have been already given. All these significations may be referred to the simple demonstrative pronoun as the radix.

ON THE DERIVATION OF WORDS FROM PRONOMINAL AND PREPOSITIONAL ROOTS.

[*Proceedings of the Philological Society. Vol. II.*]

The languages commonly called synthetic agree uniformly in this leading feature of being resolvable into a comparatively small number of elements, usually denominated *roots*. In Hebrew there are few derivative words which are not capable of being referred to their parent stem; or when this cannot be done within the limits of the Hebrew itself, the root wanted may generally be supplied from the Arabic or some other cognate dialect. We here speak of the Semitic roots as they are usually given by grammarians, and do not now enter into the controverted question whether they are primary or in reality compounded. In Welsh also there are few derivatives which may not be satisfactorily accounted for either from the radicals of that language, or from the Armorican and Gaelic dialects. In like manner the Indian grammarians have reduced the whole of the Sanscrit language to a comparatively small number of *d'hatoos* or roots; and there is no reason for doubting that in a great majority of cases the secondary and composite forms are rightly referred by them to their originals. There may be room to question their conclusions in particular instances, especially with regard to pronouns and particles; and it may be also suspected that a number of ostensible roots are in reality mere varieties of form or collateral descendants from some unascertained primitive.

These roots are commonly regarded as mere abstractions, that is, not actual practical words, but words *in posse*; and they are generally explained, either by an abstract noun in the locative case, or a verb in the third person; indeed they are almost universally represented to be *roots* of *verbs*, and consequently more nearly related to the verb than to any other part of speech. Bopp and Pott, who frequently question the positions of the Indian grammarians, do not dissent from them in this general view of the subject; except that, instead of deriving pronouns and simple particles from verbal roots, they consider them, or the elements out of which they are formed, as a class apart, neither descended from verbs, nor in any way related to them. With respect to the non-derivation of those elements from verbs, they are probably in the right; but whether, on the other hand, verbs and other parts of speech may not occasionally be derived from them, is a different question, which a small amount of research will enable us to decide in the affirmative. Proofs might be multiplied from many languages; we shall at present content ourselves with a few examples from the Old High-German.

ABA. The Old-German preposition corresponding to the Sanscr. *apa*, Gr. ἀπὸ, is *aba*, only occurring in this form in the oldest monuments of the language. From this we have the adjective *ab-uh*, sinister, perverse, i. e. *deviating*, branching into several derivative nouns, along with the verb *abahon*, to abominate. A verb more directly formed from the root may be inferred from the participial form *aband*, evening, i. e. declining, which again is enlarged into the verb *abanden*, vesperascere.

ABAR, AFAR, AVAR. This word, evidently a comparative form of the preceding, is in Gothic a preposition, with the sense of Lat. *post*; but in Old-German it is an adverb, commonly denoting *again*. From it the verb *avaron*, to repeat, is directly formed, together with a number of nouns in all the dialects; among which may be specified Goth. *afar*, series, and Ang.-Sax. *afara*, *eafora*, a descendant.

OBAR, UBAR. This preposition, found in nearly all the Indo-European dialects, forms in O. H.-Germ. the verbs *obaron*, to put off, prolong, and *ga-obaron*, to surpass, overcome. Compare Lat. *superare*.

ANU, without. Mod.-Germ. *ohne*. *Indanon*, afterwards *entanen*, to deprive.

IN—forms the verb *innon*, bearing the various meanings of to annex, bring, receive, admit, &c. along with the nouns *innod*, viscera, *innote*, indigena, and several others. From the comparative form *innaro*, inner, is derived *innaron*, to insinuate; and with the prefix *er*, *erinnern*, to remember.

UZ, out. From this come the verbs *uzon*, to renounce; *ga-uzon*, to remove, exclude. From the comparative *uzaro* is derived the present Germ. *aüssern*, to express, enunciate. The Engl. *utter* is evidently of cognate origin.

NIDAR, below, beneath. *Nidarjan*, to humble, condemn; *ganidaron*, to cast down; with many nouns and adjectives.

NAH, near, after. *Nahen*, to approach; *zuonahen*, to hasten, come near.

SAMAN, with, together. *Samanon*, to gather, congregate; with a multitude of derivatives.

SUNTAR, apart. *Suntaron*, to separate.

The above list might be greatly enlarged; but enough has been given to show, not merely the abstract possibility, but the fact of the derivation of verbs and other parts of speech from simple particles: analogies will readily suggest themselves from the Greek and other languages, but they are too obvious to be here dilated upon. It may perhaps be objected that all the above instances are of comparatively recent date, and that no similar principle of formation can be traced in the earliest stages of language. It is apprehended that we know too little of language in its infancy, either to affirm or deny this proposition on direct and positive grounds: the utmost that we can expect to accomplish is to deduce probable conclusions from the data and the analogies within our reach. It is however conceived, that there is no inherent improbability in the supposition that verbs and other words might equally be formed from similar elements at a much earlier period.

Terms expressive of local relations must have existed in every regularly organized language at least as early as some other classes, and the powers of combination and symbolical application inherent in the human mind could be as easily exercised on words expressing separation and connexion in space, as upon any other attributes cognizable by the senses. That those terms are themselves of the highest antiquity is admitted by the best philologists; indeed Bopp does not scruple to characterize them as "antediluvian." The origin of the words themselves is a question which we do not undertake to discuss. It is not perhaps absolutely impossible that they were primarily *onomatopœiæ*, or imitations of natural sounds; but there are many difficulties in the way of such an hypothesis. Wüllner, and other writers who have laboured with great ingenuity to account for the formation of language by this process, have felt the difficulty of dealing with this branch of the subject; and while they allow that pronouns and particles are an original and very important part of language, they admit that it is not easy to establish a connexion between the enunciation of a sound and the idea of a place.

Waving therefore the discussion of this point as being beyond our means of information, we proceed to inquire whether there is any evidence of particles and pronouns having actually become roots of verbs and nouns at an early stage of the Indo-European languages. We shall begin with a class of languages which have hitherto been only partially employed for purposes of general philology, but which it is believed are calculated to throw considerable light on several obscure phenomena.

The Cymric and Armorican preposition denoting *over*, *upon*, is *gwar* or *gwor*, commonly abbreviated to *gor* in the former language, but subsisting in its original form in the latter. The corresponding Gaelic term is *for*, now obsolete except in composition. Now there is a large class of words — nouns, adjectives and verbs — which may be more naturally and obviously referred to this preposition as their root, than to any other in the compass of the Celtic languages. Thus we have W. *gwarad*, covering; *gwarchau*, to enclose; *gwared*, to guard; *gwer*, a shade, and many similar words. These again have their counterparts in Germanic, Latin, and Slavonic words commencing with *w* or *v*, or in Greek words which formerly had the digamma. Many of these terms are referred by Pott, Benfey, and other German philologists to the Sanscrit *varāmi* or *varayāmi* (from the root *vrĭ*), commonly denoting to cover or to choose. Admitting this, it follows that if the Celtic terms are related to the corresponding Teutonic, &c., they must be equally so to the Sanscrit; in other words, Sanscr. *varāmi*, Goth. *warjan*, Celt. *gwarad*, &c., all denoting covering, must be of common origin. The next step in the investigation is to see what probable grounds we have for referring these terms and their cognates to a local or prepositional relation as their original root.

Pictet, in his ' Affinité des Langues Celtiques avec le Sanscrit,' observes that the Irish *frith* and W. *gwrth*=against, are the counterparts of Sanscr. *prati*, Gr. προτὶ, and that Ir. *for*, W. *gwor* or *gor*, correspond to *pra*, *parā*, Gr. πρὸ and παρά. Among the Celtic prepositions which have no formal representatives in Sanscrit or Greek, he specifies Ir. *fa*, *fo*, sub, apud, &c., W. *gwa*, *go*=under. Against the etymology of *frith* and *gwrth* there is nothing to object: with respect to *for* and *gor**, it is to be observed that they, as well as the Lithuanian *per*, always signify *over*, *upon*, and therefore are potentially equivalent to Sanscr. *upari*, Gr. ὑπὲρ, Germ. *ubar*, &c. With respect to *fa*, *fo*, &c., it is strange that Pictet did not perceive that they bear precisely the same relation to Sanscr. *upa*, Gr. ὑπὸ, that *frith*, &c. do to *prati*, προτὶ, with their cognates; a relation further borne out by the analogy of the Slavonic and Lithuanian *po*, *pod*, under, after, &c., which are clearly cognate with the corresponding Sanscrit and Greek, and also it is believed

---

* The Welsh equivalent of παρά is *ger* = by, adjoining.

with the Celtic. Thus we have a strict parallelism throughout: *gwa*, *fa* = *upa*; *gwar*, *for* = *upari*, and *gwrth*, *frith* = *prati*.

If therefore the preposition *gwar*, upon, is cognate with Sanscr. *upari*, and is at the same time the root of *gwarad*, covering, &c.—which come as naturally from it as *supero* does from *super*—it follows that *upari* and *varāmi* are related to each other, and that an element simply denoting *upon*, *over*, may be the primordial one in the latter word. If this point could be once well-established, it would lead to conclusions important in themselves, and calculated to simplify in no small degree the current ideas of the organization of language. We shall at present hypothetically assume this position, and proceed to inquire how far the actual phenomena of language are found to coincide with it.

As preliminary to the ensuing discussion we may observe, once for all, that the Cymric *gw* = Irish *f*, is convertible in Welsh to a simple guttural *g*, *c* (*ch*), or to a labial *b*, *p* (*m*): in Sanscrit it corresponds generally to *w*, occasionally to *sw*; to a labial, guttural, or palatal: in Slavonic to *v*, a labial or palatal: in German to *qu*, *w*, *g*, *b*, *p*. Correspondences with other dialects will occasionally be noticed in the sequel. *R* is also commutable with other liquids, generally with *l*, and is not unfrequently transposed; e. gr. *var*, *bar*, *par*, may become respectively *vra*, *bra*, *pra*, &c. We shall also consider the Sanscrit roots, *varn*, to colour; *vrit*, *hvri*, *dhvri*, generally denoting turning, deflection, v. t. q. *val*, to cover; *hval*, to move to and fro — the corresponding forms to which in other dialects frequently interchange significations — as etymologically related to each other and belonging to the class which we are proposing to examine. If we assume then that *gwar*, upon, over, may become the parent stem of verbs and nouns, as the Germ. *ubar* becomes *ubaron*, the words most obviously connected with it are those simply denoting superposition, covering or elevation. Among these we may class *gwarad*, *gwarch*, *gwarth*, covering; *gwarchâu*, to enclose; *gwer*, a shade; *gweryd*, turf, sward. In the Teutonic languages we have Goth. *warjan*, to cover; O. H.-Germ. *wara*, a dwelling; *werjan*, to dress; A.-S. *wreon*, to cover. In Slavonic *vrieti*, to cover or shut up, whence *vrata*, a door or gate; *vr'ch*, a summit (comp. Armen. *i werah*, over, upon); and many similar words. The Sanscrit words derived from *var* (*vri*), denoting clothing, equipment, armour, and other modes of covering, are pretty numerous; one of the most remarkable is *urnā*, wool, which it is curious and instructive to trace through the cognate dialects. The initial *v* or *w* vocalized in *urnā*, and dropt in *lana*, reappears in Slavon. *vl'na*, Lithuanian *wilna*, Goth. *wulla*, where *n* is assimilated to the preceding liquid.   The Welsh *gwlan* presents the fullest form of the word, as Gael. *ollan*, and Gr. ἐρίου the weakest.   The Latin *villus, vellus* (for *vilnus, velnus?*) are probably related.   The antiquity of the term and the attribute meant to be denoted by it are sufficiently evident. The English *flannel*, from W. *gwlanen*, which might have been a Gaelic form, is a good example of the change often made in adopted words.

Passing over for the present the numerous formations in *gwal, val, bal,* &c., believed to be connected with the above, we may next observe, that there is an easy and obvious transition from the idea of covering to that of defence or protection.   Connected with this we have in Welsh *gwared*, to guard (whence Ital. *guardare*, Fr. *garder*); *gwarant*, security; *gwersyll*, a camp; *gwerthyr*, a fortification.   In Teutonic, *warjan, werjan* (O. H.-G.), to defend; *gawer*, defensive armour; A.-S. *wer*, a wear or embankment; with a multitude of similar words in many languages.   Allied with the idea of defence is that of prohibition, examples of which are W. *gwarddu*, to forbid; Germ. *wehren*, to keep off; *warnen*, to warn.   From the notion of protecting, the transition is also easy to that of watching, observing, beholding, seeing; as may be seen in the Ital. *guardare*, to guard or watch, to observe, to look; Germ. *warten*, to beware, to perceive; analogous to which is Lat. *tueor*, to defend, to behold.   A simpler form occurs in the A.-S. *wær*, wary, Germ. ge-*wahr*, observant; with which the Gr. ὄρω, to guard, ὁράω, to see, may possibly be connected.   The Welsh *gwyliaw*, to watch; *gwyled, gweled*, to see; appear to be from the same root, substituting *l* for *r*; as may be inferred from Bret. *gwere*, Irish *faire*, watch, where *r* is preserved.   Another modification of the same idea is that of endurance, continuance; as may be seen in the German *warten*, to watch, also to expect, wait; and in a more simple form in O.-Germ. *wēren*, to abide, endure; *wirig*, permanent; and in a metaphorical sense, A.-S. *weorig*, weary, tedious.

Pott and other German philologists also refer to the same root Germ. *war*, Lat. *verus*, true; *q. d.* covered, protected, secure.   If we admit this, the W. *gwir*, Gael. *fior*, true; Slavon. *viera*, faith, belong of course to the same category. Again, what is covered may at the same time be concealed, whence A.-S. *wreon*, to hide; Dan *vraa*, O.-Eng. *wro*, a secret corner.   Comp. Lat. *velare, revelare.*

The next class of words which we propose to consider as connected with the root in question, is that involving the idea of crossing, deviating, turning, &c., both literal and metaphorical. A relation between this and the former class is easily established if we keep in mind that what lies or passes over a surface may *cross* it, or deviate from what is assumed to be its proper direction, or go beyond its natural limits. Thus *transire flumen* may be indifferently rendered to go *over the* river, or *across* it, or beyond it; and he who thus crosses a river deviates at the same time from the natural direction of its current, and may also turn from it by passing further. The most original Celtic form appears to be the Breton *gwara*, to bend; whence *gwarek*, a bow (compare Lat. *arcus*); *gwarog*, a yoke. The Welsh *gwyr*, oblique, curved; *gwyraw*, to bend; Irish *fiar*, crooked, slightly deviate in form, while the Eng. *wry* transposes the liquid. The German furnishes the full form *quer*, across, athwart; and the weaker *werran*, to disturb, confuse; ga-*werran*, to over-turn; *wir–t*, deflected, distorted. If we regard the Sanscrit *vrĭt* as connected with the simpler form *vrĭ*, we are enabled to connect with this class the Lat. *vertere*, to turn; Germ. *werden*, to become, *q. d.* to turn out; Slavon. *vratiti*, to turn; Lithuanian *wersti*, to turn, roll; A.-S. *wræthian*, to wreathe, entwine; and many other words. The list might be extended to some hundreds of terms, by including all the varieties of form caused by a substitution or modification of radicals, a few specimens of which will be given in the tables.

The secondary and metaphorical ideas connected with the relation of *turning*, are too numerous to be specified individually. A multitude of words bearing the literal significations of roll, twist, throw, variegate, corrupt, surround, shake, and the moral or metaphorical ones of err, deceive, pervert, transgress, &c., referable more or less directly to the class under consideration, will readily occur to the comparative philologist. To *choose*, Sanscr. *varayāmi*, O.-Germ. *weljon*, Lith. *weliti*, Gr. αἱϱέομαι, may be explained as *to set aside*, out of a larger number = Lat. *seligere*. To *will*, Welsh *gwyll*, *gwyllys* (voluntas), Germ. *wollen*, Lat. *volo*, Gr. βούλομαι, is evidently related, as may be seen at once from the Lat. *opto*, to wish and to choose.

The extent of the field of investigation ostensibly connected with the particular class of words under consideration, may be inferred from the circumstance that Benfey, in his 'Griechisches Wurzel-Lexicon,' traces to them nearly a thousand Greek vocables; and had he been fully aware of the resources derivable from the Cymric and Armorican dialects, he might easily have found many more. These dialects satisfactorily explain many phænomena otherwise not easily accounted for; as for instance *gwar*, *gwyr*, oblique, curved, show at once the possible connexion between Germ. *quer*, Lat. *varius*, *varus*, Engl. *wry*, Gr. γυϱὸς; to say nothing of Lat. *curvus*, Gael. *cor*, *car*, turn, twist; Gr. εὐϱὰξ, awry; with a multitude of words more or less deflecting from the original type, but easily reducible to it according to recognized analogies.

We have all along treated the word *gwar* in the light of a simple and independent radical; there is however every reason to believe that it is in reality a comparative form of *gwa* (*gwo*, *go*), as Sanscr. *upari* is of *upa*, and Goth. *ufar* of *uf*. To speak more strictly, *gwar* is a combination of two prepositional elements, *gwa* + *ar*, the latter having in itself the sense of *upon*, *over*, in all the Celtic dialects. Each of these elements is the parent of other words: thus *gwa* is enlarged into *gwadn*, base, foundation (comp. Germ. *boden*); *gwad-dawd*, dregs; *gwael*, low, base (Lat. *vilis*); *gwas*, a servant, vassal: while *ar* becomes W. *aros*, abiding, dwelling; Gael. *ard*, lofty (Lat. *arduus*); *airde*, height; *ardaighim*, to elevate, &c. That the Sanscr. *upari*, Goth. *ufar*, should be compounds is easily conceivable, if we reflect that A.-S. *butan* (our *but*) is composed of three distinct elements, *bi–ut–an*, and *abutan* (about) of four. If therefore *gwar*, to cover, turn, &c., is connected with the preposition, it is not in the strict sense of the term a primary word; and if we are correct in the view which we have all along taken of the matter, the same will apply to the Sanscrit *vṛi* and the other ostensible roots supposed to be connected with it. It is believed that they are all reducible to one leading notion, viz. that of *covering*, as included in the preposition or adverb *upon*, which again is itself probably of pronominal origin.

This view of the matter is further strengthened by the comparison of the collateral element *tar* in Gaelic, = over, upon, in conjunction with W. *tra*, *tros*, over, *trwy*, through, &c., with the Sanscrit root *trī*, to pass over, and its numerous cognates. Words apparently including this element abound in every branch of the Indo-European family; and they will be found on examination to run parallel throughout, or nearly so, with the class previously examined, in the senses of covering, preserving, watching, turning, throwing, transgressing, &c. This coincidence is easily accounted for if we suppose that both classes contain the same prepositional element *ar* = over, upon — giving pretty nearly the same force to each. It is believed that the same element, both in the simple form *ar* and the augmented *tar*, enters into the comparative forms of adjectives and particles, and various other formations in which the idea of *more*, *further*, v. t. q. is included.

It will perhaps be thought that it is a series of ungrounded assumptions to regard the words in question as connected with each other, whereas they may be independent roots. To this it may be replied, that it is equally an assumption to maintain that they are totally unconnected with each other; and if they *are* related, as the general analogy of their forms would rather lead us to believe, it is clear that they cannot be at the same time collateral and primary. The science of comparative etymology does not, like arithmetic or geometry, rest upon certain and demonstrable premises, but consists in a series of presumptive deductions from such analogies of form and meaning as can be traced in languages known or believed to be cognate. We have no direct evidence that *wary*, *warn*, *wear*, *weary*, *wry*, *wreathe*, *writhe*, are all from the same root; but it is conceived that no one who has traced them carefully through all the kindred dialects would venture to assert that they are radically and totally distinct. An attempt has been made to show that those, and multitudes of similar words may be referred to one simple local relation; and if this be really the case, it is obvious that the same principle may be applicable in many more cases. Such words as περάω, περαίνω in Greek, and *samanon*, *uzon*, &c. in German, show that particles may and actually do become the parent stems of verbs; and it is at least as intelligible and easy that *over* should become *cover*, or *cross*, as that *out* should come to denote *speak*, or *in*, remember. If it should be found, on further investigation, that this principle of derivation has prevailed to a great extent, it will follow that the doctrine of Bopp and Pott, viz. that the pronominal and prepositional roots constitute a class apart, wholly unconnected with the elements of verbs, cannot be supported. On the contrary it would seem more probable that those roots are in many cases the real primordia of the ostensible *d'hatoos* or verbal roots, and that they in fact constitute the basis of no inconsiderable portion of the Indo-European languages.

The following words, constituting a very small portion of the aggregate, seem directly referable to the Sanscrit roots *hvri̇̆*, *vri̇̈*, *vri̇̆t*, *hval*, *val*, already assumed to be related to each other. The Celtic words are Welsh when not otherwise specified.

gwal, enclosure.
gwalc, palisade (cf. Ital. palco).
gwalch, *adj.* towering, *sub.* falcon.
gwalen, Bret. a ring.
gwall, defect, error.
gwar, Bret. crooked, vaulted.
gwàr, neck (from *turning*; cf. Sl. vrat).
gwara, to fence.
gwarad, covering.
gwarant, security.
gwarch, covering.
gwarchâu, to enclose.
gwarddu, to prohibit.
gwared, to guard.
gwaremm, Bret. a warren.
gwarez, Bret. shelter, protection.
gwarog, a yoke.
gwarth, covering.
gweilging, a cross-beam.
gweili, a surplus.
gweled, to see.
gweli, an exposure.
gwell, better.

gwellt, grass, sward (cf. gwallt, hair of the head)
gwer, a shade.
gwere, Bret. a watch-tower.
gwerthyd, a spindle (Ir. fearsaid).
gweryd, sward.
gwil, turn off, start.
gwilc'hu, Bret. to squint.
gwill, apt to stray.
gwir, true.
gwladychu, to govern (cf. Germ. walten).
gwores, open, exposed.
gwrag, curved handle, *v. t. q.*
gwregys, girdle.
gwrīth, apparent.
gwrydd, a wreath.
gwylchu, to seem or appear.
gwylied, to watch.
gwyll, will.
gwyllt, wild.
gwyr, oblique.
gwyrain, to elevate.

Slavonic, Lithuanian, &c.

varati, Serv. to deceive.
variti, Sl. to proceed.
wahrpsta, Lettish, spindle.
wahrst, to bolt.
wahrstiht, to roll to and fro.
wahrti, a door.
wairitees, *verb. refl.* to beware.
wairoht, to augment.
waldiht, to govern.
walgs, cord, rope (from twisting).
warra, power.
warren, *adv.* exceedingly.
warreht, to be powerful.
wehrigs, observant.
weley, Lithuan. late.
wercziù, I turn over.
werpju, I spin.

weru, I close; at-w- = I open (cf. Welsh a-gori; Bret. di-gori, to open; Lat. a-perio, o-perio).
willoju, I seduce (Lett. wilt, to deceive).
wirrags, Lett. a whirlpool.
wirs, upon.
wirssus, Lith. a summit.
wirst, Lett. to rise upwards.
wirstu, Lith. I overturn, become (cf. Sanscr. vrĭt, to turn, to become; Germ. werden).
wirtis, a whirlpool.
wirwe, a cord.
woloju, I roll about.
z'welgiu, I see, look.
z'wairu, I squint.

The corresponding forms in the pure Slavonic dialects generally transpose the liquid, as will appear from the following examples: —

wlada, Bohem. power, government (cf. W. gwlad, country; Bret. glad, patrimony; Ir. flaith, sovereignty).
wladnauti, to move, stir.
wlati, Slav. to fluctuate.
wlna, Bohem. wool.
wrat, turn, return. Serv. vrat, neck.
wrata, a door.

wratiti, to turn.
wratky, giddy.
wreteno, a spindle.
vrieti. Slav. to shut.
vr'gu, I throw (cf. Lat. torqueo).
vr'zu, I open.
vr't, a garden.
vr'tieti, to turn round.
vr'ch, a summit.

Some of the principal Teutonic equivalents having been given in the course of the preceding paper, it will not be necessary to repeat them. The Greek forms are reserved for an inquiry which it is proposed to make into the powers and affinities of the digamma. The following Latin words may be referred with more or less probability to the same class of roots: —

valeo, to be powerful.
valgus, bandy-legged.
vallum, an entrenchment.
valvæ, folding-doors.
varioli, small-pox (cf. W. brech, variegated; also small-pox).
varius, changeable, &c.
varus, crooked (cf. præ-varico, &c).

vellus, a fleece.
velum, a veil, covering.
vertere, to turn.
vertex, summit.
verus, true.
volvere, to roll.
vortex, a whirlpool.

The above words, to which a multitude of similar ones might easily be added, correspond pretty strictly with the forms assumed as their radicals. There are, moreover, an immense number of terms which are referable to the same origin, by taking into account the changes briefly indicated above by elision, transposition, and the substitution of elements etymologically cognate. A few examples will serve to illustrate this portion of the subject.

The following are cognate forms with the elision of the labial: —

gail, the eye-lid.
gallt, a steep or cliff.
gardd, an enclosure.
garth, a rampart.
geol, a prison.

gour, Bret. slowness, leisure.
gol, a covering.
golwg, sight.
gor, Bret. a tumour.
gorch, a fence.

gorddi, to impel forward.
gored, a wear.
gorel, opening.
gores, open, exposed.
goreu, superior, best.
gori, to brood.
gormant, exuberance.
gormu, to force in, intrude (cf. ὁρμάω).

Bret. gorre, top, surface.
— gorrea, to raise.
— gorrek, slow, idle (in some dialects gwarek).
— gorroen, cream.
— gourinn, lintel of a door.
— gourzizu, to delay, put off.

In Breton, words of this description are frequently still further abbreviated by the elision or transposition of the leading vowel.

glad, patrimony;   Welsh gwlad.
glao, rain;   — gwlaw.
gleb, moist;   — gwlyb, moisture.
gliz, dew;   — gwlith.
gloan, wool;   — gwlan.
grac'h, old woman;   — gwrach.
greg, woman;   — gwraig (cf. Germ. frau).
grisien, root;   — gwraidd.

These and similar forms show that words commencing with a guttural followed by a liquid, may correspond to a Sanscrit, German or Slavonic w: e. gr. glad, to Germ. wallen; gloan, to Sanscr. urnā, Bohem. wlna, Germ. wolle. A little inquiry will enable us to discover a multitude of words commencing with a labial or guttural followed by l or r, under significations precisely analogous to the words already given, and in all probability of kindred origin. A few examples from the Lithuanian and Lettish will place this point in a clearer light.

Lith. breest, to increase.
Lett. brunnas, armour.
— glahbt, to guard, protect.
Lith. globoju, I embrace.
Lett. gredsens, a ring.
— greest, to turn.
— greests, a coverlet.
— greest-balki, cross-beam.
Lith. greju, I surround, enclose.
Lett. greiss, awry, crooked.
Lith. greziu, I turn, bore, encircle, wind (cf. Bohem. wrtiti, wrtati, to turn, shake, waver, move, churn, bore, &c.).
— grysstu, I turn, return.
Lett. klaht, to cover.
— klaidiht, to wander about.
Lith. klaupju, I kneel down.
— klesscziu, I tremble.
— kloju, I cover.
— klonoju, I bow down.
— klydeju, I wander.
Lett. krahpt, to deceive.
— krampis, a bolt.
Lith. krattau, I shake.

Lith. krauju, I heap up.
— kreikiu, I strew.
— kreiwas, crooked; cf. W. crwm; Ger. krumm.

Lith. kreipju, I turn, return.
— priess, prep. against = W. gwrth.

It is not meant to be asserted that all the above words are certainly connected with the Sanscrit and Celtic roots which we have been examining; but the connection is theoretically possible, according to known analogies. The probability of its subsistence is greatly strengthened by the Persian, in which a Sanscrit or Teutonic *w* regularly becomes a guttural: e. gr. *gurāzah*, hog or boar = Sanscr. *varāha* (comp. Lat. *porcus*, Germ. *ferch*, Eng. *barrow-pig*, Gr. χοῖρος); *gardan-iden*, to turn = Sanscr. *vrlt*, Lat. *verto*, &c.; *garm* = Germ. *warm*; *kirm* = Germ. *wurm*. The Slavonic and Lithuanian languages manifest a considerable resemblance to the Persian, both in words and characteristic elements.

It is scarcely necessary to say, that words commencing with *bal*, *bar*, *pal*, *par*, &c. are still more likely to be related to the family of words which we have been examining; indeed the affinity of many of them does not admit of a doubt. This will become obvious on comparing such words as *bal*, peak; *balch*, proud; *bar*, summit; *bern*, a heap; *parc*, enclosure; Fr. *parer*, to keep off; Span. *parar*, to stop, &c., with the preceding lists and with the Gaelic. *Gweilging*, W. a cross-beam (from *gwail*, superincumbent), becomes in Gaelic *baircin*. It is in all probability also the etymon of Engl. *balk* and Germ. *galge*, a gallows. Many similar instances might easily be collected.

ON CERTAIN INITIAL LETTER-CHANGES IN THE INDO-EUROPEAN LANGUAGES.

[Proceedings of the Philological Society. Vol. II.]

In the various branches of the great Indo-European family of languages, we find that multitudes of words differ from their cognates in form; and, to a certain extent, according to definite laws of permutation. This is more particularly the case with respect to their initial elements. If we take Sanscrit, Latin, Slavonic, or any other considerable member of the group as a standard, numerous instances occur in which a collateral language replaces an initial conjunct consonant by a simple one, or *vice versâ*, and substitutes a guttural for a labial, a palatal for a guttural, an aspirate for a sibilant, or one liquid semivowel for another. In many cases those permutations are well-understood and easily accounted for, but with regard to some of them there appears to be a little misapprehension.

It is usual to account for the substitution of a guttural for a labial, and similar phenomena, by the assumption that one is changed into the other. This appears actually to take place in a number of instances; as for example in the Neapolitan *cchiù* from *più*, Lat. *plus*: Gaelic *caisg* from *pascha*, and many others. But there are cases in which there is reason to believe that both the labial and guttural are in reality derivative sounds, collaterally descended from a more complex element, capable of producing both. The practicability of the process may be manifest by an obvious instance. If we could only compare Gr. δὶς and Lat. *bis* with each other, we should be compelled to affirm either that the labial was the representative of a dental, or that the words had no etymological connexion. But a reference to the Sanscrit *dwis*, at once shows that each has taken a portion of a more complex sound; the Greek having elided the labial, and the Latin dropped the dental. *Bellum* from *duellum* is a parallel instance. The grammarians inform us that *bonus* was originally *duonus*; and if so, it is very possible that the Welsh *duin*, beautiful, *daionus*, good, may be representatives of the ancient form, minus *u*, which in all probability emanated from a *v* or *w*.

The same observation may perhaps serve to explain certain phænomena connected with the Greek digamma. This element is supposed by some to have been a mere aspirate, and by others to have corresponded precisely with the Latin *v* or German *w*. The former supposition appears to be contradicted by the prosody of the Homeric poems: and though the latter agrees better with the collateral forms in other languages, it is not without its difficulties.

Priscian, after observing that it had commonly the force of a consonant in prosody, adds, " The Æolians are also found sometimes to have employed the digamma as a *double consonant*, as Νέστορα δὲ Ϝοῦ παῖδος." This view might be confirmed by numerous examples from Homer, in which an initial digamma frequently lengthens a preceding short vowel. As this never takes place with a Latin *v*, it is reasonable to presume that there was some difference in their respective powers; and this presumption appears to be strengthened by various phenomena presented by the Grecian dialects and the languages to which they are etymologically related. Words known to have had the digamma in the time of Homer, in other branches of the Greek language replace this element by a simple guttural or labial; and occasionally it appears to be represented by a sibilant, alone, or in connection with a labial. On this and other grounds, Mr. Donaldson (New Cratylus, p. 119 *et seq.*) argues that the original digamma must have had a complex sound, consisting of a guttural combined with a labial, the former element being also convertible into a sibilant.* It is the object of the present paper to bring further evidence in favour of the general correctness of the above theory, from some collateral sources of illustration which it did not enter into Mr. Donaldson's plan to notice.

The illustration most in point is furnished by the Welsh. In this language the digamma, with its equivalents in other tongues, is usually represented by *gw*; *w* being nearly unknown in Cymric as a primary initial consonant. It was shown on a former occasion that the labial element may either be elided, as in W. *gwlan*, wool; Bret. *gloan*; or that the conjunct consonant may become a simple labial, as *balch* from *gwalch*. Precisely the same phenomenon is presented by the various dialects of the Greek. The grammarians and lexicographers have preserved a number of words in which γ or β appears as a prefix to the vowel initial of the

---

* Hoefer, in his 'Beiträge zur Etymologik', has taken pretty nearly the same view of the subject.

ordinary dialect; and in almost every instance the words thus augmented are known, or may be strongly suspected anciently to have had the digamma.

The correctness of the forms commencing with *gamma* is admitted by Buttmann and Giesius, who agree in regarding the phenomenon as a dialectical peculiarity. On the other hand, Ahrens, in his elaborate work on the Doric dialect, is inclined to consider them as corruptions, or errors of Hesychius or his transcribers, who, not understanding the real nature of the digamma, substituted for it the character most similar in form. This summary method of deciding the point seems rather to cut the knot than to untie it; at all events it is an unsafe species of criticism to condemn everything as corrupt which we do not perfectly understand. We know that in Persian and other languages a guttural was the regular substitute for a Greek digamma,* and it is obvious that a change which took place in a cognate language might be equally admissible in a sister dialect.

As points of this kind are better illustrated by evidence than by abstract reasoning, an attempt will be made to support the genuineness of these and other apparently anomalous forms by instances from collateral languages.

Among the Hesychian glosses we find γοῖνος, οἶνος, with several derivatives, for which the critics without the smallest hesitation bid us substitute Ϝοῖνος. Undoubtedly this was a genuine form; but if we suppose, which is very possible, that the digamma was a double consonant, comprising a guttural and a labial, like the Welsh *gwyn*, or the Georgian *ghwini*, it is obvious that the former element might prevail in particular localities as the labial did in others. This view appears to be confirmed not only by the Welsh and Breton forms, but by the Armenian *gini*.

Another remarkable gloss in Hesychius is γίαρες = ἔαρ, which appears from the analogy of other words to have been a Bœotian form. Ἔαρ is well known to have had the digamma (comp. Lat. *ver*, Icelandic *vér*): but there is also the evidence of the Armenian *garoun*, in favour of the gut-

---

* Mr. Donaldson observes, after Burnouf, that Neriosergh, who translated into Sanscrit the Pehlvi version of the Yaçna, represents the Zend *v* by the Sanscrit *ghv* or *gv*; thus for *vôhumanò*, *hàvam*, *çavangh*, he writes *ghvahmana*, *hàguana*, *çaguamgha*. (New Cratylus, p. 120.) It may be further observed that the modern Persian occasionally substitutes a labial, e. gr. *bad*, wind; *hist.* 20; Sanscr. *vinsati*. It may therefore be reasonably inferred that the ancient Persian archetype of those various articulations must have had a power bearing some analogy to that which we attribute to the digamma.

16*

tural. The Persian *bahar* presents another form of the labial; the Gaelic *earrach* is exactly parallel with the ordinary Greek. Benfey and other German philologists suppose a connexion with Sanscr. *vasanta*; *s*, as is frequently the case, being softened to *r*. This idea appears to be confirmed by the Slavonic *vesna*, and perhaps by the Cornish *guantoin*, W. *gwannvyn*, where *s* or *r* may have been elided. The Lithuanian *wasara*, summer, appears to be from the same root.

Ahrens, who is unwilling to admit that the simple guttural could become a representative of the digamma, allows that there is competent authority for it in the word $\gamma o\tilde{\iota}\nu o\varsigma$, a hide or shield; which is also known to have had the digamma. Its genuineness is further attested by the Welsh *croen*, skin or hide. The Bohemian *blana* may possibly be related, *l* being frequently substituted for *r* in the Slavonic dialects. The direct affinity of the Norse *brynja*, a coat of mail, is doubtful; it being apparently from the Slavonic *brona*, which is referable to a root implying defence or protection, analogous to Germ. *wehren*.

Many other examples might be given wherein a guttural initial in other languages, or in the dialects of Greece itself, corresponds with the digamma. Some of these have been noticed in former communications, and a few others will be pointed out in the sequel. We proceed to adduce evidence in favour of other words where inscriptions or glosses appear to prefix a labial.

In the Tables of Heraclea, published by Mazochi, the digamma is regularly prefixed to the numeral *six* and its derivatives: $F\acute{\epsilon}\xi$, $F\epsilon\xi\eta\kappa o\nu\tau a$, $\vert F\acute{\epsilon}\kappa\tau o\varsigma$, &c. This is pronounced by Ahrens to be a recent corruption, since neither the Sanscrit *shash*, Lat. *sex*, nor Gothic *saihs*, show any traces of a digamma. This is true; there is however no lack of evidence for it from other quarters. The fullest form extant is the Zend *ksvas*; and it is curious to observe how the component elements of the word appear and disappear in the cognate dialects. The Welsh *chwech* has preserved the guttural and labial; the Affghan *shpaj*, or *spash*, the sibilant and labial; the Albanian *giast*, the mere guttural; while the Armenian *wetz* corresponds pretty closely with the digamma-form of the tables. The Lithuanian *szessi* agrees closely with the Sanscrit: the ordinary Greek $\acute{\epsilon}\xi$ substitutes an aspirate initial, and the Gaelic *sè* drops the final. The Heraclean forms, which doubtless agreed with the current language of the locality, are therefore not entirely unsupported by analogy; and this example may serve, among many others, to show how unsafe it is to decide points of this kind upon a narrow induction.

It is a well-ascertained peculiarity of the Æolic dialect that β was apparently prefixed to words beginning with ῥ in the ordinary language, as βρόδον for ῥόδον. Some grammarians regard this as a merely arbitrary process; but Priscian more correctly observes that it was a mutation of the digamma; and this view is fully confirmed by the analogy of the cognate languages. An excellent example is furnished by βρίζα or βρίσδα, the Æolic form of ῥίζα, which closely agrees on one side with the Gothic *vaurt-s*, and on the other with Welsh *gwraidd*, Bret. *grisien*. The Sanscrit *bradhna* may also be of the same family. Another Sanscrit term for *root*,*budhna*, has a remarkable resemblance to the Welsh *bun*, also found in Persian and in some Slavonic and Finnish dialects. If *budhna* be a mutation of *bradhna*, as it possibly may, all the above forms are reducible to a common origin. Βρόδον may be compared with the Armenian *ward*; βρά, βραΐδιος = ῥέα, ῥάδιος, with the Anglo-Saxon *hræd*, ready, where *h* represents a more ancient guttural; βράκος, a rag, with A.-S. *hracod*, ragged, and perhaps with Welsh *brat*, rag, *bratiawg*, ragged. Φρῆξις, quoted by Trypho from Alcæus, shows that ῥήσσω had the digamma; and this at once connects the verb with Germ. *brechen*, Lat. *frango*, and possibly with W. *brau*, brittle, *breuddilaw*, to comminute, and Slavon. *br'chu*, to grind.

It appears from Herodian and Hesychius that the Bœotian form of γυνή was βανά, gen. βανῆκος; respecting which Ahrens observes, after Grimm, that a comparison of the Gothic *quinō* shows that both γυνή and βανά have sprung from a more ancient γϜανά, which also illustrates the mutations of the vowel. This is so obvious and satisfactory a solution, that it is strange that Ahrens did not think of applying it in those cases where he questions the genuineness of the simple guttural. He might also have found an admirable confirmation of it in the Welsh *gwen*, in conjunction with its synonym *benyw*, which are doubtless according to the same analogy. The Irish has also the duplicate forms *coinne* and *bean*. The Armenian *kin* closely agrees with γυνή. The Slavonic *zhena* (pron. *jena*, more Gallico) turns the guttural to a palatal. The Scandinavian *kone* vocalizes the labial: the North-Yorkshire *whcan* is a softening of the Anglo-Saxon *cwen*.

In like manner the Elean Ϝράτρα for ῥήτρα, along with its primitive Ϝρέω and several cognate terms, may be referred to the Irish *briathar*, a word; Goth. *vaurd*; Lithuanian *wardas*, a name; Russ. *govoriti*, to speak; to say nothing of Lat. *verbum*. Γηρὺς, speech; the Welsh *gair*, a word, and Lat. *garrio*, are reducible to the same origin, if we suppose an elision of the labial. From a comparison of βρόγχος, frog, a word preserved by Hesychius, Benfey infers that *rana* was originally *vrahna*: the Cornish *kranag*, Fr. *grenouille*, and Armen. *gort*, equally speak for a guttural. The Yorkshire *frosk*, Germ. *frosch*, insert a sibilant; the Danish *fro* drops the final; the Lettish *warde* agrees pretty nearly with the Armenian.

An instance of the compound initial *gw* being represented by the hard labial *p*, occurs in W. *parc*, an inclosure, Eng. *park*; which we need not hesitate to connect with *gwarchâu*, to inclose; and perhaps with Γέργω, to restrain, Γέρχος, inclosure. Another, not commonly known, is furnished by Germ. *pfennig*, Eng. *penny*. Though this is found in most of the Teutonic and Slavonic dialects, it is confessedly not vernacular in any of them; and many unsuccessful attempts have been made to account for it. It is believed that the true etymon is the Breton *gwennek*, a diminutive of *gwen*, white; the coin being, as is well known, originally of silver. The Spanish *blanquillo*, and the Slovak *belizh*, from *bel*, white, are of exactly parallel import. The Welsh *ceiniawg*, together with its root *càn*, white, show an elision of the labial. Another instance would appear to be presented by Πάξος, given by Scylax as a name of the Cretan city called by Herodotus Ὄαξος, and on coins Γάξος. The genuineness of the reading in Scylax has been doubted, but the above examples show that such a form would not be absolutely impossible.

A few miscellaneous words, chiefly from inscriptions and ancient grammarians, are annexed, with illustrative forms from corresponding dialects. They are principally words known or presumed to have had the digamma.

βαδὺ = ἡδὺ . . . . . . W. *chweg*, sweet. [cf. A.-S. *swæc*, odor, sapor.]
βάρνες, *lambs* . . . . . Russ. *baran*; Pers. *barah*; Armen. *garr*.
βινζω = ἰνζω . . . . . W. *gwacddi*, to shout.
δάβω = δαίω . . . . . W. *daiv*; Gael. *daigh*; Sanscr. *dah*; to burn.
ὤβεα = ὤα . . . . . . Gael. *ubh*; A.-S. *æg*; Lat. *ovum*.
Γέσπερος . . . . Bret. *gwesker*; W. *gosper*; Gael. *feascor*; Manks. *feastor* [cf. west, western]; Lith. *wakaras*.
Γέρδω, Γέργον . . . . Germ. *werken*; W. *gorug*, made, did; Bret. *gra*, do [comp. Gr. πράσσω].

Ϝίκατι, 20 . . . . . . Ir. *fiche*, *fichit*; W. *ugaint*; Pers. *bist*.
Ϝοῖκος . . . . Lat. *vicus*; W. *gwig*, town, hamlet.
Ϝρὶς (as inferred from the Homeric prosody.) } Bret. *fri*; W. *ffroen*, the nostrils [comp. Sanscr. *ghrāna*; Ital. *grugno*; N.-Yorksh. *groon*].
γάλι = ἅλις . . . . . . W. *gwala*, enough.
γέλλαι (*u. v.* to pluck) Lat. *vello*; A.-S. *pullian?*
γελλίξαι = συνειλή-σαι; } W. *chwylaw*, to turn, revolve; Slav. *valiti*, to roll.
γεστία = ἱμάτια . . . W. *gwisg*, apparel; Lat. *vestis*.
γιτέα, osier . . . . . . W. *gwden*; Eng. *withy*.
γοῖδα = οἶδα . . . . . W. *gwydd*, knowledge; A.-S. *witan*, to know.

The application of this analogy enables us not unfrequently to recover, at least conjecturally, a form that had been lost. From a comparison of *galleria*, ambulatorium, Ihre ingeniously infers that the French *aller* was originally *galler*. This conjecture derives a collateral support from the Breton *balèa*, to walk; *bali*, avenue; in conjunction with Germ. *wallen*; and all the forms taken in conjunction lead to the conclusion that the primary Celtic verb was *gwalla*.

Most of the permutations which we have been considering may be summed up in the counterparts for *wind*, in the different branches of the Indo-European family: — Welsh *gwynt*, Sanscr. *vahanta*, Lat. *ventus*, Slavon. *vietr*, Lithuanian *wejis*, Beluchi *gwath*, Irish *gaoth*, Persian *bad*. These forms not only illustrate the changes of the initial, but the appearance and disappearance of the nasal. The Greek ἄνεμος is probably from the same root, but with a different suffix. In its present form it bears an external resemblance to the Gaelic *anail*, W. *anadl*, breath.

The above examples, to which many others might be added, lead to the belief that the commonly received theory of labials and gutturals being commutable with each other is not in all cases strictly correct; but that each has frequently had an independent origin in a more ancient complex sound. The general progress of language is towards euphony and attenuation of articulations; it is therefore much more likely *à priori* that *w* or *v* should be modifications of *gw*, or some similar combination, than that the process should have been reversed. Words commencing with *qv* in Gothic, or *cw* in Anglo-Saxon, appear in other dialects with the simple labial, *e. gr.* A.-S. *cwanian*, Germ. *weinen*; and in this and similar cases there can be little doubt which form is the more ancient.

The establishment of this theory of an original complex

sound, divisible in the way we have been supposing, would enable us to bring many apparently unconnected words together, and to diminish the number of ostensible roots. If we assume a primitive *gwal*, *qwal*, v. t. q. signifying to turn, roll, &c., it is easy to conceive how it might on one side become the parent of the Welsh *chwylaw*, to revolve; Sanscr. *hval*, to turn; A.-S. *hweol*, wheel; O.-Germ. *hwel*, crooked; Slavon. *kolo*,* a wheel, *kolievati*, to agitate; and on the other, of Slavon. *valiti*, Germ. *wälzen*, Lat. *volvere*, to roll; with many similar words in most European languages. Formerly the only method of connecting ἀλινδέω and καλινδέω together, was by supposing that a guttural had been dropped or assumed. But the knowledge that the former anciently had the digamma places the matter in a different light, and makes it at all events probable that they are in reality collateral formations, and that they, together with their cognate κυλίω, ἀλέω, to wander about; εἰλύω, to involve, &c., have a common origin with the Latin *volvo*, and the Welsh *chwylaw*, i. e. a root *gwal* or *qwal*, or something similar.

There is another remarkable mutation of the initial *w*, which though of partial occurrence, appears to be well-established. Graff observes that this element occasionally resolves itself into *ub*, e. gr. *ubisandus*, a low Latin word for *wisant*, a bison. Other examples are — *ubandus* for *wantus*, a glove (Ital. *guanto*); *ubartellus* for *quartellus*, a quarter measure. It would be worth inquiring whether a similar principle of formation may not have operated at a more ancient period; whether, for instance, the Latin *uvidus* may not be etymologically connected with our *wet*, and the Slavonic *voda*, water. The Celtic, Slavonic and Lithuanian words corresponding with Sanscr. *upa, upari*; Goth. *uf*, under; Germ. *ubar*, over; show no traces of a prepositive vowel: the initial *u* of the latter class of words may therefore have been evolved from a consonant according to the same analogy. It will not be denied that it was just as possible in the nature of things for *gwar* or *war* to become *ubar*, as for

---

* This word, with its derivative *kolasa* (Polish), a wheel-carriage, may perhaps throw some light on a disputed point of ethnology (Ovid, Trist.): —

> "Gens inculta nimis vehitur crepitante *colossa*;
> Hoc verbo currum, Scytha, vocare soles."

This remarkable word is perfectly Slavonic, both as to its root and termination. The few words of ancient Scythian that have reached us generally correspond with Slavonic, Teutonic, Medo-Persian, or some other Indo-European dialect. We may hence plausibly infer that the Scythians were not, as Rask supposes, Tschudes or Finns, but more nearly allied to the Slaves, if not their direct ancestors.

wantus to become *ubandus*. The prepositive vowel in ὄβελος, a spit, compared with Lat. *veru*, W. *ber*, may possibly be an analogous formation. Compare also ὄβριμος, ὀφρύς, with their cognates in other languages. According to the same principle, the Goth. *ubils* may be related to W. *gwall*, or Lat. *vilis*; while the Norse *ill-r* may have lost its initial. Further examples of a similar process will be given in treating of the liquids.

With respect to the letter *l*, Grimm and other German philologists observe that it is the least variable of all sounds, especially at the beginning of words. It is true that in the languages usually compared with each other, *l* as an initial is seldom replaced by any other simple consonant. The Sanscrit affords examples of inter-change between *l* and *r*: e. gr. *lōhita* and *rōhita*, red; *lōman* and *rōman*, hair; but they are not numerous. If however we take a more comprehensive induction, and inquire at the same time whether the ordinary *l* of the Greek, Latin, and Teutonic languages may not occasionally be represented by a more complex sound, we shall discover phenomena which at all events appear to deserve a careful investigation. We may observe as a preliminary to the present inquiry, that an Englishman or German is apt to take a limited view of the subject, because he only knows of one power of the letter *l*, and naturally supposes that the same is the case in all other languages. This however would be a very erroneous impression. The Armenian, for example, has two perfectly distinct elements: one, at least in the modern language, answering to the ordinary English or Latin *l*, and another, which, whatever may have been its ancient pronunciation, has now assumed that of *gh*, guttural. Several Slavonic dialects have also two distinct *l*'s; the difference between them is not however easily rendered intelligible through the medium of our own language. The Welsh also possesses a twofold element of this class: one secondary, that is, only employed in construct or compound words, and not differing in power from the same character in our own language; and another primary, usually, for want of a better sign, written *ll*.

This character, invariably used at the beginning of words not in grammatical construction, is sometimes erroneously compared to the initial *ll* in Spanish *llano*, *llamar*, &c. It has however a totally different power, bearing nearly the same relation to a simple *l* that our *th* does to *t*: indeed it is sometimes described by Englishmen as equivalent to *thl*; but though this combination approximates in some degree to the sound, it contains too much of a dental admixture. Though the same sound has not as yet been found in any other language, there is no doubt of its great antiquity; and it is believed that the existence of it in Welsh may serve as a clue for the explanation of certain apparent anomalies in other tongues.

It is scarcely necessary to say, that when people attempt to express articulations difficult or impracticable to their vocal organs, they try to represent them by the best substitutes that they can find. Englishmen, when they employed Welsh proper names learnt by the ear, were aware that their own simple *l* conveyed no adequate idea of *ll*, and the common resource was to employ *fl* in the place of it. Thus Shakspeare's Fluellin is merely a Saxon transformation of Llewelyn, and the surname Floyd, which has now become fixed, is nothing more than Llwyd or Lloyd, adapted, or attempted to be-adapted, to English organs. Now if we suppose that the sound of the Welsh *ll*, or a still older articulation out of which it was formed, existed in the parent language of the Indo-European class, and was gradually disused by various tribes in the course of their divergence from the original stock, it is obvious that substitutes would be employed for it, varying according to circumstances. Some nations might express it in one way, and some in another, but all would endeavour to convey an idea of the original sound as nearly as their vocal organs permitted them.

If therefore we take the known English instances of *Floyd* and *Fluellin* as a criterion, we might expect to find other and still older examples of the same substitution. The following list of words, which might be greatly augmented, appears to give some countenance to this supposition: —

llab, stroke	*flap*.
llac, slack, relaxed	*flaccidus*, Lat.
llawr, area	*floor*.
llawv, palm of the hand. . . .	*folme*, Ger.
llawr, many	*fleira*, Isl.
lletty, dwelling.	*fleil*, Anglo-Sax.
luath, Gael. swift.	*fliotr*, Isl.; *fleet*, Eng.

Sometimes, by an easy change, *b* or *p* appear instead of *f*.

llachiaw, to beat, lick	*plaga*, L.; *placu*, *I strike*, Lith.
llawn, full	*plenus*.
leach, Bret. place	*plecus*, Lith.; *pleck*, Lanc.
ledan, broad, Lat. latus	πλατύς; *platus*, Lith.
lyja, it rains, Lith.	*pluit*, Lat.
λούω, I wash	*plauju*, *I rinse*, Lith.

lein, Bret. summit . . . . *blean*, W.
llian, linen . . . . *bliant*, O.-Eng. *fine linen*, &c.

Sometimes a vowel seems to be inserted, in order to facilitate the pronunciation: —

llavar, speech . . . . *palabra*, Span.
llawv, palm, Gael. lamh, hand παλάμη.

This resolution into a liquid preceded by a labial is by no means the only one which the class of words under consideration appears to admit of. It has already been observed, that one of the Armenian letters related to *l* has in more recent times assumed the sound of *gh*. A similar phænomenon is presented by the Spanish language, in which the Latin *li* not unfrequently becomes a pure guttural, as in *muger* from *mulier*, and *hoja* from *folium*. Μόλις and μόγις exhibit the same species of affinity; it is therefore not surprising to find words commencing with *l* in one dialect, in another exhibiting this element in connexion with *c*, *g*, or *k*. A few examples will show the matter in a clearer light.

llavar, speech . . . . *klavre*, Dan. *to prate*.
llai, mud . . . . *clay*.
llais, voice . . . . *glas*, Slav.
llathru, to shine . . . . *glitter*.
llawd, a youth . . . . *gloit*, O.-Swed.
llavn, blade . . . . *glafwen*, O.-Swed. a lance.
læccan, A.-S. to seize ⎱ . . . . *glacaim*, Gael.
laikau, Lith. I hold ⎰
luppu, Lith. I strip . . . . . *glubo*, Lat.

There is a still further modification of this element, perhaps more extensively prevalent than any of the others. The Welsh *ll* has a sort of sibilant sound, easily reducible to *sl* by organs unable to pronounce it or the English *th*, as is notoriously the case with most of the Indo-European nations. Accordingly we find that words with this initial frequently reappear in Gaelic and Teutonic under the form *sl*, or in the modern German *schl*, as will appear from the following instances: —

llaciaw, to beat. . . . . *slacair*, Gael.
lladyr, theft . . . . *slad*, —
llai, mud . . . . , ... *slaib*, —
llath, rod, lath . . . . *slat*, —
llovyn, lock of hair . . . . . . *slamhagan*, —
llwyvan, an elm . . . . *sleamhan*, —
llu, host, army. . . . . *sluagh*, —

llivaw, to grind	*schleifen*, Germ.
llawg, swallowing	*schlucken*, —
llarp, rag	*slarfwa*, O.-Swed.

The above examples, to which many others might be added, appear to establish the fact, that words with the initial *l* are liable to have this element modified by a labial, guttural or sibilant prefix. It is not perhaps possible, with our present means of information, to lay down any single rule, capable of accounting for all those modifications. It might be conjectured that the forms with prefixes are the more original, and that the Welsh *ll* for example represents several distinct classes of conjunct consonants, in the same way as the Spanish *llamar*, *llama* and *llaga* are respectively to be referred to *clamare*, *flamma* and *plaga*. It is however a serious objection to this theory that the same root not unfrequently appears under all the different forms, and has sometimes a twofold aspect even in the same dialect.

Thus besides *llab*, a stroke or blow, we have the forms *clab*, *flap*, *slap*; German. *klopfen*, to beat; Slavon. *klepati*: along with the Germ. *lau*, lukewarm, we have W. *clauar;* Gr. χλίαρος; Belg. *flauw*; O.-Swed. *flia*, to thaw; and along with W. *llwfr*, E. *lubber*, appear the O.-Swed. *flepr*, Gael. *sliobair*, in the same sense. Again it might be supposed that the simple liquid sound is the original one, and that the labials, gutturals and sibilants are distinct prefixes, bearing some analogy to prepositions, and having formerly a distinct meaning which cannot now be traced. This is undoubtedly possible, and might be supported to a certain extent by actual examples. We know that the Anglo-Saxon *blinnan*, to cease, and Germ. *bleiben*, to remain, are no simple verbs, but compounds of *bilinnan* and *biliban;* and in the Slavonic dialects an immense number of words, commencing with *sl* or *vl*, require the removal of the initial in order to arrive at the real root.

There are however many cases in which it would be unsafe to apply this solution. Supposing the Armenian *lou* or *lov*, a flea, to be a genuine original form, it is not likely that it should be transformed into *floh*, *blocha*, *pulex* and ψύλλα, without any visible reason or change of meaning, by means of a prefix with which it could very well have dispensed. Again, the Arm. *lūsel*, to hear or listen, has in other languages the counterparts *klu*, *hlu*, *shlu*, *sru*, while in the Pali and in certain Greek forms, the supposed radical liquid entirely disappears, *e. gr.* Pali *suyatè*, he ir heard = Gr. ἀκούεται. It appears much more likely, *à priori*, that all these forms are organic modifications of the same primitive root, than that they should be compounds, made out of different elements, in languages closely related to each other.

If one might venture to hazard a conjecture on a point respecting which there is confessedly no evidence beyond that afforded by an inductive comparison of forms, it would be a suggestion analogous to that lately proposed respecting the digamma and its cognates, namely, that none of the known forms are, strictly speaking, original; but that all have branched out of some still older element, capable, according to known phonetic laws, of producing them all. It has been shown that the archetype of the digamma, whatever it was, has given birth to labials, hard and soft, gutturals, palatals, and sibilants; and that the Wesh *ll* has within the last few centuries been resolved into *fl*: it is therefore very possible that it may itself be the descendant of a stronger and fuller sound, capable of being modified in various ways. The comparison of a few cognate forms may serve as a groundwork for an attempt to reduce the varieties to one standard.

The Latin *lis, litis*, corresponds pretty accurately in form with W. *llid*, anger, strife; and with these the Anglo-Saxon *flytan*, to scold, quarrel, and the Lettish *kilda*, strife, may very well have affinity, according to analogies already pointed out. In like manner *locus* agrees regularly with Bret. *leach*, with which Lith. *plecus* and Lancash. *pleck* appear to be cognate. But further, Quintilian has preserved two remarkable archaic forms, *stlis* and *stlocus*, initial combinations of which there is only one other example in Latin, viz. *stlatarius*, apparently connected with *latus*. Now, assuming a primitive articulation bearing some analogy to the Welsh *ll*, but with a certain admixture of the guttural element, it is not difficult to conceive that *flytan* might be evolved from it in the same way as Floyd has sprung from Lloyd; *kilda*, according to the analogy of O.-Swed. *glafwen* from W. *llavn*, and *stlis*, like *starfwa* from W. *llarp*. The insertion of the dental may be explained on the principle of euphony, the combination *st* not being tolerated in Latin. A parallel instance occurs in Fr. *esclave, esclavie*, where the guttural is not radical, but inserted to prevent the collision of *s* and *l*. Benfey compares Germ. *streiten*, to strive, and Sanscr. *srīni*, an enemy; if the latter is really cognate, it would furnish another argument against the originality of the dental in *stlis* and *stlocus*.

The synonyms for *milk* show a still greater variety of forms, all of which are however reducible to one origin.

Lat. *lac*; W. *llaeth*, *blith*; Gael. *bligh*; Gr. γλάγος, γάλα; Slav. *mliek*; A.-S. *meolc*; Lat. *mulgeo*, I milk; Lith. *melzu*; Gr. ἀμέλγω. Respecting the interchange of *b* and *m* as initials, compare Sanscr. *brū*, Zend *mrū*, Bohem. *mluwiti*, to speak; Sancr. *mritas*, Gr. βρότος, a mortal; with many others.

The above examples, selected from a much greater number, show, it is conceived, that Pictet was far from being justified in broadly stating that the Celtic *l* accurately corresponds with the Sanscrit one (including of course the other cognate dialects) in every situation. It is believed, on the contrary, that few elements are capable of a greater variety of modifications, for the view we have just taken by no means exhausts the subject. Many instances might be given of *l* being completely vocalized, or converted into an articulation of a class totally distinct from its own; but they do not so properly belong to the present division of our subject, which professes only to treat of the modifications of initial sounds. It is presumed that enough has been advanced to show that the scale of permutations in the Indo-European languages, as laid down by Grimm and Pott, will admit of being considerably extended beyond the limits which they have assigned; and that it is very unsafe to fix upon Sanscrit or any other known language as a model to which all others are to be referred. It is believed that there are numerous phænomena in language of which neither Sanscrit, Greek, Teutonic, nor all in conjunction, can furnish a satisfactory solution; and that the real original articulations of speech have in many cases yet to be ascertained. This can only be attempted by a copious induction of all known varieties of cognate forms, and all that we can rationally expect to achieve is an imperfect approximation to the truth.

Reasons have now been given for believing that in many cases the initial *l* is not, strictly speaking, an original sound, but a modification of a more complex element, which was equally capable of becoming a labial, a guttural, or a sibilant combined with the simple *l*. There appear to be grounds for extending the same theory — *mutatis mutandis* — to the other liquids *r* and *n*, some of which it is proposed briefly to consider.

It has been already observed, that an Englishman only acquainted with one sound of the letter *l*, is apt to take a limited view of the subject. The same remark is equally applicable to the other liquids, especially to *r*. A native of our southern counties, accustomed to enunciate this element with a delicate, sometimes scarcely perceptible vibration, naturally thinks his pronunciation the standard and only genuine one, and regards every marked deviation from it as a defect in utterance or a provincial peculiarity. Nevertheless there are few foreigners who do not give it a much stronger dental intonation, nearly resembling the one still current in Westmoreland, while in Northumberland and some parts of Germany, the sound meant for r has no lingual vibration at all, but becomes a deep guttural, neither very easy to describe nor to imitate, but almost exactly corresponding to the Arabic غ, *ghain*.

The further we pursue the inquiry the more complicated it becomes. In Tamul there are three *r*'s, one ordinary and two cerebral; in Hindostanī two, one of which is cerebral; in Armenian a soft and a hard; in several Slavonic dialects a soft one, nearly corresponding to the Sanscrit *rĭ*, and a peculiarly harsh one, including a sibilant admixture. In Welsh, the common soft r is unknown as a primary initial of words, the aspirate form *rh* being invariably considered as the primitive. The same appears to have been the case in Greek; and in certain districts of the Tyrolian Alps, every initial r is attended by a strong aspirate, the combined sound of which, according to Schmeller, may be represented by *hhr*. In some adjoining districts the vibration entirely disappears, the aspirate alone remaining, especially in the middle of words: thus for example, *fort* becomes *fuhht*, and *garten, gahhten*.

In some languages r is frequently commutable with other letters, particularly *l* and *d*; while in others it is altogether wanting, as for example in Chinese and some African and American dialects, where *l, d, s, n*, are substituted for it, according to circumstances. We have neither the leisure nor the means for investigating and accounting for all the above variations, to which others might be added, as many of the dialects in question have neither been grammatically analysed, nor sufficiently compared with their cognates. We shall therefore, for the present, confine ourselves chiefly to that class where the element appears in intimate connexion with an aspirate or a guttural.

As the general progress of languages is towards the attenuation and softening of articulations, it may be assumed that the aspirated forms in Welsh, Greek and other languages are more original than their weaker correspondents, — the latter, at least in Welsh, being regarded as grammatical modifications of the former. In other words, the aspiration is not adventitious or capriciously employed, but inherent, and to a certain extent essential. And as we know that the aspirate is in innumerable cases a mere modification of a still stronger sound, especially of the gutturals *k* or *g*, to which in fact it is closely related, it is very possible that the Greek and Celtic aspirated *r* may not itself be original, in the strict sense of the term, but a softening of a still more primitive sound. This, like many similar theories, is neither to be dogmatically asserted nor capable of direct proof: but it is at all events lawful to inquire whether there may not be some known element of speech hypothetically capable of accounting for the various phænomena.

It has been observed, that the substitute for what we suppose to be the true sound of *r* in Northumberland and some parts of Germany, is an articulation closely resembling the Arabic *ghain*. This being formed very deeply in the throat, is obviously capable of being variously modified. It may be either attenuated to *ain*, — a guttural formed higher in the throat, — or still further to *a*: if uttered with a certain degree of vibration, it might be made nearly equivalent to *ghr*, capable of being softened into *gr;* or if prolonged with a nasal intonation, it might gradually become *gn* or *ng*. Moreover, as it is an articulation of extreme difficulty to those to whom it is not vernacular, it is easy to conceive that other races who have had occasion to adopt Arabic words including this element, would attempt to approximate to the sound, some in one way and some in another, according to the diversity of their vocal organs. Silvestre de Sacy, who observes that this element is a compound of *gh* and *r*, and that the sound of it is variously described in Roman characters by *gr*, *ghr*, *hr*, or *rh*, compares it to the Provençal *r*, which apparently does not materially differ from the burr of the Northumbrians. The Persians and Turks give it the sound of our ordinary hard *g*, while in some parts of Africa it appears to approximate to the *r*, with a greater or less admixture of a guttural or aspirate intonation. And as there is a great tendency in languages to divide complex elements, it is very possible, *à priori*, that in the case of an original sound of this nature, one tribe or nation might reject the guttural or aspirate portion of it, and that another might drop the vibration, so that words primarily commencing with *ghain*, or something equivalent, might have their representatives in others with an initial *g*, *h*, or a simple *r*, according to circumstances.

All these gradations appear in the Vedic Sanscrit *grab'h*. Icel. *greipa*, Welsh *rheibiaw*, Latin *rapio*, Irish *gabhail*. This last-mentioned form follows the analogy of the Pali, in which the *r* of *grab'h* would be elided; and as many words in most Indo - European languages are parallel with the soft forms of Pali or Pracrit rather than with the stronger ones of Sanscrit, it is very possible that *capio* and *rapio* may be different forms of the same word. Thus, the Slavonian *greblo*, an oar, would in Bohemian become *hreblo*; in Welsh we have, transposing the aspirate, *rhwyf*; in Gaelic, without the aspirate, *ramh*, Lat. *remus*; while, supposing a liquid to have been elided, the Greek χώπη may be of the same pedigree.

In the above instances and many similar ones, we have nothing but analogy to guide us; but there are cases in which the descent of a simple *r* from a more complex sound is historically certain. Not to insist upon the softening of the Greek and Welsh aspirate forms in Latin and Gaelic, there are in Icelandic a multitude of words commencing with *hr*, so strongly articulated, that the Feroese, who write entirely by the ear, regularly represent it by *kr*. Many of these have their counterparts in Anglo-Saxon, under the same form; and there are traces of the employment of the aspirate in the corresponding terms in Old High German. But in the modern dialects, German, Danish, English, &c., the *h* has entirely disappeared; and there would be no proof of its ever having existed, if we had only the present condition of these languages to guide us. A number of the above words have their counterparts in Welsh, generally under the initials *rh:* e. gr. A.-S. *hrim*, hoar-frost, W. *rhew*, Gael. *reodh*, Engl. *rime*, Germ. *reif*. The Greek χρύος is probably of the same family. The West Riding Yorkshire *hime* bears a curious resemblance to the Sanscrit *hima*, Gr. χεῖμα, and it is not impossible that a liquid may have been elided in both. If therefore we admit the Icelandic and Anglo-Saxon forms as the true representatives of the Welsh ones, and the latter again as a single organic element, it seems to follow that all may have descended from some more primitive articulation, originally employed as a simple element, but capable of being subdivided and variously modified. Whether this archetype bore some analogy to the Arabic *ghain*, or the Northumbrian *r*, or not, is a matter of speculation; it is believed that this theory is sufficient to explain most of the phænomena which we have been considering.

The originally complex nature of this element may also be inferred from the remarkable fact, that in a number of languages, particularly those of the Tartarian family, it never appears as an initial letter, at least in vernacular words.

17

Words ostensibly beginning with it in Turkish will be found on examination to have been adopted from the Arabic, Persian, or some European tongue, and even these borrowed terms are occasionally adapted to native organs by prefixing a vowel — *Orosz*, for *Rosz*, a Russian. The Manchu, Mongolian and Calmuck strictly adhere to the same analogy. The Basque regularly prefixes a vowel and doubles the consonant; a peculiarity adopted in many Spanish words, apparently through Basque influence, as may be seen by comparing *arrecife*, a reef, with Fr. *recif*, along with a multitude of others. We may here suggest that it would be a matter of curious speculation to trace the Indo-European words commencing with r or its combinations to their equivalents in the Tartarian dialects, supposing any to exist. It is clear that if they are to be found, it must be under some other form, and the identification of those forms could not fail to clear up points in philology which are at present involved in obscurity.

It is not meant to affirm that all initial *r*'s are to be accounted for by the theory that we have suggested; it is only advanced as an hypothesis capable of accounting for a certain class of them. It is generally admitted that the element in numerous instances is only secondary, being a mere mutation of s, l, n, d, and perhaps of other articulations. Lepsius expresses an opinion, that it is in no case a primary sound, but, as an initial, generally a descendant from an older l. Like many similar conjectures, this is incapable of direct proof; and it may be doubted whether it is sufficient to explain all known phenomena. It is not to be denied that it is the proper solution for particular instances.

A few examples are subjoined in illustration of the above points : —

Gael.	ramh, *an oar*;	Slav.	greblo.
—	ràn, *a cry*;	Sc.	croon.
—	ròbach, *coarse*;	Germ.	grob.
Welsh	rhad,	Lat.	gratia.
—	rhathu,	Eng.	grate.
—	rhawth, *gluttony*;	Sc.	greed.
—	rhegen, *landrail*;	—	crake.
—	rheibiaw, *to snatch*;	Eng.	grip, crib.
—	rhew, *frost*;	Gr.	κρύος.
—	rhinciaw, *to gnash*;	Fr.	grincer.
—	rholiaw, *to roll*;	Bavar.	krollen.
—	rhynu, *to shake*;	Gael.	crionaich.
Sanscr.	rud, *to weep*;	Goth.	gretan.

| Goth. | raupjan, *to pluck*; | Eng. | crop. |
| — | rikan, *to heap up*; | Welsh | crug, *a heap*. |

Sometimes the Welsh has the guttural where other languages only exhibit the simple liquid, *e. gr.*

| Welsh | grab, *cluster*, *grape*; | Germ. | rebe. |
| — | grawn, *roe*; | Sc. | raun. |

It would be easy to show that the letter *n* presents many similar analogies. Thus the Anglo Sax. *hnæcan* corresponds to Lat. *necare*, and *hnitu* to Welsh *nedden*, Eng. *nit*. In the Indo-Chinese, Tartarian and Polynesian dialects, there is an initial nasal *n*, usually represented by *ng*, capable of being variously modified. Thus the Chinese *ngo*, ego, Tibetan *nga*, becomes in Burmese *no*: while the Manchu relative postfix *nge* appears in Turkish in the form *ki*, *ghi*. Many similar instances might easily be collected.

17 *

ON THE FORMATION OF WORDS BY THE FURTHER MODIFICATION OF INFLECTED CASES.

[*Proceedings of the Philological Society, Vol. III.*]

It is pretty generally admitted by modern German philologists that the possessive pronoun in many languages is either directly formed from the genitive case of the personal, or is closely related to it. In many instances the two classes are interchangeable with each other; and there is, in a great majority of languages, a decided resemblance of form: — thus *me−us, tu−us, su−us*, are naturally referable to *me−i, tu−i, su−i*, and the German *mein−er, dein−er*, &c., with the disjunctive forms *der mein−ige, der dein-ige*, show an equally close affinity to the personal genitives *mein, dein*. Now it seems clear that a similar mode of formation is abstractedly possible in other classes of words. Adjectives, in most cases, bear the same analogy to substantives that pronouns possessive do to personal, and if one species of words could be formed on the basis of an inflected case, there seems no valid reason why another might not be equally so. Of course we do not here speak of such words as sorrowful, truthful, godlike, respecting the composition of which there is no manner of doubt; but of adjectives like δῖος, ἡμάτιος, &c., having a common base with the corresponding substantives, but distinguished from them by their application, and by terminations which appear to have no separate meaning. It is not necessary here to repeat what has been advanced on former occasions respecting the significance or non-significance of those elements; the object of the present paper being to show that there are at the least plausible grounds for believing that many of the words in question are formed from nouns, and not from the nominative or the crude form, but from oblique cases.

It has been already remarked, that in some classes of languages the whole process of formation is carried on by means of postpositions, generally of a known and determinate signification. One of the most remarkable of these appears to be the Basque. In this there are no prepositions, in our sense of the term, nor scarcely any separate particles of relation; the connection and separation of terms being shown by postfixes respectively denoting *of*, *to*, *for*, *in*, *with*, *by*, and all other ordinary relations of time, place or manner. When these postfixes are combined with nouns, they are of course equivalent to the cases of corresponding meaning in other languages, and a certain number of them are exhibited as such by the native grammarians. It is one of the many peculiarities of this language, that any case, singular or plural, is capable of becoming the basis of a fresh formation. Every case of a noun, or every person of a verb may be made to constitute a fresh stem, capable, according to circumstances, of being conjugated as a verb, declined as a new noun or adjective, or employed as an adverb. This unlimited capability of expansion is of course subject to some restrictions in practice, and the majority of derivatives obtained in this way will be found to consist of abstract nouns and adjectives. Thus L'Écluse, in his 'Grammaire Basque,' observes that four adjectives may be formed from the oblique cases of every noun, generally from those which correspond to the genitives and datives in other languages. For instance, *egun-eco*, for a day, one of the datives of *egun*, by appending the post-positive article becomes *egunecoa*, daily, which is in itself capable of being carried through a long series of inflections. In like manner, *ceru-co*, *lurreco*, datives of *ceru*, heaven, *lurrà*, earth, form *ceru-co-a*, heavenly, *lurrecoa*, earthly: gen. *cerucoaren*, *lurrecoaren*, &c. &c. The analysis is simple and obvious, the, or that, *for* heaven or earth. It is plain that similar words are equally capable of becoming substantives if used in a concrete sense.

The illustrations of this principle furnished by the Hungarian language are almost as numerous and important as those supplied by the Basque. The common sign of the genitive, both singular and plural is *é*, which is in fact itself an oblique case of the pronoun of the third person *ö*, and has the force of the Latin *sui* or *ejus*. Every noun or pronoun augmented with this element, may, as in Basque, become a fresh stem, capable of inflection through all the usual cases. Thus *ur-é*, gen. of *ur*, *dominus*, may become *ur-ét* (acc.), *dominicum*; *ur-e-töl* (ablat.), *dominico*, plur. *ur-ak-e*, quod est dominorum, &c. This process may be still further varied by the insertion of the pronominal affixes; *e. gr. ur-am* = *dominus meus*, may become *ur-am-é*, qui est domini mei, and so on through all the persons singular and plural. The application of the principle is not confined to the genitive:

several other formations with postpositions, corresponding to the cases in other languages, are equally capable of becoming new nominatives, not unfrequently used as different parts of speech. Thus the formation called the *casus substitutivus*, answering to the *nuncupativus* or predicative case of the Finnish and Lappish grammarians, may be employed either as an adverb or the stem of a verb: *e. gr. atya*, a father, *aty — ul*, as or like a father, Germ. *väter—lich*; *könyör*, mercy, *könyör—ül*, in a merciful manner, or as *v. a.* to pity. The caritive or privative case, formed in Hungarian by the post-positive *talan* or *atlan*, may equally become an inflected adjective, answering to the German formation in *— los:* e. gr. *atya—tlan*, subst. without a father, adj. fatherless; plur. *atyatlan—ok* = Germ. *vater-lose*.

The same principle prevails to a considerable extent in all the Finnish dialects. In these the caritive case is regularly employed as an adjective, sometimes unaltered, and sometimes with a slight addition, as Finn. *armo*, love, affection; caritive case *armo — tta*, without affection; adj. *armotto—m*, unfeeling; plur. *armottom—at*. Other cases may be treated in the same manner : thus *armoin—en*, merciful, is formed on the basis of the genitive plural, and *armoll—inen*, of the same signification, from the dative singular. Many of the abstract nouns in the Finnish dialects are formed upon the same or similar principles.

It is readily conceded, that no language of the Indo-European class, in its actual state, exhibits anything approaching to a parallel with the general structure of the Basque. Though there is little doubt that the formative terminations of Sanscrit, Greek, Latin, German, &c. were originally postpositions, they are now so closely incorporated with the words to which they are attached, that their separate existence and proper import can only be inferred by analogical reasoning. Nevertheless there remain partial evidences, scarcely equivocal, of the operation of the same principle of formation, leaving room to suspect that a careful investigation might bring to light many others.

· Many examples of adjectives and other words formed from cases, or terminations having the force of cases, of simple substantives, might be produced from a variety of languages, a selection from which will be given in the tables. It is obvious that derivatives from adverbs, prepositions and other particles are reducible to the same category, it being notorious that the great bulk of those words are merely oblique cases of nouns or pronouns. Thus, in Icelandic there are a number of derivatives from the conjunction *ef*, if; which

itself, as may be proved by an extensive induction, is only
an ablative or instrumental case of a pronominal root resolvable into *with that;* a phrase actually employed instead of
if, in old English poetry.

Some obvious examples are furnished by the language of
the Ossetes. In this are a multitude of nouns ending in *aen*,
denoting the place appropriated to any particular action,
regularly inflected through a variety of cases in both numbers. They are all however mere dative cases of the corresponding abstract nouns: e. gr. *zaunaen*, a walking-place
(ambulatorium), is the dative of *zaun*, ambulatio, being in
fact an elliptical expression of [place] *for* walking. Several
other classes of words are formed from oblique cases of
nouns in a manner exactly analogous. The Georgian language furnishes a curious parallel to the above-specified
formation. The particle *sa*, having, according to Brosset,
the force of *for*, is, when postfixed to a noun, the sign of
the dative case, e. gr. *marili*, salt, maril*sa*, to salt. But
when prefixed, it converts the noun either into a substantive
implying *use, application, instrument*, v. t. q., or into an adjective of possession, quality, &c. Thus *sa*-marile is a
thing *for* salt, *i. e.* salt-cellar; while from *wardi*, rose, dat.
ward-*sa*, are formed *sa*-warde, adj. rosy, and *sa*-wardi,
subst. a rosary or chaplet. It is obvious that the force of
the particle is the same, whether postfixed or affixed, and
that the slight difference in application is merely for the
sake of distinction. Most of the ordinary adjectives of the
Ossetes and many Armenian ones are either simple genitives,
though capable of inflection when used substantively, or
formed from the genitive case with a slight change of form.

Similar phenomena are presented by languages of a more
decidedly Indo-European structure. For example, in German there is an unequivocal instance of the formation of an
adjective from a dative in the word *vorhandener*. This is
regularly inflected as an adjective of three terminations, both
in the indefinite and definite form, and does not differ either
in form or application from the great body of words of the
same grammatical class. Nevertheless, it is a mere secondary formation from the dative plural of *hand*, in construction with the preposition *vor*, being in fact nearly equivalent
in its composition to the Basque *aurre-coa* (present = *pro
facie* or *conspectu*). Several other compounds from *hand* follow the same analogy.

Another example, equally decisive, is furnished by the
Greek *ἴφιος*, generally allowed by philologists to be formed
from *ἴφι*, the ancient dative or instrumental of *ἴς*, force;

which is also used adverbially by Homer and other epic writers. In fact, the word consists of three distinct elements: *ι*, the root — *φι*, sign of the dative or instrumental case — and *ος*, a postpositive pronoun or article bearing the same relation to the aspirated *ὁ* that the Sanscrit root *a* does to *sa*; and is altogether the precise counterpart, as to its structure, to the Basque *lurre - co - a*, earthly, and a multitude of similar words *.

It is hardly credible that there should be only one word in the Greek language formed upon this principle; and a little inquiry will show us a multitude of adjectives, which, judging from their form, may be according very well to the same analogy. Thus there is no difficulty in referring *ἡμερή-σιος* to the Ionic dative plural *ἡμέρῃσι*; and if this is admitted, it will follow that *ἡμάτιος* may be equally from the dative singular of *ἦμαρ*, and *βίαιος*, with a profusion of similar terms, from *βία*, anciently *βίαι*. Certain cases extant in Sanscrit and other languages, though not formally existing in Greek and Latin, have nevertheless left traces of their influence; for instance, the Latin *ruri*, *domi*, Gr. *οἴκοι*, and several local adverbs, &c. in *ι*, may be naturally referred to the Sanscrit locative in *i* or *ē = ai*. And as the ancient Attic form for *οἴκοι* was *οἴκει*, this may very well lie at the root of the adj. *οἴκεῖος*. In like manner Greek and Latin adjectives in *νος*, *nus*, may possibly be connected with the Sanscrit instrumental case *-ēna* (for *-aīna*). Thus, supposing *βίαιος* to be formed from the dative singular, *ἡμέρινος* may equally be connected with an ancient instrumental, *ἡμέριος* with a locative, and *ἡμερήσιος* with the dative plural. *Lapide - us*, *marmore - us*, and a variety of other terminations, may with more or less probability be referred to existing or obsolete inflections of the cognate nouns.

The above brief sketch might be augmented by examples from nearly all known classes of synthetic languages, there being few which do not in one way or other adopt an inflected case, or a composition equivalent to a case, as the basis of a new formation. We trace similar phænomena even in languages commonly, though very incorrectly, supposed to be destitute of grammatical relations. In Burmese, simple nouns may become adjectives by means of a prefixed or affixed pronominal particle, sometimes equivalent to a case, and this adjective may again be declined with all postposi-

---

* If we assume an ancient dative of *vis*, corresponding in form to *tibi*, *sibi*, the proper name Vibius might be formed from it on precisely the same principle as *ἴφιος* from *ἴς*.

tives usually employed as signs of cases. In Tibetan, which appears to form the connecting link between the Indo - Chinese and the Tartarian languages, adjectives and other parts of speech are formed by the addition of demonstrative pronouns to the noun - substantive, and the new word thus arising may itself be inflected through a variety of cases singular and plural. If we pass to the Manchu, the Mongolian and other cognate tongues, we find abundant evidence of the same nature; of which we may briefly notice a single item.

In a former paper on the origin of the genitive case, it was observed, that in the Turco-Tartarian languages that case is formed by the postfix *ning* (Western Turkish *uñ - nuñ*, presumed on strong inductive grounds to have been originally a relative pronoun. Thus the Eastern Turkish *men - ing*, genitive of *men*, I, is used in conjunction with a substantive, just like Lat. *meus*. In ordinary Turkish it is indeclinable; but in the Tschuwaschian dialect it is inflected through all the cases: e. gr. *manyng*, meus, *manyng - yng*, mei; and so on through both numbers. In all the proper Turkish dialects the disjunctive possessive pronoun is formed by the addition of the ordinary relative *ki* to the conjunctive form. Thus, Western Turkish *ben - um - ki*; Tschuwaschian *manyng - ki* = Germ. *der meinige*; the final element being regularly inflected according to circumstances, as *manyng - ki - nyng* = *des meinigen*, where the original pronoun substantive *man* is augmented by the agglutination of three pronominal endings.

In Galla the same class of elements concur to form a possessive pronoun in a somewhat different order: *ko*, the oblique form of the pronoun of the first person, has for its dative *ko - ti*, which in its turn becomes a perfect pronoun possessive by prefixing the relative *kan*: *kan - ko - ti* = ὁ ἐμός. In the Turkish form, the analysis is *me - of - who*, in Galla *who - me - to*.

When we inquire whether any of the corresponding Indo-European terms are capable of a similar resolution, we find in Sanscrit two sets of possessive pronouns: one — *madīya*, *twadīya*, &c. — apparently formed on the basis of the ablative, with a suffix identical in form with the ordinary relative; another — *māma - ka*, *tāva - ka* — manifesting the same relation to the genitive, with a suffix corresponding to the interrogative pronoun, also capable of being employed as a relative. If analogical reasoning is to be allowed in such cases — and we have frequently no other clue to guide us — we are naturally led to the belief that the above - specified Turkish, Galla, and Sanscrit terms, to which many others might be added, are all composed of similar elements and were originally combined on similar principles.

A few examples illustrative of the above views are subjoined.

The system of adopting an inflected case as the basis of a new formation is carried out with great regularity, and in the most unequivocal manner, in the Armenian adjective pronouns. The examples furnished by this language are peculiarly important from its being of the Indo-European family.

1. es, ego.	. . . . .	*Gen.*	im, mei, meus.
2. dou	. . . . . .	—	kho, tui; khoh, tuus.
3. [iu].	. . . . . .	—	iur, sui, suus.
Plur. 1.	. . . .	—	mer, nostri, noster.
2.	. . . .	—	dser, vestri, vester.
— Wanting.			

Demonstratives.

sa, hic	. . . .	— so-ra	} ὁ τούτου
da, iste	. . . .	— do-ra	}
na, ille	. . . .	— no-ra	ὁ ἐκείνου

Excepting the slight variation in the second person singular, all the words in the second column are equally genitives of the primitives, and nominatives of the possessive or adjective pronouns. In the latter capacity they can be regularly declined in all cases of both numbers. This principle of super-formation is applicable in a partial degree to other cases: thus, *i 'menj*, ablative plural of *es*, I, may become *i 'menj-kh* = οἱ ἀφ' ἡμῶν, *i 'menj-itz* = τῶν ἀφ' ἡμῶν, &c. &c. Even the relative pronoun *or*, qui, appears to be an abbreviated genitive of ὁ, quis?

The Georgian adjective pronouns closely follow the same analogy:

1 pers. me	. . . .	*Gen.*	cheni, mei, meus.
2 — shen	. . . . . .	—	sheni, tui, tuus.
3 — ighi	. . . . . .	—	misi, sui, suus.
Plur. 1 —	. . . .	—	chweni, nostri, noster.
2 —	. . . .	—	thkweni, vestri, vester.
3 —	. . . .	—	mathi, αὐτῶν, ὁ αὐτῶν.

All the above forms are regularly inflected throughout; thus *cheni*, as a possessive, makes gen. *chenisa*, dat. *chensa*, and so of the rest.

In Basque, the possessive pronoun is formed directly from the genitive of the personal by appending the article:

ene, nere, mei;	ene-a, nere-a, meus.
hire, tui;	hirea, tuus.
bere, sui;	berea, suus.
gure, nostri;	gurea, noster.
zure, vestri;	zurea, vester.
beren, αὐτῶν;	berena, ὁ αὐτῶν.

The disjunctive or definite possessive form of the Ossetes is according to the same principle, being produced by appending the demonstrative element *on* to the simple genitive, which is also employed as a conjunctive possessive:

az, ego . . . . *Gen.* ma, man, mei, meus.
— man-on = Fr. le mien.

It is believed that the distinctive terminations *as*, *os*, *us*, in Sanscrit, Greek and Latin, had a similar origin.

It would be endless to multiply examples, as there are few declinable adjective pronouns which do not manifest the same process of formation. Let it be conceded that the Latin possessive *cuj – us*, *cuj – a*, *cuj – um*, is formed from the genitive of *quis*, and it immediately follows that *meus*, *tuus*, *suus*, with the corresponding forms in the cognate languages, must be placed in the same category. It equally follows that other parts of speech, adjectives for example, might follow the same analogy. To the examples already given the following may be subjoined:

Mordwinian (*Finnish Dialect*).

Gen.	käv-en, of a stone, and	stony.
Dat.	sälme-nen	oculatus.
Caritive.	präv-teme	ἄφρων.
Abl.	pak (body), pak-es	pregnant.

Ossete.

Gen.	lag-ij, of a man, and	manly.
Dat.	bon-æn	daily.
—	zaun-æn	ambulatorium.
Abl.	dor-ej	stony.

Basque.

Gen. sing.	guizon-aren-a,	of man, human.
— *plur.*	guizon-en a	ὁ ἀνθρώπων
Dat.	egun-e-coa	daily.
—	ceru-co-a	heavenly.

Adjective proper. Bayona-eo-a, Fr. Bayonnais.
Plur. Indiet-a-co-a, one from the Indies.

All the above words can be regularly inflected, the oblique case being taken as a new nominative. There is reason to believe that a multitude of apparent nominatives in nearly all synthetic languages are, in reality, oblique cases of more primitive forms, or formed from them by a slight modification. North American-Indian, and Australian names of places are almost invariably in the locative case, with the force of *at, in*. Europeans never hearing them in any other form, naturally regard them as nominatives, and regularly use them as such[*]. It is easy to conceive that many similar phenomena might occur, particularly when the force of the component elements of words came to be less understood.

We now proceed to a question of considerable importance in philology, namely the true force and analysis of the present participle in the Indo-Germanic family of tongues.

It may be assumed as a general maxim, that analytic forms in one language may, and often do potentially correspond with synthetic ones in another, consisting in fact of the same or equivalent elements differently arranged. Though this principle has not been sufficiently kept in view, it is believed that it is capable of illustrating a number of points which have hitherto been misunderstood, or involved in a good

---

[*] Compare the Turkish *Istamboul* from εἰς τὴν πόλιν, containing nearly the same elements in an inverse order.

Note. Dr. Donaldson remarks as follows upon some ideas broached in this essay (*New Cratylus*, pp. 474— 475, second edition.) 'Mr. Garnett seems to have overlooked the distinction between those nouns which are formed from oblique cases by the mere appendage of a new system of inflexions, and a different class of secondary structures which affix to the new crude-form the pronominal terminations enumerated in a preceding chapter. Thus it is plain to see on the one hand that δημό-σιο-ς is merely the genitive δημό-σιο made the vehicle of a new set of case-endings and that χρύσεος, χιόνεος &c. are similarly derived from weaker forms of the genitive. But it is equally clear, on the other hand, that a form like ἴφιος contains something more than an oblique case and a new system of case-endings; and a comparison of Ἰφιxλῆς, Οἰ-λεύς &c. would lead us to doubt whether the first part is to be regarded as merely the dative of ἴς ...... There seems to us to be the same objection to Mr. Garnett's theory respecting the derivation of the participle from an ablative of the verbal root '. Dr. Donaldson adduces several other instances in support of his views, the essence of which, however, has been already given. The second edition of the New Cratylus appeared only a short time before Mr. Garnett's death, and whether the latter might or might not have seen occasion to modify the doctrine of his paper in accordance with the suggestions of his distinguished critic cannot now be known. ED.

deal of obscurity. It is well known that in Sanscrit, Greek, Latin, with their descendants, and all the Teutonic and Slavonic dialects without exception, the participles of the present tense are reducible to a common origin, of which the Lat. *amans, amantis*, may conveniently be given as the type. But even within the limits of the British islands we find two languages of considerable importance — the Welsh and the Irish, which have, strictly speaking, no present participle, but express it periphrastically by means of the infinitive or verbal noun combined with a preposition: *e. gr.* W. *yn sefyll*, in standing; Ir. *ag seasamh*, on standing = in statione, ἐπὶ τῷ ἱστάναι. If therefore these analytic forms are equal in power to a present participle, it follows that the synthetic participle itself may have been originally an ablative, instrumental or locative case; at least in particular languages, for it is not meant to assert that it could not be expressed in any other manner.

It may not be unknown to the readers of Mr. Donaldson's 'Varronianus' that the writer several years ago expressed an opinion that the Sanscrit present participle was originally an ablative of the verbal root, and that the following up of this position would lead to important consequences in philology. Subsequent researches having tended to confirm this idea, it is now proposed briefly to consider a few of the data on which it is founded.

The crude form or base of the ordinary present participle active in Sanscrit regularly terminates in *-at*, some of its inflections being regularly deducible from this stem and others from one augmented with a nasal, analogous to the Lat. *-ans**, *-antis*. Adjectives having the same ending appear to have been originally participles: for instance *mah–at*, great, may either be an adjective or a modification of the participle present from the root *mah*, to grow. In the first place then it is to be observed, that the syllable *at* is the regular termination of the ablative case of the *a*-declension of masculine nouns, that is to say, of the great body of nouns in the language. Again, we have reason to believe from the analogy of the Zend, the Oscan, and the ancient Latin, that *as*, the present ending of the ablative in nouns terminating in consonants, is not the true ancient form, but either a softening of *at*, or what is more probable, a genitive employed as a substitute for the ablative, the two cases being

---

* It is however important to observe, that the nasal element is by no means essential to the participial formation; there being whole classes of verbs in which it disappears altogether.

identical in form, in the singular, in most of the declensions. * The existence of a more ancient ablative in *ût*, analogous to the Zend, may be inferred from the pronominal ablatives *mat, tvat, asmat, yushmat*=*me, te, nobis, vobis*, which may have had their counterparts in the consonantal declension of nouns, either in Sanscrit or in some still more primitive language. It is generally admitted that the personal pronouns have, *cœteris paribus*, preserved the greatest proportion of ancient forms. It has already been shown that in the Celtic languages the periphrastic forms *in* or *on*-standing, are equivalent to the Lat. *stans* or Germ. *stehend*: to which we may add the familiar phrase *a* (i. e. *on*) *hunting*, precisely corresponding with the Gaelic *ag sealgadh*. The next step in the investigation is to find actual oblique cases of verbal nouns employed in the same manner. These are so numerous that it will be necessary to confine ourselves at present to a few select instances of this particular construction.

In the Basque language the great majority of verbs consist, in the present tense, of an ostensible participle in *en* or *ean*, combined with the auxiliary *am* or *have*. This supposed participle may be employed separately and inflected like any other noun or adjective, and is commonly dismissed by the native grammarians without any particular remark, as being nearly parallel to an ordinary Greek or Latin participle of the present tense. But the Abbé Darrigol, ** the only writer who has discerned the true analysis of the Basque verb, will teach us in what light it ought to be regarded.

"The expression *erortean* signifies *in falling*; but by what secret? It is this: the point *where* one is (*ubi*) is expressed by the positive case (*i. e.* locative, or case of position): as *barnean*, in the interior; *etchean*, in the house, *ohean*, in the bed, &c. Now, the action which one is at present performing may be regarded as the point where one is, and thence be also expressed by the positive case; whence the phrase *erortean* is nothing more than the infinitive (verbal noun) *erortea*, the act of falling, put in the positive case: therefore it signifies literally *in the falling* (dans le tomber). We are now in a condition to appreciate properly an infinite number of words, commonly called verbs. Let us take for example the ostensible verb "to fall;" it makes in the present tense

---

* Compare the French *de*, employed both as the sign of the genitive and the ablative.

** Dissertation critique et apologétique sur la Langue Basque, published anonymously, but known to be the work of M. Darrigol.

erorten niz, I fall; *erorten hiz*, thou fallest &c.   If what we have said of the expression *erortean* is correct, the phrase *erortean niz* must denote I am in the falling, or in the act of falling.   It is true that we say by syncope *erorten* for *erortean*; but of what consequence can the suppression of the *a* be, since we say indifferently according to the dialect, *etchean*, *etchen*, or *etchin*, in the house? If however any importance is to be attached to this vowel, we may be allowed to believe that its absence denotes the absence of the article, which does not appear improbable.   It follows from this observation that in the formulæ of the present tense, *erorten niz*, *erorten hiz*, &c., the word *erorten*, which expresses the action of falling, is not a verb, but, in reality, a noun in the positive case."

The author proves with equal evidence that the other tenses of the Basque regular verb are formed on the same principle, and correspond to different cases of nouns, the perfect to a dative signifying *to*, and the future to another dative with the sense of *for*.   This is so completely the case, that the very same words are indifferently oblique cases of nouns or tenses of verbs according to circumstances. *Baratcen*, *baratceri*, *baratceco*, may either be *in*, *to*, or for a *garden* (*q. d.* a resting-place), or with the proper auxiliaries may denote *cesso*, or *quiesco*, *cessavi*, *cessabo*.   It is highly creditable to the sagacity of the Abbé Darrigol to have satisfactorily resolved a point which had not only escaped the notice of the Basque grammarians, but even of the illustrious William Humboldt.

By the aid of the light derived from this language we may be enabled to discover similar phenomena in many others.   In a multitude of languages in all parts of the world, we find tenses of verbs formed from the verbal noun by means of postpositions, which again often correspond with the cases of the same element employed as a substantive or adjective.

In the structure of the participle, the Hungarian, especially as written in the fifteenth century, equals the Basque in the importance and clearness of its forms, and exceeds it in their variety.   More than a dozen different forms equivalent to the Latin participle in -*ans* or -*ens* occur in the ancient Gospels published by Döbrentei, nearly every one of which is resolvable into the verbal root, accompanied by postfixes denoting *for*, *in*, *on*, *with*.   The one ending in -*va*, -*ve*, commonly used in construction, is, when employed absolutely, nearly equivalent to the Latin gerund in *do*, or ablative absolute; thus *ditser-ve*, from the root *ditser*, praise, might be rendered *laudando, laudante*, or simply *laudans*. For the sake of further emphasis it may be augmented by the particle *an, en* = *super*, *in: mond–va–n*, saying; *ditser–ve–n*, praising. These are the forms commonly used in the modern language; and taken analytically, they are rather gerunds than participles in apposition, as this part of speech is commonly understood. But in the ancient language, those ostensible gerunds are capable of being regularly inflected through cases and numbers: e. gr. *rak–va*, *ædificans*, dat. *rak–va–nak* = *ædificanti*, acc. *rak–va–t* = *ædificantem*, plur. *rak–va–k* = *ædificantes*. These forms admit of no other analysis than *cui*, *quem*, *qui* — *in ædificatione*, or *in ædificando*, being in fact precisely equivalent to the Welsh *y rhai yn adeiladu*, those building. For the sake of rendering the logical copula more precise and complete, this form is often augmented with pronominal suffixes *in statu obliquo*: e. gr. *mond–va–m*; dicens (ego); *mond–va–d*, dicens (tu); *mondva-jok*, dicentes (illi). This presents a remarkable analogy to the Galla language, in which the presents participle, being in fact a dative case of the verbal noun, is construed with pronominal suffixes in exactly the same manner: as *adema*, act of going; dat. *ademe-ti*, *ademe-ne-ti*, I going; literally, for going of me. The Welsh *yn ei dywedi* = dicens (ille), literally, in ejus dictione, contains the same elements expressed in a more strictly analytic form.

Other examples of Hungarian participles, equally clear in their analysis, and important in their bearing upon the theory in question, will be given in the tables. The investigation of the cognate forms of the Finnish family of tongues is rendered difficult by the recent state in which we now possess them, and the extreme imperfection of most of their grammars. Nevertheless they occasionally present valuable illustrations of the operation of the same principle. Gamander and Rask long ago observed that the Lappish present participle is nothing more than an oblique case of the verbal noun: as *orrom*, state of being; particip. *orrom–en*, literally, in or for being. Castren remarks that other dialects present the same construction with slight variations in form.

Passing over for the present the examples afforded by the Tartarian and some African languages, we shall proceed to those of the Indian peninsula. In most of the Hindustanī dialects the tenses of the regular verb are composed of participles combined with an auxiliary, which participles again often correspond in form with the oblique cases of nouns. We shall at present confine our attention to the

Mahratta, which appears to present several interesting phæ-nomena.

Dr. Stevenson observes, in his Mahratta Grammar, that *sutūn*, a past participle of *sut-anē*, to get loose, is formed from the root by means of the postposition *-ūn*. The same element is also employed in the formation of the ablative case: e. gr. *ghar–ūn*, from *ghar*, a horse. Dr. Stevenson does not give the analysis of the other participles, but it is obvious that the preterite *sutalā* has a close resemblance to the dative *gharālā* = equo, and the present participle *sutat*, an equally close one to the locative *ghar–āt*. According to this analysis the Mahratta and Basque participles would run pretty nearly parallel to each other, the sense deducible from the latter being equally applicable to the former. Other Indian dialects present similar phenomena; but the point which we are at present most interested in ascertaining is, what evidence there is for regarding the Sanscrit present participle, with which that of most European languages is closely connected, as an oblique case of the verbal root, considered as an abstract noun.

It might be supposed that if confirmations of this theory were to be found anywhere, they would be most likely to occur in the oldest monuments of the language. The grammatical peculiarities of the Vedas are unfortunately little known, at least to the public, but it is believed that evidence of some importance may be gleaned from Rosen's confessedly imperfect Notes on the Rig-Veda. One doubt which suggests itself is, whether an ablative or other oblique case could govern another noun in the same way that a Latin participle appears to govern an accusative or dative. On this point Rosen observes, p. lv., with respect to the expression *sūrgam dri'sē* (nearly parallel to Gr. ἥλιον ὁράματι, instead of ἡλίου), "This employment of the mere verbal root, placed in the sense of a *nomen actionis*, and accompanied by an accusative, is repugnant to the custom of the more recent language." He gives a number of examples of verbal roots inflected in various cases, some governing other nouns, and some not; but serving to establish two points, first, that the verbal root is capable of being inflected like a noun. and secondly, that it may ostensibly govern an accusative case *.

The next question which arises is, whether the crude participle ever appears to perform the functions of the fuller form. On the compound *vidadvasum*, q. d. knowing treasure,

---

* Compare the construction in Plautus: "Quid tibi *eam* est tactio.'' The writer is indebted for this important illustration to Professor Key.

Rosen remarks, "I now prefer believing that this is compounded of the participle *vidat* and the substantive *vasu*, so that the latter depends on the former. Compare the fragment of an ancient poem, quoted by Yāska, *vidadvasur*, thesaurorum gnarus. This license which we see employed by the ancients, of forming compounds in such a manner that the participle of the verb active is prefixed to a noun, which, if the composition is dissolved, is found to be governed by the verb, afterwards became obsolete. Examples of words thus compounded are: *bharadvāja*, sacra ferens; *mandayatsakha*, amicos exhilarans; *kshayad-vīra*, viros necans, &c. Unless I am mistaken, examples of this construction abound in the writings of the Greek poets, but under a somewhat altered aspect. For in the first place, the dental letter, the proper termination of the crude participle (*bharat, kshayat*: compare τυπτοντ- *amant-*, instead of the primitives τυπτοτ-*amat-*) according to a well known law of Greek euphony, is changed into the sibilant, so that φερέσ–βιος, λιπεσ–ήνωρ, Δαμάσ–ιππος stand for φερέτ–βιος, λιπετ–ήνωρ, Δαμάτ–ιππος, &c."

This analysis of the Greek compounds must be allowed to be ingenious and plausible; what we are chiefly concerned to observe is, that the crude form of the participle was regularly employed in composition by the most ancient Sanscrit writers, virtually, if not formally, affecting the noun with which it was joined. The same form also appears to be employed absolutely in the Vedas: thus *dravat* (Rig-Veda, p. 3, 1. 2), rendered *celeriter* by Rosen, seems to be formed from *dru*, currere, according to the analogy of *bhavat* from *bhu*, and might be indifferently rendered (accedite) *currentes*, *currendo*, *cursu*, or *cursim*.

With respect to the termination of the Sanscrit ablative, Bopp regards it as formed by the postposition *at*, itself a modification of the pronominal root *a*. It is not unimportant to observe that this element appears to exist in an independent form in the Vedas. On the participle *at* (Rig-Veda, p. 9, 1. 1) Rosen remarks, "Probably *at* is the ancient ablative of the same pronominal theme *a*, the genitive of which is *asya*, discharging the office of an adverb, and employed in the same sense as *tatah*, *atah* . . . . The Zend adverb *aat*, *tunc*, *deinde*, is doubtless of the same origin and structure."

The Lithuanian and Lettish languages also present some interesting phenomena, which are more valuable on account of the close relationship confessedly subsisting between these tongues and the Sanscrit. In the former, the present participle — e. gr. *jesskas* (the latter vowel nasal), fem. *jesskanti* from *jesskau*, I seek — shows at once its identity with the Sanscrit and its congeners, being evidently a softening of *jesskan-t-s*, as Lat. *aman-s* of *aman-t-s*. This form of the Lithuanian participle does not differ materially in construction or inflection from its correspondent in Sanscrit, except that the development of the neuter gender is more restricted. But there is an indeclinable modification of it in *-ant*, sometimes employed as an infinitive, sometimes as a gerund, and, in certain constructions, as a participle, which bears a remarkable analogy to the crude form of the Sanscrit; — *jessk-ant*, to seek, in seeking, or simply, seeking. The relation of this element to the inflected participle is proved by the fact that each of the four participles, present, imperfect, perfect, and future, has its corresponding indeclinable. That it has moreover the force of an ablative, instrumental, or locative case, may be inferred not only from its employment as a gerund in *do-jesskant* = *quærendo* — but moreover from its being regularly used in construction with a dative or ablative noun: *dienui dudant* = *Deo dante; dukterei jesskant* = *filia quærente*, exactly equivalent to Latin ablatives absolute, except that the participial element does not appear to be declined, it being considered unnecessary to add further inflection to a word already containing the force of an ablative within itself.

The Lettish forms present a remarkable analogy to those Sanscrit participles which reject the nasal. The absolute or indeclinable form *dohdoht*, almost identical with Sanscrit *dadat*, by adding a terminational *s*, the sign of the masculine gender in Lithuanian and Lettish as well as Gothic, becomes a present participle, capable of inflection throughout both numbers, *dohdohts* = δίδων, fem. *dohdoti*. Both forms have in various constructions the force of a dative or ablative: e. gr. es dsirdeju *eijoht*, I heard while going, i. e. *in* going; saulitei *lezzoht* = sole oriente: — also in phrases expressing contingency: ne weens *essoht* mahjas, if, lest, v. t. q. no one be at home, *i. e.* no one *in being*: at-*eeschoht*, if he comes, *i. e.* in (the case or circumstance of) his coming. The original structure of these forms can only be inferred by inductive and analogical reasoning; as nothing like direct historical testimony can be expected with regard to the phenomena of a language of which there are no monuments older than the sixteenth century. But the theory that the so-called infinitives or gerunds, Lith. *jesskant*, Lett. *dohdoht*, were originally ablative forms, convertible into declinable parti-

18*

ciples by the addition of a pronominal termination, is supported both by external and internal evidence, and appears amply sufficient to account for the peculiar force of the words and all other phenomena.   If this be conceded respecting the Lithuanian and Lettish, it must be equally so with regard to Sanscrit, Greek, Latin, and Teutonic, the present participle being indisputably formed on the same model in all.

With respect to the participle, the evidence may be briefly stated at follows: — Languages destitute of this element supply its place analytically by means of the verbal noun combined with a preposition. 2. Other languages represent it by an oblique case of the verbal noun, generally the ablative, locative or dative, which case in certain instances is itself capable of further inflection. 3. Various oblique cases of the verbal root are in ancient Sanscrit employed in a manner analogous to participles, and are even capable of governing nouns. 4. The crude state of the Sanscrit present participle presents a decided analogy to certain forms of the ablative, not only in that language, but in other ancient dialects. 5. Various adjectives in Greek and other tongues appear to be formed from oblique cases of substantives, by adding the sign of the gender; it is therefore à priori possible that a participle may be formed in the same way.

It is not meant to be denied that there are certain difficulties and objections in the way of this theory, as far as Sanscrit and its immediate cognates are concerned, some of which may possibly be removed when we become better acquainted with the language and the grammar of the Vedas. The strength of the case, it is conceived, lies in the combination of evidence afforded by the analytic languages, and those in which the precise force of the component parts is known.   Thus, supposing *dravat* to signify *running*, it is equivalent to the Welsh *yn rhedeg*, the Basque locative *eyaten*, the Lapland *warremen*, the Lat. *currens*, *currendo*, *cursu*, *cursim*, and the Greek δράμων, δρόμῳ and δρομάδην. Some of those forms are either decided ablatives or locatives, or potentially equivalent; it is therefore very possible that they may lie at the root of *currens*, Germ. *laufend*, &c., though not formally conspicuous. It is certain that this analysis is perfectly adequate to account for the peculiar force and application of the participle, and is capable of being supported by a much larger induction than it has been found consistent with present limits to give. Some philologists, it is true, regard the formative suffixes of words as a kind of *otiosa elementa*, originally destitute of signification, but by degrees employed to modify the meaning of the terms to which they had been affixed by accident or caprice. It might be replied, that it is difficult to conceive how an element totally unmeaning in itself can modify the meaning of anything, and that no such arbitrary process is known to be exercised in any part of the world, in which we have languages exhibiting every possible shade of barbarism and refinement. But there is a consideration which seems to place the improbability of the theory in a still stronger light. When connected language is logically analysed, it is found to consist of a series of subjects, leading and subordinate, connected with certain predicates, either by simple juxtaposition or by means of a grammatical copula. This copula is frequently a qualifying suffix, and though formally attached to the predicate, it does not, as a qualifying element, belong to it, but invariably to the *subject*. This applies to the personal terminations of verbs, the finals of compound adjectives and adverbs, and the characteristic endings of inflected participles. For instance, the –μι of ἵστημι belongs as much to the subject or person as *I* in 'I stand,' and in the phrase *lionlike hero*, it is the hero who is characterized as being *like* something — not the lion. These, and thousands of similar phrases may be expressed analytically; and when this is the case, we find that people, if they mean to make themselves understood, employ terms obviously expressing or implying the particular relation which they wish to convex to the mind of the hearer. No man, describing a local relation, says *in* when he means *out*, or *towards* instead of *from* — still less does he employ words totally destitute of signification; knowing that in the first case he would convey a false idea, and in the latter no definite idea whatever. Participation in an action is equally expressed by terms significant of the *connection* between the subject and the object. A Welshman does not resolve *ego currens* by means of a negative, disjunction, or unmeaning term; but says, quite rationally, *myfi yn rhedeg*, I *in* (or *a = on*) running — the particle *in* belonging subjectively to *I* and only objectively to the act of running. The Hungarian arranges the same materials in a different order: *I running-in*, or occasionally *running-in-my*; and though the phrases appear to be synthetically enunciated, they are just as capable of analysis, and as truly significant in every part as their Celtic equivalents. To deny this, — to assert, for example, that *ben* in *menö-ben*, a Hungarian participial phrase for *going*, is destitute of signification, though when prefixed to pronouns, *ben-nem*, *ben-ned*, &c., it clearly denotes *in* me, *in* thee, — would be as absurd as to maintain that though *cum*, employed separately, means *with*, it has no intrinsic meaning in *mecum, tecum*.

Reasoning analogically from the above premises, we may argue, that as the characteristic terminations of Greek and Sanscrit participles, –ων, –ουσα, –ον, &c., belong subjectively to the person or thing in concord with them, they were originally placed there to express the relation between that subject and the action predicated of it, and that a term or combination of terms intrinsically denoting that relation would not fail to be chosen. Of this we possess a twofold evidence, that of analytic languages, and synthetic languages of which the analysis is certainly known; while all the reasonings on the other side amount simply to the *argumentum ad ignorantiam*: "we do not know the meaning of this element, therefore it never meant anything." Some persons, for example, would maintain that the Sanscrit suffix –*vat*, used as a formative of adjectives, adverbs and participles, is naturally void of significance, though in the two former cases it closely corresponds with the German *lich* = *like*; and though there was a logical reason for employing it in every instance where it occurs; namely, it qualifies the subject of the proposition, not the term to which it appears to be joined. The origin and primary force of the suffix is matter of conjecture: a theory capable of explaining many of its applications is, that like the Latin so-called adverb *qui*, it is an ablative or locative case of the pronominal root *va*, and consequently capable of denoting *how, thus, in what manner, like**. The subsequent incorporation of elements expressing gender, number and case is a distinct process, every branch of which is to be explained on its own grounds. In some languages, Hungarian for example, those additions are unequivocally to be recognized as such: in Greek and Sanscrit, in which euphonic considerations have exercised so powerful an influence, they are often only to be inferred from analogical reasoning. The peculiar force of the Sanscrit or Slavonic locative is expressed in a whole multitude of languages formally destitute of that case, by a preposition plainly denoting *in*; we may therefore rationally conclude that the locative termination had originally a similar meaning, either expressly or by implication; and that it would never have been employed to express a twofold rela-

---

* Compare ὡς, *as*, *thus*, with the terminations of καλῶς, κακῶς, &c. Com are also the Ossete adjectives in - *ay* = *how*: svallon - *ay* , child-like, childish.

tion between subject and predicate, one moreover absolutely necessary to be made clearly intelligible, unless it had conveyed the notion of *in* to the mind the very first time it was used. In all investigations of this sort we may confidently lay down the following rule: "Every combination in language is an act of the will and reason of man: consequently it was made upon rational grounds, and must be explained on rational principles, and no others."

Some select examples illustrative of the above views are subjoined:

Chinese. — The relative or demonstrative particles *che, chi,* are extensively employed in the ancient language: — 1. As formatives of adjectives and abstract nouns: shing-*che*, holy, ching-*che*, perfection. 2. To express the genitive case: tien-*chi*, of heaven. 3. To form the participle: ngwei-*che*, doing.

The correspondent in the modern language is *ti*: e. gr.

> *Adj.*   pe-*ti*, white.
> *Gen.*   tung-*ti*, of copper.
> *Particip.* mai-*ti*, selling.

Burmese. (*Pru*, verbal root.)

> *Gen. postfix* i * (eng.), *part.* pru-i, doing.
> *Abl.* ka, *particip. indef.* pru-ka.
> — mha,   pruh-mha.
> *Instrumental.* nhæn, *part. pluperf.* pru-nhæn-prih **.
> —— præn, *part. indef.* pru-sa ** — præn.
> —— si (thang, thi), *part. pres.* prusi.
> *Locative* . . . mu-kah, *part. aorist*, pru-mu-kah.

All the above participles can be regularly declined in both numbers. Several others are formed by postpositions, equivalent to signs of cases, though not formally used as such. The particle *si* (more properly *thang* or *thi*), originally a demonstrative pronoun, is remarkable for its strict parallelism with the Chinese *chi* or *ti*. Compare the various offices of the Sanscrit element *ya* as a relative, a sign of the genitive case, a formative of adjectives and participles, &c. &c.

Tibetan. — *Pres. particip.* (construct. form), *gen.* jed-pei, doing. Several other participles are formed upon the same principle.

The analogy appears to run through the Manchu, Mongol,

---

* For the sake of uniformity and more ready reference, the orthography of Schleiermacher's 'Grammaire Barmane' has been followed.

** *Prih* is a sign of a completed action; *sa*, a connective particle.

and Turco-Tartarian languages, somewhat modified in the last by the employment of auxiliary verbs. Thus, in Manchu, the future participle is formed by adding the particle *ra*, *re*—khoacha-*ra*, about to nourish—which may in its turn have various signs of cases after it. Dr. W. Schott has shown, by a copious induction from the different dialects, that this formative is a particle denoting *for, towards*, employed in that sense both with nouns, verbs, and particles. It is remarkable that this element is employed in the same acceptation in a great variety of apparently unconnected languages.

> *Basque.* — *Pres. particip. Locative.* ethorteen, coming.
>   *Preterite* . . . *Dative*. . ethorri.
>   *Future* . . . . *2nd Dat.* ethorrico.

Many other participial forms in Basque are equally cases of the verbal noun, or analogous to them in structure.

> *Lapland.* — *Locative*, orrom-en, being.
> *Hungarian.* — *Present or aorist*, *mutative case*, mond-*va*, saying.
>   *Preterite, ancient locative*, ditser-*t*, having praised.
>   *Augmented forms.* . . . . men-ve-*n*, going.
>   mene-*öl*, —
>   menö-*ben*, —
>   mene-*te*, —
>   eleven-*t*, living.

The above forms, used for greater precision or emphasis, are a sort of compound cases: -*n*, -*ben*, -*t* = *in*, representing the locative, and -*öl*, -*ul* = like, as — the *casus substitutivus*. Several are obsolete, or nearly so, in the modern language. Some are found regularly declined by old writers *.

> *Galla.* — *Pres. particip., Dative* . ademe-*ti*, going.
>   *Past particip., Ablat.* . ademna-*ni*, having gone.
> *Sechuana.* — *Pres. part. Ablat.* . rek-*ang*, buying.
> *Haussa.* — *Pres. part.* . *Gen.* **. na-soh, }
>   (postfixed) . . *song*, } loving.
> *Mahratta.* — *Pres. part. Locative* chalat, walking.
>   —   *Pret.* . . . *Dative* . chalalā, —
>   —   *Pluperf.* . *Ablat.* . chal-ūn, —

---

* It is believed that the participles of the languages of the Deccan, — Tamul, Teloogoo, &c., to which the Singhalese may be added, are organized on the same principles as those of the Tartarian stock.

** This is a remarkable instance of a distinct nasal element changing its position and becoming incorporated with the verbal noun. Several analogous cases are furnished by the Polynesian languages.

Bengali. . . . . *Locative* kari-tē, doing.
Doogra. . . . . *Locative* māra-dē, leaping.
Punjābi. . . . . *Gen.* . . kar-dā, doing.

The other Indian dialects related to the Sanscrit generally correspond with the Hindi, and appear for the most part to be ablative, instrumental, or locative cases, slightly modified. Thus in the Braj-Bhasha, which may be conveniently assumed as the type of all the rest, the ablative terminates in - *tēn*, and the present participle in *at*, *'tu*, or *ū*—*marat*, mār-*tu*, marī, striking. The Ujjein chala-*tān* approaches still more nearly to the form of the Braj. ablative: and it is certain that in nearly all the *bhashas* or subsisting dialects, the participles are formed by postfixes closely analogous to those employed in the declension of nouns. A good comparative analysis of the different forms would be of great importance, as the whole structure of the verb depends upon them *.

The few present participles occurring in the old Persian inscription at Behistun end in *aniya*, chartan-iya, &c., which also occurs as a termination of the locative. We also find the ablative in - *at*, paruvi-*yat*, ab antiquo.

Sanscrit. — *Pres. part. Ablative?*   sās-at.
           (crude form) . . . .   tan-vat.
           Vedic form . . . . .   dra-vat.
Lithuanian. — Gerundial form. .   sukant, in turning.
         Pres. part. . . . . . .   sukas-f-anti, turning.
Lettish. — Gerundial form. . . .   essoht, in being.
         Pres. part. . . . . . .   essots-f-essoscha, being.
Carinthian Slavonic. — *Pres. part.*   delajoch-f-ocha, doing.

This last form is evidently the same as the Lettish, without the final *s*, which does not appear as a sign of gender in the proper Slavonic dialects. Several of them however append a demonstrative pronoun in the definite form, which amounts to the same thing.

---

* The writer is indebted to Professor D. Forbes for interesting and valuable information on the above points.

ON THE RELATIVE IMPORT OF LANGUAGE.

[Proceedings of the Philological Society.   Vol. II.]

The ordinary definition of words in general is, that they are names of things.   Though this position was maintained by Horne Tooke with great ingenuity, it is far from being satisfactory.   The analysis of language shows that names of material objects are uniformly descriptive epithets, and consequently not original; and there are moreover multitudes of words which are certainly not names of *things*, according to any legitimate meaning of the term.   The statement that they are *pictures* of *ideas* appears still more liable to objection; in fact, it scarcely conveys any definite idea to the mind, so long as the terms idea and picture are so vaguely employed as is the case at present.

In an essay on the subject in a well-known periodical, words were defined by the writer as being indicative of the qualities or attributes of things.   Though this might be defended, it is liable to the objection that things are often designated from qualities which they do *not* possess.   A slight examination of the articles commencing with *an*, *in*, *un*, in a Greek, Latin, or English lexicon, will supply abundant examples of this, and a *negative* quality is, as far as property is concerned, no quality at all.   It is therefore proposed, in lieu of the above definition, to state that they express the *relations* of things; and this, it is believed, is strictly applicable to every word in every language, and under every possible modification.   Names of material objects express the individual qualities or the relations of those objects; names of mental faculties or phenomena are borrowed from the sensible properties of matter; and all other words, without exception, help to denote some category, circumstance or mode of existence.   This existence may be either past, present or future, actual or hypothetical; but in one or other of these ways it must be at the root of all language; for *ex nihilo nihil fit.*   As the arithmetician cannot operate upon mere cyphers, so language cannot deal with absolute nonentities, for this simple reason, that nullities cannot stand in any possible relation towards each other. As the able translator * of Sir William Hamilton's Essays well observes. "Not only all knowledge, but even all thought is ontological, inasmuch as every judgment, every nation, every thought, has for its object an *existence* actual or possible, real or ideal. Everything that is affirmed or denied is affirmed or denied respecting *being*, and being is what is affirmed or denied of all things. As, in the reality of things, besides being there is nothing, in like manner, in the human mind, there is not a single thought which has not being for its principle, its foundation, and its object. There is therefore no question whether our reason can know being; for in reality it does not and cannot know anything."

The following remark by the same author is worthy of particular attention; as though not made by him with reference to that point, it appears to constitute the very foundation of the true philosophy of language:—"Our knowledge of beings is purely indirect, limited, relative; it does not reach to the beings themselves in their absolute reality and essences, but only to their accidents, their modes, their relations, their limitations, their differences, their qualities; all which are manners of conceiving and knowing which not only do not impart to knowledge the absolute character which some persons attribute to it, but even positively exclude it......Matter (or existence, the object of sensible perception) only falls within the sphere of our knowledge through its qualities; mind, only by its modifications; and these qualities and modifications are all that can be comprehended and expressed in the object. The object itself, considered absolutely, remains out of the reach of all conception."

It is of the utmost importance to keep the above observation in mind in all speculations upon the nature of language. We are incapable of knowing any particle, aggregate or modification of matter as it is in itself; we only know it in its relations of similarity, diversity, or whatever else they may be, towards other objects of our perception. And as we *know* relations only, it follows that they are all that we can *think of* or *talk about*. A further consequence is, that no words are in their origin of concrete signification.

---

* M. Louis Peisse: 'Fragmens de Philosophie par M. W. Hamilton.' Pref. p. 88.

All indicate phenomena which have no distinct independent existence, but only a relative one.

The relations in which the objects of our perceptions stand towards each other may be and are manifold and various. They may be near or distant, like or unlike, higher or lower, better or worse, united or separate, or in any conceivable degree of affinity or nonaffinity. Now, of objects standing in such relation towards each other, the word descriptive of that relation may become the name by which any one of them is popularly designated. They may be characterized from what they do or do not do to each other, or from any possible shade of resemblance or contrast. Of course, the most obvious and prominent relations are most likely to be fixed upon; but this is by no means necessarily the case: a terrestrial object, for instance, might receive its name from the sun, the moon, or the polar star, if any relation, real or supposed, could be traced between them. Either term of the relation may acquire its appellation from it: supposing A and B to be considered with reference to each other; A might be designated from some phænomenon connected with B, or *vice versâ*; or either of them might be characterized from something derived mediately through A or B from C or D. In scholastic language, such names may be either *subjective* or *objective*, a point which, though hitherto greatly overlooked, is of the utmost importance in the analysis of language. A few examples will place the matter in a clearer light.

In most Indo-European languages the numeral or adjective *one* forms various compounds and derivatives, often bearing apparently opposite significations. Thus, from the Irish *aon* we have *aonach*, a waste or moor, also a fair or great assembly; *aonta* and *aontugadh*, celibacy, also a joint vote or consent; with another derivative, *aontumadh*, marriage. In Welsh, *untref* (*un*, one + *tref*, town or habitation) means, of the same abode, townsman; while *untuawg* (*un*, one, *tu*, side) does not denote on the same side or allied, but *one-sided*, *partial*; Germ. *einseitig*. In like manner the Latin *unicus* implies solitude or singularity, and *unitas* association or community. The concord of this discord is easily found, if we consider that the term *one* may either refer to *one* as an *individual*, or in the sense of an *aggregate*. In its first acceptation *aonach* denotes *solitude*, implying that wastes or moors are commonly destitute of population; in its second it denotes aggregation, or the meeting of a multitude of people with a general unity of purpose. In like manner, the words *other*, *another*, may either express difference or addition, according as they are taken in a disjunctive or conjunctive sense.

In Anglo-Saxon the abstract noun *œmta* or *œmetta* means leisure, idleness, and its adjective *œmtig*, idle, vacant, empty. The Old-German *emazzig*, modern *emsig*, is the same word, but with a totally opposite meaning; namely, busy, industrious, occupied. The clue to this may be found in the Latin *vacare*, which, taken absolutely, denotes being vacant or idle; but when joined with *negotio* or some similar word, is equivalent to *occupari*, and implies diligence and close attention. The same diversity of meaning occurs in σχόλη and σχολάζειν. Σχόλη means leisure, idleness and at the same time a school, with its manifold occupations, — not because people necessarily idle away their time at school, but because they are free from manual labour and all similar interruptions of their studies. Thus *vacans negotio* and *emsig* express vacuity or leisure — not absolute and entire, but from all business except that in hand; and, by implication, time and power to attend to it alone. Had our word *emptiness* followed the same course as the Latin and German, it might very well have acquired the sense of diligence or industry along with its present one, the primary idea being the same in all. It may be observed, once for all, that as every voltaic current has its positive and negative pole, so every relation has its positive and negative, or subjective and objective aspect, either of which may give its character and complexion to the word used to express it. To borrow Euler's excellent illustration of negative quantities, a man's debts are negative as far as relates to right of property, but positive with respect to his obligation to pay them; while, with respect to his creditors, the same debts are negative as to actual possession, but positive as to right. The word may pass from its positive to its negative acceptation, or *vice versâ:* for instance, when we speak of a deceased merchant's debts, we are supposed to mean the sums due from him; but when we talk of his good and bad debts, we are understood to imply those owing to him by others.

The following may serve as a familiar example of the same thing receiving different names from its different attributes. In Icelandic, *lyckill*, a key, is derived, naturally enough, from *lyckia*, to shut or lock; and the German *schlüssel* (from *schliessen*), the Greek κλεῖς, with many other terms in various languages, follow the same analogy. But a key may be employed to open as well as to shut, and therefore it is with equal propriety in Welsh called *agorad*, from *agori*, to open. In other languages it is designated by terms implying crookedness, from its usual form; and it might be equally denominated from the idea of access, security, confinement, prohibition, or any other notion connected directly or indirectly with a key or its offices.

Again, the word *lee*, as applied to the side of a ship, is referred by etymologists — and it is believed rightly — to the Anglo-Saxon *hleo*, shelter, as being covered or protected from the direct action of the wind. Dr. Jamieson excepts to this derivation, on the ground that it is not applicable to *lee-shore*. A little consideration would have shown him that there is no real ground for the objection. When a ship ascends the Thames with a cross north wind, the Essex side is the weather-shore and the Kentish the lee-shore — not because they are respectively exposed to and sheltered from the wind, the reverse being the case, but with relation to the weather-side and lee-side of the ship that is passing. The term is subjective as applied to the ship, and objective with reference to the shore. This example, with many similar ones, may serve to show, that as rays of light may be refracted and reflected in all possible ways from their primary direction, so the meaning of a word may be deflected from its original bearing in a variety of manners; and consequently we cannot well reach the primitive force of the term unless we know the precise gradations through which it has gone. Had lee-side been lost or forgotten, we should have been not a little puzzled to give a rational explanation of lee-shore.

There is perhaps no more remarkable instance of the intrinsically relative nature of language than the names of the points of the compass, at least in certain classes of tongues. Everybody admits that these points vary according to locality, and that the north of London is not the north of New York. Most people however would suppose that, with reference to a fixed point, Greenwich Observatory for example, the terms for the cardinal divisions could not with propriety interchange with each other. This may be true as to the Teutonic languages, in which the precise original import of the terms is uncertain. But there are tongues in which, paradoxical as it may seem, any given point might have been designated by the name of any other. In the Semitic languages, and to a great extent in the Celtic, east, west, north, south, are respectively equivalent to *before, behind, left, right*. The congruity and propriety of the appellations evidently depend on the ancient practice of directing the view towards the rising sun, specifically for devotional purposes. But there was clearly no natural invincible necessity for taking this precise point of view and no other. The direction fixed upon might just as easily have been the setting sun, the meridian, or the north pole. In the first case every present designation would have been completely reversed. *Kedem* (front), now *east*, would have become *west; yamin* (right), *south*, would have been transformed to *north*, and so of the rest. In the second case all the points would have shifted ninety degrees sunwards; in the third they would have made a similar move in the opposite direction: thus all might travel by just stages round the horizon, and four different Semitic or Celtic tribes might have come to employ the same set of words in four perfectly distinct acceptations. It now remains to show that this is not mere theory, but that it has to a certain extent been realized in practice.

In Mosblech's 'Vocabulaire Français-Oceanien,' art. NORD, we find the following passage:—"The Islanders (Marquesans, Hawaiians, &c.) turn to the *west* in order to find the cardinal points; whence it comes that they call the north, right side, and the south, left side." A glance at the comparative tables in Humboldt and Buschmann's great work, 'Ueber die Kawi-Sprache,' will confirm the accuracy of this statement with respect to various tribes of Polynesians, western as well as eastern. When an Arab visits Java, he turns in the same direction as a Javanese to look at the southern cross; but if asked to express this direction in words, the Arab will say that it is *right* (yemen), and the Javanese *left* (kidul). In like manner, while looking out for omens, the Greek augur faced towards the north, the Roman to the south; consequently the *left*, ἀριστέρα, of the former was the western quarter, while the *lœva* of the latter was the direct contrary. Thus, while each looked towards the east for auspicious omens, they denoted them by names of diametrically opposite import. As connected in some degree with this subject, it may be observed, that our Anglo-Saxon ancestors called the right hand *se swiðre*, the stronger or better hand, while the Greek ἀριστέρα, also meaning *better*, was applied to the *left*. The Saxon simply meant to express physical superiority; while the superstitious Greek, both in this case and in that of the synonymous term εὐώνυμος, strove to avoid words of inauspicious import. Thus we find that the word *left* has been, in point of fact, employed by different races to denote east, west, north and south, and that the simple relation itself may be, and is expressed by terms in one language, which in another have a totally different meaning.

The above examples, to which thousands of similar ones might be added, may serve to illustrate the positions advanced above, that words express the relations of things, and that those relations may be indifferently positive or negative, objective or subjective.

———————

ON THE NATURE AND ANALYSIS
OF THE VERB.

[Proceedings of the Philological Society. Vol. III.]

It is well known that there has been great difference of opinion among philologists as to the priority and relative importance of the different parts of speech, as they are commonly classified by grammarians. Nearly all have concurred in regarding nouns and verbs as the two principal classes; and though a few, among whom may be specified M. Court de Gebelin and Professor Lee, have maintained the necessarily higher antiquity of the noun, the opinion of those who consider verbs as the roots of all language appears to have met with more general acceptance.

In certain languages, for example in Hebrew, Arabic and Sanscrit, the primitives or roots have been diligently collected, and those roots are generally regarded either as actual verbs, or, at all events, more closely allied to verbs than any other part of speech. There is again much discrepancy of opinion as to what constitutes a verb, and in what essential particular it differs from a noun. The definitions most commonly given are, that its essence consists in expressing *motion*, or *action*, or *existence*; and most grammarians seem to be possessed with the idea that the verb is endowed with a sort of inherent vitality, making it to differ from a noun much in the same way that an animal does from a vegetable. It is believed that not one of the above theories will bear examination. There are many verbs which express neither motion, action, nor existence, but their exact opposites, while at the same time many other words express those ideas with precision without being verbs. Moreover all words, whatever they may signify, being mere sounds, expressed by the same vocal organs, it is hard to see how one can be possessed of more vitality than another. They may *represent* life or action something in the same way as pictures or statues do, but they cannot themselves partake of those attributes.

It is believed that much of the misapprehension and error prevalent on this subject has originated in confounding the *finite verb* with the root from which it is formed. It has

19

been admitted that the essence of this part of speech consists in predication or assertion, a view to which no objection can be made. But this immediately destroys its claim to be considered as a primitive element of speech. There can be no predication in the concrete without a given *subject*; every verb therefore must have its subject; that is, speaking grammatically, it must be in a definite person. The term expressing this person is an element perfectly distinct from the root; and when it is taken away, there is no predication and consequently no verb. In short, a verb is not a simple, but, *ex necessario*, a complex term, and therefore no primary part of speech.

It may be said that though the Semitic and Sanscrit roots are not actually verbs, they are capable of becoming so by the aid of certain adjuncts, and therefore may be regarded as verbs *in posse*. Admitting this to be true, it is no special peculiarity of the words in question. In Sanscrit, almost any noun may become what is called a denominative verb; and in Basque and many American languages, not only nouns, but adverbs, conjunctions, in short, nearly all terms in the respective vocabularies, may be conjugated through a long array of moods and tenses. If therefore there is any occult principle in Sanscrit or Semitic roots, predisposing them to become verbs, it is by no means their exclusive property, any more than liability to electric influences is peculiar to metals.

Philologists who admit the greater antiquity of nouns, and regard verbs as formed from them, commonly analyse the latter as consisting of a noun connected with a subject or nominative by means of a verb substantive understood. This theory is totally untenable, for the plain reason that it involves the logical absurdity of identifying the subject with the predicate. "Ego (sum) somnium" can by no legitimate grammatical or logical process be brought to mean "ego somnio," any more than "ego (sum) navis" could denote "ego navigo." Yet it is not possible to find a better solution, so long as we entertain the currently received notions of the form and nature of the pronominal subject, and regard the predicate as a simple noun in apposition with it. We believe that this popular view of the subject has tended, more than any other cause, to obscure the true nature and origin of the verb. Grammarians have not been able to divest themselves of the idea that the subject of the verb must necessarily be a nominative; and when it was ascertained that the distinctive terminations of verbs are in fact personal pronouns, they persisted in regarding those pronouns, as *bonâ fide* nominatives, abbreviated indeed from the fuller forms, but still performing the same functions.

The writer has long felt a conviction that the usually received theory can neither be reconciled with the principles of logic, nor with the actual phenomena of language. Some of his ideas on the subject were submitted to the public in an article printed in a wellknown periodical in the year 1836. In this, an opinion was advanced that the root or predicative part of a simple verb is, or originally was, an abstract noun, and that the personal terminations are pronouns — not however nominatives in apposition, but *in regimine*, or oblique cases. This idea was grounded in the first instance on an induction from the actual phenomena presented by the Welsh language. Edward Lhuyd observed, a century and a half ago, that the personal terminations of verbs in Cornish are manifestly pronouns; and in our own time Dr. Prichard, in 'Eastern Origin of the Celtic Nations,' has made the same remark respecting the Welsh. But it was observed in the article already alluded to, that the terminations in question have not in Welsh, as might be expected, the *forms* of nominatives, but those of oblique cases — precisely such as appear in combination with prepositions, or under the regimen of nouns. It was also shown that this connexion *in regimine*, assuming it to be real, furnishes a sufficient copula between the subject and the predicate, which no ingenuity can extract from a nominative in apposition with a simple noun. The possibility of a combination of this sort assuming the functions of a verb, was further shown by a remarkable instance from the Syriac. In this language a periphrastic present tense is formed by combining the plural of the abstract substantive *ith* = existence, being, with the oblique cases of the personal pronouns: e. gr. *ithai-ch*, existentiæ tui = es; *ithai-hun* existentiæ illorum = sunt.

The analysis of these phrases is clear and certain. *Ithai* is unequivocally a noun substantive, in the plural number, in the construct form and in regimen of a pronoun in an oblique case, answering to our genitive, while we find that the combination of those elements is equivalent to a word commonly supposed to lie at the root of all verbal expression. Another remarkable instance is furnished by the Feejee language. In this, besides the ordinary Polynesian verb formed by a combination of the root with prefixed particles and pronouns, there is a more simple one arising out of the union of a noun with a pronominal suffix *in obliquo*. Thus *loma*, literally denoting *heart*, and metaphorically *mind*, *will*, is regularly employed in conjunction with the

19 *

genitives of the personal pronouns in the sense of the Latin verb *volo*: e. gr. *loma - qu*, literally, heart of me == I will; *loma - munu* == thou wilt; *loma - na* == he will; *loma - mudou* == ye will or wish.

The above instances, to which multitudes of similar ones might be added, are decisive as to the *possibility* of the functions of a verb being performed by a noun in combination with the oblique form of a pronoun, and they moreover include categories commonly regarded as peculiarly essential to the part of speech at present under consideration. *Being* and *will* are usually regarded by metaphysical grammarians as the two ideas necessarily inherent in the verb, and in fact constituting the difference between it and the noun. But, if *beings of me* can be made equivalent to *I am*, and *heart of me* to *I will*, it follows *à fortiori*, that any other verbal category may be enunciated in a similar manner.

It is not meant to be asserted that every finite verb in every language is capable of being analysed in precisely the same manner. At present it is only contended that a noun in construction with a pronoun is *capable* of being employed as a verb, and that there is no lack of instances in which it actually is so. It is also clear that if verbs are necessarily complex terms, they cannot be the primordia or roots of language, and that the definitions usually given of them are erroneous or incomplete. The true definition of the verb appears to be, that it is a term of relation or predicate in grammatical combination with a subject, commonly pronominal. In some languages, any word in any given part of speech is capable of being made the basis of a verb, and of being regularly conjugated through moods, tenses and persons; in others this license is considerably restricted. Generally speaking, simple abstract nouns are the most convenient materials, and may be regarded as the basis of the oldest forms, but prepositions and other particles are equally capable of being employed. The form of the combination between the predicate and its pronominal subject may also vary according to circumstances and the genius of particular languages. To specify every actual modification would require an analysis of all languages spoken on the face of the globe; but most of those which have been examined appear to be reducible to two leading classes: 1. abstract nouns, and occasionally other parts of speech in grammatical connexion with pronominal subjects in oblique cases, analogous to the examples already given; 2. participles, or *nomina actoris*, in construction with a subject in the nominative, or more rarely in the instrumental, ablative or locative case. This latter class comprises the Tibetan, Mongolian, Basque, and many other languages; and is not unknown in Indo-European and Semitic. As a general rule it may be stated, that if the predicate is a nominative, the subject is *in obliquo*; and conversely, if the subject is nominative the predicate is an oblique case, a participle, or in regimen by a preposition. Occasional variations will be pointed out in the sequel.

In proceeding to give practical illustrations of the theory now advanced, we may conveniently begin with the Coptic, both as being an isolated language and on account of the peculiarity and originality of its grammatical forms. Notwithstanding the comparatively recent state in which the bulk of its literature has reached us, there is no reason to doubt that it has preserved a considerable portion of the ancient language of Egypt, and what is of no small importance, without any material disturbance of its grammatical character. Champollion observes, 'Grammaire Égyptienne,' chap. 3, that the greatest part of the words of the Egyptian language are to be found in the hieroglyphic and hieratic texts, expressed in phonetic characters, and only differing from the same words written in the Grecian letters called Coptic by the absence or different position of some vowels, rarely by the transposition of certain consonants; and that there is no language which does not exhibit still greater orthographical changes in an equal lapse of time. He further shows that nearly all the articles, pronouns and formative particles may be identified in the hieroglyphic and hieratic texts; and that when phonetically expressed, the Coptic forms are with slight exceptions mere transcriptions of them. In both classes the nominatives of the personal pronouns, employed separately, are accurately distinguished from the oblique cases, used as affixes and suffixes in construction with nouns, verbs and particles. Again, what are called the roots of verbs are at the same time nouns (or occasionally pronouns or particles), and Peyron observes that there is no way of distinguishing between a Coptic finite verb and the corresponding noun with pronominal affixes, except that the latter usually has the article, which is wanting in the former. In the Coptic and recent demotic texts, the pronouns in construction precede the noun and the verb; but in the hieroglyphic and hieratic monuments they are regularly postfixed, a transposition which, as Lepsius observes, frequently appears as a mark of distinction between the modern and the ancient state of a language.

What is most essential to our present purpose is to observe, that in both states of the language the pronouns em-

ployed as oblique cases in construction with nouns and prepositions, and those serving to indicate the persons of verbs,
are perfectly identical. *Ti*, for example, is indifferently *to
give* or *gift*; and in an ancient text, *ti-k*, *ti-f*, *ti-n*, or *ti-en*,
would generally correspond to Lat. *das*, *dat*, *damus*. But if
the definite article is prefixed, the same phrases immediately
become *thy*, *his*, *our gift*, and so on through all the persons. It seems inconceivable that the pronominal suffixes
-k, *-f*, *-n*, should mean *of me*, *of him*, *of us* in the latter
instances, and *thou*, *he*, *we* in the former, words for which
the language affords perfectly distinct terms: or that *ti*, merely
meaning *gift* in one class of terms, should by some unknown
mystical process become invested with an active character
and be transmuted into a word of a totally different class.

If it be conceded that *ti* is in both classes essentially the
same word, it necessarily follows that the pronominal adjuncts of each have precisely the same power; in other words,
they have the construction of oblique cases, not of nominatives, as nominatives are usually understood. *Gift I*, for
I give, would be a downright absurdity; but *gift of me* or
by me necessarily implies *I give*, or *did*, or *shall give*, according to circumstances. The same remarks might be extended
to the entire conjugation of the Egyptian verb. Let any
one, previously divesting his mind of the usually received
notions of the essential difference between nouns and verbs,
examine the paradigm of *taka*, ostensibly *to destroy*, in Tattam's Grammar, together with the words classed under the
same root in Peyron's Coptic Lexicon, and he will find that
under every modification, *tako* considered separately means
destruction, and nothing else; other supposed senses are not
inherent, but depend altogether on the qualifying adjuncts.
With the articles it is a noun substantive, with the relative
pronoun it becomes an adjective or a participle, and when
predicated of a given subject, according to the forms above
specified, it assumes the functions of a verb. Take this
predication away and all traces of the verb immediately
vanish. What are called the auxiliary and substantive verbs
in Coptic are still more remote from all essential verbal
character. On examination they will almost invariably be
found to be articles, pronouns, particles, or abstract nouns,
and to derive their supposed verbal functions entirely from
accessories, or from what they imply.

An attempt has now been made to show that the basis
or root of the verb is a simple predicate, usually an abstract
noun, and that its supposed distinctive character arises entirely out of its combination with a subject, commonly a

presonal pronoun in an oblique case. Special illustrations of those positions have been given from the Coptic and other languages. It is now intended to consider some phenomena presented by the Semitic dialects.

The analysis of the ordinary verb in the Semitic tongues, especially in Hebrew, Syriac and Arabic, is not so obvious and certain as it is in Coptic. Many euphonic changes have taken place; and the singular structure of the future in particular has not been satisfactorily explained by any philologist.

The resemblance of the personal terminations in the preterite to the pronouns attracted however the attention of grammarians at an early period, and it has been pretty generally allowed, that those endings are in point of fact personal pronouns, modifications of them. They are commonly regarded as abbreviations of the ordinary nominatives, and this opinion appears to be countenanced by Dr. Lee in his Hebrew Grammar. He has however pointed out several instances in which the forms do not correspond, and when we attempt to carry the principle throughout the cognate dialects, we find the discrepances so numerous and serious, as to excite considerable doubts respecting its soundness. For example, there is a periphrastic present tense in Syriac indubitably formed by the addition of the nominative personal pronouns to the present participle. But the terminations thus obtained are so different from those of the ordinary preterite, that it is scarcely possible to refer them to a common origin. To go no further than the first person, *qetleth = occīdi* can hardly be composed of the same materials as *qotel–no = ego occīdens* or *occīdo*. In the latter the termination is simply *eno = ego*, with a quiescent initial; but if the dental ending of the latter ever was a nominative, it must have been totally different from any nominative now found in the languages.

It is believed that the Ethiopic and Amharic dialects furnish the most satisfactory explanation of the true structure of the Semitic verb. In both these the conjugation of the verb presents several peculiarities, and if we are not mistaken, those peculiar forms have a more original and organic cast than the corresponding ones in the more cultivated dialects. One remarkable distinct is, that in several persons the Ethiopic substitutes gutturals, accompanied by fuller vowel sounds for the dentals of the Hebrew and other dialects. For example, the Hebrew forms *lamad–ti*, doceo; *lamad–t*, doces; *lemad–tem*, docetis, would in Ethiopic be *lamad–ku, lamad–ka, lamad–kemmu*. The reason for regarding the latter forms as more original than their Hebrew cognates is, that they correspond in general with the oblique cases of the pronouns employed in construction with nouns and prepositions.

When the forms of the verb and noun happen to correspond, their respective combinations with pronominal suffixes are often perfectly identical. Thus *naggar*, noun subst., denotes speech, discourse; and as the base of a verb of the second conjugation, analogous to the Heb. *piel*, meaning to relate or speak, *naggar-ka*, considered absolutely, may either denote *sermo tuus* or *tu locutus es;* and in the plural *naggarna*, *sermo noster* or *locuti sumus; naggar-kemmu*, *sermo vester* or *locuti estis*. Some of the above forms cannot without violence be deduced from the nominatives of the personal pronouns. *Na*, the suffix of the first person plural, might possibly be a fragment of *nehna*, but it is not so easy, by any legitimate process, to extract *ka* from *anta*, or *kemmu* from *antmu*. On the other hand, identity of form may be fairly regarded *à priori* as an indication of original identity of power, at least till we have some proof to the contrary. If the strongly marked form *kemmu*, in combination with a noun, means *vestrûm* and not *vos*, it seems more rational to conclude that it had originally the same power in the verb, than to assume without a shadow of proof that it was once a nominative, or to deduce it from a word organically different.

It is admitted that this identity of the personal terminations of verbs and the pronominal suffixes of nouns in Ethiopic is not carried through all the persons of the ordinary preterite. The discrepances may however either be accounted for by the process of abbreviation in forms frequently and familiarly employed, which is common to many languages, or may be partially explained by reference to other dialects. There is however a formula frequently employed as a substitute for the ordinary verb, in which the nature and construction of the pronominal suffixes is perfectly unequivocal. In many constructions, and more particularly in order to express a contingent future, what is called the infinitive, but, as is also the case in other Semitic languages, in reality is a mere abstract noun, is employed in both numbers and in all persons, with precisely the same suffixes as any ordinary substantive. Thus *gabir*, to do, or more properly *act of doing*, is employed in combination with suffixes according to the following paradigm: —

Sing. 1. gabir-ya.   2. gabir-ka.   3. gabir-ō
Plur. 1. gabir-na.   2. gabir-kemmu.   3. gabir-omu.

Taken absolutely, these combinations simply denote *doing of*

me, *thee*, *him*, &c., but in connected composition they are
used extensively to signify *when I go*, or *when I shall go*,
&c., through all the persons. A similar construction occurs
in Hebrew, but it is employed in a much more partial manner. In Amharic it is used much in the same way as in
Ethiopic, with some slight variations in form. The remarks
of Isenberg on this idiom, which he designates the constructive mood, may help to throw some light upon its nature:—

"This (the constructive) is a singular mood which has nothing corresponding either in European or in other Semitic
languages; although its form, as far as the simple one is
concerned, answers the Ethiopic infinitives *gabir* and *gabrö*;
but this mood is not an infinitive. It has nothing of a substantive character; whereas the infinitive is the first verbal
substantive, possessing both the characters of substantive
and verb. Nor is there any other mood to which it exactly
corresponds; neither participle nor gerund nor finite verb
will answer it, although it may be occasionally translated
by either, and sometimes by an adverb. It occupies an intermediate station between the infinitive and the finite verb;
has four forms, one of which is simple, one augmented, and
two compound; and is flexible like the finite verb, having
afformatives, resembling the suffixed pronouns, partly of the
noun and partly of the verb. The simple form is used for
amplifying; the other forms, on account of the auxiliaries
which are attached to them, for constituting sentences. When
the nature of this mood is understood, we hope the designation *constructive* will be justified, not having been able to fix
upon any better.

"The simple form *kabr* (a modification of the radix *kĕbr*,
'honour,' which may be considered as containing the idea
of an agent, and of an action or a concrete being, and an
abstract state or condition, &c.) assumes peculiar forms of
pronouns, which must not be taken as possessive (nominal),
but as personal (verbal); nor as the other verbal suffixes
which are in the accusative, but they are nominatives." —
Isenberg, Grammar of the Amharic Language, pp. 69, 70.

It is not difficult to perceive that while the premises are
here correctly stated, the author's reasonings upon them
are, like those of most grammarians, influenced by the
hackneyed idea of the necessarily intrinsic difference between the noun and the verb. Ludolf, rightly as we believe, treats the Amharic construction as perfectly analogous
to the Ethiopic one already analysed; and it will be obvious
on examination that the root is a mere verbal noun, commonly denoting state or action, and that the pronominal

endings are nothing more than the ordinary oblique cases of the personals, in some cases slightly modified. *Kabr* for example, taken absolutely, means nothing more than the state or category of being honourable; and *kabr–ē*, with the suffix of the first person, means *my being honourable*, or more simply, *my dignity*, just as much as *beth–ē* means *my house*. It may indeed, in connected discourse, require to be rendered by *when I am or shall be honourable*; but this sense depends on the combined power of the elements, not upon anything inherent in the root.

The arguments for the hypothesis now advanced, deducible from the Semitic languages, may be briefly stated as follows: — 1. In most of them a mere abstract noun with oblique pronominal suffixes is unequivocally employed ׳to express the verb substantive, commonly regarded by grammarians as the verb *par excellence*. 2. The personal terminations of the Ethiopic and Amharic preterites generally correspond with the pronominal suffixes employed with nouns, the difference in meaning being often only determinable by the context. The preterite, in other dialects, is evidently formed upon the same *principle*: whether the Ethiopic or the Hebrew has preserved the more ancient type is a question of fact not easy to be decided from such data as we now possess. 3. The infinitive — in other words, the verbal noun — is regularly employed in the Abyssinian dialects in combination with oblique pronominal suffixes to supply a deficient tense of a regular verb; the literal resolution of the phrase being *act* or *state of me*, *of thee*, *of him*, &c., according to circumstances. These forms are probably more recent than the regular preterite; but in them, as well as in the periphrasis of the verb substantive already alluded to, there appears to have been an intention to proceed upon the original *principle* of formation. In the older as well as in the more recent, there is no doubt that the pronominal termination stands for the subject of the proposition, and the root for the predicate; the only dispute is, what is the nature of the connexion between them? No reason appears to have been hitherto assigned why it may not be the same in one case as in the other, except the assertion that the roots of verbs are and must be intrinsically different from nouns, which in fact amounts to begging the entire question at issue.

There are other phenomena in the Semitic languages apparently tending to confirm the hypothesis now advanced, which will be more conveniently discussed in another division of the general subject.

We proceed to consider the evidence deducible from a class of languages nearly related to the Turco-Tartarian family, namely the Tschudish or Finnish, of which the Lappish and Hungarian are now generally admitted to be members. The Hungarian was indeed for a long time regarded as a language *sui generis*; but in the last century, Sajnovics, and subsequently Gyarmathi, brought abundant evidence to show that it is closely related to the Lappish, Finnish, and Esthonian, both in words and construction. Though their demonstration was in some respects more empirical than scientific, and was capable of being carried much further, it was sufficient to establish their leading position; insomuch that Adelung, whose ideas respecting the origin of language inclined him to believe in the existence of perfectly isolated ones, admitted that the connexion could not be denied.

A still greater step was made in our own time by Dr. W. Schott of Berlin, who showed by an able and extensive induction, that the Manchu, Mongolian, Calmuck, Turco-Tartarian, Tschudish, and Hungarian are all members of one great family of tongues, divisible indeed into classes, but still bearing abundant marks of a community of origin. One general point of agreement among them is, that they have no single class of words bearing the distinct and exclusive character of roots of verbs. The abstract noun forms most commonly the basis of the conjugational system, but by no means necessarily and peculiarly so; other parts of speech, not excluding particles, being often capable of construction with pronominal terminations, so as to be perfectly equivalent to verbs in other languages.

The following remarks of Gabelentz, in his valuable sketch of the Grammar of the Mordwinian language in Lassen's 'Zeitschrift für die Kunde des Morgenlandes,' will help to place the capabilities of this member of the great Finnish family in a clearer light. After observing that it is important to study all the languages of the class in conjunction, in order to form an adequate idea of the variety and copiousness of their forms, he adds: —

"In this point of view, the Mordwinian is not one of the least interesting. One circumstance in particular is well calculated to attract the attention of the philologist. It has hitherto been considered a distinctive characteristic of the American languages — at all events of the greater part of them — that they can employ almost every word as a verb, and represent the varied relations for which other languages employ auxiliaries, particles, pronouns, and suchlike, by

the forms of the verb itself. As these forms are rather su-
peradded to the verb from without than developed from it
inwardly, those languages have been called polysynthetic,
with the intention of thereby designating a peculiar class of
tongues. But the Mordwinian furnishes evidence that the
Old Continent can produce an instance of polysynthesis,
though it may be not quite so perfect. Or could such forms
as *asodav–tasamisk*, 'you will not let me know'; *maronzolt*,
'they were along with him'; *kostondädo*, 'whence are you?'
prävevtemelt, 'they were without understanding'; *pazonän*,
'I am the Lord's'; *tsüratan*, 'I am thy son'; and many similar ones, be well regarded in any other light*?"
    It will be sufficient to observe for the present, that though
the above combinations are employed as verbs, and have
regular conjugational endings, they are for the most part
nothing but particles or nouns in construction with pronominal suffixes *in obliquo*. Thus the base of *maronzolt* is simply
the particle *maro = apud*; and of *kostondädo*, *kosto = unde;*
prävevtemelt being a formation on the caritive case of an abstract noun, *pazonän* a similar one on the genitive of *paz*,
'Lord,' and *tsüratan* a combination of a concrete noun with
the suffixes of two personal pronouns, equivalent to υἱός
–σου –μου, *q. d.* 'son of thee — [condition] of me.' It is
sufficiently obvious that no one of the above combinations is
or can contain in itself a verb, as that part of speech is
usually conceived by grammarians, and that their apparent
verbal character consists in the predicative form in which
they stand, and nothing else whatever.
    The so-called regular verbs in this family of languages
will be found on examination to consist of the same or very
similar materials. The analysis of the forms is more clear
and certain in some than in others, owing to a variety of
causes. Several of those tongues, particularly the Finnish
and Esthonian, are remarkably sensitive to peculiar laws
of euphony, in obedience to which vowels are modified and
consonants changed or elided so as greatly to disguise the
original forms of words. In some also the so-called inflexions of the verb do not appear to be simple modifications
of pronouns, but coalitions of the oblique pronoun with particular case-endings or postpositions of the verbal noun,
occasionally so transposed, abbreviated or softened down as
to render the analysis of them somewhat difficult.
    There are however several languages in which the con-
formity between the respective persons of the verbs and

---

* Zeitschrift für die Kunde des Morgenlandes , vol. ii pp. 256, 257.

ordinary nouns in construction with oblique personal pronouns is almost complete. In the Wotiak, nouns ending in vowels are combined with this class of pronouns according to the following paradigm:—

pī [for pi-ĭ]	*filius mei.*
pi-ed	—— *tui.*
pi-ez	—— *ejus.*
pi·my . . .	—— *nostri.*
pi·dy . . .	—— *vestri.*
pi-zy . . .	——— *eorum.*

In verbs, the endings of the simple preterite are as follow:—

Singular.	Plural.
1. bera-i, *dixi.*	bera-my, *diximus.*
2. bera-d, ——	bera-dy, ——
3. bera-z, ——	bera-zy, ——

Here it is evident, that, with the exception of the coalition . of two short vowels into the corresponding long one in *pī*, the two sets of terminations are perfectly identical.

In Tcheremissian the noun is combined with pronouns according to the following scheme:—

ata-m	*pater mei.*
ata-t	—— *tui.*
ata-*sha . . .	—— *sui, ejus.*
ata-na.	—— *nostri.*
ata-da.	—— *vestri.*
ata-sht	—— *eorum.*

Compare the conjunctive form of the verb:—

Singular.	Plural.
1. ischtene-m, *faciam.*	ischtene-na, *faciamus.*
2. ischtene-t, ——	ischtene-da.
3. ischtene-she, ——	ischtene-sht.

Here again the agreement is complete, except that the third person singular ends in *-she* instead of *-sha.*

The endings of the present and perfect indicative *ischte-m* facio; *ischtena-m*, feci, are perfectly analogous, as far as the first and second persons of both numbers are concerned. In the third person there is some discrepancy; but Wiedemann, in his elaborate Tcheremissian Grammar, p. **122**,

---

Pronounced like *s* in *pleasure.* The English sound of *sh* is expressed by *sch*.

shows clearly that the third person singular of the present
tense, *ischta* or *ischtesch*, has no pronominal ending or proper
sign of person at all, being in fact a mere verbal noun,
employed indifferently as substantive, adjective, or verb;
and that the third person singular of the preterite, *ischten*,
is another verbal noun, having frequently the construction
of a present or aorist participle, or a Latin gerund in *do*.
In fact, *ischt-esch* has precisely the form of the predicative
case, used in various Finnish dialects to express the category, circumstances or condition of a given subject, as the
instrumental is in Slavonic. According to this analysis,
ischtesch denotes in the act or category of doing, just as
mar-esch signifies in the character, condition or category of
a man. Frequently this form requires to be rendered *for*,
in which case it is nearly equivalent to a dative. *Ischt-en*,
used as the third person of the preterite, seems to bear a
like analogy to an ablative or locative, not unlike the Welsh
construction of the preposition *yn* with nouns, adjectives, and
infinitives. It is believed that the conjunctive form given
above has the same element for its basis: *e. gr. ischtenesh-em*,
in [the case of] my doing = if I do.

It is unnecessary to enter minutely into the investigation
of the corresponding forms in Finnish and Esthonian. For
the most part they are of the same origin as those already
specified, *m* being usually attenuated to *n*, *t* to *d*, &c., apparently for the sake of euphony. It is somewhat remarkable
that in Syrianian the personal endings of verbs differ from
the suffixes of nouns throughout the singular and closely
agree with them throughout the plural. In Lappish, the
pronominal suffixes employed with nouns do not appear in
any single tense of the verb, but most of them may be
elicited from the various parts of the entire conjugation. In
Mordwinian also, the adjuncts of the noun not found in the
indicative tenses present themselves in the conjunctive and
the imperative.

The reason of these discrepancies appears to be, that in
their earlier state those languages, like many others, had
duplicate and even triplicate sets of pronouns, some of
which were employed in one kind of construction and some
in another. For example, the termination of *soda-tado*, 'ye
know,' does not bear the smallest resemblance to that of
tel-ante, 'your body.' But that *tado* is really a pronoun of
the second person plural is proved by its being employed in
the definite conjugation, in which the verb and its regimen
are included in the same combination: — *e. gr. soda-tady-z*,
'he judges you,' where the final consonant is the regular

sign of the third person, abbreviated from *zo* = *ejus*, and *tady* the regimen or objective case = *ὑμᾶς*. In fact, a general comparison of the dialects shows that the guttural and dental forms are used interchangeably with nouns and verbs, and that one is often merely a modification or mutation of the other. Thus in Hungarian and Lappish the plural of nouns ends in *k*, in Finnish in *t*, and in Esthonian in *d*. As all the languages have the same origin, it is reasonable to conclude that the dental forms are mere softenings of the guttural, like our modern *mate* from the Old-English *make*, A.-S. *mæg*.

The last language of this class which we shall have occasion to consider is the Hungarian, perhaps as remarkable as any for the distinctness of its forms and the striking similarity of the two classes of words which it is at present attempted to identify with each other. As in most languages of the class, the place of pronouns possessive is supplied by suffixes attached to the noun, and it his hardly possible to compare these suffixes with the personal endings of the verb without admitting a community of origin. For example *kéz*, 'hand,' is connected with oblique forms of pronouns as follows: —

kéz-em,	kéz-ed,	kéz-e.
manus mei,	— *tui*,	— *ejus*.
kéz-ünk,	kéz etek,	kéz-ek.
— *nostri*,	—· *vestri*,	— *eorum*.

Compare the preterite of the definite conjugation, *i. e.* of a verb followed by a regimen with a definite article, an objective personal pronoun, *v. t. q.*

Singular.	Plural.
1. esmert-em, *cognovi*.	1. esmert-ük [indef. conj. esmert-ünk].
2. esmert-ed, ——	2. esmert-étek.
2. esmert-e, ——	3. esmert-ék.

It will be seen that the correspondence of the two sets of endings is perfect, with the exception of *ük* instead of *ünk* in the first person plural; which form however duly appears in the indefinite conjugation. Some of the remaining tenses, both of the definite indicative and conjunctive, differ slightly, in one or two persons, chiefly as it seems for the sake of euphony, or through the retention of older forms. There is considerable discrepancy between the inflexions of the definite and the indefinite conjugations, owing to the latter having adopted forms of pronouns now obsolete in other combinations.

The resemblance between the two classes of endings did not escape the notice of the Hungarian grammarian Márton, who however strangely assumes that the pronominal suffixes of nouns, — and infinitives, which have precisely the construction of nouns, — are *borrowed* from the finite verb; thus taking it for granted, without evidence, that the verbal combination is the older of the two. Another native grammarian, Reváy, whose acumen unfortunately was not quite equal to his industry, shows by an elaborate induction that the endings of finite verbs are all of pronominal origin, and that those of the definite conjugation are identical with the suffixes of nouns. On these and similar phenomena he grounds some speculations respecting the rudimentary state of the language, which appear to contain a strange mixture of truth and error.

After observing that the radical terms employed to denote action, passion, or state, had originally rather the force of nouns than verbs, and that they became verbs first by the annexation of personal pronouns, and then by the progressive augmentation of the forms of moods and tenses, he remarks: —

"In the early state of languages the primary names of things were chiefly monosyllables, which also furnished verbs in their most simple form, before the more enlarged and artificial forms made their appearance. There remain, even at the present day, some nouns of this kind, being at the same time verbs; for example, *fagy*, signifying both 'frost' and 'it freezes'; also *lak**, 'habitation,' which, augmented by the affixing of a pronoun, is used as a verb, *lak-ik*, 'habitat.' In the infancy of the language, the forms *fagy-en*, *fagy-te*, *fagy-ö*, arose from the inartificial annexation of the pronoun, having both the force of the noun and of the verb, when predicated of persons: primarily denoting *gelu*, ego, tu, ille, instead of *gelu*, meum, tuum, suum, and then *gelasco*, *gelascis*, *gelascit*. Afterwards, by a more perfect formation which is still in use, a distinction was made between them in this way, namely that *fagy-om*, *fagy-od*, *fagy-a* or *-ja*, *lak-om*, *lak-od*, *lak-ja*, where employed as nouns, and *fagy-ok*, *fagy-oz*, *fagy*, *lak-om*, *lak-ol*, *lak-ik*, as verbs."

That the rudimentary words of language were nouns, and that verbs arose out of them by the annexation of personal pronouns, are positions which we feel by no means inclined

---

* Now only used in composition.

to dispute. But that the pronouns thus employed as the subjects of propositions were, as Reváy imagines, originally *nominatives*, is not only unsupported by evidence, but repugnant to the very nature of things. It is totally incredible that *habitatio ego* could ever be used in regular and connected speech to express either *habitatio mei* or *habito*. All known languages are constructed on strictly logical principles, and one in which no distinction could be made between *asinus ego* and *asinus mei* would be unfit for the purposes of intercourse between man and man. From the very earliest period there must have been some method of expressing *attribution;* and when pronouns were employed, this was done either by putting them in oblique cases, or by means of possessive pronouns, nearly all of which are formed on oblique cases; and in many languages more than one pronoun is employed in order to render the attribution more clear. Sometimes, as in Welsh and Finnish, the nominative is used pleonastically along with the oblique case for the sake of emphasis; but the proof that the oblique form is the essential element is, that it is optional to omit the former, but not the latter. Even in ancient Chinese, a marked distinction is made between apposition and attribution. Notwithstanding this fundamental error as to the nature of the relation between the noun employed as a verb and its pronominal affix, Reváy's remarks, as applied specifically to the Hungarian language, are extremely valuable and contain the germ of an important principle. He gives elsewhere various examples of nouns which are at the same time verbs, and observes that many more such were current in an earlier state of the language. The formal difference which he attempts to establish between the verb and the noun is fallacious, as the examples which he gives are both in the *indefinite* conjugation. When the definite conjugation is employed, there is, as we have already shown, no external difference worth mentioning. For instance, *tér* may be indifferently noun, adjective, or verb, in the respective acceptations of *spatium, spatiosus, spatium habeo*, or *transeo;* and *tér-em, tér-ed, tér-i*, might either denote *spatium mei, tui, sui*, or, as verbs in the definite conjugation, *transeo, transis, transit*. Thus *ir-om* may be either *unguentum mei* or *scribo; tudat-om, scientia mei* or *scire facio; vadasz-om, venator mei* or *venor; nyom-om, vestigium mei* or *calco;* and *lep-em, tegimen mei* or *tego*. In modern Hungarian, *eső* denotes *pluvia*, and *es-ik, pluit*; but in the fifteenth century the simple root *es* was employed in both senses. There is little doubt that at an early period this identity of the verbal root with the noun was a general law of the language. At present the abstract noun commonly differs from the simplest form of the verb by the addition of a formative syllable, usually *as* or *at:* e. *gr.* *ir*, scribit; *iras*, scriptio; *ir–at*, scriptum. Such formatives, introduced for the sake of explanation or distinction, often belong to a comparatively recent period of a language, as may be seen by comparing Gothic with modern German.

The observation already made respecting the Turco-Tartarian verb, that it is almost entirely an aggregation of participles and pronouns, is in a great measure equally applicable to the Hungarian. The present tense has been already analysed, as consisting of the simple root in construction with personal pronouns, *in obliquo.* The imperfect *esmeré–m*, anciently *esmereve–m* or *esmereje–m*, is formed on a modification of the present participle: the perfect *esmert–em* is nothing but the perfect participle *esmert*, with the usual pronominal endings; and *esmertend–ö*, the future participle, is equally the basis of the future tense, *esmertend–em*. In a former paper, "On the Origin of the Present Participle," the writer took occasion to show that the Hungarian participles have generally the forms and the construction of ablative or locative cases. We have also seen that the personal endings of the definite conjugation are recognized by the native grammarians as identical with the pronominal suffixes regularly employed with nouns. If we admit both parts of this analysis, it seems to follow that there is an oblique relation in both constituents of the verb, constituting the same kind of double attribution that has already been pointed out in Burmese and Tibetan. It is not a little remarkable moreover, that in Tibetan and Hungarian this phenomenon is exhibited in verbs with a definite regimen, or in the language of Latin grammarians, transitive verbs. A similar construction also prevails in Basque and Greenlandish; in the latter of which the subject of the transitive verb has regularly the form of a genitive. Now we can scarcely conceive anything more repugnant to the ideas usually entertained of the finite verb, than that it should be formed out of the combination of an ablative base in construction with a pronominal genitive; yet this is the case in a variety of languages, if identity of form is to be trusted. The simpler form, in which the pronoun alone is put in the oblique case, occurs however more frequently. It is indeed asserted by some grammarians, that those apparent oblique cases are, in the conjugation of the verb, really abbreviated nominatives; but this explanation will not account for instances where the element is lengthened instead of being shortened, nor for those where the actual nominatives have nothing in common with the verbal inflexions, being in fact composed of letters of totally different organs. It seems much more legitimate and rational to consider identity of form as an indication of identity of power and meaning, till some good reason is given to the contrary.

It may not be amiss to add a few supplementary remarks on some Caucasian languages, the exact place of which has not as yet been accurately determined, but exhibiting some points of resemblance with the Finno-Tartarian family. In the principal of these, the Georgian, the conjugation of the verb is singularly intricate, and the attempts of grammarians to analyse it have not been very successful. Many of the paradigms in Brosset's Grammar are confessedly erroneous; and Bopp's attempt to account for the characteristic forms from the Sanscrit is little calculated to produce conviction. Thus much may be affirmed, that the root of the verb is regularly an abstract or verbal noun, which becomes a verb by the instrumentality of particles and personal pronouns. It is remarkable that these elements, indicating the person or subject, are not, as in the Indo-European and most other languages, terminational, but prefixed, and in some dialects curiously infixed in the middle of the verb. In some tenses they are only employed in a fragmentary manner, but in others their correspondence with the personal pronouns is pretty exact; and what is of most consequence to our present argument, they have the forms of the oblique cases, which are totally different from the regular nominatives. Thus the root *qwar*, 'to love,' forms its pluperfect tense in the singular number by inserting, after the formative particle *she*, the syllables *mi*, *gi*, *ù*, as follows: —

1st pers. *she-miqwarebia*, amaveram.
2nd — *she-giqwarebia*, ——
3rd — *she-ùqwarebia*, ——

The above elements *m*, *g*, *ù*, are precisely those employed as the dative or objective cases of the personal pronouns in construction with transitive verbs, though the first person agrees pretty well with *me* = ego, the second and third are totally unlike, *shen* = tu, *igi* = ille. To say therefore that they are nominatives, or ever were, is a mere arbitrary assumption. Even Bopp admits that they are oblique cases, both in form and construction, but assumes that this and similar tenses are in reality in the passive voice, without making the smallest attempt to prove them so.

The Lazian, Suanian, and Mingrelian, on which light has

20 *

been recently thrown by the researches of Rosen, are languages of the same class as the Georgian; and it will be sufficient to say of them that they exhibit the same characteristics as have already been specified, some more and some less completely: and where the forms differ, the principle is obviously the same.

In all there has evidently been a great abrasion of characteristic forms, especially of the pronominal prefixes. In the Suanian, some tenses accurately distinguish the three persons singular and plural; in others, as also in Georgian and Mingrelian, the singular and plural forms of those elements are the same; while in Lazian scarcely any personal characteristic has survived beyond an obscure indication of the first person. There is however a class of dialects which it is conceived clearly exhibits the original principle of organization in the whole Caucasian group; namely the Abchassian and Circassian, with their immediate cognates. The Circassian is at present unfortunately only known to us by the notoriously inaccurate statements of Klaproth; but as it is admitted to be closely related to the Abchassian, we will abstract the extremely interesting and important remarks of Rosen respecting the structure of the verb in the latter: —

"The Abchassian verb, interesting on account of its great simplicity, exhibits equal completeness and consistency in its formation. We here find the personal conception or characteristic, indispensable to the finite verb, completely detached from the termination, so that the plurality of the subject is not, as is still the case in the Suanian, expressed by a modification of the ending, but, more naturally, by means of the pronominal prefixes of the several persons. The termination simply and abstractedly denotes the verbal action with its relation to time, and in this capacity can admit of alteration neither on account of number nor person. The pronominal prefixes, on the other hand, are different according to the six relations of person which they represent, and cannot on their part undergo alteration according to tense or time."

Rosen proceeds to remark that the six personal characteristics are perfectly identical with the personal pronouns, being respectively: —

Sing. 1.	s, z,	*Plur.* 1.	h,
2.	w, u,	2.	sh,
3.	i,	3.	r.

which are generally prefixed to the verbal root, but sometimes infixed or intercalated in what appears to us a singular manner. He makes however no observation on a point which we conceive to be of some consequence, namely that the above elements are not nominatives, but oblique cases, employed indifferently as genitives in construction with nouns, as datives or objective cases with transitive verbs, and as pronominal subjects with all verbs without exception. For example, *ab*, 'father,' is attributed to the different persons in the following manner: —

s-ab,	pater mei.		*h-ab*,	pater nostri.
w-ab,	—— tui.		*sh-ab*,	—— vestri.
i-ab,	—— ejus.		*r-ab*	—— eorum.

Compare with the above present tense of the verb *neh-oit*, ' to pray': —

Sing. 1. *s-nehoit*, oro.
    2. *u-nehoit*, oras.
    3. *i-nehoit*, orat.

Plur. 1. *ha-nehoit*, oramus.
    2. *sh-nehoit*, oratis.
    3. *r-nehoit*, orant.

Here we see that the forms of the pronominal elements are perfectly identical in both classes; and there seems no reason to doubt that the force or construction is, or originally was, the same in both. We may venture to affirm that *s-nehoit* primarily denoted *oratio mei*, just as *s-ab* means *mei pater*.

When the dialects more immediately connected with the Abchassian are better known, we shall doubtless be able to derive important conclusions from them. The opinion of Rosen, who has enjoyed better means of information than any other European, is, that the Iberian and Circassian divisions all originally belong to one family of tongues, though in various stages of development; the Abchassian having preserved most of the original type, and the Georgian having deviated the most widely from it; owing probably to the greater amount of cultivation bestowed upon it and mixture with other tribes. If our remarks on the nature of the relation between the Abchassian verbal root and its pronominal subject are well-founded, it is obvious that the same principle of formation may have originally operated in the entire family; a point, which, if well-established, would afford no small confirmation to the argument of the present series of papers.

The next division of the general subject which it is proposed to consider, is that of the great family of Polynesian languages; a class equally remarkable for its peculiar structure and the immense extent of territory over which it is spoken.

It is still a controverted question how far this family may be affirmed to consist of several distinct races partially intermixed, or to be in reality reducible to one common type. If physical characteristics were to form a criterion, there appears a marked distinction between certain light- and dark-coloured populations, and several writers have supposed that there is nothing in common between the two except a few borrowed words. On this ground the Australians, the Papuans, the Feejees, the Harafooras of the Philippine and Molucca islands, and the Malagassy, have been sometimes separated from the proper Malayan and Polynesian tribes, and assumed to be radically distinct from them, both in race and language.

The Australian languages certainly differ materially from those of the Malayan type, though a similarity of structure may be traced. Respecting the Papuan Negrito, there is great want of information, especially as to grammatical character; however, the vocabularies hitherto collected present a number of Malayan words. But if language is to be regarded as a criterion, the Feejee, the Moluccan Harafoora, and the Malagassy are closely connected with the main stock; in fact they are in several respects more perfectly organized than the Malay or Javanese. We may therefore venture to include them in the class of which we are now treating, and reason from the phænomena which they present.

It was observed in the first paper of the present series, that in the Feejee language the functions of a verb may be discharged by a noun in construction with an oblique pronominal suffix, *e. gr. loma-qu = heart*, or *will of me*, for *I will*. Though there are examples of this in other languages of the family, it is not the ordinary way in which the Polynesian verb is formed. So far is the finite verb from being a simple original element, that it commonly requires to be equipped with an array of particles, prefixed, infixed, or postfixed, as the case may be, before it can act in that capacity; and the basis on which this complex expression rests is generally a noun, sometimes a mere adverb or preposition. The peculiar organization of the class is most fully exhibited by the languages of the Philippine Islands, and next by the Malagassy; the Malay and Javanese having lost a good deal of their original type, though they exhibit traces of it in particular instances.

Almost all philologists who have paid attention to the Polynesian languages, concur in observing that the divisions of parts of speech received by European grammarians are, as far as external form is concerned, inapplicable, or nearly so, in this particular class. The same element is admitted to be indifferently substantive, adjective, verb or particle, and the particular category in which it is employed can only be known by means of its accessories. Thus Roorda, in his notes to Gericke's Javanese Grammar, observes that the root of every verb is necessarily a noun, and that its verbal character depends entirely on the pronouns and particles by which it is modified. William Humboldt also, in his great work 'Ueber die Kawi-Sprache,' repeatedly states that no very distinct line of discrimination can be drawn between nouns and verbs, and that the passive verb in particular, the class most commonly employed in the more perfectly organized tongues, can only be resolved into a formation equivalent in force and construction to an abstract noun.

In Tagalá there are two principal modes of formation, commonly called active and passive. In the former, the ostensible verb is construed with the nominatives of the personal pronouns, according to the following paradigm: —

	1.	2.	3.
1st Future Sing. *susulat* . .	*aco,*	*ca,*	*siya,*
Plur. ——— . .	*tayo,*	*cayo,*	*sila;*

usually considered as equivalent to *scribam, scribes,* &c.

In the passive voice the personal pronouns are regularly appended in the genitive case; *e. gr.,*

	1.	2.	3.	
Sing. *susulatin,*	*co,*	*mo,*	*niya,*	} *scribar,* &c.
Plur. ———	*atin,*	*inyo,*	*nila,*	

Here it might be alleged, that in the active voice the personal pronouns are plainly nominatives, and consequently *susulat,* the base to which they are appended, must have the true force of a verb.

It is however easy to show that the formations above specified are neither actives nor passives, nor verbs at all, in the sense in which that part of speech is commonly understood. The root of the formation is a noun — *sulat,* Arab. *surat,* writing. The aggregation of particles expressing the various modifications of time, converts it into a *nomen actoris,* nearly equivalent to an active participle, in the former class; and into a *nomen actionis* or *passionis* in the latter. The proof of this is, that the entire phrase in both classes is convertible into a virtual participle by merely prefixing the definite article, thus: —

Active Pres. . . *ang sungmusulat* . . ὁ γράφων.
—— Perf. . . *ang sungmulat* . . . ὁ γεγράφως.
—— Fut. . . *ang susulat* . . . . . ὁ γράψων.
Passive Pres. . *ang sinulat* = τὸ γραφόμενον, &c.

In this construction the force is the same whether the personal pronoun is expressed or not. *Ang sungmusulat aco* is simply *scribens ego*, and *ang sinulat co*, — *scriptum* or *scriptio mei*. This explains at once the reason why nominatives are employed in the so-called active form and oblique cases in the passive. It is also completely subversive of the supposed verbal character of the phrase. Ὁ γράφων ἐγὼ is sufficiently intelligible; but it is not so easy to make sense or grammar of ὁ ἐγὼ γράφω.

Another strong argument against this presumed verbal character is furnished by the remarkable fact, that in transitive constructions the so-called passive form is preferred to the active, especially with a definite regimen. When the object of the action is a personal pronoun, a noun in construction with a possessive pronoun or a definite article, or anything of which the individuality is plainly specified, the passive form of construction is indispensably requisite. Thus the absolute phrase, *I will eat*, is expressed by the active voice, with the personal pronoun in the nominative, *cacan-aco*; but, *I will eat the rice*, by the passive, *cacanin-co ang palay*, the personal pronoun being here in the genitive. This is seemingly analogous to the Latin construction *comedetur a me;* but the true analysis is, *the eating of me*, or *my eating*, [*will be*] *the rice*, = *comestio mei*, or *mea*. The supposed verb is in fact an abstract noun, including in it the notion of futurity of time (forthwith, hereafter, *v. t. q.*), in construction with an oblique pronominal suffix; and the ostensible object of the action is not a regimen in the accusative case, but an apposition. It is scarcely necessary to say how irreconcileable this is with the ordinary grammatical definition of a transitive verb; and that too in a construction where we should expect that true verbs would be infallibly employed, if any existed in the language.

The Malagassy stands next to the Philippine dialects in the regularity of its forms and the apparent complexity of its structure, being capable, by means of its numerous prefixes and affixes, of expressing the times, circumstances and other relations of actions with great nicety of discrimination. In one particular it seems at a first glance to differ materially from the branch which we have just been considering. Each of the fifteen voices of the Tagalá has its corresponding passive, the

oblique form of construction already noticed prevailing in all.
But the thirteen voices of the Malagassy verb, as classed by
grammarians, have all the forms of actives or neuters, and
though the oblique form of expression is not absolutely unknown, it is of comparatively infrequent occurrence. This
difference is however more apparent than real. The place
of the passive forms is sufficiently supplied by participial or
abstract nouns, having precisely the same oblique form of
construction as the Philippine passives, and often modified
by prefixes and affixes in a similar manner.

The rule of employing the oblique construction with a definite regimen does not appear so imperative as in Tagalá;
but, whether necessary or not, it is a very common idiom,
examples occurring in almost every page of the Malagassy
version of the Scriptures. Thus, 'I love' may be expressed
by the simple form *izaho tia*, or with the pronoun in the genitive, *tia ko*. It is equally permissible to say *fitiava' ko*,
the literal rendering of which is simply *amor mei*. Mr. Freeman observes, in the short sketch of grammar appended to
his 'Account of Madagascar,' that verbal roots are transformed into participles by prefixing the particles *voa*, *ova*, or
a; and that the pronominal affixes again convert these participles into verbs; *e. gr. ova* = change; *a–ova* = changed;
a–ova–ko = I changed. He further observes that another
form is made by giving a participial termination to the root,
adding *–ena*, *–ina*, *–ana* or *–aina*, and sometimes *–vina*, *–vana*,
–zena, *–zana*, or some similar adjunct; the final syllable
being rejected when the pronominal affix is appended, as
fantatra, known; *fantatr' ao*, thou knowest, or knewest;
fanta–ny, he knows or knew.

It is stated in the Malagassy dictionary that there has been
a difference of opinion among the Missionaries as to some
of those forms being really participles, or more properly
participial nouns. There are ample grounds for believing
that, in point of fact, there is not such a thing as a true
participle, analogous to a Greek or Latin one, either in Malagassy or in any other Polynesian language. Their place is
supplied, as in the Celtic languages, by a circumlocution
with the abstract noun and particles expressive of time,
place, or some similar adjunct; and the formative syllables,
as well as the grammatical construction, are those of nouns,
and not those of verbs. *Fitiavana*, for example, corresponds
accurately to *dilectio*, and is currently employed in that sense;
though, with a suitable pronominal affix, it is used as equivalent to a verb. The form of the personal pronoun clearly
shows the true character of the word. If it were analogous

to the passive participle *dilectus*, or the active aorist φιλήσας, it would be construed with the nominative, *izaho fitiavana*—not with the genitive, *fitiava'-ko*.

The above examples from the Tagalá and Malagassy, to which many similar ones might be added from other languages, are of considerable value as establishing one important point in the general argument. Whatever may be thought of the proposition that all verbs were originally nouns, there can be no question that nouns in conjunction with oblique cases of pronouns may be and, in fact, are employed as verbs. Some of the constructions above specified admit of no other analysis; and they are no accidental partial phenomena, but capable of being produced by thousands. They may therefore be safely regarded as organically belonging to the languages in which they are found; and they are the most marked and prevalent in the most fully organized tongues, and employed precisely in those constructions in which, according to European ideas, a *bona fide* verb would appear to be most imperatively called for.

The true character of many of the forms to which we have adverted is so obvious, that it was hardly possible that it could altogether escape the notice of philologists. Thus, Roorda observes, that in the Harafoora of Ceram, a language allied in some respects to Malay, and in others to Javanese, but presenting more of the original type than either, the personal pronouns used in conjugating verbs are often in the oblique or genitive form; and that many combinations called verbs are in reality nothing but nouns. For instance, *pina–sanih–an*, the ostensible passive of *sanih*, to agree, immediately acquires the sense of *agreement, determination*, through the mere prefixing of the indefinite or definite article.

William Humboldt also admits that the Tagalá passive forms and the Malagassy participial ones are in reality to be resolved by abstract nouns, and that the noun lies at the base of all the verbal formations. But being unable to divest his mind of the prevalent idea of an essential and radical difference between the verb and other parts of speech, he endeavours to make it appear that this character resides in the verb substantive, which is to be supplied by the mind in all cases where the functions of the verb proper are to be called in requisition. This theory presupposes the existence of a verb substantive in the languages in question, and consciousness of that existence and of the force and capabilities of the element in those who speak them. Unfortunately the Spanish grammarians, to whom we are indebted for what knowledge we possess of the Philippine dialects, unanimously concur in stating that there is no verb substantive either in Tagalá, Pampanga, or Bisaya, nor any means of supplying the place of one, except the employment of pronouns and particles. Mariner makes a similar remark respecting the Tonga language, and we may venture to affirm that there is not such a thing as a true verb substantive in any one member of the great Polynesian family.

It is true that the Malayan, Javanese and Malagassy grammarians talk of words signifying *to be;* but an attentive comparison of the elements which they profess to give as such, shows clearly that they are no verbs at all, but simply pronouns or indeclinable particles, commonly indicating the time, place or manner of the specified action or relation. It is not therefore easy to conceive how the mind of a Philippine islander, or of any other person, can supply a word totally unknown to it, and which there is not a particle of evidence to show that it ever thought of. To say that it is sufficient for the mind to supply the *idea* of existence, would attempt to prove too much, it being clear that the mind is equally capable of supplying it in any other case whatever. A more suitable opportunity may perhaps occur of showing that many of the current notions respecting the nature and functions of the verb substantive are altogether erroneous, and that they have been productive of no small confusion in grammar and logic.

A second theory respecting the so-called Polynesian verbs is, that their essential character resides in the formative prefixes employed to distinguish the different tenses and voices. This will be found on examination to be equally untenable. Those formatives cannot communicate the character of a verb to any other part of speech; for this plain reason, that they do not possess any such character themselves. They are in fact mere particles, indicating some attendant circumstance, and occurring in other combinations in the unequivocal senses of *to*, *for*, *after*, *further*, *like*, or something similar. Thus the Malayan *de*, the formative of the so-called passive voice, is simply *in*, *on*, *at*; the Malagassy *ho*, interpreted *shall*, or *shall be*, in reality means *for*; and the Harafoora *toro*, also a formative of the future, answers pretty exactly to the Fr. *pour* or Germ. *um* = in order that. It is evident therefore that the combination of such elements with nouns or adjectives cannot convert them into verbs, any more than the prefixing a Greek or Latin preposition can make a verb out of a word that is not one already. Explanations of this sort, which are in fact mere suggestions of a *non causa pro causa*, are little calculated to advance the progress of philology, and only lead one to suspect that there is something unsound and unsubstantial in the hypothesis which they are advanced to support.

We now come to a class of tongues, which, when the circumstances of those who speak them are considered, might *à priori* be thought as likely as any to exhibit the phenomena of language in nearly their original state, namely those of the great Continent of America. Our knowledge of them indeed only dates from the sixteenth century; but we also know, that before that time they had neither been corrupted by the caprices of writers nor the refinements of grammarians. We then may safely regard all principles of formation common to them and those of the Old World as equally original, and inherent in the very nature of language.

The scanty and unsatisfactory nature of the materials at present accessible, renders a general connected analysis of the verb in the South American languages an undertaking of no small difficulty. Many dialects are barely known by name; of many others we have nothing beyond meagre and inaccurate vocabularies; and those that have been grammatically analysed, have been commonly treated by men disposed to refer everything to classical models, and to find everywhere something like Latin cases, moods and tenses. The multiplicity of forms and the uncertainty of their proper analysis is another great obstacle. Besides the absolute, oblique and possessive forms of the pronouns, we often find triplicate and even quadruplicate sets employed in the conjugation of the verb, each tense having its appropriate one. Sometimes those variations may be accounted for as being combinations of several elements, namely of particles denoting the time of the action, and very frequently of other pronouns in the objective or dative case, which coalesce with the proper subject of the verb in such a manner as to make it hardly distinguishable.

In other cases this solution is only matter of conjecture, or to be inferred by analogical reasoning. But, amidst much that is at present obscure and doubtful, there is no lack of instances in which the analysis of the simple tenses of the verb is perfectly certain. The pronouns employed in conjugation are readily recognised as such, and when this is the case, it is important to observe that they commonly agree with the oblique forms employed as possessives, scarcely ever with the absolute form of the nominative, except in a few cases where the same word is indifferently used in both capacities. For example in the Lule, a language spoken to the west of the Paraguay, the personal pronouns are as follows:—

	1.	2.	3.
Nominative Sing.	*quis*,	*ue*,	*meolo*.
—————— Plur.	*ua*,	*mil*,	*meolo*.
Genitive or ｝Sing.	*s, c*,	*ce*,	*p*.
Possessive ｝Plur.	*cen*,	*lom*,	*pan*.

The latter set of forms is identical with the personal endings of the ordinary verb; *e. gr., mait-ce*, thy will; *loot-ce*, thou art; *tanta-cen*, our bread; *lopsaui-cen*, we forgive.

The identity of the oblique cases of the pronouns with the personal formatives of verbs is equally close in the Moxan, the Maïpurian, and the Mixtecan. In the Araucanian, the Betoi, the Mexican, and several other languages, the resemblances of the two classes are considerable, but do not amount to perfect identity. In Guarani and some other tongues the same forms serve both as absolute nominatives and as possessives, the personal characteristics of verbs being totally different, while in others no resemblance can be traced in any of the three classes; and again in some there are five, six or seven sets of personal pronouns, with scarcely a single element in common. It would be vain to attempt to reconcile all these discrepancies with the aid of our present means of information; the comparison of a number of kindred dialects might possibly help to clear up a part of them.

Some points, from which interesting and important conclusions may be drawn, have been obscured by the erroneous views taken of them by European philologists. W. Humboldt, in the introductory part of his work 'Ueber die Kawi Sprache,' vol. i. pp. 188—9, among some remarks on the structure of the South American verb, all ingenious, but occasionally questionable, has the following observations on the conjugation of the Maya dialect:—

"The affixed pronoun of the second leading class is also employed as a possessive pronoun in conjunction with substantives. It betrays a total misapprehension of the difference between the noun and the verb to allot a possessive pronoun to the latter,—to confound *our eating* with *we eat*. This however appears to me in those languages which are guilty of the fault, to consist chiefly in a want of properly discriminating the different classes of pronouns from each other. For the error is evidently more trifling when the conception of the possessive pronoun is not laid hold of with due precision, and this I believe to be the case in the present instance. In almost all American languages, the perception of their structure is to be deduced from the pronoun; and this, in the manner of two great branches, winds itself around the noun as a possessive, and around the verb as governing or governed; and both parts of speech usually remain united with it. Commonly the respective languages have different forms of pronouns for each class. But when this is not the case, the idea of the person is connected with either part of speech in an uncertain, changeable und indeterminate manner."

The illustratious author seems to regard the agreement of the possessive and conjugational pronouns as a sort of error in language, originating in the want of due discrimination on the part of those who commit it. It is apprehended that the error is not in the language, or the people who speak it, but in ourselves, when we attempt to adjust apparently novel grammatical phænomena to our own preconceived ideas. Were the instance of the Maya language a solitary one, there might be room for suspecting some error or corruption in the matter. But when we find a multitude of languages in all parts of the known world in the same predicament, we may venture to affirm that there must be some good reason for it. This reason we believe to be, that there is no essential difference between the simple noun and the verb; and that in an early stage of language *our eating* might very well mean precisely the same thing that *we eat* does at present. With respect to the Maya language in particular, the framers of it can hardly be suspected of inability to discriminate between the different classes of pronouns, there being few nations who make so many distinctions as they do. They have four different sets of conjunctive pronouns: one employed before the verb or noun as a sort of auxiliary or verb substantive; another in the same capacity after them; a third serving as possessives and conjugational pronouns with nouns commencing with consonants; and a fourth employed with the same parts of speech when they begin with vowels. Besides all these they have long and distinctly marked forms for nominatives absolute: *tinmen*, ego; *tinmenel*, tu; *lumen*, ille; *tamen*, nos, &c. Now they could certainly employ the last-mentioned class in conjugating the verb, if they entertained the same ideas about nominatives and their necessary conjunction with verbs that are current among European grammarians. But instead of saying *tamen zaatzic*, we forgive, as according to Humboldt's reasoning they ought to have done, they choose to employ *c'zaatzic*, just as they say, *c'ziipil*, our sin; or *ca–yum*, our father. We may surely give them credit for knowing how to combine the elements of their own language in a proper manner and according to rational principles. And if we find it difficult to reconcile their system with our own *I, we, ye, they love*, it may be as well to inquire whether they or ourselves have departed furthest from the original principle of formation.

With respect to the North American dialects, at least some of the principal ones, our means of information are tolerably ample. Much light has been thrown on their organization by the labours of Eliot, Zeisberger, Heckewelder, Schoolcraft, and more recently by Howse, whose Grammar of the Cree language contains, along with a good deal of questionable reasoning, a valuable collection of materials. It is pretty universally recognized that these Northern languages do not differ as to their general character from those of Southern and Central America. Du Ponceau does not hesitate to say, that all the languages from Greenland to Cape Horn are formed upon the same principle. This is rather a hazardous assertion to make, while there are so many of which we know absolutely nothing; but it is believed to be substantially correct, as far as our present means of information extend. The most remarkable feature of the family to an European is the polysynthetic character of the verb; in other words, its capability of aggregating the component parts of an entire clause of a sentence into a single word, or at least what appears as such to the ear, and is written as such by grammarians.

There has been however a great deal of exaggeration and misapprehension on the subject. It would be a mistake to suppose that every person of every tense is an intricate polysynthetic combination. Many such doubtless occur; but there are many others just as simple as the ordinary verbs in other languages, and substantially formed upon the same principles. The error has been in regarding elements as integral portions of the verb which are mere accessories, variable according to circumstances. An Indian, for example, if he wished to say, "I give him the axe," would not only embody the subject *I*, the dative *him*, together with an objective pronoun *it*, in one combination, but would moreover intercalate *axe*, in an abbreviated form perhaps, but still distinguishable by one familiar with the language. It is however clear that *him*, *it*, *axe*, are no integral or necessary elements. The verb still remains a verb when they are omitted; the only essentials of it being the subject and the root or verbal noun. The point which we are most concerned to investigate is the nature of the connection between the two.

It was observed at an early period by grammarians that there is no difference between the Indian possessive forms used in combination with nouns, and the personals employed in conjugating verbs. Du Ponceau remarks, that Eliot, in his Grammar of the Massachusetts language, does not consider the pronoun as a part of speech, but only speaks of it as a *possessive form* of the noun and the verb; and that this is in fact the principal part which it plays in those languages. He further states that there is no difference in them between the personal and the possessive pronoun in the inseparable form; they are distinguished by the sense of the phrase and the nominal or verbal terminations of the word to which they are joined. Heckewelder also observes in his grammar of the Lenni Lenape or Delaware, that the possessive pronoun is the same as the personal, separable and inseparable, which is used in a possessive sense, and that no ambiguity results from this similarity; the meaning being always understood from the context, or the form or the inflection of the word with which the pronoun is combined. Howse also states in his Cree Grammar, that the possessive pronouns before nouns are expressed in the same manner as the personal before verbs; and his paradigms show that the forms are the same in both cases.

In the Sahaptin, an Oregon dialect, it is remarkable that there is a duplicate conjugation of the verb, the personal pronouns in one division being nominatives, and in the other regularly genitives; the form of the root also being different for each. For example, 'he is,' according to the former construction, is expressed by *ipi hiwash;* but according to the second by *ipnim ush; ipnim* being the genitive of the pronoun of the third person. It seems evident that in the first instance the supposed verbal element is in the capacity of being put in apposition with its subject, bearing in fact some analogy to our present participle, but that in the second it can only be attributed to it in the manner of a noun substantive.

It may be observed in general terms, that there are many differences of detail in the Northern Indian languages. Scarcely any two have precisely the same personal pronouns throughout, or arrange them in the same order in construction. But the agreement of those employed in conjugating the simple verb with the possessives used in conjunction with nouns is a general feature among them. This does not arise from poverty of forms, there being commonly a distinct and marked form for the absolute nominatives. These, in Cree for example, are in the singular: 1. *netha*, I; 2. *ketha*, thou; 3. *wetha*, he, or it; while the possessives and formatives of verbs are, 1. *net*, 2. *ket*, 3. *oot*; or still more briefly, *ne*, *ke*, *oo*. If therefore the possessives have the force and construction of oblique cases, it is difficult to assign a valid reason why the conjugational ones, identical with them in form, and admitting of the same analysis, should not partake of the same character.

The Greenland, of which the Esquimaux is merely a dialect, was for a time supposed to be generically distinct from the so-called American Indian languages, but it is now allowed that it agrees with them in all their most marked peculiarities of structure. It differs from all of them hitherto known in its vocabulary; but it has the same polysynthetic character, embodying as they do the subject and predicate along with all their accessories, in one compact phrase; being one word to the ear, or to the eye when written, but sometimes capable of being resolved into a dozen. The same remarks that have been made respecting the pronouns of the Northern Indian tongues are applicable to the Greenland or Esquimaux. The arrangement differs, the possessives and verbal formatives being commonly prefixed in the former and postfixed in the latter; but the personal terminations of the simple tenses regularly resemble the pronominal suffixes of nouns, not the absolute forms or nominatives. It is true that several forms are used with nouns which do not occur in the conjugation of the verb, but this is owing to a regard to euphony, not to any radical difference in the elements themselves.

It has already been observed that very exaggerated and erroneous ideas have been advanced respecting the structure of the class of languages of which we have been treating in the present paper. They have been represented as the products of deep philosophic contrivance, and totally different in organization from those of every known part of the Old World. The author of 'Mithridates' regards it as an astonishing phenomenon, that a people like the Greenlanders, struggling for subsistence amidst perpetual ice and snow, should have found the means of constructing such a complex and artificial system. It is conceived that there cannot be a greater mistake than to suppose that a complicated language is, like a chronometer or a locomotive engine, a product of deep calculation and preconceived adaptation of its several parts to each other. The compound portions of it

21

are rather formed like crystals, by the natural affinity of the component elements; and, whether the forms are more or less complex, the principle of aggregation is the same.

There is a logical faculty inherent in the mind of attributing its proper relations to each given subject, and, when enunciated in words, those subjects and relations which belong to each other are naturally and properly placed in juxtaposition. In the Indian languages, and probably in many others when in their original and inartificial state, there is moreover an evident anxiety to leave nothing *implied* that is capable of being expressed within a given compass. In the abstract, *giving* is a single word, denoting a simple action; but in the concrete, there are implied the accessory notions of a person giving,—a thing given and a receiver;—all of which an American Indian would think it necessary to express in mentioning a specific act. Languages in a more advanced state are less solicitous about formally enunciating what can be readily supplied by the understanding. In the well-known passage in Alciphron, "I want fifty pieces of gold, and not letters — εἴ με φιλεῖς, δός," it is clear from the context that the full meaning of the last word is, "give [*me money*]." Nevertheless an Algonquin would think that he left the matter imperfect if he did not say, "money — give — thou — it — me," or something equivalent. A Basque would embody all the pronouns with the verb, but would separate the word *money*; a Mordwinian would perhaps strike out the objective pronoun *it*, as superfluous, carefully retaining "give — me — thou"; an European thinks the simple δός sufficiently significant and more emphatic. In none of the combinations, long or short, is there anything marvellous, or anything implying the exercise of profound ingenuity or previous calculation. On this point Mr. Albert Gallatin well observes: — "The fact, that, although the object in view was, in every known Indian language without exception, to concentrate in a single word those pronouns with the verb, yet the means used for that purpose are not the same in any two of them, shows that none of them was the result of philosophical researches and preconcerted design. And in those which abound most in inflections of that description, nothing more has been done in that respect, than to effect, by a most complex process, and with a cumbersome and unnecessary machinery, that which in almost every other language has been as well, if not better, performed through the most simple means. Those transitions, in their complexness and in the still visible amalgamation of the abbreviated pronouns with the verb, bear in fact the impress of primitive and unpolished languages*."

To this we may add, that the same method of formation is not unknown in other languages, modern as well as ancient. In the Semitic dialects, for example, the objective pronoun is regularly incorporated with the different persons of the finite verb, just as it is in Basque or American Indian. Du Ponceau observes, that the French phrase "tu m'étourdis," only differs from the corresponding Algonquin in the method of writing it. He might have remarked that the Italian combination, *darottelo* = dare-habeo-tibi-illud, embodies in itself more elements than many of the American polysynthetic forms represented as so very wonderful, but which we may be assured were formed in the same manner and on exactly the same principles.

There are two points connected with the leading object of the present essay which it may not be amiss to notice. The first is, that in the American languages generally, in the Basque, and to a great extent in the Mordwinian dialect of the Finnish, the capability of receiving conjugational inflections is not limited to one particular class of words, but extends to all parts of speech. Not only substantives and adjectives, but adverbs, prepositions, conjunctions, interjections, and even certain classes of pronouns receive the pronominal affixes and are carried through the different persons according to the usual analogy of a transitive or intransitive verb. Now it may be fairly inferred that where *all* words are or may be verbs, *none* are essentially or peculiarly so. Their capability of assuming personal forms evidently depends upon some principle common to all, not the property of a single class. This we believe to be nothing more or less than *predication*. All words express relations, and all relations may be predicated of the subjects to which they belong. When those subjects are represented by pronouns, their union with the predicates, if according to certain grammatical forms, becomes to all intents and purposes a verb, whatever the term might originally denote, or whatever class of words it might belong to.

The same extensive principle of formation may be traced in other classes of languages. To say nothing of denominative verbs from nouns, we have εὐδαιμονίζω, μακαρίζω, *cum plurimis aliis*, from adjectives: χωρίζω from an adverb; — Germ. *innen*, *ubaron*, — our own *utter*, and many other

---

* Archæologia Americana, vol. ii. pp. 202—3.

21*

Teutonic verbs from prepositions;—the Icelandic *efa*, dubi-
tare, from a conjunction; αἰάζω and the Germ. *ächzen*, to
groan, from interjections.   The fact is, that the current
ideas of primitive verbs, constituting a sort of native pri-
vileged class or aristocracy in language, is totally unfounded.
There is no *intrinsic* difference between them and the ordinary terms constituting the mass of language, though there
is an *adventitious* one, resulting from their combination with
an additional element.

The other point appearing to call for notice is the apparently singular practice in the Greenland and many American languages of employing a different verb for every different manner in which an action may be done.   Thus in
Chilian, *elun* is, to give; *eluguen*, to give more; *eluduamen*,
to desire to give; *elurquen*, to appear to give; and so on,
through a long list of possible modifications.   Gallatin remarks of the Northern Indian languages, that by affixing,
prefixing, or inserting an arbitrary particle, or rather an
abbreviated noun, verb, adverb, preposition, or conjunction,
the verb is made to designate the specific modification of the
action; each modification apparently constituting a different
mood or voice of the primitive verb.

In the Greenland language this principle is carried to an
almost unlimited extent.   Fabricius gives in his grammar a
list of nearly three hundred postpositions, by the aid of which
complex verbs may be formed from simple ones, and this
by no means exhausts the number.   Some of those postpositive elements correspond to Greek or Latin prepositions in
composition; others are adverbs, or similar words expressive
of the manner or circumstances of the action; and not unfrequently three, four, or even more, are appended in closely consecutive series; the last regularly receiving the pronominal conjugational affixes.   All this seems very strange
and intricate to us; but it depends in reality on a very
simple principle.   In such Greek words as ἐπιπροχέω, οἰο-
πολέω (*solus degere*), ἀλλοφρονέω, ἑτεροπροσωπέω, the modifying elements are *prefixed* to the verb, the combination
being regarded as one word and capable of being predicated
of one given subject.   In Greenland similar elements are
regularly *postfixed*, and with less restriction as to their number.   All however relating to the same subject are considered as forming one aggregate, and are predicable in the
aggregate of that subject, just as the Greek combinations
above specified are of theirs, only in a different order.   As
the genius of the language requires the personal terminations
to be placed last, they thereby become immediate appen-

dages of the adverb or other modifying word, instead of the leading verb, and frequently with a separation of many syllables from it. This shows clearly that the personal terminations are no inherent portions of the verb, evolved as it were out of its substance, like the branches of a tree out of its trunk, otherwise they would have adhered to it more closely. There is no want of parallel examples in languages of the Old World, some of which we may find occasion to advert to in the further prosecution of the subject.

We now come to the most important and perhaps the most difficult portion of the general subject, namely the application of the principle attempted to be established to the great and important family of Indo-European languages. Many of the phenomena noticed in the languages of which we have previously treated are both obvious and unequivocal, as far as outward form is concerned. They are indeed admitted in particular cases by philologists who hold the ordinary opinion respecting the distinct elementary nature of the verb. But in the greatest part of the Indo-European languages the analysis of the component elements of this part of speech is by no means so simple and self-evident as it is in some other families. Various causes may be assigned for this, one of which is, that in the early period of the parent language a number of elements were employed as personal terminations which cannot now be traced among the separate personal pronouns. Another reason is, that in some of the leading tongues, more particularly in Sanscrit and Greek, a vast number of articulations have been sacrificed to considerations of euphony, the restoration of which is often a matter of conjecture, and sometimes altogether impracticable. One point however is conceded, even by some who would be disposed to deny that the theory of the original identity of noun and verb is applicable to languages of this type, namely that the personal terminations of the simple verb, or at all events a portion of them, are of pronominal origin. This concession at once establishes a certain degree of analogy between them and the tongues of which we have already treated. It now remains to inquire how far this analogy may be presumed to extend.

It would be both tedious and unnecessary to examine in detail all the members of the family now under consideration. They are all confessedly descended from the same general stock, and if a great leading principle of organization can be established respecting any one of them, it must equally apply to all. It is proposed at present to examine the Celtic portion, more especially the Welsh, which appears to exhibit phænomena of considerable interest and importance to the comparative philologist.

It was observed nearly a century and a half ago by Edward Lhuyd, that the distinctive terminations of the Cornish verb were clearly connected with the pronouns. It is but justice to a meritorious and ill-requited scholar, to give his own words on the subject, which show how far he was in advance of his age as a scientific philologist:— "We may observe, that the verbs have derived their distinction of persons originally from the pronouns, in regard we find yet some footsteps of them in their termination. For the last letter in Guelav [I see] is taken from *vi*, I; the last of Guelon [we see], from *ni*, we; of Gueloch and Gueloh [ye see], from *chui* and *hui*, ye; and in Guelanz, the third person plural, the pronoun [which] is almost wholly retained for *anz*, *onz*, or *oinz*, is but the same with our Welsh *uynt* or *huint*, they*."

Dr. Prichard, who does not appear to have been aware of the above statement of Lhuyd, makes a perfectly analogous one with respect to the personal terminations of the verb in Welsh, in his well-known work, 'The Eastern Origin of the Celtic Nations.' Both those eminent scholars refer those terminations to the ordinary nominatives of the personal pronouns, of which they consider them to be abbreviated forms. As far back as A. D. 1836, the writer believed that he saw reason to allege strong objections to this view of the matter, which he expressed in the following terms in a critique on Dr. Prichard's work:— "We have observed that Dr. Prichard's statements respecting the Celtic languages throw a new and important light on the formation of language; and this we hold to be particularly the case with respect to the verb. He has shown that the personal terminations in Welsh are pronouns, and that they are more clearly and unequivocally so than the corresponding endings in Sanscrit or its immediate descendants. However, he lays no stress upon a fact which we cannot but consider highly important, viz. that they are evidently *in statu regiminis*, not in apposition or concord: in other words, they are not nominatives, but oblique cases, precisely such as are affixed to various prepositions. For example, the second person plural does not end with the nominative *chwi*, but with *ech*, *wch*, *och*, *ych*, which last three forms are also found coalescing with various prepositions — *iwch*, to you;

---

* Archæologia Britannica, vol. iii. p. 246.

ynoch, in you; *wrthych*, through you. Now the roots of Welsh verbs are confessedly nouns, generally of abstract signification: ex. gr. *dysg* is both *doctrina* and the 2nd pers. imperative, *doce*; *dysg-och* or *-wch* is not, therefore, *docetis* or *docebitis vos*; but *doctrinâ vestrûm*, teaching *of* or *by* you. This leads to the important conclusion that a verb is nothing but a *noun*, combined with an *oblique case* of a personal pronoun, virtually including in it a connecting *preposition*. This is what constitutes the real *copula* between the subject and the attribute. *Doctrina ego* is a logical absurdity; but *doctrina mei*, teaching *of* me, necessarily includes in it the proposition *ego doceo*, enunciated in a strictly logical and unequivocal form*."

The above theory was supported by a reference to the Syriac periphrastic verb substantive, also alleged at the commencement of the present series of papers. The application of the whole process of induction from the Coptic, Semitic, Finno-Tartarian and other classes of languages is too obvious to be here insisted upon. No one capable of divesting his mind of preconceived systems who compares the Welsh prepositional forms *er-ov*, *er-ot*, *er-o*, *er-om* *er-och*, *er-ynt*, for me thee, &c., with the verbal forms *car-ov*, *car-ot*, *car-o*, *car-om*, *car-och*, *car-ont* or *car-wynt*, I, &c. will love, will deny the absolute formal identity of the respective sets of endings, or refuse to admit that the exhibition of parallel phænomena in languages of all classes and in all parts of the world, furnishes a strong *primâ facie* ground for the belief of a general principle of analogy running through all.

The above Welsh terminations are easily identified with the corresponding ones in Sanscrit, Greek, Latin, &c., with the exception of the second person singular in *t*, and the second plural in *ch*. The former may be readily understood to be an older form than the ordinary sibilant, especially if we compare the Doric or Latin *tu* with the Ionic συ. The guttural form of the second person plural is not so easily reducible to the ordinary dental endings in other languages. A comparison with the Irish *sibh*, *vos*, and other etymological data, seems to indicate a connexion with the reflective pronouns *sva*, *sui*, &c., *self*, which are frequently employed to represent more than one person. Compare the Greek dual forms σφῶι, σφὼ, and the Sanscrit *sva*, suffix of the second pers. imperative in the Atmanepadam or middle voice.

* Quarterly Review, vol. lvii. pp. 93, 94.

The Armoric and Cornish terminations are for the most part mere dialectical varieties of the Welsh. The Irish verb differs considerably, the entire conjugation having every appearance of being a fragmentary collection of synthetic and analytic as well as active and deponent forms. The third person singular of every tense is most commonly analytic, while the terminations –*maid*, –*maoid*, –*maois*, which have no counterparts in Welsh or Armorican, exhibit a remarkble resemblance to the Greek μεϑα and the Zend–*maidhe*. Many of the other synthetic forms agree more or less closely with their correspondents in other dialects, sometimes with one branch and sometimes with another. Thus the termination of the conditional –*fann* or –*finn*, unknown in Welsh, appears in the Breton *kan*–*fenn*, I would sing; and the dental characteristic of the second person plural in several tenses, for which in Welsh we find a guttural, also occurs in the Breton present and future *kani*–*t*, ye sing, *kanot*, ye will sing.

The most ancient and genuine forms of the preterite also manifest a general community of origin with their Cymric counterparts; *ex. gr.*

Irish. — Sing.	1. ghlanas.		Plur.	ghlansam.
	2. ghlanais.			ghlanabhar.
	3. ghlanastar.			ghlansat.
Welsh. — Sing.	1. gwelais.		Plur.	gwelsam (or -som).
	2. gwelaist.			gwelsach (or -soch).
	3. gwelodd (or gweles).			gwelsant.

It may be here observed, that the Irish third pers. plural, as well as many other cognate words, regularly elides the nasal element of the Armorican and Cymric dialects. The remarkable termination of the second person plural, –*bhar* — unknown, it is believed, in all other Indo-European dialects — is referred by Pictet to the Sansc. *vas, vos*. Bopp, with his usual eagerness to find a Sanscrit archetype for everything, likely or unlikely, endeavours to extract it from –*dhvam*, the termination of the second pers. plural of the Sanscr. middle voice. It is conceived that it would be a much more obvious process to refer it to the oblique case of the personal pronoun *bhar = vestrúm*, which is not only the same word formally, but furnishes a very appropriate meaning. Even admitting Pictet's identification with *vas*, which involves no impossibility, it would not, if an original Sanscrit element, be the nominative [*yuyam*], but the genitive, dative, or accusative. In fact, examples of forms identical with actually existing nominatives, employed as personal terminations of synthetic Indo-European verbs, have

yet to be produced, and ·it is presumed that such are not
readily to be found. Pictet indeed alleges from the Welsh
"Englynion clywed" the formula *"a glywaisti == audivistine ?"*
as an example of the full nominative form *ti*, employed as
an inflexional termination. He might equally have quoted
from several poets *caravi*, I love, as a parallel instance of
the use of the nominative *mi*. Every Welsh scholar however
knows them to be mere euphonic abbreviations of *glywaist
ti, carav vi*, the nominative being annexed as in Latin or
Italian, for the sake of emphasis or metre.

Besides the evidence deducible from the identity of the
personal terminations of verbs and the prepositional forms
of pronouns in Welsh, there is another of no small weight,
furnished by the consideration of the formation and structure
of the entire body of verbs in the language. In Sanscrit
and the classical tongues, verbs are usually divided into
two distinct classes, primitive and derivative, a large proportion of which latter class are styled denominatives, as
being formed directly from nouns. Thus *cano* is supposed
to be a primary or radical word, while *vulnero, puerasco,*
&c. are allowed to be formed from *vulnus* and *puer*. Such
words are, it is well known, very numerous in Greek, and
they are perhaps still more so in Welsh, which is excelled
by no language of the family in the power and variety of
its synthesis. The following example will give some idea
of its copiousness and plastic power, and of the manner in
which verbs are formed from nouns, simple and derivative,
abstract and concrete: —

llyw, guide, ruler;	*llywed, llywedu, llywiaw*, to guide.
llywawd, guidance;	*llywodu*, to conduct.
llywiad;	*llywiadu.*
llywiant;	*llywiannu.*
llywodraeth, governance;	*llywodraethu*, to govern.
llywodri;	*llywodru.*
llywydd, a president;	*llywyddu*, to preside.
llywyddiad, presidency;	*llywyddiadu.*
llywyddiaeth;	*llywyddiaethu.*

To which may be added, as of the same origin, *llyweth*, a
muscle, *i. e.* a *guider*; *llywethu*, to be muscular.

Here we see that a series of nouns from the same stem,
denoting *guide, ruler*, or *guidance, governance*, become respectively the bases of verbs of cognate import. It is also
obvious that the shorter and the longer forms are all on
the same footing; *llywed* and *llywiaw* being as clearly formed
from *llyw*, as *llywyddiaethu* from *llywyddiaeth*. Except in the

number and variety of forms, this phænomenon is in no way remarkable, and presents itself in one shape or other in most languages. In all of them the concrete or abstract noun is predicated of the usual pronominal subjects, according to recognized forms, and thus becomes a verb. But it is of no small importance to observe, that it is impossible to establish any distinction in this respect between Welsh denominative verbs and those which correspond to the so-called primitives in other tongues. It has already been observed that the roots of verbs in this language are confessedly nouns; *dysg*, for example, being at the same time *teaching, instruction*, and the root of the verb *dysg—u*, to teach. In like manner, *can—u*, to sing; *car—u*, to love; *cas—au*, to hate; *cel—u* and *cudd—io*, to conceal; *cwyn—o*, to complain; with multitudes of others, have for their roots the still simpler forms and ideas, *càn*, song; *càr*, love; *càs* hatred; *cel, cudd*, covering, concealment; *cwyn*, murmur; and the same may be affirmed of almost every verb in the language. The correctness of the view taken by the native grammarians in regarding the noun as the root may be supported by many considerations. In the noun both *notion* and *form* are simple, either as subjects or predicates; in the finite verb they are complex, necessarily comprising both subject and predicate, each element capable of being separately conceived. Again, if the supposed primary verbs and the denominatives are traced either in ascending or descending series, it is impossible to discover that any one link of the chain is formed on a different principle from the rest. *Car—u*, to love, is as readily and legitimately referable to *càr* as its basis, as its cognate *car—ueiddiaw* is to *caruaidd*, or *llywodraeth—u* to *llywodraeth*.

If this is conceded respecting the Welsh, it must equally hold good with respect to Greek, Latin, German, and other languages, now universally admitted to be cognate with Celtic. *Can—o, cel—o, κενϑω*, Germ. *ich weine*, anciently *wein—em*, must have been formed in the same manner and on the same principle as their counterparts *can—af, cel—af, cuddi—af, cwyn—af*; and if one class originally meant *song, concealment, lamentation of* or *by me*, the others must at one time have had the same import. If the writer is not mistaken, this view receives a strong confirmation from the Vedic Sanscrit, in which, as Rosen observes, the assumed d'hatoo or verbal root is frequently employed as a *nomen actionis*, and regularly inflected through most of the ordinary cases. Thus, as to outward form, those roots appear to be exactly on the same footing as the Welsh primitives of which we have been speaking; and when combined with the usual personal terminations, or other words when in the form of finite verbs, they are capable of exactly the same analysis. In fact, the writer believes that they admit of no other, either as to form, the known analogies of other languages, or the principles of logic.

But it will perhaps be objected that the simple Welsh forms *can*, *cel*, &c., though allowed to be nouns, are equally imperatives of the second person, and that this is the true root of the verb. This objection, though specious, admits of an easy reply. A little consideration will show that no part of the verb approaches so nearly in its nature to a noun as the second person of the imperative, and that a simple noun is, in point of fact, often employed in the place of it. When the crier of the court calls "silence!" or the drill-serjeant "attention!" the effect produced is exactly the same as if verbs were used instead. The person addressed construes the term, noun though it be, as a command to perform or refrain from a certain specified action, and does accordingly. Consequently according to the axiom, "things equal to the same thing are equal to each other," it seems that if nouns may be imperatives, imperatives may very well be nouns.

Nor is this faculty restricted to the noun, a simple particle being equally capable of exercising the same functions. The German interjectional adverb *fort*! Eng. *away*! may be legitimately rendered by *abi*! or *abito*! the Ital. *via*. originally a noun, having precisely the same force. In the phrase "away with you!" a pronominal adjunct is introduced, and in this familiar expression we see the germ of the process by which the simple noun or particle became arrayed with personal suffixes, so as to put on the character of the complex term called the verb. We may at the same time discern the precise nature of the copula or connexion between them, which, when the pronominal element is *in obliquo*, is necessarily a virtual preposition. Many proofs indeed may be given that personal terminations are neither the exclusive property nor integral portions of such verbs as we find in Greek and Latin. In the Semitic languages many particles are construed with oblique suffixes, the combination having all the force of a verb: *e.x.* עוֹדֶנִי (*odeni*), literally yet of me = I am yet. The compound preposition לְעַל (*la-al*), over, upon, is in Ethiopic conjugated throughout as a verb, in the sense to be over, surpass, &c. The Gothic phrases *hirjats* = πάρεστον, *hirjith* = πάρεστε, are said by grammarians to be dual and plural imperatives; and so they are, as to

import and outward form; but when analysed, they are confessedly mere modifications of the adverb *her*, which in its turn
is of pronominal origin.   Many words, supposed to be primary and radical verbs, would, if properly examined, turn
out to be of similar descent.

In the writer's paper "On the Formation of Words from
Particles," many instances were given of Old-German verbs
formed directly from prepositions and other indeclinables;
and many others might have been produced from Welsh.
At present, a couple of examples may suffice.   The adverb
or conjunction *mal*, like, as, so, is obviously the basis of
the verb *mal-u*, to guess, imagine, *q. d.* to liken* (Gr.
εἰκάζω).   In the same manner the preposition *rhag*, before,
is the parent of *rhag-u*, to go before, also to oppose.   Both
are regularly conjugated throughout, and their respective
imperatives are *mal, rhag*.   Now we may fairly ask, if these
supposed radical imperatives really are radical in this particular application;   whether, in short, they are anything
more than particles employed with reference to a particular
subject? whether, in short, our own *forward!* is not, to all
intents and purposes., as good an imperative as *rhag*?   If
this is not the case, by what process did the particle become a word of a totally different class?

Some persons who still cling to the same species of mystical jargon in philology that has been so long exploded in
natural philosophy, will be ready to say that the word used
as a verb is endued with an *occulta vis*, or innate vital
energy, rendering it capable of expressing action or motion;
in short, that *càn*, sing! differs from *càn*, song, in the same
degree that a magnetized steel bar differs from.an ordinary
one, or a charged Leyden jar from a discharged one.   It
will be time enough to consider this assumed energetic
principle when it has been made manifest by something like
a rational analysis.   At present the writer expresses his
total disbelief of its existence; nay, even of the possibility
of its being infused into any sort of word whatever.   There
is indeed such a principle connected with language, but it
resides in the human *mind*, not in the elementary sounds
or combinations of sounds of which human speech is composed.

A few remarks on the formation of the causative verb in
Celtic may serve to close this branch of the discussion.
Pictet, who is as usual followed by Bopp, has the following
theory on the subject: —

---

* Still used for *guess* in some parts of Lancashire.

"Verbs of the tenth class [in Sanscrit] adding *ay* to the root, which *ay* equally distinguishes the causatives and a portion of the denominatives, find their representatives in the Irish verbs in *igh* or *aigh*, also comprehending causatives and denominatives. In Welsh, the formation of causatives and denominatives is operated by the insertion of *ia* or *i*, another modification of the Sanscrit *ay;* thus *bhavayámi*, I cause to be (causative of *bhù*), is in Welsh *bywiwyv*, I vivify; in the infinitive *bywiaw*. An example of a Sanscrit verb of the tenth conjugation, having its analogous one in Irish, is *bhush*, to adorn, forming in the present *bhùshayámi*. The Irish *beos - aigh - im*, I adorn, from the root *beos*, whence the adjective *beosach*, beautiful, is the complete facsimile of it*."

The identification of the Celtic causative verb with the Sanscrit form, would lead to consequences which Pictet was far from contemplating. The Irish terminations which he gives are the ordinary, though by no means the only ones in that dialect; but his statement of the Welsh forms gives a very insufficient view of the matter. Verbs implying causation are very frequent in this latter language, which possesses an almost illimitable faculty of forming them. The point of most consequence for our present investigation is, that the great mass of them is based, not upon what are called primary verbs, but on nouns and adjectives, most commonly on the latter. Either the simple or the derivative adjective may become the stem, and as derivative forms are pretty numerous, the array of causative verbs, of synonymous or slightly varying import, is in a similar ratio. This will appear clearly from an analysis of the example adduced by Pictet himself; *bywiaw*, to vivify. This has nothing whatever to do with Sanscr. *bhavayámi* or its root, being directly formed from the adjective *byw*, living, which it is hardly necessary to say is cognate with Gr. βιος, Lat. *vivus*, &c., referred by Bopp himself to the Sanscrit root *jiv*. Similar verbs are formed from the derivatives of *byw*, as may be seen from the following list:—

byw, living;	*bywâu*, to vivify.
	bywiaw.
bywaidd;	*byweiddiau*.
bywiawg;	*bywioccàu*.
	bywiogi.
bywiawl;	*bywioli*.

* De l'Affinité des Langues Celtiques, pp. 148, 149.

Here we see that the simple adjective and its three enlarged forms have branched out into six verbs, all signifying *to cause to live*. Theoretically speaking, every adjective in the language is capable of being treated in the same way, and examples of causatives from nearly every known form might easily be collected. That the first two verbs in the list are formed from the adjective, and not from a more primitive verb, is proved first by the analogy of many thousands of similar formations; and secondly by the fact that no simple verb analogous to Lat. *vivo* exists either in Welsh or any other Celtic dialect. 'I live' can only be expressed by 'I am living,' or more properly by 'I am *in* living,' similar to '*in vivis sum*,' or the Old-English 'I am on live,' of which *alive* is merely a various form.

With respect to the form *bywiogi* (from *bywiawg*), it is important to remark that it is etymologically cognate with the Irish forms in *aighim*, or more frequently in *uighim*, also derived by the best Irish grammarians from nouns or adjectives in *ach*. Thus, among multitudes of similar instances, Ir. *salach*, filthy; *salaighim*, I pollute; *torrach*, pregnant; *torraighim*, *ingravido*, are etymologically the same words as Welsh *halawg*, *halogi; torawg, torogi*. We may therefore feel assured that Pictet's example *beosaighim* is formed according to the same analogy, directly from the adjective *beosach*, not from the imaginary root *beos*; and consequently if it is formally identical with Sanscrit *bhushayâmi*, it follows that the base of the latter is equally an adjective or a noun. That this is a possible supposition would appear from the circumlocutory form of the perfect, *bhushayâm—babhuva*, &c., where the first word has both the form and the construction of a noun. This is in fact admitted by modern Sanscrit grammarians, though they are not exactly agreed as to the analysis of the phrase. Bopp resolves it into the accusative feminine, but Dr. Trithen observes, that though this solution may suit the formations with the auxiliary *chakâra = feci*, it will not do so well for those with *âsa* or *babhuva = fui*. A locative case would be most according to the analogy of other languages; but this differs from the Vedic locative masculine *sivayâ* in the nasal termination, and from the ordinary locative feminine *sivâyâm* in the quantity of the penultimate*. It can however hardly be separated from the

---

* Forms with a long penultimate are however found in particular roots, as well as in many denominatives based upon nouns and adjectives: thus in *panâyâm chakâra = laudavi*, the first word has precisely the form of a locative of the *â* declension. It may not be irrelevant here to observe that the Indian grammarians usually define the d'hatoos or roots by an abstract

base of the entire verb, and consequently if it be a noun, that must be equally so, or at all events closely related to that part of speech.

Denominatives, which are confessedly formed from nouns, have nearly the same form of conjugation, and indeed there seems no invincible reason why a causative should not be formed from a noun or adjective in Sanscrit as well as in other languages.

The Welsh forms *bywiawl*, *bywioli*, are of interest, from the circumstance that we know their precise analysis. The termination *awl* is etymologically the same as Gael. *ail*, Ir. *amhail* = like, so that *bywiawl* is literally 'life-like.' We may here observe that *lich* is a common element in German causative verbs: *ex. gr. ver – herr – lich – en*, to glorify. Many examples of a similar employment of the same element in Old - High - German may be found in Graff's Sprachschatz, Art. LIK. It is also remarkable that in many Polynesian languages the causative is formed by the prefix *maca*, or some dialectical variation of it, which as a separate particle denotes *like, as, how*. There is reason to believe that many of the formative suffixes in a multitude of languages had originally the same import, and that this apparently simple element has exercised no small influence on the organization of human speech.

Except as to the great variety of forms in Welsh, the connexion of the causative verb with the adjective is no special peculiarity of that language. It Lithuanian, almost every adjective has its corresponding causative, and nearly every page of a Greek, Latin, or German Dictionary will furnish examples of the same class of words formed according to the same or a similar analogy. Nor will it avail to say that they may be in reality formed from the original verbal root, and not from the noun or adjective derived from that root. It is notorious that many of them are based directly upon augmented forms, of which they include the full signification, and of which the Lat. *melior – are*, Germ. *besser – n*, *ärger – n*, *verherrlich – en*, are sufficient instances. Now, if it

---

noun in the locative case: *ex. gr.* the numerous roots signifying *to go*, are commonly explained by *gatau* = in going, Welsh *yn myned*. This is, in fact, the nearest approach that can be made to the abstract notion of a verb, and would, in combination with a subject in the nominative, be exactly equivalent to a Manchu or Mongolian one. It is however evidently not a simple but a complex expression, combining the idea of an abstract relation with an element denoting *place*, and parallel in every respect, except that of form, to the analytic phrases with *in* or *on* in Celtic and other languages.

be of the essence of a verb to denote motion or action, and the faculty of doing this resides in the roots of primitives, it might be expected that terms expressing *action* causing *another action*, would, *à fortiori*, be entitled to rank in the same category; or at all events that their relation to words endued with the supposed characteristic would be clear and unmistakeable. On the contrary, we find that while many of the so-called primitive verbs are *neuters*, those possessed of this double energy are formed in countless multitudes from that third-rate part of speech, the adjective, and may even come from particles, words still lower in the grammatical scale. Thus *vacare*, to be empty, a term neither expressing motion, action, nor result, nor anything in short beyond absolute negation, is allowed to enjoy all the native dignity of a primary verb, including of course the motive and active energies distinguishing that part of speech from others; while *vacuare*, which *does* express an action performed and an effect produced, must get its energies as it can, through the medium of the adjective *vacuus*. This may be philosophical, but it seems hardly reconcileable to the principles of common sense; it is however only one out of thousands of glaring inconsistencies which the usual theory involves.

The truth is, that the definition of a verb, as a word intrinsically denoting action or motion, is exactly on a par with the old one of a bird as a creature whose esssential characteristic is to fly, of which the production of an ostrich or an apteryx is a sufficient refutation. The following appears to the writer a more legitimate view of the question. All words denote relations, and every relation is capable of being predicated of a suitable subject. When this is done according to certain grammatical forms, the combined predicate and subject become a verb, whatever the nature or import of the former may be. Some languages, as was observed in the first paper of the present series, can carry this principle of formation to an almost illimitable degree; in others it is more restricted in general practice. There are however abundant traces in the latter class of the original operation of the principle. Almost every Indo-European language furnishes instances of verbs formed from nouns, adjectives, pronouns aud particles; and those secondary and tertiary formations are found capable of expressing all the same modifications of idea as their supposed primitives — in some cases still more emphatically. On the other hand, the roots of those primitives are found in whole classes of languages to be identical with simple nouns of cognate meaning, while in others the noun only differs from the assumed root in an adventitious termination, commonly of pronominal origin. We may therefore rationally conclude that the simple verb is formed from a simple noun, pronoun or particle, and the derivative one from a form that has received some augmentation; but that, as to the original and characteristic principle of structure, there is not the smallest difference between the two.

In closing, for the present, the discussion of this extensive subject, it is proposed to make a few remarks upon the so-called verb-substantive, respecting the nature and functions of which there has perhaps been more misapprehension than about any other element of language.

It is well known that many grammarians have been accustomed to represent this element as forming the basis of all verbal expression, and as a necessary ingredient in every logical proposition. It would seem to follow, from this statement, that nations so unfortunate as to be without it, could neither employ verbal expression nor frame a logical proposition. How far this is the case will be seen hereafter: at present we shall make some brief remarks on this verb, and on the substitutes usually employed in dialects where it is formally wanting. It will be sufficient to produce a few prominent instances, as the multiplying of examples from all known languages would be a mere repetition of the same general phenomena.

In the portion of the essay relating to the Coptic, it was observed: "What are called the auxiliary and substantive verbs in Coptic are still more remote from all essential verbal character (than the so-called verbal roots). On examination they will almost invariably be found to be articles, pronouns, particles, or abstract nouns, and to derive their supposed verbal functions entirely from their accessories, or from what they imply." In fact any one who examines a good Coptic grammar or dictionary will find that there is nothing formally corresponding to our *am, art, is, was*, &c., though there is a counterpart to Lat. *fieri* (*sthopi*) and another to *poni* (*chi*, neuter passive of *chē*); both occasionally rendered *to be*, which however is not their radical import. The Egyptians were not however quite destitute of resources in this matter, but had at least half-a-dozen methods of rendering the Greek verb-substantive when they wished to do so. The element most commonly employed is the demonstrative *pe, te, ne*; used also in a slightly modified form for the definite article; *pe* = *is*, having reference to a subject in the singular masculine; *te*, to a singular feminine; and *ne* = *are*, to both genders in the plural. The past tense is indicated by the addition of a particle expressing remoteness. Here then we find as the counterpart of the verb-substantive an element totally foreign to all the received ideas of a verb; and that instead of its being deemed necessary to say in formal terms *'Petrus est,' 'Maria est,' 'homines sunt,'* it is quite sufficient, and perfectly intelligible, to say, *'Petrus hic,' 'Maria hæc,' 'homines hi.'* The above forms, according to Champollion and other investigators of ancient hieroglyphics, occur in the oldest known monumental inscriptions, showing plainly that the ideas of the ancient Egyptians, as to the method of expressing the category *to be*, did not exactly accord with those of some modern grammarians.

Another word employed to represent the verb-substantive is *ouon*, used nearly in the same manner as *pe* to denote *is*, and with the addition of a demonstrative particle, *was*. Sometimes, with a slightly varied form of construction, it is used in the sense of *have*, nearly as the Latin formula *est mihi*. The radical import is however neither *is* nor *has*, nor that of a verb of any sort, it being simply the indefinite pronoun corresponding to *aliquis, some one*, and occasionally employed in the sense of *unus*. Thus the literal rendering of *Petros ne ouon*, is simply, 'Peter then one, or some one,' = *Petrus erat*. Here then we find another pronominal element used as the counterpart of *is* or *was*, much in the same way as the demonstrative already indicated, except that the original signification is more vague and indefinite. Several other words are employed for the same purpose, among which may be specified *a, o, are, er, el,* all apparently pronouns or pronominal particles, and not differing materially in use or construction from *pe* or *ouon*.

There is however another and a very common method of expressing the verb-substantive, capable of more extensive development, and of much greater variety of modification. Whoever refers to Peyron and Tattam for the detailed conjugation of the verb *to be*, will find a most imposing assemblage of forms, varied through all persons singular and plural, and nominally comprising more tenses than Greek or Latin can boast of. A little examination will however show that all this array consists of nothing more than the suffixes of the personal pronouns, — exactly the same as those employed in construction with nouns and verbs, combined with particles of time and place that modify the sense of the phrase according to circumstances. Thus the masculine suffixes of the three persons in the singular, either emloyed absolutely, *ti, k, f,* or with the preformatives *a* or *e*, respectively denote *sum*, *es*, *est*, and by varying the preformative particles, they are made to express almost every possible modification of time or contingency. Again the consuetudinal tense formed by the combination of the suffixes with *sha*, — *sha-ti*, *sha-k*, *sha-f*, &c., 'to be usually, or habitually,' — is commonly rendered *soleo esse*, and most grammarians regard the formative as a *bonâ fide* auxiliary verb, having the force of the Latin one. It is however no verb at all, but a mere particle, having, among other significations, that of *usque*, and therefore well-suited to express the continuance or habituality of an action.

It will perhaps be said that such an abnormal language as the Coptic is not to be taken as a criterion of others, which may be organized on totally different principles. There might be some force in the objection, if other languages presented us with no instances of parallel constructions. This negative argument will not however hold good, nearly every apparent Coptic peculiarity having its counterpart in languages belonging to almost every quarter of the globe. Thus, every Semitic scholar knows that personal pronouns are employed to represent the verb-substantive in all the known dialects, exactly as in Coptic, but with less variety of modification. In this construction it is not necessary that the pronoun should be of the same person as the subject of the proposition. It is optional in most dialects to say either *ego ego, nos nos,* for *ego sum, nos sumus,* or *ego ille, nos illi.* The phrase ,,ye are the salt of the earth,'' is in the Syriac version literally "you *they* (*i. e.* the persons constituting) the salt of the earth." Nor is this employment of the personal pronoun confined to the dialects above specified, it being equally found in Basque, in Galla, in Turco-Tartarian, and various American languages.

It will be said that there are in all the Semitic dialects verbs regularly conjugated in the acceptation of *am, was,* &c., and defined as verbs-substantive by grammarians. This is true; but at the same time it may be observed, that the numerous substitutes employed show that it would have been very possible to do without them. Neither does it follow that every word conjugated as a verb is formed on a true verbal root. The Syriac periphrastic form already noticed more than once, *ithá-i, ithai-ch*, &c., is indisputably based on a construct noun in the plural number, and the etymologically cognate Hebrew *yesh*, which, with the exception of the root being singular instead of plural, has precisely the same construction, must be regarded as standing on the same footing.   In other Semitic words, the signification 'to be' is not the primary one.   The Arabic *kan* is currently used in this sense, but a comparison with the other dialects shows that the primary import is simply 'to stand,' a word, as it is scarcely necessary to say, used as a substitute for the verb-substantive in a variety of languages.

With respect to the term most commonly employed in Hebrew and Aramaic (Heb. *hayah*, *havah*, Syriac *hvo*, &c.), the resemblance to the pronoun of the third person *hu*, *hi*, is so obvious, that many of the best modern Semitic scholars regard the latter as the real base of the verb.   The possibility of this is readily conceived, if we consider that when the pronouns themselves were familiarly used to denote *is*, *was*, &c., it was a very easy matter to add the personal terminations, *pro re natâ*.   Several eminent German philologists, among whom may be specified Hoffmeister and Schwarze, have generalized this theory, regarding for example the Sanscrit *as–mi* = Lat. *sum*, with all their Indo-European cognates, as no proper verbal root, but a formation on the demonstrative pronoun *sa*, the idea meant to be conveyed being simply that of local presence.   Professor Newman seems to give some countenance to this theory, in a paper lately published in the 'Classical Museum.'

Finally, we may briefly observe that particles, sometimes with pronominal suffixes, and sometimes without them, are used in various parts of the world in place of the verb-substantive, some nations in fact having no other way of expressing it; while others neither employ verb, pronoun, noun nor particle, but leave the predication to be gathered from the arrangement of the terms of the proposition.   This is in fact often done in languages which have a verb-substantive, or even several; and in practice scarcely any difficulty or ambiguity is ever found to arise from this so-called ellipsis.   The Magyars, for example, have words denoting *to be*, or capable of being employed in that sense.   It is however considered rather inelegant to use them in formal composition, and in the best writers whole consecutive pages may be found without an *is* or a *was* enunciated in terms.

Now it seems that the above-specified facts, to which a multitude of analogous ones might easily be added, justify us in entertaining a doubt whether the ordinary theory of the verb-substantive as a sort of *sine-qua-non* in language and logic, can be rationally or consistently maintained.   Whatever intrinsic vitality there may be in *is* or *was*, it does not seem easy to extract much from *this* or *that*; still less from *here* or *there*, words currently used as substitutes.   Nor are our difficulties lessened by finding that millions of people are totally destitute of the term, or of any means of supplying its place, not having in fact the smallest conception of the existence of such an element. Indeed the writer believes that a verb-substantive, such as is commonly conceived, vivifying all connected speech, and binding together the terms of every logical proposition, is much upon a footing with the phlogiston of the chemists of the last generation, regarded as a necessary pabulum of combustion, that is to say, *vox et prœterea nihil*.

He further believes that many of the extravagances promulgated on the subject have arisen from the utterly erroneous idea of an intrinsic meaning in words, constituting them the counterparts and equivalents of thought. They are nothing more, and can be nothing more than signs of relations, and it is a contradiction in terms to affirm that a relation can be inherent. Nor had those employed to express mental categories originally that power; all, without exception, being metonyms adopted from terms indicating the sensible relations of matter; it is therefore obviously out of the question that they should at the same time be capable of intrinsically expressing the phænomena of mind. Moreover, of all mental categories, the idea of *being* was perhaps the least capable of being so expressed. Let any man endeavour to form a clear idea of the nature of existence in the abstract, and explain in what it consists; he will then see how likely it is that persons in a rude state of society should find a term intrinsically expressing what the profoundest metaphysician is unable to give a tolerable definition of. Happily there is no need for any such effort of the intellect, there being scarcely any category capable of being enunciated in so many different ways, all and any of them amply sufficient for practical purposes. There is surely nothing profoundly intellectual in the Latin words *exsisto* and *exsto*, taken in their ordinary and literal acceptations. The former, *vi termini*, denotes to put forth, present; the latter, to stand forth, or out; yet both are currently employed in a secondary sense, to express *existence* or *being*. But though the primary words *say* nothing about *being*, they both clearly *imply* it, and this in fact is all that is wanted. What is put forth or stands forth is prominent; what is prominent is conspicuous; and what is conspicuous may be lawfully presumed to exist. The same holds good of the innumerable other terms used as substitutes for the cabalistic *to be*. If a given subject be 'I,' 'thou,' 'he,' 'this,' 'that,' 'one'; if it be 'here,' 'there,' 'yonder,' 'thus,' 'in,' 'on,' 'at,' 'by'; if it 'sits,' 'stands,' 'remains,' or 'appears,' we need no ghost to tell us that it *is*, nor any grammarian or metaphysician to proclaim that recondite fact in formal terms. The same principle is applicable in a great measure to language as a whole. Words are not to be interpreted so much from what they actually say, as from what they imply; and they perform every function that they can be reasonably expected to perform, when the implication is understood by the speaker and the hearer.

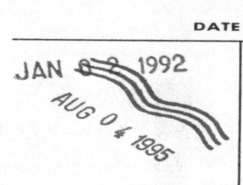

3 9015 02246 4500

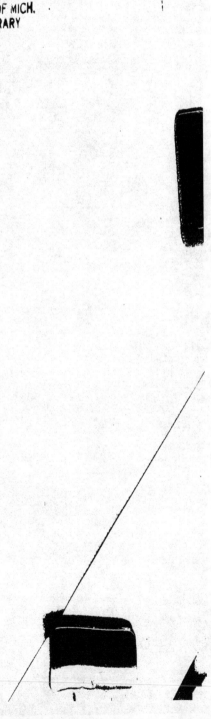

CPSIA information can be obtained
at www.ICGtesting.com
Printed in the USA
BVHW081819220819
556561BV00020B/4428/P

9 781407 638447